THE MARRIAGE
OF FIGARO

THE MARRIAGE OF FIGARO

Wolfgang Amadeus Mozart

TEXT BY ROBERT LEVINE

Additional commentary by William Berger

BLACK DOG
& LEVENTHAL
PUBLISHERS
NEW YORK

Published by
Black Dog & Leventhal Publishers, Inc.
151 West 19th Street
New York, NY 10011

Distributed by
Workman Publishing Company
225 Varick Street
New York, NY 10014

Manufactured in China

Cover and interior design by Elizabeth Driesbach

Archive Photos: pgs. 10, 14, 26, 32; Getty Images: p. 12;
Jack Vartoogian: pgs. 16-17, 21, 31, 34; New York Public Library: pgs. 19, 23, 35;
Bridgeman Art Library: pgs.27/Mozart Museum, Vienna, 33/Roger-Viollet, Paris;
Culver Pictures: p. 47; Beth Bergman: pgs. 49, 50; Stills: p. 51/Lebedinsky;
National Gallery, Budapest, Hungary/ET Archive, London/SuperStock: p. 55

ISBN-13: 978-1-57912-512-7

h g f e d c b a

Library of Congress Cataloging-in-Publication Data available on file.

The Marriage of Figaro is the result of one of the greatest creative collaborations in history. Mozart's musical genius, da Ponte's skillful realism and Beaumarchais's courageously honest subject matter combine to create perhaps the most successful opera buffa of all time. *Figaro* takes us through a single 'mad day' in the Almaviva household; unique in its chaos but wonderfully typical in its players, their lives and their relationships with each other. The music is joyful and complex, the characters are endearing and real and the plotlines are boisterously entertaining: *Figaro's* success is well-deserved.

You will hear the entire opera on the two compact discs included on the inside front and back covers of this book. As you explore the text, you will discover the story behind the opera and its creation, the background of the composer, biographies of the principal singers and conductor and the opera's libretto, both in the original Italian and in an English translation. Special commentary has been included throughout the libretto to aid in your appreciation and highlight key moments in the action and score.

Enjoy this book and enjoy the music.

ABOUT THE AUTHOR

*R*obert Levine is a New York based music and travel writer whose work has appeared in dozens of newspapers and periodicals around the world. In addition to his being Senior Classical Music Advisor to Amazon.com, he contributes to *Stereophile, Fanfare, Opera News* and *BBC Music Magazine* and acts as advisor to a handful of European opera companies and artists.

ACKNOWLEDGEMENTS

The author would like to thank Paul Harrington for his help in preparing the manuscript.

THE MARRIAGE OF FIGARO

*I*n 1785 Wolfgang Amadeus Mozart was the most sought-after composer in Vienna. *Die Entführung aus dem Serail (The Abduction from the Seraglio)*, the exotic opera he had written three years prior, had made him famous in Viennese society. Immediately after its premiere, he found himself invited regularly to perform for Emperor Joseph II, Count Esterhazy, the Court Counselor and lesser courtiers. Even the great Franz Joseph Haydn recognized his talent and sought out his company. Nevertheless, Mozart and his new wife, Constanze (they were married in 1782), found themselves under constant financial stress; his

Wolfgang Amadeus Mozart (1756–1791)

The Viennese Opera House

carousing, entertaining and gambling increased with his artistic successes. Certainly these problems were related to his immaturity—at 29, he had been independent of his father for only a short time. Mozart seems to have assumed his income would increase commensurate with his rising fame, but this was not happening at the rate he had expected. He needed to cement his place in Viennese music and his young family's financial well-being.

Although this was the most fertile period in his career, Mozart had not written an opera since *Abduction*. Opera was the most significant art form in Vienna, and could make or break a composer's reputation. To achieve the stability his family needed, it was clear that he should assume one of the court's musical positions—but this goal could be achieved only through renown. Accordingly, despite the impressive number of instrumental compositions he wrote during this period, Mozart also sought a libretto with which to secure his standing.

Mozart had a very fine understanding of what made an opera great. He wrote to his father, "In an opera the poetry must perforce be the obedient daughter of the music"; he knew what people listened for, and knew that the words could make an opera magical, or they could sap the music of its meaning and appeal. He had learned this after spending his childhood (Mozart wrote his first opera when he was 12) composing music for librettos handed to him as *faits accomplis* by his teachers and patrons. As an adult he worked closely with his librettists on all the operas he composed; he claimed to have read, and tossed out, hundreds of librettos in search of those worthy of his composition.

Lorenzo da Ponte was the librettist with whom Mozart wrote three of his greatest operas, *Le Nozze di Figaro, Don Giovanni* and *Cosi Fan Tutte*, and he could not have found a more appropriate partner. If Mozart was a rascal, he was a well-heeled one; he was always a good son and husband. However, da Ponte was a true adventurer, the sort of "bad boy" Mozart could never be. Born to Jewish parents in the Venetian city of Ceneda in 1749, his birth name was Emmanuele Conegliano until he was 14, when his widower father decided to marry a Christian and converted to Catholicism. All the children were baptized by the Bishop of Ceneda, who gave his own name, Lorenzo da Ponte, to Emmanuele, the eldest son.

The new Lorenzo went on to become an ordained priest and led a life of amorous adventure in Venice. (Remember, this was the Age of Reason, and priests could do that sort of thing.) Eventually he became a teacher of rhetoric at the University of Treviso, but was dismissed in 1776 for writing poems seen as seditious and defamatory. Da Ponte's dismissal from the University was just the beginning of his colorful journey. His libertine ways caught up with him following an affair with a married woman (which produced a child) and a stint as a violinist in a brothel; in 1779 he was banished from the state of Venice entirely. From Venice he went to Germany and Austria; in Vienna he was appointed poet to the Imperial Theater, and met Mozart.

Da Ponte lived in Vienna until 1791 but he fell out of favor with Emperor Leopold II, Joseph II's successor. After publishing some vituperative attacks upon the new Emperor, he found himself banished from Austria as well. He next landed in Paris, then London, working for a time as a theater impresario and bookseller, but his stay there was cut short by money problems and he eventually fled again—this time to New York. He survived there by taking up jobs as a grocer and a distiller, eventually becoming the first Professor of Italian at Columbia College, where he wrote his famous and controversial memoirs. He died at 89 in 1838, and is buried in the Roman Catholic cemetery on East 11th Street in New York City.

Joseph II of Austria (1741–1790), King of Germany 1764–1790, Holy Roman Emperor 1765–1790, King of Austria, 1780–1790

The Count begs for forgiveness
in the final scene, Metropolitan
Opera, 1985.

The Marriage of Figaro was a well-known play by Pierre-Augustin Caron de Beaumarchais (1732–99) when Mozart discovered it in 1785. The son of a watchmaker, Beaumarchais was one of his century's more colorful figures. He gave harp lessons to the daughters of Louis XV, speculated in grandiose business schemes, spent several years tied up in one of the age's most scandalous lawsuits, acted as a secret agent for France during a period of exile in England, published the first complete edition of Voltaire's works, ran guns to the American revolutionaries and founded the French Society of Dramatic Authors.

As a "dramatic author," Beaumarchais wrote several plays, and two of his comedies gained immortality. The first of these, *Le Barbier de Séville (The Barber of Seville)*, was first produced in 1775. An immensely important work during its time, it ingeniously blended the tradition of Molière and the figures from the classical Italian *commedia dell' arte*. The youthful lover (Count Almaviva) and the miserly, pompous old man (Doctor Bartolo) contend for the hand of Rosine, and the Barber (Figaro), through sheer ingenuity, enables the Count to win.

The social criticism floating behind the comedic elements of *Le Barbier* was seen even more clearly in its 1778 sequel. *Le Mariage de Figaro (The Marriage of Figaro)* was an even more daring play, one that would have serious social and political reverberations. In it, Beaumarchais showed that the Almaviva marriage was less than successful, and that Figaro (now the Count's valet) finds himself pitted in another battle of wits, this time with the Count himself.

Almaviva, being an "enlightened" ruler, has recently done away with the *droit de seigneur*, an ancient privilege of the aristocracy that allowed them first-night privileges with any of their servants who marry. After abolition of this ancient custom, however, the Count's eyes have fallen upon Susanna, his wife's maid and Figaro's fiancée. Finding himself passionately enamored of her, he attempts to convince Susanna to sell him the "right" he so recently—and gallantly—gave up. Not only the servants stand against the Count; even the Countess is forced to seek their aid and side with them in their machinations. Eventually she and they win: Figaro and Susanna marry, the Count and Countess's marriage is renewed and

Susanna, Cherubino and the Countess Almaviva,
in a 1928 illustration by H. Montassier

order is restored. In *Le Barbier de Séville* Beaumarchais parodies contemporary social conventions and touches upon political matters; in *Figaro* he goes even further. While the Count tries, like so many aristocrats of the period, to be enlightened, he finds himself very much at odds with this enlightenment. The common people are shown to be not only smarter, but also ethically and morally superior. Any aristocrat seeing this play could not have missed the meanings behind the clever repartee: It questioned their very right to rule.

The Marriage of Figaro's criticism of its time's social and political order (just five years before the bloody French Revolution) ensured the play a rocky start; it faced stiff censorship from the beginning. It was not until 1784, after some of Louis XVI's courtiers saw a private production and convinced him to allow a public performance, that the play was seen by the general public. It immediately became one of the greatest successes of the French theater.

Of course, any cultural event so well-received in Paris would become the talk of Europe, and the play was soon translated and spread throughout the continent. In early 1785, a Viennese theater troupe led by Emanuel Schikaneder (later to be the librettist of Mozart's *The Magic Flute*) began rehearsing a German language version. Not surprisingly, the Imperial Censor did not allow the planned performance, though he permitted the play to be published.

Mozart brought a copy of the play to da Ponte, who wrote in his memoirs that he turned it into a libretto in six weeks. Apparently he was not alone in either his inspiration or hard

Cecilia Bartoli (Susanna) and Bryn Terfel (Figaro) at the Metropolitan Opera, 1998

work, for da Ponte also reported that, "As fast as I wrote the words, Mozart set them to music." The rascality that the two seem to have shared enabled them to work as an impressive team. However, it was more than shared character traits with his librettist that inspired Mozart in composing *Figaro*, for there was much in the play with which he could identify. Figaro, like Mozart, was in constant conflict with his superiors. Just a few years earlier, Mozart had angrily rebelled and been (literally) booted out of the service of the Archbishop of Salzburg. Since then he had found himself competing with jealous men in superior positions who would stop at nothing to impede his progress.

Once the opera was completed, it was da Ponte who convinced the Emperor to allow it to be performed, but this was no simple matter. Joseph II was no fan of the original play, fearing its political implications, and both the Abbé Casti (da Ponte's chief rival) and Antonio Salieri (Mozart's chief rival), as well as the court's opera manager Count Orsini-Rosenberg, tried to prevent its production. (Salieri, Joseph II's court composer, was the most famous of Mozart's competitors. He recognized Mozart's superior talent, and acted whenever possible to ensure that his own position would not be endangered by the younger composer. Contrary to what was presented in the play and movie *Amadeus*, however, there is no evidence that Salieri was instrumental in Mozart's death.) Only after the Emperor was satisfied that the inflammatory scenes from the original play had been removed or rewritten, and that it had been turned into a harmless farce, did he give permission to perform *Figaro*.

The significance of *Figaro* was recognized at its premiere on May 1, 1786 at the court theater. Mozart conducted from the keyboard, and the audience's reception was generally favorable. The opera's popularity grew astoundingly with each repetition, and by the third performance it is said there were so many encores that in order to keep performances from running all night, the Emperor banned the repetition of ensemble pieces.

Antonio Salieri (1750–1825)

While this tale is certainly evidence of the public's feelings about the opera, written reviews from the time are equally telling. Not long after the premiere, a reviewer wrote in the *Wiener Realzeitung*:

"The public. . .did not really know on the first day where it stood. It heard many a bravo from unbiased connoisseurs, but obstreperous louts in the uppermost story exerted their hired lungs. . .to deafen singers alike with their ST! and Pst!; and consequently opinions were divided at the end of the piece. . .Apart from that, it is true that the first performance was none of the best owing to the difficulty of the composition. But now, after several performances, one would be subscribing either to the cabal or to tastelessness if one were to maintain that Herr Mozart's music is anything but a masterpiece of art."

Oddly, *Figaro* played for only nine days in Vienna. Why was its run so short? We do not know to what extent the machinations of Salieri or any of Mozart's other rivals might have been responsible. One must not forget that despite da Ponte's editing (and in some way, perhaps, because of it) the social and political criticism contained within *Figaro* could not have pleased the powerful nobility who must have felt the sting that Mozart so artfully delivered.

In December 1786 *Figaro* was staged in Prague so successfully that Mozart traveled there in January 1787 to conduct a performance. He was clearly thrilled with Prague's acceptance

Costume sketch for Figaro and Susanna, 18th century Austrian engraving

of his work, as he wrote to a friend, "Here they talk about nothing but *Figaro*. Nothing is played, sung or whistled but *Figaro*. No opera is drawing like *Figaro*. Nothing, nothing but *Figaro*." The commission for a new opera (which would be *Don Giovanni*) that the company gave him further confirmed that Mozart had written a masterpiece.

From the beginning of Figaro, the music signals that we are about to hear an intense and complex story. Its overture is playful and conspiratorial, with an unmistakable tension. This manic tension, not unlike Warner Brothers's cartoon music of a century and a half later, prepares us for the madcap adventures we are about to witness; however, unlike with cartoon music, there is real sobriety behind the tomfoolery. Indeed, it might be said that this juxtaposition of cheerfulness and tension hammers home the seriousness of Figaro's themes. It presents us with an aural warning of larger issues at hand.

Figaro is very much more than lovely music. Unlike classical drama and classical opera, which is populated by gods and goddesses, *Figaro* is peopled with real characters and real issues that resound even for modern audiences. (Indeed, the 1980s saw opera director Peter Sellars update the action—successfully, intelligently and non-anachronistically—to today in New York's Trump Tower!) Beyond the political commentary in the opera, and perhaps even more important, was the theme of order in disordered times. This was, after all, the Age of Enlightenment, and the eve of a long and bloody revolution.

Mozart's study in Vienna, where he composed *Le Nozze di Figaro*

Without doubt, Mozart sensed the political undercurrents, and one is therefore struck by the hopefulness behind even the saddest pieces in the opera; there is always a smile somewhere behind the tears. At the same time, deceit, another major theme, is used effectively only by characters who have no other recourse. The Count, for example, is a schemer, but he's not very good at it, and fails whenever he attempts to match wits with his servants. The servants and the Countess succeed in their intrigues simply because they lack the Count's power. They have no other way to foil his plans. But it should also be noted that nobody in *Figaro* actually harms anyone else.

These are not one-dimensional characters. We see this even in the Count and Countess. Whether they emerge triumphant in the end or not, Mozart still reserved his most powerful musical portraits for the aristocracy. The Count is the villain of the piece—but not a cardboard, mustache-twirling one. In him we see a man coming to terms with his age. He represents order, power, stability (even if his actions seem to undermine everything he represents), and Mozart pokes plenty of fun at him. However, despite his buffoonery, the Count is realistic and frightening; these qualities lie just beneath the surface, and sometimes explode. For example, in the third act, after he overhears Susanna and Figaro plotting against him—actual evidence at last that he is being played for a fool—he expresses his outrage in a vicious (and very challenging vocally) recitative and aria, "*Vedro, mentr'io sospiro (Shall I live to see a servant of mine happy and enjoying pleasure, while I am left to sigh. . .Only the hope of vengeance. . .makes me*

rejoice)." By using an instrumental technique combining small
phrases which are different from each other but still linked,
Mozart shows the Count's mounting rage and his frayed emotional state, culminating in a desire for revenge.

In the Countess we see a grace and dignity that is at times
awe-inspiring. *The Barber of Seville* ended with her as the happy

wife of Almaviva, but in *Figaro* she is an older, wearied woman. Her deep sadness and the decency with which she accepts it, while acting to "fix" things for herself, impresses us most. Her actions are an attempt to right a sinking ship. The Count no longer returns her affections and chases servant girls, yet leaving him is not an option—not only is it simply not done, but it also would only add to the disintegration taking place throughout the palace. As Countess she must solve these problems and return propriety and enlightenment to her home. This is precisely what she does at the end of the opera, when the Count apologizes with a melody so simple and lovely that only a heart of stone would turn him down. But while the Countess is attempting to reestablish order in the palace, she has no choice but to turn to her maid, Susanna, for assistance.

The impact of the Countess's character is heightened by the fact that she does not appear until the second act. We know from Mozart's letters that this was an intentional ploy: Act One introduced us to the farce, but the Countess, who opens Act Two, must make us realize that there are real feelings involved as well. We meet her as she sings a plea for love, "*Porgi amor (Return my loved one to me, or let me die)*," and a sobering influence sets in. As if to protect herself from her own sorrow, she goes along with Susanna's and Figaro's machinations. It diverts her; despite her station above her servants, she becomes one with them—she's empathetic and feels their predicament as well. But when she's alone her sadness, doubts and humiliation return. In her third act recitative, "*E Susanna non vien,*" she voices her embarrassment: "*To what shame am I reduced by a cruel husband?*" And in the aria which follows, "*Dove sono (Where are the happy moments of sweetness and pleasure?),*" she wishes her constancy would change "*his ungrateful heart.*" Despite this disgrace, she pushes on to fulfill her duties, yet this charming, sympathetic character still manages to enjoy herself. It is this underlying *joie de vivre* that makes the Countess, and Mozart unique and so exquisite.

Frederica von Stade as Cherubino

But what of Figaro and Susanna? "*Cinque. . .dieci. . .venti,*" the opening piece of Act One, shows Figaro and Susanna preparing for their wedding day. He is innocently—but a little randily—measuring the room to see if the bed the Count has so generously given them will fit. She's trying on a hat—but abandons that to let him in on the Count's ulterior motives after calling the naïve Figaro a "dolt." Figaro is horrified—he believes that the Count has given them this bed and a room located strategically near his own out of kindness and to make Figaro's job easier. Susanna is the worldly one—she has no doubt that the Count wants her close so he can seduce her more conveniently.

Susanna's realism and insight is a recurring theme. She understands what occurs in the castle and has the Countess's ear—it is Susanna who hatches the plans that make up the witty complications in the plot. She never loses her dignity, and only once—briefly—misreads a situation: the moment

The Opera House in Prague

after Figaro discovers that Marcellina is his mother, a twist that
even Susanna could not have foreseen.

Once aware of the Count's intentions toward Susanna,
Figaro angrily sings, "*Se vuol ballare (If, my dear Count, you feel
like dancing, I'll play the tune on my little guitar)*." The aria changes
tempo three times, moving from Figaro's sarcasm to his right-
eous anger, to his refusal to allow the Count to bully him. "It
shall not be: Figaro has said it," he concludes. He has react-
ed, but he has no way to solve the problem. (This task, as do
most tasks, falls to Susanna.) And Figaro remains the same
throughout the opera: He reacts. In the final act, when he
thinks Susanna might be betraying him, he delivers a diatribe
on the fickleness of women ("*Aprite un po' quegli occhi*") in an

aria which took the place of a tirade against the upper classes that appeared in the Beaumarchais original. Figaro remains likeable and sympathetic, yet again, his judgment is off.

Cherubino, the Count's page, is another pivotal character. Just coming into adolescence, this young man (always played by a woman), even more than Figaro, is in opposition to the Count. He is in love with the Countess (and every other woman in the palace, for that matter), and the lonely Countess cannot help but be charmed by his attentions. But he bunglingly shows up at all the wrong times, and can't seem to help reminding the Count of the aging process and the fact that the Count is vainly attempting to hang onto his youth by pursuing every available beauty. This young punk continually reveals the Count's unraveling dignity. The Count exiles him (often) and the others ridicule him, but it's impossible not to like him, so ardent and unprotected are his feelings, as exhibited by his breathless, panting first-act aria and almost embarrassingly sincere second-act aria.

Figaro, in an engraving by Emile Antoine Bayard (1837–1891)

Metropolitan Opera production of *Figaro*, 1985

If *Figaro* is a musical masterpiece, as well as a masterpiece of social satire, its politics, no less masterful in a subtle presentation, did not help Mozart further his career. Its initial popularity in Vienna did not stop the production's run from ending quite abruptly. And though the fervor with which it was accepted in Prague led to more operatic commissions for him, even these successes did not have the required effect for Mozart. The most important, lucrative commissions and audiences were in Vienna.

Even today one can't help but be struck by this vital and overwhelmingly rich work. In *Figaro*, Mozart does more than write brilliant music to a wonderful libretto; he creates a vibrant story that contemporary audiences can still comprehend. How many men going through a mid-life crisis might understand the Count's issues and feel his rising rage, so palpable in the music? Certainly the predicament—and the sadness—of the Countess is not unknown to wives (and husbands, for that matter) today. How many young couples might recognize the challenges Figaro and Susanna face in learning to trust one another? And Cherubino? Well, most of us remember what it was like to be an adolescent coming to terms with sexuality and its resulting challenges and awkwardness.

Celebrated artist Al Hirschfeld's rendering of the 1986 cast of *Figaro*, in an advertisement for a televised production.

The political message that seems to have limited Mozart's financial and professional success during his lifetime was quickly overcome with the passage of a few years, yet the compelling and sensitive characterizations in this work remain to keep *The Marriage of Figaro* relevant to modern ears. More than two centuries after its premiere, audiences still clamor for its outrageousness, its truths, its slapstick, its tears and its message of forgiveness.

THE STORY OF THE OPERA

Act 1

The curtain rises on the wedding day of Count Almaviva's valet, Figaro, and the Countess's maid, Susanna. We see Figaro and Susanna in a sparsely furnished room in the Count's palace, Aguafrescas, near Seville. Figaro is measuring the space for their connubial bed, but when Susanna learns that this room is to be theirs, she warns him that the location is unwise because of the Count's designs on her. Figaro, astonished and furious, determines to thwart his master's aims.

They leave and Dr. Bartolo and Marcellina, the Count's middle-aged housekeeper, enter. She tells Bartolo that Figaro owes her money, and has promised to marry her if he cannot pay off the debt. Bartolo rejoices at the idea of forcing Figaro to marry this older woman, rather than the youthful and beautiful Susanna. He harbors old hostility toward Figaro, and sees a glimmer of potential revenge. As Marcellina is leaving, Susanna enters and there is a brief but acrimonious encounter between these rivals. Next the Count's page, Cherubino, enters and tells Susanna he is to be sent into exile, as yesterday the

Count caught him with Barbarina, the daughter of the gardener, Antonio. Cherubino tells Susanna he does not want to leave, for he is in love with the Countess (and the rest of womankind). Before he can leave, Cherubino spies the Count approaching and dives behind a nearby chair. The Count, entering, begins to tell Susanna of his desire for her, but not long into his impassioned speech they hear Don Basilio's voice; now the Count hides behind the chair as Cherubino deftly slips around to sit in it, covered by a lady's robe. Basilio, Susanna's music teacher and the Count's factotum, tells her how Cherubino adores the Countess; this infuriates the jealous Count, who comes out of hiding. He relates his recent discovery of Cherubino at Barbarina's, and while doing so un-covers the page once more in a lady's chamber.

Figaro enters with a group of peasants who sing the Count's praises for recently abolishing the *droit du seigneur*. Figaro asks the Count to place a white, virginal headdress on Susanna's head and give her away in marriage, but the Count avoids the issue by postponing the ceremony with a "generous" offer of a lavish party in their honor later in the day. The peasants leave and the Count punishes Cherubino by ordering him to take a commission and foreign posting in his own regiment. Figaro lightheartedly warns the nervous young officer about the rigors of military life.

Act 2

In her chamber, the Countess mourns the fading of her husband's love. Susanna enters, then Figaro. Figaro tells the Countess he has hatched a plot to distract the Count from Susanna. He has had a note delivered to the Count saying that the Countess has an assignation that evening with a lover; he also has Susanna invite the Count to meet her, and plans to send Cherubino, disguised as Susanna, in her place to the assignation. Figaro leaves and Cherubino arrives. He sings a love song he has written, then Susanna playfully begins to dress him as a woman. She rushes off to find a piece of ribbon, and he is in his shirtsleeves with the Countess when the Count knocks on the door. Cherubino hides in the dressing room, but upon entering the jealous, suspicious Count senses his wife's confusion. The combination of Figaro's note and her uncharacteristically locked door convinces him that she has a lover within. When there is a noise from the dressing room, the Countess tells the Count that it is only Susanna, and refuses to give him the key to check the room for himself. The Count decides to go get tools to break down the door, taking his wife with him and locking the door from the outside.

Susanna, who was in her own room and had entered unnoticed during the argument, tells Cherubino he may safely come out; he escapes by jumping out the window. She takes his place in the dressing room and re-locks door. Upon the couple's return, the Countess admits that it is a partly dressed Cherubino in the dressing room. As the enraged Count, his sword drawn, approaches the door, Susanna demurely steps out; the Count can only apologize to his equally nonplussed wife.

Now Figaro enters with news that the musicians have assembled for the wedding. The Count questions him about the letter he received earlier, having just learned from the Countess and Susanna that Figaro was its author. Figaro denies knowledge of it, and Antonio bursts into the room: Some of his prize plants have been destroyed by someone leaping from the window in this chamber. Figaro, who knows the situation, says that it was he who jumped from the window. Antonio goes to hand him a paper dropped near the broken pots, but the Count intercepts it. He questions Figaro about it; fortunately the Countess recognizes the paper as Cherubino's commission and is able to furtively inform Figaro of this fact. He explains that he had the paper because (after being prompted again by the Countess) it needs the Count's seal. Marcellina, Bartolo and Basilio now enter and demand justice for Marcellina, ending the act in a complete muddle.

Act 3

In the main hall, the Count reflects on the situation. Susanna enters and tells him she is willing to comply with his desires. She plans to use the dowry he had promised her in return for her compliance to pay off Figaro's debt to Marcellina. As she leaves, the Count overhears her passing remark to Figaro, "Our case is won." Realizing that he is being tricked, and furious to think that his servant may enjoy what he cannot, the Count is left to stew.

Figaro, Marcellina, Dr. Bartolo and Don Basilio meet with the Count who, as lord of the land, rules on the advice of the lawyer Don Curzio that Figaro must pay Marcellina or marry her. But now, to everyone's amazement, the story unfolds that Figaro is a foundling—he is Marcellina's long-lost son (not the son of a nobleman, as he had thought)—and his father is none other than Dr. Bartolo. Just as Figaro embraces his newly discovered mother, Susanna enters. Her initial anger and confusion turns to happiness when she learns what has transpired. The Count, meanwhile, is once more frustrated, learning of the true situation. Thereupon Marcellina and Bartolo decide to make that evening's festivities into a double wedding.

The Count departs; Cherubino and Barbarina pass through the hall, talking of the plan to dress him as a girl. The Countess, alone in her chamber, laments her lost happiness and the stratagem to which she is reduced in the hope of regaining her husband.

Next, in the Countess's chamber, the Countess and Susanna continue the plot to catch the Count and end his philandering. The Countess dictates a letter to Susanna—to be signed by Susanna—setting up a rendezvous. They seal it with a pin, to be returned in acknowledgment. A group of peasant girls, led by Barbarina, come to bring flowers to the Countess. Cherubino, disguised as a girl, is amongst them, but is revealed by Antonio, who enters with the Count. The Count's anger is quickly diverted when Barbarina reminds him that he has promised her a favor in return for her affections, and she claims Cherubino as that favor.

Entering, Figaro urges that the party and dancing begin. A march is heard as peasants enter, sing once again in praise of the enlightened Count, and dance a fandango. The marriage ceremony follows, during which Susanna surreptitiously slips her note to the Count. Although Figaro did not see her hand it to him, he notes that the Count has apparently pricked his finger on a sealing pin while opening a love letter. Finally, the Count promises a fabulous party that evening to celebrate the weddings.

Act 4

We find Barbarina in the garden looking for the pin the Count
had given her to return to Susanna; she has dropped it. Figaro
enters and she tells him she has lost the pin the Count asked
her to bring to Susanna. Not knowing about this plot, Figaro
assumes the worst. He tells Marcellina, who runs to warn Susanna. Meanwhile, Figaro assembles Bartolo, Basilio and most of
the other characters to hide in the garden and help him uncov-
er his new wife's infidelity. He conceals himself as Susanna and
the Countess enter. They have exchanged clothes, and Susanna, having spotted Figaro hiding, sings raptly but ambiguously
of her approaching bliss. Figaro, his suspicious mind reeling,
bursts with an impassioned rant about woman's infidelity.

The Countess, disguised as Susanna, awaits the Count. But
Cherubino stumbles once more upon the proceedings and
makes a pass at her; that ends abruptly when the Count enters.
The Count leads "Susanna" to an arbor, but hearing Figaro
pass by noisily, goes to hide himself. Figaro spots the "Countess" (Susanna in costume) and tells her that the Count is with
Susanna. Susanna forgets to conceal her voice, Figaro recognizes her and at last realizes what is going on. Unable to resist

teasing her, he pleads passionate love to the "Countess." Not seeing through Figaro's game, Susanna punches him. Figaro quickly explains that he knew it was she, and the reconciled pair continue the charade for the returning Count. The Count, enraged at discovering Figaro and a woman he thinks is the Countess making love, summons everyone to witness his wife's betrayal. Everyone begs him to forgive her, but he is adamant—until he hears the true Countess's voice join the crowd. He immediately realizes what he has done, and kneels to beg her forgiveness; she cannot withhold it. As the opera ends, all joyfully "hasten to the revelry" that the Count had earlier promised.

THE MARRIAGE OF FIGARO

Wolfgang Amadeus Mozart
(1 7 5 6 - 1 7 9 1)

Dietrich Fischer-Dieskau . . . . Count Almaviva
Heather Harper . . . . Countess Almaviva
Judith Blegen . . . . Susanna
Geraint Evans . . . . Figaro
Teresa Berganza . . . . Cherubino
Birgit Finnilä . . . . Marcellina

Daniel Barenboim
Conductor, English Chamber Orchestra

THE PERFORMERS

DIETRICH FISCHER-DIESKAU (Count Almaviva) Acknowledged as one of the great baritones of the 20th century, Fischer-Dieskau was born in Berlin in 1925 to a self-taught musician father and an amateur pianist mother. His musical education began with piano lessons at the age of 9 and voice at 16. In 1942–43, he continued his voice study with Hermann Weissenborn at the Berlin Musikhochschule. Drafted into the army in 1943, he was captured by the Americans while serving in Italy in 1945. He returned to Germany after his release in 1947, and made his first professional appearance as a soloist in the Brahms *Deutschen Requiem* in Badenweiler. He resumed his study with Weissenborn in Berlin and performed on radio broadcasts during this time. In 1948 he made his operatic debut in the bass role of Colas in a broadcast of Mozart's youthful opera *Bastien und Bastienne*. He débuted on stage a few

Dietrich Fischer-Dieskau (Count Almaviva) and Kiri te Kanawa
(Countess Almaviva), 1984

months later as Rodrigue, Marquis of Posa in Verdi's *Don Carlos* at the Berlin Städtische Opera, where he remained an invaluable member for 35 years.

Although Fischer-Dieskau continued to pursue his operatic career at leading opera houses and festivals in Europe, it was as a *lieder* and concert artist that he became world-famous. In 1955 he made his American debut with the Cincinnati Symphony Orchestra, and soon after his recital debut at New York's Town Hall. His best-known operatic roles included Count Almaviva, Don Giovanni, Papageno, Macbeth, Falstaff, Hans Sachs, Mandryka and Wozzeck. He created the role of Gregor

Mittenhofer in Henze's *Elegy for Young Lovers* (1961) and the title role in Reimann's *Lear*. Among the honors he received were membership in the Berlin Akademie der Künste (1956), the Mozart Medal of Vienna (1962), Kammersanger of Berlin (1963), the Grand Cross of Merit of the Federal Republic of Germany (1978), honorary doctorates from Oxford University (1978) and the Sorbonne in Paris (1980) and the Gold Medal of the Royal Philharmonic Society of London (1988).

HEATHER HARPER (Countess Almaviva) The distinguished Irish soprano Heather Harper was born in Belfast in 1930. While studying at Trinity College of Music in London, she also took voice lessons with Helene Isepp and Frederic Husler. In 1954 she debuted as Lady Macbeth with the Oxford University Opera Club. She joined the English Opera Group (1956–75); performed for the first time at the Glyndebourne Festival in 1957, at Covent Garden as Helena in *A Midsummer Night's Dream* in 1962 and at the Bayreuth Festival as Elsa in 1967. In 1969 she sang in the United States and South America. Her final public appearance as a singer was in 1990.

Some of Harper's best-known roles included Arabella, Marguerite, Gutrune, Hecuba, Anne Trulove in *The Rake's Progress*, The Woman in *Erwartung*, Ellen Orford in *Peter Grimes* and the role of Nadia in Tippett's *The Ice Break* (1977), which she created. She later became a professor at the Royal College of Music in London and director of singing studies at the Britten-Pears School. In 1965, Harper was made a Commander of the British Empire.

Judith Blegen as
Susanna, 1975

JUDITH BLEGEN (Susanna) Judith Blegen was born in Missoula, Montana in 1941. She studied violin and singing at the Curtis Institute of Music in Philadelphia (1959–64). After studying with Luigi Ricci in Italy, she sang at the Nuremberg Opera from 1964 to 1966. Her American debut was at the Santa Fe Festival in 1969, as Emily in Menotti's satirical opera *Help, Help, the Globolinks!*, written especially for her. In 1970, Blegen debuted at the Metropolitan Opera as Papagena in *Die Zauberflöte*; her light, silvery soprano found an ideal home in Mozart's operas. She continued to appear at the Met in a variety of roles, debuted at the Paris Opéra in 1977, and sang at several other European opera houses as well.

GERAINT EVANS (Figaro) Sir Geraint Evans was a world-famous baritone from Cilfynydd, Wales, born in 1922. He began voice study in Cardiff at the age of 17, but World War II interrupted his education. After serving in the RAF he resumed his studies in Hamburg with Theo Hermann, then studied with Fernando Carpi in Geneva and Walter Hyde at the Guildhall School of Music in London. His operatic debut was as the Night-watchman in *Die Meistersinger von Nürnberg* at Covent

Garden in London (1948), where he became a leading member of the company. From 1960 through 1961 he sang at the Glyndebourne Festival; his first United States appearance was with the San Francisco Opera. He debuted at Milan's La Scala (1960), the Vienna State Opera (1961), the Salzburg Festival (1962), the Metropolitan Opera (1964) and the Paris Opéra (1975). His best-known roles include Figaro, Leporello, Papageno, Beckmesser, Falstaff, Don Pasquale and Wozzeck. In 1984 he gave his final opera performance, as Dulcamara, at Covent Garden. For his notable performances and his work as an opera producer, Evans was made a Commander of the British Empire in 1959, and in 1969 he was knighted.

TERESA BERGANZA (Cherubino) Mezzo-soprano Teresa Berganza was born in Madrid in 1935. She studied at the Madrid Conservatory, and sang at the Florence May Festival and Aix-en-Provence in 1957. The next year she made her United States debut (in Dallas), as well as at the Glyndebourne Festival and in 1960 sang at Covent Garden in London. Cherubino was the role in which she debuted

Teresa Berganza, 1993

at the Metropolitan Opera. Berganza was an admired Rosina *(Il Barbiere di Siviglia)*, Carmen, Dorabella *(Cosi Fan Tutte)* and Zerliná *(Don Giovanni)*.

BIRGIT FINNILÄ (Marcellina) This Swedish contralto was born in Falkenberg in 1931. She studied voice in Göteborg and with Roy Henderson at the Royal Academy of Music in London. Since her 1963 concert debut in Göteborg, she has performed with major European, American, Australian and Israeli orchestras.

DANIEL BARENBOIM (Conductor, English Chamber Orchestra)Born in Buenos Aires, Argentina in 1942, this talented pianist and conductor began his musical education with his parents. His first public performance (at the piano) was in Buenos Aires when he was seven years old. In 1952 the Barenboims settled in Israel, and during the summers of 1954 and 1955 he studied piano in Salzburg with Edwin Fischer and conducting under Igor Markevitch. From 1954 to 1956 he studied music theory with Nadia Boulanger in Paris and enrolled at the Accademia di Santa Cecilia in Rome, where in 1956 he became one of the youngest students ever to receive a diploma. During this period he also studied conducting with Carlo Zecchi at the Accademia Musicale Chigiana in Siena. After giving recitals in Paris (1955) and London (1956), he made his American debut at Carnegie Hall in New York, performing Prokofiev's First Piano Concerto with Leopold Stokowski.

Barenboim's debut as a conductor occurred in Haifa in 1957. Ten years later he led the Israel Philharmonic on its tour of the United States, and a year after that he conducted the London Symphonic Orchestra in New York. Barenboim's debut as an opera conductor was at the Edinburgh Festival in 1972. In 1975 he was named music director of the Orchestre de Paris. Barenboim was named artistic director of the new Bastille Opera in Paris. In 1988, but after a headline-making falling out with the French Minister of Culture he left (in 1989) to succeed Sir Georg Solti as music director of the Chicago Symphony Orchestra, a post he still holds. He is also the General Music Director of the Deutsche Staatsoper Berlin.

The Libretto

Act 1

OVERTURE

DISC NO. 1/TRACK 1

Count Almaviva's Castle near Seville. (A half-furnished room with a large armchair in the centre. Figaro is measuring the floor. Susanna is trying on a hat in front of a mirror.) The celebrated Overture does not use any material from the opera itself, as was traditional in most opera overtures. However, it is a perfect encapsulation of the world about to unfold: conspiratorial and secretive yet with an elegance always on the brink of being torn away by disorder.

DISC NO. 1/TRACK 2

No. 1: Duettino The curtain rises on Figaro and Susanna in their new bedroom. Their playful music and subtly risqué banter let us know that they are a perfect match for each other, despite the tribulations to come.

FIGARO
Cinque…dieci…venti…Trenta…trentasei…
quarantatre…

FIGARO
Five…ten…twenty…thirty…thirty-
six…forty-three…

SUSANNA
Ora sì. Ch'io son contenta, Sembra fatto
inver per me.

SUSANNA
How happy I am now you'd think it had
been made for me.

FIGARO
Cinque…

FIGARO
Five…

SUSANNA
Guarda un po', mio caro Figaro.

SUSANNA
Look a moment, dearest Figaro.

FIGARO
dieci…

FIGARO
ten…

SUSANNA
guarda un po' mio caro Figaro...

SUSANNA
Look a moment, dearest Figaro.

FIGARO
venti...

FIGARO
twenty...

SUSANNA
guarda un po',

SUSANNA
Look a moment.

FIGARO
trenta...

FIGARO
thirty...

SUSANNA
guarda un po', guarda adesso il mio cappello!

SUSANNA
Look a moment, look here at my cap!

FIGARO
trentasei...

FIGARO
thirty-six...

SUSANNA
guarda adesso il mio cappello.

SUSANNA
Look here at my cap.

FIGARO
quarantatre...

FIGARO
forty-three...

SUSANNA
guarda un po', mio caro Figaro, *ecc.*

SUSANNA
Look a moment, *etc.*

FIGARO
Sì, mio core. Or è più bello, sembra fatto
inver per te.

FIGARO
Yes, dear heart, it's better that way; you'd
think it had been made for you.

SUSANNA
Guarda un po', *ecc.*

SUSANNA
Look a moment, *etc.*

FIGARO
Sì, mio core, *ecc.*

FIGARO
Yes, dear heart, *etc.*

SUSANNA
Ora sì ch'io son contenta, *ecc.*

SUSANNA
How happy I am now, *etc.*

FIGARO
Sì, mio core, *ecc.*

SUSANNA, FIGARO
Ah il mattino alle nozze vicino,

SUSANNA
quant'è dolce a l mio tenero sposo,

FIGARO
quant'è dolce al tuo tenero sposo,

SUSANNA, FIGARO
questo cappellino vezzoso, che Susanna ella
stessa si fe', *ecc.*

FIGARO
Yes, dear heart, *etc.*

SUSANNA, FIGARO
Ah, with our wedding day so near…

SUSANNA
How pleasing to my gentle husband.

FIGARO
How pleasing to your gentle husband.

SUSANNA, FIGARO
is this charming little cap which Susanna
made herself! *etc.*

RECITATIVO

SUSANNA
Cosa stai misurando, caro il mio Figaretto?

FIGARO
Io guardo se quel letto, che ci destina il
Conte, farà buona figura in questo loco.

SUSANNA
In questa stanza?

FIGARO
Certo, a noi la cede generoso il padrone.

SUSANNA
Io per me te la dono.

FIGARO
E la ragione?

SUSANNA
What are you measuring, you dear little
Figaro?

FIGARO
I want to know whether the bed which the
Count is giving us will look good in this spot.

SUSANNA
In this room?

FIGARO
Certainly, this one was granted us by our
generous patron.

SUSANNA
Then I turn it over to you.

FIGARO
Your reason?

SUSANNA *(Sì tocca la fronte)*
La ragione l'ho qui.

FIGARO
Perché non puoi far, che passi un po' qui?

SUSANNA
Perché non voglio; sei mio servo, o no?

FIGARO
Ma non capisco perché tanto ti spiace la
più comoda stanza palazzo.

SUSANNA
Perché io son la Susanna, e sei pazzo.

FIGARO
Grazie; non tanti elogi, guarda un poco, se
potria sì meglio star in altro loco.

SUSANNA *(tapping her forehead)*
The reason is up here.

FIGARO
Why can't you let it out for a moment?

SUSANNA
Because I don't wish to. Are you my humble servant or not?

FIGARO
I don't understand why you are so dis-
pleased with the most comfortable room in
the palace.

SUSANNA
Because I am Susanna, and you are insane.

FIGARO
Thank you, spare the compliments; but
consider whether any other place would be
better.

DISC NO. 1/TRACK 3
No. 2 Duettino **This little "ringing bells" duet plays on the ominous undercurrents beneath
the veneer of life's pleasantries in the Count's household.**

FIGARO
Se a caso Madama la notte ti chiama,
dindin, in due passi da quella puoi gir.
Vien poi l'occasione che vuolmi il padrone,
dondon, in tre salti lo vado a servir.

FIGARO
If perchance Madame should call you at
night, ding ding: in two steps from here
you'd be there. And then when the time
comes my master wants me, dong dong: in
three bounds I am ready to serve him.

59

SUSANNA

Così se il mattino il caro contino, dindin, e
ti manda tre miglia lontan, dindin, dondon, a mia porta il diavol lo porta, ed ecco
in tre salti...

SUSANNA

Likewise some morning the dear little
Count, ding ding: may send you some
three miles away, ding, ding, dong dong:
the devil may send him to my door, and
behold, in three bounds...

FIGARO

Susanna, pian pian, *ecc.*

FIGARO

Susanna, hush, hush, *etc.*

SUSANNA

ed ecco, in tre salti...dindin...dondon...
Ascolta!

SUSANNA

and behold, in three bounds...ding, ding...
Listen!

FIGARO

Fa presto!

FIGARO

Quickly!

SUSANNA

Se udir brami il resto, discaccia i sospetti,
che torto mi fan.

SUSANNA

If you want to hear the rest, drop those suspicions that do me such wrong.

FIGARO

Udir bramo il resto, i dubbi, i sospetti
gelare mi fan.

FIGARO

I will hear the rest; dubious suspicions
make my spine shiver.

RECITATIVO

SUSANNA

Or bene; ascolta e taci.

SUSANNA

Then listen, and be quite.

FIGARO

Parla, che c'è di nuovo?

FIGARO

Speak, what's the news?

SUSANNA

Il signor Conte, stanco d'andar cacciando
straniere bellezze forestiere, vuole ancor nel
castello ritentar la sua sorte; né già di sua
consorte, bada bene, l'appetito gli viene.

SUSANNA

My lord, the Count, tired of going hunting
for new beauties in the country, wishes to
try his luck once more in the castle; nor is
it for the Countess, mind you, that his
appetite moves him.

FIGARO
E di chi dunque?

SUSANNA
Della tua Susannetta.

FIGARO
Di te?

SUSANNA
Di me medesma, ed ha speranza ch'al nobil
suo progetto utilissima sia tal vicinanza.

FIGARO
Bravo! Tiriamo avanti.

SUSANNA
Queste grazie son, questa la cura ch'egli
prende di te, della tua sposa.

FIGARO
Oh guarda un po', che carità pelosa!

SUSANNA
Chetati, or viene il meglio: Don Basilio,
mio maestro di canto, e suo mezzano, nel
darmi la lezione, mi ripete ogni dì questa
canzone.

FIGARO
Chi! Basilio! Oh birbante!

SUSANNA
E credevi che fosse la mia dote merto de
tuo be muso?

FIGARO
Me n'era lusingato.

FIGARO
For whom, then?

SUSANNA
For your little Susanna.

FIGARO
For you?

SUSANNA
For none other, and he hopes that for his
noble endeavor our proximity will be most
useful.

FIGARO
Marvelous! Go on.

SUSANNA
Hence his favours, hence the solicitous
attentions he pays you, and your bride.

FIGARO
Oh, look out for his easy-going charity!

SUSANNA
Hush, now comes the best part: Don Basilio,
my singing teacher and his go-between,
when he gives me my lesson, every day
repeats for him the same old tune.

FIGARO
Who! Basilio? Oh, the rogue!

SUSANNA
And you thought that he gave me my
dowry to reward your good service?

FIGARO
So I flattered myself.

SUSANNA	**SUSANNA**
la destina per ottenere da me certe mezz'ore	It is intended to obtain from me certain
che il diritto feudale…	favours that the lord of the manor…
FIGARO	**FIGARO**
Come! Ne' feudi suoi non l'ha il Conte	What! Hasn't the Count abolished such
abolito?	rights in his lands?
SUSANNA	**SUSANNA**
Ebben, ora è pentito, è par che tenti riscot-	Perhaps, but he's changed his mind and
tarlo da me.	wants to get them back from me.
FIGARO	**FIGARO**
Bravo! Mi piace! Che caro signor Conte! ci	Admirable! So be it: my beloved lord and
vogliam divertir, trovato avete… Chi suona?	master! We are at the mercy of your whim!
La Contessa.	You have found… Who is ringing? The
	Countess.
SUSANNA	**SUSANNA**
Addio, addio, addio, Figaro bello.	Farewell, farewell, my handsome Figaro.
FIGARO	**FIGARO**
Coraggio, mio tesoro.	Courage, my treasure.
SUSANNA	**SUSANNA**
E cervello.	Keep your wits about you.

(She goes off.)

DISC NO. 1/TRACK 4

No. 3: Cavatina Having been told by his bride-to-be, Susanna, that his employer, the Count, has designs on her, Figaro sings a mockingly courtly ballad to him: The rhythms are easy-going but the text is bitter and provoking, and Figaro practically speaks the words, some quietly, some at the top of his voice. Despite the defiant message, Mozart keeps the mood light—the plucked strings which "imitate" the guitar Figaro would play for the Count to dance to are charming—plain and simple. Here is the character of Figaro in a nutshell—reacting quickly, far from subservient, witty—and angry with the situation he has found himself in.

FIGARO
Bravo, signor padrone! Ora incomincio a
capir il mistero, e a veder schietto tutto il
vostro progetto: a Londra, è vero? Voi ministro, io corriero, e la Susanna segreta ambas-
ciatrice, non sarà, non sarà! Figaro il dice!

FIGARO
Bravo, my lord! Now I begin to understand
the mystery, to see plainly your entire project: to London, is it? You the minister, I
the courier, and Susanna secret ambassadress.
It shall not be! Figaro speaks!

Se vuol ballare, signor contino, il chitarrino
suonerò, sì, se vuol venire nella mia scuola,
la capriola insegnerò, sì. Saprò, saprò, ma
piano, meglio ogni arcano dissimulando
scoprir potrò. L'arte schermendo, l'arte
adoprando, di qua pungendo, di là
scherzando, tutte macchine rovescierò. Se
vuol ballare, *ecc.*

If you would dance, my pretty Count, I'll
play the tune on my little guitar. If you will
come to my dancing school I'll gladly teach
you the capriole. You will learn quickly
every dark secret, you will find out how to
dissemble. The art of stinging, the art of
conniving, fighting with this one, playing
with that one, all of your schemes I'll turn
inside out. If you would dance, *etc.*

(He leaves. Bartolo and Marcellina enter, she with a contract in her hand.)

RECITATIVO

BARTOLO
Ed aspettaste il giorno fissato per nozze a
parlarmi di questo?

BARTOLO
And you waited until this day appointed
for the wedding to tell me this?

MARCELLINA
Io non mi perdo, dottor mio, di coraggio
per romper de' sponsali più avanzati di
questo bastò spesso un pretesto; ed egli ha
meco, oltre questo contratto, certi impeg-
ni...so io...basta...conviene la Susanna atter-
rir, convien con arte impuntigliarla a rifi-
utare il Conte; egli per vendicarsi prenderà
il mio partito, e Figaro così fia mio marito.

MARCELLINA
Not yet, my dear Doctor, have I lost hope;
to break off marriages nearer completion
than this one needs only a pretext, and that
I have here, and, besides this contract, definite promises. I know...but enough! Now is
the time to harass Susanna; we must con-
trive an imbroglio with the Count. He, to
get revenge, will take my side and Figaro
will thus become my husband.

BARTOLO *(prende il contratto)*
Bene, io tutto farò; senza riserve tutto a me
palesate.

BARTOLO *(taking the contract)*
Excellent. I shall do everything: keep me
well posted.

(aside)

Avrei pur gusto di dare in moglie la mia serva antica a chi mi fece un dì rapir l'amica.	I shall be only too glad to marry off my old servant to the man who once ruined my chances with Rosina.

DISC NO. 1/TRACK 5

No 4: Aria Bartolo, alone, reveals his lowest instincts in this staple of the bass repertory. The dark sounds of the orchestra are a parody of great revenge arias in opera, and suggest that the heroic posturing of many operatic "heroes" might be prompted by baser motives.

La vendetta, oh, la vendetta, è un piacer serbato ai saggi, l'obliar l'onte, gli oltraggi, è bassezza, è ognor viltà. Coll'astuzio… Coll'arguzia, col giudizio, col criterio..sì potrebbe…il fatto è serio, ma credete sì farà. Se tutto il codice dovessi volgere, se tutto l'indice dovessi leggere, con un equivoco, con un sinonimo, qualche garbuglio sì troverà. Se tutto il codice, *ecc.* Tutta Siviglia conosce Bartolo, il birbo Figaro vinto sarà, *ecc.*	Revenge, oh, sweet revenge is a pleasure reserved for the wise; to forgo shame, bold outrage, is base and utter meanness. With astuteness, with cleverness, with discretion, with judgment if possible. The matter is serious; but, believe me, it shall be done. If I have to pore over the law books, if I have to read all the extracts, with misunderstandings, with hocus-pocus he'll find himself in a turmoil. If I have to pore over, *etc.* All Seville knows Bartolo, the scoundrel Figaro shall be overcome!

(He goes.)

RECITATIVO

MARCELLINA

Tutto ancor non ho perso: mi resta la speranza. Ma Susanna sì avanza, io vo' provarmi…fingiam di non vederla. E qualla buona perla la vorrebbe sposar!	**MARCELLINA** I haven't been stopped yet: my hopes are very good. Ah, Susanna is coming: we'll see. I'll pretend not to notice her. And this is the bright pearl whom he's going to wed!

(enter Susanna)

SUSANNA
Di me favella.

SUSANNA
She's chattering about me.

MARCELLINA
Ma da Figaro alfine non può meglio sperar-si: l'argent fait tout.

MARCELLINA
But I suppose she couldn't do better than Figaro. L'argent fait tout.

SUSANNA
Che lingua! Manco male, ch'ognun sa quanto vale.

SUSANNA
(What a tongue!) It takes troubles to bring out a person's character.

MARCELLINA
Brava! Questo è giudizio! Con quegli occhi modesti, con quell'aria pietosa, e poi…

MARCELLINA
Splendid! Here's justice! With those modest eyes! With that pious air, and still…

SUSANNA
(Meglio è partir!)

SUSANNA
(Now's the time to leave.)

MARCELLINA
(Che cara sposa!)

MARCELLINA
(A pretty little wife!)

(They both want to leave and meet at the door.)

DISC NO. 1/TRACK 6

No 5: Duettino **This tells us all we have to know about the relationship between Marcellina and Susanna—they hate each other. In two minutes Mozart gives us a portrait of one of the supremely bitchy relationships in opera.**

(fa una riverenza)
Via, resti, servita, madama brillante.

(making a curtsy)
Go on, I'm your servant, magnificent lady.

SUSANNA *(fa una riverenza)*
Non sono sì ardita, madama piccante.

SUSANNA *(making a curtsy)*
I should not presume too much, sharp-witted dame.

MARCELLINA *(fa una riverenza)*
No, prima a lei tocca.

MARCELLINA *(making a curtsy)*
No, you go first.

SUSANNA *(fa una riverenza)*
No, no, tocca a lei.

MARCELLINA *(fa una riverenza)*
No, prima a lei tocca.

SUSANNA *(fa una riverenza)*
No, no, tocca a lei.

MARCELLINA, SUSANNA
(fa fanno una riverenza)
Io so i dover miei, non fo inciviltà, *ecc.*

MARCELLINA *(fa una riverenza)*
La sposa novella!

SUSANNA *(fa una riverenza)*
La dama d'onore!

MARCELLINA *(fa una riverenza)*
De conte la bella!

SUSANNA
Di Spagna l'amore!

MARCELLINA
I meriti…

SUSANNA
L'abito!…

MARCELLINA
Il posto…

SUSANNA
L'età…

SUSANNA *(making a curtsy)*
No, no, after you.

MARCELLINA *(making a curtsy)*
No, you go first.

SUSANNA *(making a curtsy)*
No, no, after you.

MARCELLINA, SUSANNA
(making a curtsy)
I know my position, and do not breach
good manners, *etc.*

MARCELLINA *(making a curtsy)*
A bride-to-be!…

SUSANNA *(making a curtsy)*
A lady of honour…

MARCELLINA *(making a curtsy)*
The Count's favourite…

SUSANNA
All Spain's beloved…

MARCELLINA
Your merit…

SUSANNA
Your fine dress…

MARCELLINA
Your position…

SUSANNA
Your age…

MARCELLINA
Per Bacco, precipito se ancor, se ancor resto
qua.

MARCELLINA
By Bacchus, I might grow rash if I stay here
longer.

SUSANNA
Sibilla decrepita, da rider mi fa.

SUSANNA
Decrepit old Sibyl, you make me laugh.

MARCELLINA *(fa una riverenza)*
Via, resti servita, *ecc.*

MARCELLINA *(making a curtsy)*
Go on, I'm your servant, *etc.*

SUSANNA *(fa una riverenza)*
Non sono sì ardita, *ecc.*

SUSANNA *(making a curtsy)*
I should not presume so much, *etc.*

MARCELLINA *(fa una riverenza)*
La sposa novella! *ecc.*

MARCELLINA *(making a curtsy)*
The bride-to-be, *etc.*

SUSANNA *(fa una riverenza)*
La dama d'onore! *ecc.*

SUSANNA *(making a curtsy)*
A lady of honour, *etc.*

(Marcellina goes off in a rage.)

RECITATIVO

Va là, vecchia pedante, dottoressa arro-
gante, perchè hai letto due libri, e seccata
Madama in gioventù...

Go on, you old pedant, you ill-tempered
schoolmistress, just because you've read two
books and harassed Madame in her youth...

(Cherubino comes in.)

CHERUBINO
Susannetta, sei tu?

CHERUBINO
Little Susanna, is it you?

SUSANNA
Son io, cosa volete?

SUSANNA
It is I; what do you want?

CHERUBINO
Ah, cor mio, che accidente!

CHERUBINO
Ah, my heart, what a misfortune!

SUSANNA
Cor vostro? Cosa avvenne?

CHERUBINO
Il Conte ieri, perchè trovommi sol con Barbarina, il congedo mi diede, e se la Contessina, la mia bella comare, grazia non m'intercede, io vado via, io non ti vedo più, Susanna mia.

SUSANNA
Non vedete più me! Bravo! Ma dunque non più per la Contessa segretamente il vostro cor sospira?

CHERUBINO
Ah, che troppo rispetto ella m'inspira! Felice te, che puoi vederla quando vuoi, che la vesti il mattino, che la sera la spogli, che le metti gli spilloni, i merletti...Ah, se in tuo loco...Cos'hai li'? dimmi un poco...

SUSANNA
Ah, il vago nastro e la notturna cuffia di comare sì bella.

CHERUBINO
Deh dammelo, sorella, dammelo per pietà.

(He snatches the ribbon.)

SUSANNA
Presto quel nastro.

SUSANNA
Your heart! What happened?

CHERUBINO
Yesterday, the Count, because he found me alone with Barbarina, gave me orders to go away: and if the dear Countess, my beloved protectress, doesn't grant her protection, I must go, and see you no more, my Susanna.

SUSANNA
See me no more! Bravo! So then it's not for the Countess now that your heart secretly yearns!

CHERUBINO
Ah, what great respect she inspires in me! Happy are you who can see her whenever you wish! You who dress her in the morning, you who undress her in the evening, pin up her hair, tie on her lace...Ah, to be in your place! What do you have there? Just tell me...

SUSANNA
Oh, just a pretty ribbon and the nightcap of your beautiful protectress.

CHERUBINO
Come, give it to me, my sister, give it to me for pity's sake.

SUSANNA
Quick, give it back.

CHERUBINO
Oh caro, oh bello, oh fortunato nastro! lo
non te'l renderò che colla vita!

CHERUBINO
O dearest, prettiest, most fortunate ribbon!
I shall not give thee up, but with my life!

SUSANNA
Cos'è quest'insolenza?

SUSANNA
What does this insolence mean?

CHERUBINO
Eh via, sta cheta! In ricompensa poi questa
mia canzonetta io ti vo' dare.

CHERUBINO
Oh, please, don't tell! In payment I'll give
you this canzonetta of mine.

(He takes a song to the Countess outof his pocket.)

SUSANNA *(cogliendo il foglio)*
E che ne debbo fare?

SUSANNA *(accepting it)*
And what would I do with it?

CHERUBINO
Leggila alla padrona; leggila tu medesma,
leggila a Barbarina, a Marcellina…leggila ad
ogni donna de' palazzo!

CHERUBINO
Read it to our patroness, read it to yourself,
read it to Barbarina, to Marcellina, read it
to every woman in the palace!

SUSANNA
Povero Cherubin, siete voi pazzo!

SUSANNA
Poor Cherubino, are you mad!

DISC NO. 1/TRACK 7

No 6: Aria **Here is Cherubino, the hormonally-driven youth who loves all women (the role is
one of the most famous of all "trouser roles," ie.: the part of an adolescent boy sung by a female
mezzo-soprano). The breathless quality of this little aria again tells us as much about the character as the words—here is an anxious, passionate, panting youth, ready to explore and explode.**

CHERUBINO
Non so più cosa son, cosa faccio, or di
foco, ora sono di ghiaccio, ogni donna can-
giar di colore, ogni donna mi fa palpitar.
Solo ai nomi d'amor, di diletto, mi sì turba,
mi s'altera il petto e a parlare mi sforza
d'amore un desio ch'io non posso spiegar.

CHERUBINO
I no longer know what I am, what I do;
now I'm all fire, now all ice; every woman
changes my temperature, every woman
makes my heart beat faster. The very men-
tion of love, of delight, disturbs me, changes
my heart, and speaking of love, forces on

Non so più cosa son, *ecc*. Parlo d'amor vegliando, parlo d'amor sognando, all'acqua, all'ombre, ai monti, ai fiori, all'erbe, ai fonti, all'eco, all'aria, ai venti, che il suon de' vani accenti portano via con sé. Parlo d'amor vegliando, *ecc*. E se non ho chi m'oda, parlo d'amor con me.

me a desire I cannot restrain! I no longer know what I am, *etc*. I speak of love while I'm awake, I speak of love while I'm sleeping, to rivers, to shadows, to mountains, to flowers, to grass, to fountains, to echoes, to air, to winds, until they carry away the sound of my useless words. I speak of love while I'm awake, *etc*. And if no one is near to hear me I speak of love to myself.

(The Count's voice is heard outside. Cherubino dives behind the armchair.)

RECITATIVO

CHERUBINO
Ah! Son perduto! Che timor...Il Conte! Misera me!

CHERUBINO
Ah! I'm lost! How awful...It's the Count; how unlucky!

(The Count enters.)

CONTE
Susanna, tu mi sembri agitata e confusa.

COUNT
Susanna, you seem nervous and confused.

SUSANNA
Signor...io chiedo scusa...ma, se mai qui sorpresa...per carità partite!

SUSANNA
Sir, I beg your pardon, but if someone... found you here; I beg you leave me.

(The Count sits on a chair; takes her hand.)

CONTE
Un momento, e ti lascio. Odi.

COUNT
One moment, and I'll leave you. Listen.

SUSANNA
Non odo nulla.

SUSANNA
I won't hear anything.

CONTE
Due parole: tu sai che ambasciatore a Londra il re mi dichiarò: di condur meco Figaro destinai.

COUNT
Two words. You know that the king has appointed me ambassador to London; I have decided to take Figaro with me.

SUSANNA
Signor, se osassi…

CONTE
Parla, parla, mia cara! E con quel dritto,
ch'oggi prendi su me, finché tu vivi, chiedi,
imponi, prescrivi.

SUSANNA
Lasciatemi, signor, dritti non prendo, non
ne vo', non ne intendo. Oh me infelice!

CONTE
Ah, no, Susanna, io ti vo' far felice! Tu ben
sai quant'io t'amo; a te Basilio tutto già
disse, or senti se per pochi momenti meco
in giardin sull'imbrunir del giorno…ah per
questo favore io pagherei…

BASILIO *(dietro quinte)*
E uscito poco fa.

CONTE
Chi parla?

SUSANNA
Oh dei!

CONTE
Esci, ed alcun non entri.

SUSANNA
Ch'io vi lascio qui solo?

BASILIO *(sempre dietro quinte)*
Da Madama sarà, vado a cercarlo.

SUSANNA
Sir, if I dared…

COUNT
Speak, speak, my dear, and by that right
you assume today for as long as you live,
ask, request, demand.

SUSANNA
Leave me, signor; I am assuming no right
and do not intend to. Oh, unhappy me!

COUNT
Ah no, Susanna, I want to make you
happy! You know how much I love you.
Basilio has already told you everything.
Now listen. If for a few minutes you meet
me in the garden this evening…Ah, for this
favour I would pay…

BASILIO *(outside)*
He just left.

COUNT
Who is speaking?

SUSANNA
Ye gods!

COUNT
Go, and don't let anyone in…

SUSANNA
And leave you here alone?

BASILIO *(outside)*
He must be with Madame. I'll look for
him there.

CONTE (*additando la poltrona*)
Qui dietro mi porrò.

SUSANNA
Non vi celate.

CONTE
Taci, e cerca ch' parta.

SUSANNA
Ohimè! Che fate!

(The Count hides behind the chair. Cherubino, unobserved by him, scrambles into the seat and Susanna covers him with a dress as Basilio enters.)

BASILIO
Susanna, il ciel vi salvi: avreste a caso veduto il Conte?

SUSANNA
E cosa deve far meco il Conte? Animo, uscite.

BASILIO
Aspettate, sentite, Figaro di lui cerca.

SUSANNA
(Oh cielo!) cerca chi dopo voi più l'odia.

CONTE
Vediam come me serve.

BASILIO
Io non ho mai nella moral sentito ch'uno ch'ama la moglie odii il marito, per dir che il Conte v'ama…

COUNT (*pointing to the chair*)
I can go behind this.

SUSANNA
Don't hide here.

COUNT
Hush, and try to get rid of him.

SUSANNA
Oh dear! What are you doing?

BASILIO
Susanna, Heaven bless you: have you by chance seen the Count?

SUSANNA
And what would the Count be doing here? Just go away!

BASILIO
Wait, and listen; Figaro is looking for him.

SUSANNA
(Heavens!) Then he's looking for the man who, after you, hates him most.

COUNT
We'll see how he serves me.

BASILIO
I've never heard any moral law that says that he who loves the wife must hate the husband. Which is to say that the Count loves you.

SUSANNA
Sortite, vil ministro dell'altrui sfrenatezza:
io non ho d'uopo della vostra morale, del
Conte, del suo amor…

BASILIO
Non c'è alcun male. Ha ciascuno i suoi
gusti; io mi credea che preferir doveste per
amante, come fan tutte quante, un signor
liberal, prudente e saggio, a un giovinastro,
a un paggio…

SUSANNA
A Cherubino!

BASILIO
A Cherbubino, a Cherubin d'amore, ch'oggi sul far del giorno passeggiava qui d'intorno per entrar.

SUSANNA
Uomo maligno, un'impostura è questa.

BASILIO
È un maligno con voi, chi ha gli occhi in
testa. E quella canzonetta, ditemi in confi-
denza, io sono amico, ed altrui nulla dico,
è per voi, per Madama?

SUSANNA
(Chi diavol gliel'ha detto?)

BASILIO
A proposito, figlia, istruitelo meglio, egli la
guarda a tavola sì spesso, e con tale immod-
estia che s'il Conte' s'accorge…e sul tal
punto, sapete, egli è una bestia.

SUSANNA
Get out, you pander to another's lascivious-
ness. I do not aspire to your system of
morality, nor to the Count's love.

BASILIO
There's no harm in it! Everyone to his own
taste; I should have thought that you
would prefer as a lover, as most women
would do, a generous gentleman, discreet
and wise, to a stripling, to a page…

SUSANNA
To Cherubino!

BASILIO
To Cherubino, love's cherubim, who today
at daybreak was seen on his way to this place.

SUSANNA
Wicked man! What a falsehood that is!

BASILIO
Is one evil just because one has eyes in his
head? And that canzonetta? Tell me, in
confidence: I am your friend and will tell
no one else: Is it for you? For Madame?

SUSANNA
(What devil told him about it?)

BASILIO
Apropos, my daughter, instruct him more
wisely; he stares at her so at the table, and
with such immodesty, that the Count is
beginning to notice: In this, you know, he
can be a terror.

SUSANNA Scellerato! E perchè andate voi tai men- zogne spargendo?	**SUSANNA** Villain! And why do you come here to spread such lies?
BASILIO Io! Che ingiustizia! Quel che compro io vendo, a quel che tutti dicono io non aggiungo un pelo.	**BASILIO** I! You do me wrong! What I sell, I also buy. I have not added a hair to what everyone is saying.
CONTE *(mostrandosi improvvisamente)* Come! Che dicon tutti?	**COUNT** *(coming forward)* How's that, what is everyone saying?
BASILIO Oh bella!	**BASILIO** Oh, perfect!
SUSANNA Oh cielo!	**SUSANNA** Oh, Heavens!

DISC NO. 1/TRACK 8

No. 7: Terzetto **The first of a number of great ensembles in the opera, we here discover how nasty the Count can be, how sniveling Basilio (the Music-Master) can be, and how well Susanna can react under pressure. Listening carefully to the text, one can also hear Basilio sing "Cosi fan tutte le belle" ("Women are all alike"): Is this the first notion Mozart and da Ponte had with regard to working together on an opera based on such a theme?**

CONTE Cosa sento! Tosto andate, e scacciate il seduttor.	**COUNT** What do I hear! Go at once, and throw the seducer out!
BASILIO In mal punto son qui giunto; perdonate, o mio signor.	**BASILIO** I came here at the wrong moment! Pardon me, my Lord.
SUSANNA Che ruina, me meschina, son oppressa dal terror!	**SUSANNA** I'm ruined, unhappy me! I'm crushed with fright!

CONTE Tosto andate, *ecc.*	**COUNT** Go at once, *etc.*
BASILIO In mal punto, *ecc.*	**BASILIO** At the wrong moment, *etc.*
SUSANNA *(quasi svenuta)* Che ruina, *ecc.*	**SUSANNA** *(she appears to faint)* I'm ruined, *etc.*
CONTE, BASILIO *(sostenendola)* Ah! Già svien la poverina! Come, oh Dio, batte il cor, *ecc.*	**COUNT, BASILIO** *(supporting her)* Ah, the poor dear is fainting! Oh God, how her heart beats!
BASILIO Pian pianin, su questo seggio...	**BASILIO** Softly, softly, on to this chair.
SUSANNA *(rinvenendo)* Dove sono! Cosa veggio! Che insolenza, andate fuor, *ecc.*	**SUSANNA** *(recovering and drawing away)* Where am I? What is this? What insolence, get out of here! *etc.*
BASILIO Siamo qui per aiutarvi, è sicuro il vostro onor.	**BASILIO** We are here to help you, and your honour is perfectly safe.
CONTE Siamo qui per aiutarti, non turbarti, o mio tesor.	**COUNT** We are here to help you; don't be alarmed, my treasure.
BASILIO Ah del paggio quel ch'ho detto, era solo un mio sospetto.	**BASILIO** Ah, what I said about the page was only a suspicion of mine.
SUSANNA È un'insidia, una perfidia, non credete all'impostor, *ecc.*	**SUSANNA** It is a malicious scandal, don't believe the impostor, *etc.*
CONTE Parta, parta il damerino, *ecc.*	**COUNT** No, the young reprobate must go! *etc.*

SUSANNA, BASILIO
Poverino! *ecc.*

CONTE
Poverino! Poverino! Ma da me sorpreso
ancor!

SUSANNA
Come?

BASILIO
Che?

SUSANNA
Che?

BASILIO
Come?

SUSANNA, BASILIO
Come? Che?

CONTE
Da tua cugina, l'uscio ier trovai rinchiuso;
picchio, m'apre Barbarina paurosa fuor del-
l'uso, io, dal muso insospettito, guardo,
cerco in ogni sito, ed alzando pian pianino
il tappeto al tavolino, vedo il paggio.

SUSANNA, BASILIO
Poor boy! *etc.*

COUNT
Poor boy! But I've caught him again!

SUSANNA
How's that?

BASILIO
What!

SUSANNA
What!

BASILIO
How's that?

SUSANNA, BASILIO
How's that? What?

COUNT
Yesterday I found your cousin's door was
locked; I knocked and Barbarina opened
much more sheepishly than usual. Suspicious
at her manner I went searching in every corner, and raising up the table covering as
gently as you please, I found the page!

(He shows them what he means and lifting the dressing-gown on the chair discovers Cherubino.)

Ah, Cosa veggio!

SUSANNA
Ah, crude stelle!

BASILIO
Ah, meglio ancora!

Ah, what's this I see?

SUSANNA
Ah, cruel fortune!

BASILIO
Ah, better yet!

CONTE
Onestissima signora, or capisco come va!

COUNT
Most virtuous lady, now I understand your ways!

SUSANNA
Accader non può di peggio; giusti Dei, che mai sarà!

SUSANNA
It couldn't have turned out worse; ye just gods, what next!

BASILIO
Così fan tutte le belle non c'è alcuna novità! Ah, del paggio quel che ho detto era solo un mio sospetto..

BASILIO
All pretty women are the same, there's nothing new in this case! Ah, what I said about the page, was only a suspicion of mine.

(The following portion of the libretto is not included on the enclosed CDs but has been left here as text for your enjoyment. Please resume listening at page 82, disc no. 1/track 9).

CONTE
Basilio, in traccia tosto di Figaro volate; io vo' ch'ei veda...

COUNT
Basilio, take wing and track down Figaro this instant; I want him to see...

SUSANNA
Ed io che senta; andate.

SUSANNA
And I want him to hear, go on.

CONTE *(a Basilio)*
Restate, che baldanza! E Quale scusa se la colpa è evidente?

COUNT *(to Basilio)*
Stay here: what nerve! What excuse is there if the facts are plain?

SUSANNA
Non ha d'uopo di scusa un'innocente.

SUSANNA
Innocence needs no excuse.

CONTE
Ma costui quando venne?

COUNT
But when did this fellow come in?

SUSANNA
Egli era meco, quando voi qui giungeste. E mi chiedea d'impegnar la padrona a intercedergli grazia; il vostro arrivo in scompiglio lo pose, ed allor in quel loco sì nascose.

SUSANNA
He was with me when you arrived, and was asking me to beg our patroness to intercede for him with you; your coming threw him into a panic, and he hid himself there.

CONTE	COUNT
Ma s'io stesso m'assisi, quando in camera entrai!	I myself sat there when I came into the room!

CHERUBINO	CHERUBINO
Ed allora di dietro io mi celai.	I was hiding behind it then.

CONTE	COUNT
E quando io là mi posi?	And when I went back there?

CHERUBINO	CHERUBINO
Allor io pian mi volsi e qui m'ascosi.	I slipped around quietly and got in here.

CONTE	COUNT
Oh ciel! Dunque ha sentito quello ch'io ti dicea!	Oh Heavens! Then he heard everything I said to you?

CHERUBINO	CHERUBINO
Feci per non sentir quanto potea.	I tried as hard as I could not to hear.

CONTE	COUNT
Oh perfidia!	Wicked boy!

BASILIO	BASILIO
Frenatevi, vien gente.	Control yourself, someone's coming.

CONTE *(a Cherubino)*	COUNT *(to Cherubino)*
E voi restate qui, piccio! serpente.	As for you, stay here, young serpent.

NO. 8: CHORUS

(enter peasants, followed by Figaro with a white veil in his hand)

CORO	CHORUS
Giovani liete, fiori spargete davanti il nobile nostro signor. Il suo gran core vi serba intatto d'un più bel fiore l'almo candor.	Carefree girls, scatter flowers before this noble master of ours. His great heart watches over you, the spotless flower of a noble soul.

RECITATIVO

CONTE Cos'è questa commedia?	**COUNT** What is this farce?
FIGARO *(piano, a Susanna)* Eccoci in danza: secondami, cor mio.	**FIGARO** *(softly, to Susanna)* Now is the time: stand behind me, dearest.
SUSANNA Non ci ho speranza.	**SUSANNA** It is useless.
FIGARO Signor, non isdegnate questo del nostro affetto meritato tributo: or che aboliste un diritto sì ingrato a chi ben ama...	**FIGARO** Sir, do not spurn this expression of gratitude you deserve so well: since you abolished a lordly right so distasteful to all true lovers...
CONTE Quel dritto or non v'è più, cosa sì brama?	**COUNT** That right no longer exists: what's the commotion?
FIGARO Della vostra saggezza il primo frutto oggi noi colgierem: le nostre nozze si son già stabilite, or a voi tocca costei, che un vostro dono illibata serbò, coprir di questa, simbolo d'onestà, candida vesta.	**FIGARO** We gather today the first fruit of your wisdom: our wedding is arranged, now it is your duty to hand over your gift unspotted, dressed in this symbol of honesty, pure white raiment!
CONTE *(tra sé)* Diabolica astuzia! Ma fingere convien. *(forte)* Son grato, amici, ad un senso sì onesto! Ma non merto per questo né tributi, né lodi, e un dritto ingiusto ne miei feudi abolendo a natura, al dover lor dritti io rendo.	**COUNT** *(aside)* Diabolical cleverness! But I must play the game. *(aloud)* I welcome, friends, such good-hearted sentiments. But I deserve for this neither tribute nor praise; by abolishing that unjust right in my lands I only did my natural duty.
TUTTI Evviva, evviva, evviva!	**ALL** Hurrah, hurrah, hurrah!

SUSANNA
Che virtù!

FIGARO
Che giustizia!

CONTE
A voi prometto compier la cerimonia.
Chiedo sol breve indugio: io voglio in faccia de' miei più fidi, e con più ricca pompa
rendervi appien felici.
(tra sé)
Marcellina, si trovi?
(forte)
Andate, amici.

NO. 8A: CHORUS

CORO
Giovani liete, fiori spargete, *ecc.*

(The peasants leave.)

FIGARO
Evviva!

SUSANNA
Evviva!

BASILIO
Evviva!

FIGARO *(a Cherubino)*
E voi non applaudite?

SUSANNA
È afflitto, poveretto, perché il padron lo
scaccia dal castello.

SUSANNA
What virtue!

FIGARO
What justice!

COUNT
I promise to fulfill the ceremony. I ask only
for your brief indulgence while I speak to
my most loyal subjects, and with the richest
of festivities I shall make you most happy.
(aside)
Marcellina, where are you?
(aloud)
Go forth, friends.

CHORUS
Carefree girls, *etc.*

FIGARO
Hurrah!

SUSANNA
Hurrah!

BASILIO
Hurrah!

FIGARO *(to Cherubino)*
And why aren't you cheering?

SUSANNA
He's saddened, poor boy, that his master is
chasing him out of the castle.

FIGARO
Ah! In un giorno sì bello!

SUSANNA
In un giorno di nozze!

FIGARO *(al Conte)*
Quando ognuno v'ammira.

CHERUBINO
Perdono, mio signor.

CONTE
No! meritate.

SUSANNA
Egli è ancora fanciullo.

CONTE
Men di quel che tu credi.

CHERUBINO
È ver, mancai; ma dal mio labbro alfine…

CONTE
Ben, mio, io vi perdono; anzi farò di più, vacante è è un posto d'uffizial nel reggimento mio, io scelgo oi, voi, partite tosto, addio.

SUSANNA, FIGARO
Ah! Fin domani sol…

CONTE
No, parta tosto.

CHERUBINO
A ubbidirvi, signor, son già disposto.

FIGARO
Ah, on such a beautiful day!

SUSANNA
On a wedding day!

FIGARO *(to the Count)*
When everyone is praising you!

CHERUBINO
Pardon, my lord!

COUNT
You don't deserve it.

SUSANNA
He's still a boy.

COUNT
Less so than you think.

CHERUBINO
True, I've been at fault; but now I swear…

COUNT
Very well; I pardon you. I will do even more: there is vacant an officer's post in my regiment; you may have it; go immediately; farewell.

SUSANNA, FIGARO
Ah! Tomorrow morning!

COUNT
No, he goes now.

CHERUBINO
Sir, I am ready to obey you.

CONTE	COUNT
Via, per l'ultima volta la Susanna abbracciate.	Go then, for the last time embrace your Susanna.
(tra sé)	*(aside)*
Inaspettato è il colpo.	The blow was unexpected.

(The Count and Basilio leave.)

FIGARO	FIGARO
Ehi, capitano, a me pure la mano. Io vo' parlarti pria che tu parta. Addio, picciolo Cherubino! Come cangia in un punto il tuo destino!	Well, captain, give me your hand. I want to speak to you before you depart. Farewell, little Cherubino; how your destiny has changed in a moment!

DISC NO. 1/TRACK 9

No 9: Aria **This is the opera's first big hit, one that was such a resounding smash that Mozart used it again in Don Giovanni in an irresistible, self-referential way. In it, Figaro bids formal farewell to Cherubino as the youth is about to embark on an uninvited, unwanted military career. The jaunty march tune is Mozart at his most mischievous and captivating, yet the vocal line includes a threatening quality that reveals Figaro's own prickly nature and tendency to anger.**

Non più andrai, farfallone amoroso, notte e giorno d'intorno girando, delle belle turbando il riposo, Narcisetto, Adoncino d'amor, *ecc.* Non più avrai questi bei pennacchini, quel cappello leggiero e galante, quella chioma, quell'aria brillante, quel vermiglio donnesco color. Non più andrai, *ecc.* Tra guerrieri poffar Bacco! Gran mustacchi, stretto sacco, schioppo in spalla, sciabola al fianco, col'o dritto, muso franco, o un gran casco, o un gran turbante, molto onor, poco contante, ed invece del fandango, una marcia per il fango, per montagne, per valloni, colle nevi, e i

No more will you, amorous butterfly, flit around the castle night and day, upsetting all the pretty girls, love's little Narcissus and Adonis, *etc.* No more will you have those fine plumes, that soft and stylish hat, those fine locks, that striking air, those rosy, girl-like cheeks. No more will you, *etc.* Among warriors swearing by Bacchus! great mustacchios, holding your pack, a gun on your shoulder, a sabre hanging at your right, musket ready, or some great helmet or a turban, winning honours, but little money, and in place of the fandango a march through the mud. Over mountains,

solleoni, al concerto di tromboni, di bombarde, di cannoni, che le palle in tutti i tuoni all'orecchio fan fischiar. Cherubino alla vittoria, alla gloria militar!

over valleys, through the snow and burning sun. To the music of trumpets, of shells and cannons, with balls sounding thunder, making your ears ring. Cherubino, on to victory, on to victory in war!

(They leave, marching like soldiers.)

The Countess's boudoir

DISC NO. 1/TRACK 10
No. 10: *Cavatina* The only thing missing from the opera so far is its most sympathetic character—what a terrific move on Mozart's part (letters attribute the idea to composer, not librettist)! Here the Countess sings an inward, calm plea—to love, disembodied—to return her husband's love to her, or to allow her to die.

(To the right is a door, to the left a closet. A door at the back leads to the servants' rooms; on one side, a window. The Countess is alone.)

CONTESSA
Porgi, amor, qualche ristoro, al mio duolo, a' miei sospir! O mi rendi il mio tesoro, o mi lascia almen morir! Porgi amor, *ecc.*

COUNTESS
Grant, love, that relief to my sorrow, to my sighing. Give me back my treasure, or at least let me die. Grant, love, *etc.*

(Susanna comes in.)

Recitative Exchanges between the Countess, Susanna, and Figaro show us the natural affinity between them, all underscored in the most economcal manner by the harpsichord. Figaro reminds everyone that he has the wits to oppose the Count by singing a snippet of his aria (02:49).

Vieni, cara Susanna, finiscimi l'istoria.	Come, dear Susanna, finish the story.
SUSANNA	**SUSANNA**
È già finita.	It's already finished.
CONTESSA	**COUNTESS**
Dunque volle sedurti?	Then he tried to seduce you?
SUSANNA	**SUSANNA**
Oh, il signor Conte non fa tai complimenti colle donne mie pari; egli venne a contratto di danari.	Oh, his lordship pays no such compliments to women of my rank; he only thinks of it as a business matter.
CONTESSA	**COUNTESS**
Ah! il crudel più non m'ama!	Ah! The cruel man loves me no more!
SUSANNA	**SUSANNA**
E come poi è geloso di voi?	Then why is he so jealous of you?
CONTESSA	**COUNTESS**
Come lo sono i moderni mariti! Per sisterma infedeli, per genio capricciosi e per orgoglio poi tutti gelosi. Ma se Figaro t'ama ei sol potria...	That's how all modern husbands are! Systematically unfaithful, brilliantly capricious, and out of vanity all jealous. But if Figaro loves you only he can...
FIGARO *(entrando)*	**FIGARO** *(singing as he enters)*
La, la, la, la, la, la...	La, la, la, la, la, la...
SUSANNA	**SUSANNA**
Eccolo; vieni, amico, Madama impaziente...	Here he is; come, my friend, madame is getting impatient...

FIGARO

A voi non tocca stare in pena per questo.
Alfin di che si tratta? Al signor Conte piace
la sposa mia; indi segretamente ricuperar
vorria il diritto feudale; possibile è la cosa e
naturale.

CONTESSA

Possibil?

SUSANNA

Natural?

FIGARO

Naturalissima, e se Susanna vuol, possi-
bilissima.

SUSANNA

Finiscila una volta.

FIGARO

Ho già finito. Quindi, prese il partito di
sceglier me corriero, e la Susanna con-
sigliera segreta d'ambasciata; e perch'ella
ostinata ognor rifiuta il diploma d'onor che
le destina, minaccia di protegger Marcellina; questo è tutto l'affare.

SUSANNA

Ed hai coraggio di trattar scherzando un
negozio sì serio?

FIGARO

Non vi basta che scherzando io ci pensi?
Ecco il progetto: per Basilio un biglietto io
gli fo' capitar, che l'avvertisca di certo
appuntamento, che per l'ora del ballo a un
amante voi deste…

FIGARO

Madame, you should not concern yourself
in this matter. In short, what does it come
to? The Count is pleased with my bride,
and through her he means to recoup his
feudal right; it's all possible, and natural.

COUNTESS

Possible?

SUSANNA

Natural?

FIGARO

Most natural, and if Susanna agrees, most
possible.

SUSANNA

Finish your story.

FIGARO

I've already finished. Therefore he has decided to choose me as his courier, and Susanna
secret counsellor of the embassy; and since
she has stubbornly refused the high creden-
tials destined for her, he threatens to favour
Marcellina; that's the whole situation.

SUSANNA

And you have the nerve to joke about such
a serious matter?

FIGARO

Isn't it enough that I think while I joke?
Here's my plan: With Basilio's help I'll see
that he finds a letter informing him of a
certain assignation while the ball is going
on between you and your lover.

CONTESSA
Oh ciel! Che sento! Ad un uom sì geloso…

FIGARO
Ancora meglio, così potrem più presto imbarazzarlo, confonderlo, imbrogliarlo, rovesciargli i progetti, empierlo di sospetti, e porgli in testa che la moderna festa ch'ei di fare a me tenta, altri a lui faccia. Onde qua perda il tempo, ivi la traccia, così quasi ex abrupto e senza ch'abbia fatto per frastornarci alcun disegno vien l'ora delle nozze, e in faccia a lei non fia ch'osi d'opporsi ai voti miei.

SUSANNA
È ver, ma in di lui vece s'opporrà Marcellina.

FIGARO
Aspetta! Al Conte farai subito dir che verso sera attendati in giardino. Il picciol Cherubino, per mio consiglio non ancor partito, da femmina vestito, faremo che in sua vece ivi sen vada; questa è l'unica strada, onde Monsù, sorpresioda Madama, sia costretto a far poi quel che si brama.

CONTESSA
Che ti par?

SUSANNA
Non c'è mal.

CONTESSA
Nel nostro caso…

COUNTESS
Heavens! What are you saying? With such a jealous man!

FIGARO
All the better, that way we can embarrass him faster, confound him, entangle him, upset his schemes, banish his suspicions, and make him know that another can play this modern game he's trying to play. And so we'll gain time, as I've planned it, and ex abrupto, you might say, and if nothing happens to disturb our plans, the hour will come for the wedding, and with Madame on our side, he won't dare to prevent our vows.

SUSANNA
True, but in his place Marcellina will rear her head.

FIGARO
Wait! Immediately I'll let the Count know that toward evening you will be waiting for him in the garden. Little Cherubino, upon my advice, hasn't left yet, and in female attire we'll have him here in your place. This is the only way whereby Monsieur, discovered by Madame, can be forced to practise what he preaches.

COUNTESS
What do you think?

SUSANNA
Not bad.

COUNTESS
In our position…

SUSANNA
Quand'egli è persuaso...

CONTESSA
E dove è il tempo?

FIGARO
Ito è il Conte alla caccia, e per qualch'ora
non sarà di ritorno. Io vado, e tosto
Cherubino vi mando; lascio a voi la cura
di vestirlo.

CONTESSA
E poi?

FIGARO
E poi? Se vuol ballare, signor contino, il
chitarrino le suonerò, sì, *ecc.*

(He leaves.)

CONTESSA
Quanto duolmi, Susanna, che questo
giovinotto abbia del Conte le stravaganze
udite! Ah! Tu non sai! Ma per qual causa
mai da me stessa ei non venne? Dov'è la
canzonetta?

SUSANNA
Eccola, appunto facciam che ce la canti.
Zitto, vien gente; è desso; avanti, avant,
signor uffiziale.

(Cherubino enters.)

CHERUBINO
Ah, non chiamarmi con nome sì fatale! Ei
mi rammenta che abbandonar degg'io
comare tanto buona.

SUSANNA
If he can be persuaded...

COUNTESS
Is there time?

FIGARO
The Count has gone hunting, and won't
return for about an hour. I'll go, and right
away send Cherubino to you. I leave to you
the job of dressing him.

COUNTESS
And then?

FIGARO
And then? If you would dance, my pretty
Count, I'll play the tune on my little guitar, *etc.*

COUNTESS
How it pains me, Susanna, that this youth
heard the foolish words of the Count! Ah!
You can't imagine! But why in the world
didn't he come to see me himself? Where is
the canzonetta?

SUSANNA
Here it is; in fact let's make him sing it for
you. Quickly, someone's coming. It's he;
forward. Sir Officer!

CHERUBINO
Ah, don't call me by that awful name! It
reminds me that I must abandon such a
generous protectress.

SUSANNA
E tanto bella!

CHERUBINO
Ah, sì certo.

SUSANNA
Ah, sì certo; ipocritone! Via. presto, la canzone che stamane a me deste, a Madama cantate.

CONTESSA
Chi n'è l'autor?

SUSANNA
Guardate, egli ha due brace di rossor sulia faccia.

CONTESSA
Prendi la mia chitarra, e l'accompagna.

CHERUBINO
Lo sono sì tremante; ma se Madama vuole…

SUSANNA
Lo vuole, sì, lo vuol. Manco parole.

SUSANNA
And beautiful?

CHERUBINO
Ah, yes, certainly.

SUSANNA
Ah, yes, certainly. Hypocrite! Now quickly, the poem that you read for me this morning, sing it for Madame.

COUNTESS
Who is the author?

SUSANNA
Look, there are two streaks of red on his cheeks.

COUNTESS
Take my guitar and accompany him.

CHERUBINO
I am so nervous; but if Madame desires…

SUSANNA
She does desire it. Enough with words.

DISC NO. 1/TRACK 12

No. 11: Canzona Art within art emerges here: Cherubino meekly sings a song he's composed about love (what else?) and we (and the Countess and Susanna) are bowled over by its directness, its simplicity. Who wouldn't feel for this guy?

CHERUBINO
Voi, che sapete che cosa è amor, donne vedete, s'io l'ho nel cor. Quello ch'io provo, vi ridirò, e per me nuovo, capir nol so. Sento un affetto pien di desir, ch'ora è

CHERUBINO
You who know what love is, ladies, see whether it's in my heart. What I experience I'll describe for you; it's new to me, I don't understand it. I feel an emotion full of

diletto, ch'ora è martir. Gelo, e poi sento l'alma avvampar, e in un momento torno a gelar. Ricerco un bene fuori di me, non so chi 'l tiene, non so cos'è. Sospiro e gemo senza voler, palpito e tremo senza saper; non trovo pace notte, né dì, ma pur mi piace languir così. Voi, che sapete, *ecc.*

desire, that is now pleasure, and now suffering. I freeze, then I feel my soul burning up, and in a moment I'm freezing again. I seek a blessing outside myself, from whom I know not or what it is. I sigh and moan without meaning to, palpitate and tremble without knowing it. I find no peace night or day, and yet I enjoy languishing so. You who know what love is, *etc.*

DISC NO. 1/TRACK 13

Recitative Susanna's sly comment to the Countess at the beginning of this recitative (00:06) is typical of da Ponte's sophisticated suggestiveness throughout the libretto. It seems that everyone in this household has a secret or two. . .

CONTESSA
Bravo! Che bella voce! Io non sapea che cantaste sì bene.

COUNTESS
Bravo! What a fine voice! I didn't know you sang so well!

SUSANNA
Oh in verità, egli fa tutto ben quello ch'ei fa. Presto, a noi, bel soldato: Figaro v'informò…

SUSANNA
Oh, truly, he does everything well. Quickly, come here, handsome soldier. Figaro told you?

CHERUBINO
Tutto mi disse.

CHERUBINO
He told me all.

SUSANNA
Laciatemi veder: andrà benissimi: siam d'uguale statura…giù quel manto.

SUSANNA
Let me see; it will work very well, we're the same height. Off with your coat.

CONTESSA
Che fai?

COUNTESS
What are you doing?

SUSANNA
Niente paura.

SUSANNA
Don't be afraid.

CONTESSA
E se qualcuno entrasse?

SUSANNA
Entri, che mal facciamo? La porta chiuderò. Ma come poi acconciargli i capelli?

(She closes the door.)

CONTESSA
Una mia cuffia prendi nel gabinetto. Presto!

(Susanna goes into the dressing room.)

Che carta è quella?

CHERUBINO
La patente.

CONTESSA
Che sollecita gente!

CHERUBINO
L'ebbi or or da Basilio.

CONTESSA
Dalla freetta obliato hanno il sigillo.

SUSANNA *(tornando)*
Il sigillo di che?

CONTESSA
Della patente.

SUSANNA
Cospetto! Che premura! Ecco la cuffia.

COUNTESS
And if someone came in?

SUSANNA
Let him come, what are we doing wrong? I'll shut the door. But how can we do his hair?

COUNTESS
Get one of my caps out of the closet. Quickly!

What paper is that?

CHERUBINO
My commission.

COUNTESS
What solicitous people!

CHERUBINO
I just got it from Basilio.

COUNTESS
In their hurry they forgot the seal.

SUSANNA *(returning)*
The seal for what?

COUNTESS
For the commission.

SUSANNA
Good lord, What haste! Here is the cap.

CONTESSA	COUNTESS
Spicciati; va bene; miserabili noi, se il Conte viene.	Hurry, we still have time. Unlucky us if the Count comes.

DISC NO. 1/TRACK 14

No. 12: Aria **Susanna sings a lovely little ditty while she gets Cherubino up in "drag." It is all quite trifling — or is it? She certainly seems quite taken with the handsome youth. . .**

SUSANNA	SUSANNA
Venite, inginocchiatevi, restate fermo li! Pian, piano, or via giratevi, bravo, va ben così, la faccia ora volgetemi, olà! Quegli occhi a me, drittissimo, guardatemi, Madama qui non è. Più alto quel colletto, quel ciglio un po' più basso, le mani sotto il petto, vedremo poscia il passo quando sarete in piè. Mirate il bricconcello, mirate quanto è bello! Che furba guardatura, che vezzo, che figura! Se l'amano le femmine, han certo il lor perché.	Come here, get down on your knees, and stay still there! Gently, now turn around again. Bravo, that's just fine. Now turn your face around, ha! Don't make such eyes at me; keep looking straight on ahead, Madame is not there. Pull this collar a bit higher, keep your eyes down lower, your hands across your chest, we'll see how you walk when you're on your feet. Look at the little colt, look how handsome he is! What a crafty expression, what an outfit, what a figure! If women fall in love with him, they have their reasons why.

DISC NO. 1/TRACK 15

Recitative **The door-slamming, hiding-in-closets features of this comic farce begin in this scene, yet underneath the farce there are sharp recriminations between the Count and the Countess (02:46 and 03:12).**

CONTESSA	COUNTESS
Quante buffonerie!	What foolishness!

SUSANNA	SUSANNA
Ma se ne sono io medesma gelosa! Ehi! serpentello, volete tralasciar d'esser sì bello?	I'm even jealous myself! Hey! You little serpent, will you stop being so handsome?

CONTESSA
Finiam le ragazzate; or quelle maniche oltre il gomito gli alza, onde più agiatamente l'abito gli si adatti.

COUNTESS
Let's finish these pranks. Now lift his sleeves up above his elbows so that the dress can be fitted more comfortably.

SUSANNA *(eseguendo)*
Ecco!

SUSANNA *(raising the sleeve)*
There!

CONTESSA
Più indietro, così; che nastro è quello?

COUNTESS
Further back, there; what is this ribbon?

SUSANNA
È quel ch'esso involommi.

SUSANNA
It's the one he stole from me.

CONTESSA *(snodando il nastro)*
E questo sangue?

COUNTESS *(taking the ribbon)*
And this blood?

CHERUBINO
Quel sangue...io non so come, poco pria sdrucciolando...in un sasso la pelle io mi sgraffiai...e la piaga col nastro io mi fasciai.

CHERUBINO
That blood...I don't know how but I slipped a while ago...on a rock...I scratched the skin... and I bound the wound with the ribbon.

SUSANNA
Mostrate: non è mal; cospetto! Ha il braccio più candido del mio! Qualche ragazza...

SUSANNA
Let's see it: it's not bad. Look here! His arm is whiter than mine; like a girl's...

CONTESSA
E segui a far la pazza? Va nel mio gabinetto, e prendi un poco d'inglese taffetà, ch'è sullo scrigno.

COUNTESS
Are you still playing games? Go into my closet, and bring out some sticking plaster – it's on the jewel box.

(Susanna goes into the dressing room.)

In quanto al nastro...inver...per il colore mi spiacea di privarmene.

As for the ribbon...really...because of the colour, I'd be sorry to lose it.

SUSANNA *(rientrando)*
Tenete, e da legargli il braccio?

SUSANNA *(reappearing)*
Wait, how will we bind up his arm?

CONTESSA	COUNTESS
Un altro nastro prendi insiem col mio vestito.	Bring another ribbon with the dress.

(Susanna goes off through the door at the back with the page's cloak.)

CHERUBINO	CHERUBINO
Ah! Più presto m'avria quello guarito!	Ah! That one would have healed me sooner!

CONTESSA	COUNTESS
Perchè? Questo è migliore.	Why? This one is finer.

CHERUBINO	CHERUBINO
Allor che un nastro…legò la chioma…ovver toccò la pelle…d'oggetto…	Because the ribbon…that has tied the hair…or touched the skin…of one whom…

CONTESSA	COUNTESS
Forestiero, è buon per le ferite, non è vero? Guardate qualità ch'io non sapea!	…someone else, it's good for wounds, is it? It possesses qualities I never suspected!

CHERUBINO	CHERUBINO
Madama scherza, ed io frattanto parto.	Madame is joking, and I must leave.

CONTESSA	COUNTESS
Poverin! Che sventura!	Poor boy! How unhappy!

CHERUBINO	CHERUBINO
Oh me infelice!	Oh miserable me!

CONTESSA	COUNTESS
Or piange…	Now he's weeping…

CHERUBINO	CHERUBINO
Oh ciel! Perché morir non lice! forse vicino all'ultimo momento…questa bocca oseria…	Heavens! Why can't I die! Perhaps at my last moment…this mouth might dare…

CONTESSA	COUNTESS
Siate saggio, cos'è questa follia?	Are you mad? What is this nonsense?

(hearing a knock at the door)

Chi picchia alla mia porta?	Who is beating at my door?
CONTE *(fuori)* *Perché chiusa?*	**COUNT** *(outside)* Why is it shut?
CONTESSA Il mio sposo! Oh Dei! Son morta. Voi qui senza mantello! In questo stato…un ricevuto foglio, la sua gran gelosia…	**COUNTESS** My husband! Ye gods! I'm finished! And you without a coat! In here dressed like that…Figaro's letter…his tremendous jealousy!
CONTE Cosa indugiate?	**COUNT** What's taking so long?
CONTESSA Son sola…ah sì…son sola…	**COUNTESS** I am alone…yes…I am alone…
CONTE E a chi parlate?	**COUNT** Whom are you talking to?
CONTESSA A voi…certo, a voi stesso.	**COUNTESS** To you…of course, to you.
CHERUBINO Dopo quel ch'è successo…il suo furore…non trovo altro consiglio…	**CHERUBINO** After what has happened, and his anger, I have no other alternative!

(He runs and hides in the dressing room.)

CONTESSA Ah! Mi difenda il cielo in tal periglio!	**COUNTESS** Ah, Heaven defend me in such danger!

(The Countess takes the key of the dressing room then goes to admit the Count.)

CONTE Che novità! Non fu mai vostra usanza di rinchiudervi in stanza.	**COUNT** This is new! You never used to lock yourself in your room!

CONTESSA È ver; ma…io stava qui mettendo…	**COUNTESS** True; but I…I was here putting away…
CONTE Via, mettendo…	**COUNT** Go on, putting away…
CONTESSA Certe robe; era meco la Susanna, che in sua camera è andata.	**COUNTESS** some robes; Susanna was with me, but she has gone into her own room.
CONTE Ad ogni modo voi non siete tranquilla. Guardate questo foglio.	**COUNT** At any rate, you are not very calm. Look at this letter.
CONTESSA *(tra sé)* Numi! È il foglio che Figaro gli scrisse.	**COUNTESS** *(aside)* Ye gods! It's the letter Figaro wrote him!

(Cherubino knocks against a chair in the dressing room.)

CONTE Cos'è codesto strepito? In gabinetto qualche cosa è caduta.	**COUNT** What's that uproar? Something fell down in the closet.
CONTESSA Io non intesi niente.	**COUNTESS** I heard nothing.
CONTE Convien che abbiate i gran pensieri in mente.	**COUNT** You must have important thoughts in your head.
CONTESSA Di che?	**COUNTESS** About what?
CONTE Là v'è qualcuno.	**COUNT** Someone's in there.
CONTESSA Chi volete che sia?	**COUNTESS** Who could it be!

CONTE Lo chiedo a voi; io vengo in questo punto.	**COUNT** You tell me. I have just arrived.
CONTESSA Ah sì…Susanna…appunto…	**COUNTESS** Ah yes, Susanna, certainly.
CONTE Che passò, mi diceste, alla sua stanza.	**COUNT** Didn't you say she went into her own room?
CONTESSA Alla sua stanza, o qui, non vidi bene.	**COUNTESS** To her room or in there, I didn't notice.
CONTE Susanna, e donde viene che siete sì turbata?	**COUNT** Susanna! And how is it that you are so upset?
CONTESSA Per la mia cameriera?	**COUNTESS** On account of my maid?
CONTE Io non so nulla; ma turbata senz'altro.	**COUNT** I don't know, but certainly upset.
CONTESSA Ah questa serva più che non tuba me, turba voi stesso.	**COUNTESS** Ah, this girl has you more upset than me.
CONTE È vero, è vero! E lo vedrete adesso.	**COUNT** True, true, and now you'll witness it.

(Susanna enters through the door at the back and stops as she sees the Count who has not seen her.)

No. 13: Terzetto **The lies and the suspicions are ratcheted up a notch in this trio and in the subsequent recitative (track 17), marked by little spasms in the orchestra (01:18) reminiscent of those in the overture.**

(knocking on the door of the closet)

Susanna, or via sortite, sortite, così vo?

Susanna, now, come out. Come out, I order you.

CONTESSA
Fermatevi, sentite, sortire ella non può,

COUNTESS
Wait, and listen; she cannot come out.

SUSANNA
Cos'è codesta lite? il paggio dove andò?

SUSANNA
What has happened? Where has the page gone?

CONTE
E chi vietarlo or osa? Chi?

COUNT
And who dares to forbid it? Who?

CONTESSA
Lo vieta, lo vieta l'onestà. Un abito da sposa provando ella si sta.

COUNTESS
Modesty forbids it. She's in there trying on her new gown for the wedding.

CONTE
Chiarissima è la cosa, l'amante qui sarà, *ecc.*

COUNT
The matter's quite clear: her lover is in there.

CONTESSA
Bruttissima è la cosa, chi sa, cosa sarà, *ecc.*

COUNTESS
A brutal situation: who knows what will come of it?

SUSANNA
Capisco qualche cosa, veggiamo come va, *ecc.*

SUSANNA
I think I understand. Let's see what happens.

CONTE
Susanna,

COUNT
Susanna,

CONTESSA Fermatevi!	**COUNTESS** Wait!
CONTE or via sortite!	**COUNT** come out!
CONTESSA Sentite!	**COUNTESS** Listen!
CONTE Sortite!	**COUNT** Come out!
CONTESSA Fermatevi!	**COUNTESS** Wait!
CONTE Io così vo'!	**COUNT** I order you!
CONTESSA Sortire ella non può.	**COUNTESS** She cannot come out.
CONTE Dunque parlate almeno, Susanna, se qui siete?	**COUNT** Well then, speak at least, Susanna, if you're in there.
CONTESSA Nemmen, nemmen, nemmeno, io v'ordino, tacete.	**COUNTESS** No, no, no, no, no, no, I order you to be quiet.
CONTE Consorte mia, giudizio, un scandalo, un disordine, schiviam per carità!	**COUNT** My wife, be reasonable, a scandal, an uproar, can be avoided, I beg you!
SUSANNA Oh ciel! Un precipizio, un scandalo, un disordine, qui certo nascerà!	**SUSANNA** Heavens! A disaster, a scandal, an uproar, will certainly result!

CONTESSA
Consorte mio, giudizio, un scandalo, un disordine, schiviam per carità!

COUNTESS
My Lord, be reasonable, a scandal, an uproar, can be avoided, I beg you!

RECITATIVE

CONTE
Dunque voi non aprite?

COUNT
Then you won't open?

CONTESSA
E perché deggio le mie camere aprir?

COUNTESS
And why should I open my own chambers?

CONTE
Ebben lasciate, l'aprirem senza chiavi. Ehi, gente.

COUNT
Very well, then, we'll open it without a key. Ho, servants!

CONTESSA
Come? Porreste a repentaglio d'una dama l'onore?

COUNTESS
How's that? Would you play games with a lady's honour?

CONTE
È vero, io sbaglio, posso senza rumore, senza scandalo alcun di nostra gente, andar io stesso a prender l'occorrente. Attendete pur qui - ma perché in tutto sia il mio dubbio distrutto anco le porte io prima chiuderò.

COUNT
You're right. I lost my head. I can, without noise, without a scandal among our people, go after the necessary equipment. Wait here…but no: to completely satisfy my doubts I'll even shut the door first.

(He locks Susanna's door.)

CONTESSA
Che imprudenza.

COUNTESS
What foolhardiness.

CONTE
Vio la condiscendenza di venir meco avrete. Madama, eccovi il braccio, andiamo!

COUNT
Please condescend to accompany me. Madame, here is my arm. Let us go.

CONTESSA
Andiamo!

COUNTESS
Let us go.

CONTE	COUNT
Susanna starà qui finché torniamo.	Susanna will be here when we return.

(They leave. Susanna rushes out of the alcove where she had been hiding, and runs to the closet door.)

DISC NO. 1/TRACK 18

No. 14: Duettino **Susanna's fears and Cherubino's impulsive nature are perfectly portrayed in this breathy little duet, culminating in a leap out the window that elicits a delighted laugh from Susanna. The situation my be dire, but the brightest people always find something amusing even in crises.**

SUSANNA	SUSANNA
Aprite, presto, aprite, aprite, è la Susanna; sortite, via sortite andate via di qua.	Open, quickly, open; open, it's Susanna. Come out, now, come out, come on out of there.

CHERUBINO *(escendo tutto confuso)*	CHERUBINO *(entering, confused and out of breath)*
Ohimè, che scena orribile! Che gran fatalità!	Oh dear, what a terrible scene! What a disaster!

SUSANNA	SUSANNA
Di qua…di là…	This way, that way…

CHERUBINO	CHERUBINO
Che gran fatalità!	What a disaster!

SUSANNA, CHERUBINO	SUSANNA, CHERUBINO
Le porte son serrate, che mai sarà?	The doors are locked, What will happen next?

CHERUBINO	CHERUBINO
Qui perdersi non giova.	No use to stay here.

SUSANNA	SUSANNA
V'uccide se vi trova.	He'll kill you if he finds you.

CHERUBINO *(appressandosi alla finestra)*	CHERUBINO *(looking out of the window)*
Veggiamo un po' qui fuori,	Look down here a moment,

(getting ready to jump)

dà proprio nel giardino.	it opens on the garden.

SUSANNA *(trattenendolo)*
Fermate, Cherubino, fermate, per pietà!

SUSANNA *(restraining him)*
Wait, Cherubino, wait, for pity's sake!

CHERUBINO
Qui perdersi non giova,

CHERUBINO
No use to stay here,

SUSANNA
Fermate, Cherubino,

SUSANNA
Wait, Cherubino!

CHERUBINO
m'uccide se mi trova,

CHERUBINO
He'll kill me if he finds me,

SUSANNA
Tropp'alto per un salto. Fermate per pietà!

SUSANNA
It's too high to jump. Wait, for pity's sake!

CHERUBINO
Lasciami, lasciami! Pria di nuocerle, nel foco volerei! Abbraccio te per lei! Addio! Così si fa!

CHERUBINO
Leave me, leave me! To save her I would leap into flames! I embrace you for her! Farewell! So be it.

(He jumps out of the window.)

SUSANNA
Ei va a perire, oh dei! Fermate per pietà!

SUSANNA
He'll kill himself, ye gods! Wait, for pity's sake!

(She runs to the window.)

DISC NO. 1/TRACK 19

Recitative Fact and fiction become blurred in this exchange between husband and wife. Note the sound of guilt in the Countess's voice as she confesses that her closet contains a boy (01:18).

Oh guarda il demonietto come fugge! È già un miglio lontano; ma non perdiamci invano: entriam nel gabinetto; venga poi lo smargiasso, io qui l'aspetto.	Oh, look at the little devil! How he flies! He's a mile away already! But let's not lose everything. I'll go into the closet. Then when the bully comes, I'll be waiting.

(She goes into the dressing room. The Count enters with the Countess.)

CONTE
Tutto è come il lasciai: volete dunque aprir voi stessa, o deggio…

COUNT
Everything is as we left it; now do you wish to open it yourself, or must I…

CONTESSA
Ahimè! Fermate, e ascoltatemi un poco: mi credete capace di mancar al dover?

COUNTESS
Ah, wait, and listen to me a moment. Do you think me capable of failing in my duty.

CONTE
Come vi piace, entro quel gabinetto chi v'è chiuso vedrò.

COUNT
Whatever you say, I'm going into that closet to see who is shut up inside.

CONTESSA
Sì, lo vedrete, ma uditemi tranquillo.

COUNTESS
Yes, you'll see. But listen to me calmly.

CONTE
Non è dunque Susanna?

COUNT
Then it's not Susanna?

CONTESSA
No, ma invece è un oggetto che ragion di sospetto non vi deve lasciar: per questa sera… una burla innocente…di farsi disponeva… ed io vi giuro chel'onor…l'onestà…

COUNTESS
No, instead it's something that because of your suspicions I can't let you see: for this evening…we are planning an innocent prank…and I swear that my honour…my purity…

CONTE
Che è dunque? dite…L'ucciderò.

COUNT
Who is it then? Say…I'll kill him.

CONTESSA
Sentite…ah non ho cor!

COUNTESS
Listen…ah, I haven't the heart!

CONTE	COUNT
Parlate!	Speak!

CONTESSA	COUNTESS
È un fanciullo...	It is a boy.

CONTE	COUNT
Un fanciul?	A boy?

CONTESSA	COUNTESS
Sì...Cherubino...	Yes...Cherubino...

CONTE	COUNT
E mi farà il destino ritrovar questo paggio in ogni loco! Come? Non è partito? Scellerati! Ecco i dubbi spiegati, ecco l'imbroglio, ecco il raggiro onde m'avverte il foglio.	Then it is my destiny to find that page everywhere I go! How's that? He hasn't left? Villains! These are my justified suspicions, here's the mess, the plot of which the letter warned me.

DISK NO. 1/TRACKS 20–24

No. 15: Finale **Here begins 20-or-so minutes of the greatest—and most entertaining—music ever penned. Mozart invented the form of this finale, in which a duet turns into a trio, which, in turn, becomes a quartet, and so on, with the rhythm changing even more often than the number of characters and the tension, albeit comic tension, mounting by the minute. By the time it's over every character has been, at one time or another, tickled by the turn of events. Susanna has had to navigate some very tricky waters, (at track 23) the drunken gardener, Antonio, enters and almost destroys all of Susanna's and the Countess's plotting, Figaro, after almost giving away the ruse, begins to take an active part in it and saves it, and (at track 24) as if the confusion weren't rich enough, Marcellina, Basilio and Bartolo enter and publicly announce that in order to pay off an old debt, Figaro has to marry Marcellina. The act ends with the trio of Susanna, Figaro and the Countess absolutely stupefied and the quartet of Marcellina, the Count, Basilio and Bartolo gloating—all at the same time. It doesn't get much better than this.**

(going impetuously to the door of the dressing room)

Esci ormai, garzon malnato, sciagurato, non tardar.	If you're coming out, low-born brat, you wretch, don't be slow about it.

CONTESSA

Ah! signore, quel furore, per lui fammi il cor tremar.

COUNTESS

Ah sir, your anger makes my heart tremble for him.

CONTE

E d'opporvi ancor osate?

COUNT

And yet you dare to oppose me?

CONTESSA

No, sentite.

COUNTESS

No, listen.

CONTE

Via parlate!

COUNT

Go on, speak!

CONTESSA

Giuro al ciel, ch'ogni sospetto…e lo stato in che il trovate, sciolto il collo, nudo il petto…

COUNTESS

I swear by Heaven, that every suspicion, and the state in which you'll find him, his collar loosened, his chest bare…

CONTE

Sciolto il collo! Nudo il petto! Seguitate!

COUNT

Collar loosened, his chest bare…go on!

CONTESSA

Per vestir femminee spoglie…

COUNTESS

Was to dress him in girl's clothing.

CONTE

Ah, comprendo, indegna moglie, mi vo' tosto vendicar.

COUNT

Ah, I understand, worthless woman, and I'll soon get my revenge.

CONTESSA

Mi fa torto quel trasporto; m'oltraggiate a dubitar.

COUNTESS

Your outrage wrongs me, you insult me by doubting me.

CONTE

Ah, comprendo, indegna moglie, mi vo' tosto vendicar.

COUNT

Ah, I understand, worthless woman, and I'll soon get my revenge.

CONTE

Qua la chiave!

COUNT

Give me the key!

CONTESSA Egli è innocente...	**COUNTESS** He is innocent...
CONTE Qua la chiave!	**COUNT** Give me the key!
CONTESSA Egli è innocente. Voi sapete...	**COUNTESS** He is innocent, you know it...
CONTE Non so niente! Va lontan dagli occhi miei, un'infida, un'empia sei, e mi cerchi d'infamar!	**COUNT** I know nothing! Get far out of my sight, You are unfaithful and impious, and you're trying to humiliate me!
CONTESSA Vado...sì...ma...	**COUNTESS** I'll go, but...
CONTE Non ascolto.	**COUNT** I won't listen.
CONTESSA ma...	**COUNTESS** but...
CONTE non ascolto.	**COUNT** I won't listen.
CONTESSA *(dà la chieve al* Conte*)* ...non son rea!	**COUNTESS** *(giving him the key)* I am not guilty!
CONTE Vel leggo in volto! Mora, mora, più non sia ria cagion del mio penar.	**COUNT** I read it in your face! He shall die and be no longer the source of my troubles.
CONTESSA Ah! La cieca gelosia, quale eccesso gli fa far!	**COUNTESS** Ah! Blind jealousy, what excesses you bring about!

(The Count unsheathes his sword and opens the closet door. Susanna comes out.)

CONTE
Susanna!

CONTESSA
Susanna!

SUSANNA
Signore! Cos'è quel stupore? Il brando prendete, il paggio uccidete, quel paggio malnato vedetelo qua.

CONTE
Che scola! La testa girando mi va!

CONTESSA
Che storia è mai questa, Susanna v'è là!

SUSANNA
Confusa han la testa, non san come va!

CONTE *(a Susanna)*
Sei sola?

SUSANNA
Guardate, qui ascoso sarà.

CONTE
Guardiamo, qui ascoso sarà, *ecc.*

(He goes into the dressing room.)

CONTESSA
Susanna, son morta…il fiato mi manca.

SUSANNA
Più lieta, più franca, in salvo è di già.

COUNT
Susanna!

COUNTESS
Susanna!

SUSANNA
Sir! What is this amazement? Take your sword and kill the page, that low-born page, you see before you.

COUNT
A revelation! I feel my head spinning!

COUNTESS
What a strange tale, Susanna was in there!

SUSANNA
Their heads are muddled. They don't know what happened!

COUNT *(to Susanna)*
Are you alone?

SUSANNA
See yourself whether anyone is in there.

COUNT
We'll look, someone could be in there, *etc.*

COUNTESS
Susanna, I'm finished, I cannot breathe.

SUSANNA
Softly, don't worry, he's already safe.

CONTE (*escendo confuso dal gabinetto*)
Che sbaglio mai presi! Appena lo credo; se
a torto v'offesi perdono vi chiedo, ma far
burla simile è poi crudeltà.

COUNT (*emerging from the dressing room in confusion*)
What an error I made! I hardly believe it;
if I've done you wrong, I beg your pardon,
but playing such jokes is cruel, after all.

CONTESSA, SUSANNA
Le vostre follie non mertan pietà.

COUNTESS, SUSANNA
Your foolish acts deserve no pity.

CONTE
Io v'amo!

COUNT
I love you!

CONTESSA
Nol dite!

COUNTESS
Don't say it!

CONTE
Vel giuro!

COUNT
I swear!

CONTESSA
Mentite! Son l'empia, l'infida ch'ognora
v'inganna.

COUNTESS
You're lying. I'm unfaithful and impious,
and trying to humiliate you.

CONTE
Quell'ira, Susanna, m'aita a calmar.

COUNT
Help me, Susanna, to calm her anger.

SUSANNA
Così si condanna chi può sospettar.

SUSANNA
Thus are condemned the suspicious.

CONTESSA
Adunque la fede d'un'anima amante, sì
fiera mercede doveva sperar?

COUNTESS
Should then a faithful lover's soul expect in
return such harsh thanks?

CONTE
Quell'ira, Susanna, *ecc.*

COUNT
Help me, Susanna, *etc.*

SUSANNA
Così si condanno, *ecc.* Signora!

SUSANNA
Thus are condemned, *etc.* My lady!

CONTE
Rosina!

CONTESSA
Crudele! Più quella non sono! Ma il misero oggetto del vostro abbandono che avete diletto di far disperar. Crudele, crudele! Soffrir sì gran torto quest'alma non sa.

CONTE
Confuso, pentito, son troppo punito; abbiate pietà.

SUSANNA
Confuso, pentito, è troppo punito; abbiate pietà.

CONTE
Ma il paggio rinchiuso?

CONTESSA
Fu sol per provarvi.

CONTE
Ma il tremiti, i palpiti?

CONTESSA
Fu sol per burlarvi.

CONTE
E un foglio sì barbaro?

SUSANNA, CONTESSA
Di Figaro è il foglio, e a voi per Basilio…

CONTE
Ah, perfidi…io voglio…

COUNT
Rosina!

COUNTESS
Cruel man! I am now no more than the miserable object of your desertion, whom you delight in driving to despair. Cruel, cruel man! This soul cannot bear to suffer such wrong.

COUNT
Confused, repentant, I've been punished enough; have pity on me.

SUSANNA
Confused, repentant, he's been punished enough; have pity on him.

COUNT
But the page locked inside?

COUNTESS
Was only to test you.

COUNT
But the trembling, the excitement?

COUNTESS
Was only to ridicule you.

COUNT
And that wretched letter?

SUSANNA, COUNTESS
The letter is from Figaro and for you through Basilio.

COUNT
Ah, tricksters! If I could…

SUSANNA, CONTESSA
Perdono non merta chi agli altri non dà.

CONTE
Ebben, se vi piace, comune è la pace; Rosina inflessibile con me non sarà.

CONTESSA
Ah quanto, Susanna, son dolce di core! Di donne al furore chi più crederà?

SUSANNA
Cogli uomin, signora, girate, volgete, vedrete che ognora si cade poi là.

CONTE
Guardatemi!

CONTESSA
Ingrato!

CONTE
Guardatemi!

CONTESSA
Ingrato!

CONTE
Guardatemi, ho torto, e mi pento.

SUSANNA, CONTESSA, CONTE
Da questo momento quest'alma a conoscerla/mi/vi apprender potrà, *ecc.*

(Figaro enters.)

SUSANNA, COUNTESS
He deserves no pardon who withholds it from others.

COUNT
Well, if you please, let us make peace; Rosina will not be unforgiving with me.

COUNTESS
Ah, Susanna, how soft I am in the heart! Who would believe again in woman's anger?

SUSANNA
With men, my lady, we must hesitate and falter, you see how honour soon falls before them.

COUNT
Look at me!

COUNTESS
Ungrateful.

COUNT
Look at me!

COUNTESS
Ungrateful!

COUNT
Look at me! I was wrong and I repent!

SUSANNA, COUNTESS, COUNT
From this moment on he/I/you will try to learn to understand each other, *etc.*

FIGARO
Signori, di fuori son già i suonatori, le
trombe sentite, i pifferi udite, tra canti, tra
balli de' vostri vassalli, corriamo, voliamo le
nozze a compir.

FIGARO
My lords, the musicians are already outside.
Hear the trumpets, and listen to the pipes.
With singing and dancing for all the peas-
ants...let's hurry out to perform the wedding!

CONTE
Pian piano, men fretta...

COUNT
Calm down, less haste.

FIGARO
La turba m'aspetta.

FIGARO
The crowd is waiting.

CONTE
Pian piano, men fretta, un dubbio togliete-
mi in pria di partir.

COUNT
Calm down, less haste, relieve me of a
doubt before you go.

SUSANNA, CONTESSA, FIGARO
La cosa è scabrosa, com ha da finir, *ecc.*

SUSANNA, COUNTESS, FIGARO
A nasty situation; how will it all end? *etc.*

CONTE
Con arte le carte convien qui scoprir, *ecc.*

COUNT
Now I must play my cards carefully, *etc.*

CONTE
Conoscete, signor Figaro, questo foglio chi
vergò?

COUNT
Do you know, my good Figaro, who wrote
this letter?

(He shows him a letter.)

FIGARO
Nol conosco!

FIGARO
I don't know.

SUSANNA
Nol conosci?

SUSANNA
You don't know?

FIGARO
No!

FIGARO
No.

CONTESSA
Nol conosci?

COUNTESS
You don't know?

FIGARO
No!

CONTE
Nol conosci?

FIGARO
No!

SUSANNA, CONTESSA, CONTE
Nol conosci?

FIGARO
No, no, no!

SUSANNA
E nol desti a Don Basilio?

CONTESSA
Per recarlo...

CONTE
Tu c'intendi?

FIGARO
Oibò, oibò!

SUSANNA
E non sai del damerino...

CONTESSA
Che stasera nel giardino...

CONTE
Già capisci?

FIGARO
Io non lo so.

FIGARO
No.

COUNT
You don't know?

FIGARO
No.

SUSANNA, COUNTESS, COUNT
You don't know?

FIGARO
No, no, no.

SUSANNA
Didn't you give it to Don Basilio?

COUNTESS
To take it...

COUNT
Do you understand?

FIGARO
Alas, alas!

SUSANNA
And don't you remember the young fop?

COUNTESS
Who tonight in the garden...

COUNT
Now you understand?

FIGARO
I don't know.

CONTE
Cerchi invan difesa e scusa, il tuo ceffo già
t'accusa, vedo ben che vuoi mentir.

COUNT
In vain you look for defences, excuses, your
own face accuses you; I see very well you're
lying.

FIGARO
Mente il ceffo, io già non mento.

FIGARO
My face may be lying, but not I.

SUSANNA, CONTESSA
Il talento aguzzi invano, palesato abbiam
l'arcano, non v'è nulla da ridir.

SUSANNA, COUNTESS
You've sharpened your wits in vain; the whole
secret is out, and there's no use complaining.

CONTE
Che rispondi?

COUNT
What's your answer?

FIGARO
Niente, niente!

FIGARO
Simply nothing.

CONTE
Dunque accordi?

COUNT
Then you admit it?

FIGARO
Non accordo!

FIGARO
I do not!

SUSANNA, CONTESSA
Eh via chetati, balordo, la burletta ha da
finir.

SUSANNA, COUNTESS
Go on, keep quiet, you fool, the little game
is over.

FIGARO
Per finirla lietamente, e all'usanza teatrale,
un'azion matrimoniale la faremo ora seguir.

FIGARO
To give it a happy ending as is usual in the
theatre, we'll proceed now to a matrimonial
tableau.

SUSANNA, CONTESSA, FIGARO
Deh signor, nol contrastate, consolate i
miei/lor desir.

SUSANNA, COUNTESS, FIGARO
Come sir, don't be obstinate; give in to
my/their wishes.

CONTE
Marcellina! Marcellina! Quanto tardi a comparir! *ecc.*

COUNT
Marcellina, Marcellina, how long you delay in coming! *etc.*

(Antonio comes in, rather drunk, holding a pot of crushed carnations.)

ANTONIO
Ah! Signor, signor!

ANTONIO
Ah! Sir, sir!

CONTE
Cosa è stato?

COUNT
What has happened?

ANTONIO
Che insolenza! Chi'l fece? Chi fu?

ANTONIO
What insolence! Who did it? Who?

SUSANNA, CONTESSA, CONTE, FIGARO
Cosa dici, cos'hai, cosa è nato?

SUSANNA, COUNTESS, COUNT, FIGARO
What are you saying, what's this, what is it?

ANTONIO
Ascoltate!

ANTONIO
Listen to me!

SUSANNA, CONTESSA, CONTE, FIGARO
Via parla, di' su!

SUSANNA, COUNTESS, COUNT, FIGARO
Go ahead, speak up!

ANTONIO
Ascoltate! Dal balcone che guarda in giardino mille cose ogni dì gittar veggio, e poc'anzi, può darsi di peggio, vidi un uom, signor mio, gittar giù.

ANTONIO
Listen to me! From the balcony that looks out on the garden I've seen a thousand things thrown down; but just now, what could be worse? I saw a man, my lord, thrown out!

CONTE
Dal balcone?

COUNT
From the balcony?

ANTONIO *(additandogli i fiori)*
Vedete i garofani,

ANTONIO *(showing the pot)*
See these carnations!

CONTE
In giardino?

COUNT
Into the garden?

ANTONIO
Sì!

SUSANNA, CONTESSA *(sotto voce)*
Figaro, all'erta!

CONTE
Cosa sento?

SUSANNA, CONTESSA, FIGARO
Costui ci sconcerta, quel briaco che viene a far qui?

CONTE *(ad Antonio)*
Dunque un uom, ma dov'è gito?

ANTONIO
Ratto, ratto, il birbone è fuggito, e ad un tratto di vista m'uscì.

SUSANNA *(a Figaro)*
Sai che il paggio…

FIGARO *(a Susanna)*
So tutto, lo vidi.

(laughing loudly)

Ah ah ah ah!

CONTE
Taci là!

FIGARO
Ah ah ah ah!

ANTONIO
Cosa ridi?

ANTONIO
Yes!

SUSANNA, COUNTESS *(quietly)*
Figaro, get ready!

COUNT
What's this I hear?

SUSANNA, COUNTESS, FIGARO
The fellow has upset everything; What is that drunkard doing here?

COUNT *(to Antonio)*
That man, where did he land?

ANTONIO
Quick as a flash, the scoundrel fled right away out of my sight!

SUSANNA *(to Figaro)*
You know, the page…

FIGARO *(to Susanna)*
I know everything, I saw him.

Ha ha ha ha!

COUNT
Be quiet over there!

FIGARO
Ha ha ha ha!

ANTONIO
Why are you laughing?

FIGARO
Ah ah ah ah! Tu sei cotto dal sorger del dì.

CONTE *(ad Antonio)*
Or ripetimi, ripetimi: un uom dal balcone?

ANTONIO
Dal balcone.

CONTE
In giardino?

ANTONIO
In giardino.

SUSANNA, CONTESSA, FIGARO
Ma signore, se in lui parla il vino.

CONTE
Segui pure; né in volto il vedesti?

ANTONIO
No, nol vidi.

SUSANNA, CONTESSA
Olà, Figaro, ascolta!

CONTE
Sì?

ANTONIO
Nol vidi.

FIGARO
Vidi piangione, sta' zitto una volta! Per tre soldi da fare un tumulto: giacché il fatto non può stare occulto, sono io stesso salta-to di lì!

FIGARO
Ha ha ha ha. You're tipsy from break of day.

COUNT *(to Antonio)*
Tell me again, a man from the balcony?

ANTONIO
From the balcony.

COUNT
Into the garden?

ANTONIO
Into the garden.

SUSANNA, COUNTESS, FIGARO
But sir, it's the wine talking!

COUNT
Go on anyway; you didn't see his face?

ANTONIO
No, I didn't.

SUSANNA, COUNTESS
Hey, Figaro, listen!

COUNT
Yes?

ANTONIO
I didn't see him.

FIGARO
Go on, old blubberer, be quiet for once. Making such a fuss for threepence! Since the fact can't be kept quiet, it was I who jumped from there!

CONTE
Chi! Voi stesso?

SUSANNA, CONTESSA
Che testa! Che ingegno!

FIGARO
Che stupor!

ANTONIO
Chi! Voi stesso?

SUSANNA, CONTESSA
Che testa! Che ingegno!

FIGARO
Che stupor!

CONTE
Già creder nol posso.

ANTONIO *(a Figaro)*
Come mai diventasti sì grosso? Dopo il salto non fosti così.

FIGARO
A chi salta succede così.

ANTONIO
Ch'il direbbe?

SUSANNA, CONTESSA *(a Figaro)*
Ed insiste quel pazzo?

CONTE *(ad Antonio)*
Tu che dici?

ANTONIO
A me parve il ragazzo…

COUNT
You? Yourself?

SUSANNA, COUNTESS
What a brain! A genius!

FIGARO
What an upset!

ANTONIO
You? Yourself?

SUSANNA, COUNTESS
What a brain! A genius!

FIGARO
What an upset!

COUNT
I cannot believe it.

ANTONIO *(to Figaro)*
When did you grow so big? When you jumped you weren't like that.

FIGARO
That's how people look when they jump.

ANTONIO
Who says so?

SUSANNA, COUNTESS *(to Figaro)*
Is the fool being stubborn?

COUNT *(to Antonio)*
What are you saying?

ANTONIO
To me it looked like the boy.

116

CONTE Cherubin!	**COUNT** Cherubino!
SUSANNA, CONTESSA Maledetto! Maledetto!	**SUSANNA, COUNTESS** Damn you!
FIGARO Esso appunto, da Siviglia a cavallo qui giunto, da Siviglia ove forse sarà.	**FIGARO** At this moment he must be on horseback, arriving at Seville.
ANTONIO Questo no; che il cavallo io non vidi saltare di là.	**ANTONIO** No, that's not so; I saw no horse when he jumped out of the window.
CONTE Che pazienza! Finiam questo ballo!	**COUNT** Patience! Let's wind up this nonsense!
SUSANNA, CONTESSA Come mai, giusto ciel, finirà?	**SUSANNA, COUNTESS** How, in the name of Heaven, will it end?
CONTE Dunque tu?	**COUNT** So then you…
FIGARO Saltai giù…	**FIGARO** Jumped down.
CONTE Ma perché?	**COUNT** But why?
FIGARO Il timor…	**FIGARO** Out of fear…
CONTE Che timor…?	**COUNT** What…fear?
FIGARO Là rinchiuso, aspettando quel caro viset- to…tippe, tappe un sussurro fuor d'uso voi	**FIGARO** Here inside I was waiting for that dear face… When I heard an unusual noise…you

gridaste... lo scritto biglietto... saltai giù dal terrore confuso, e stravolto m'ho un nervo del piè.

ANTONIO *(mostrando una carta)*
Vostre dunque saran queste carte che perdeste...

CONTE *(cogliendole)*
Olà, porgile a me!

FIGARO
Sono in trappola.

SUSANNA, CONTESSA
Figaro, all'erta.

CONTE *(apre il foglio poi lo chiude tosto)*
Dite un po', questo foglio cos'è?

FIGARO *(cava di tasca alcune carte e finge di guardarle)*
Tosto, tosto ne ho tanti, aspettate!

ANTONIO
Sarà forse il sommario dei debiti?

FIGARO
No, la lista degli osti.

CONTE *(a Figaro)*
Parlate?

(to Antonio)

E tu lascialo.

---

were shouting...I thought of the letter...and jumped out confused by fear, and pulled the muscles in my ankle!

ANTONIO *(showing the page's papers)*
Then these papers must be yours, and you lost them?

COUNT *(seizing them)*
Here, give them to me.

FIGARO
I am in a trap.

SUSANNA, COUNTESS
Figaro, get ready.

COUNT *(quickly glancing at the papers)*
Tell me now, what letter is this?

FIGARO *(taking some papers from his pocket and looking at them)*
Wait, I have so many...just a moment.

ANTONIO
Perhaps it is a list of your debts.

FIGARO
No, the list of innkeepers.

COUNT *(to Figaro)*
Speak.

You leave him alone.

SUSANNA, CONTESSA, FIGARO
(ad Antonio)
Lascialo/mi, e parti.

ANTONIO
Parto sì, ma se torno a trovarti...

SUSANNA, CONTESSA, CONTE
Lascialo.

FIGARO
Vanne, vanne, non temo di te.

SUSANNA, CONTESSA, CONTE
Lascialo, e parti.

ANTONIO
Parto sì, *ecc.*

FIGARO
Vanne, vanne, non temo di te.

SUSANNA, CONTESSA, CONTE
Lascialo, e parti.

(Antonio leaves.)

CONTE *(il foglio in man)*
Dunque?

CONTESSA *(piano a Susanna)*
O ciel! La patente del paggio!

SUSANNA *(piano a Figaro)*
Giusti dei! La patente!

CONTE
Coraggio!

SUSANNA, COUNTESS, FIGARO
(to Antonio)
Leave/him/me alone, and get out.

ANTONIO
I'm leaving, but if I catch you once more...

SUSANNA, COUNTESS, COUNT
Leave him alone.

FIGARO
Get out, I'm not afraid of you.

SUSANNA, COUNTESS, COUNT
Leave him alone.

ANTONIO
I'm leaving, *etc.*

FIGARO
Get out, I'm not afraid of you.

SUSANNA, COUNTESS, COUNT
Leave him alone, and get out.

COUNT *(opening the papers)*
Well now?

COUNTESS *(softly to Susanna)*
Heavens! The page's commission!

SUSANNA *(softly to Figaro)*
Ye gods! The commission!

COUNT
Speak up!

FIGARO
Ah che testa! Quest'è la patente che
poc'anzi il fanciullo mi diè.

CONTE
Perché fare?

FIGARO
Vi manca…

CONTE
Vi manca?

CONTESSA *(piano a Susanna)*
Il suggello!

SUSANNA *(piano a Figaro)*
Il suggello!

CONTE
Rispondi!

FIGARO *(fingendo d'esitare ancora)*
È l'usanza…

CONTE
Su via, ti confondi?

FIGARO
È l'usanza di porvi il suggello.

CONTE
Questo birbo mi toglie il cervello, tutto è
un mistero per me, sì, *ecc.*

SUSANNA, CONTESSA
Se mi salvo da questa tempesta, più non
avvi naufragio per me, no, *ecc.*

FIGARO
Oh, what a brain! It's the commission that
the boy gave me a while ago.

COUNT
What for?

FIGARO
It needs…

COUNT
It needs…?

COUNTESS *(softly to Susanna)*
The seal!

SUSANNA *(softly to Figaro)*
The seal!

COUNT
Your answer?

FIGARO *(pretending to think)*
It's the custom…

COUNT
Come on now, are you confused?

FIGARO
It's the custom to place a seal on it.

COUNT
This rascal drives me crazy; the whole
thing's a mystery to me.

SUSANNA, COUNTESS
If I survive this tempest I won't be ship-
wrecked after all, *etc.*

FIGARO
Sbuffa invano e la terra calpesta! Poverino
ne sa men di me, *ecc.*

FIGARO
He pants and paws the ground in vain.
Poor man, he knows less than I do, *etc.*

(Marcellina, Bartolo and Basilio enter.)

MARCELLINA, BASILIO, BARTOLO
Voi signor, che giusto siete, ci dovete or
ascoltar.

MARCELLINA, BASILIO, BARTOLO
You, sir, who are so just, you must listen to
us now.

SUSANNA, CONTESSA, FIGARO
Son venuti a sconcertarmi qual rimedio a
ritrovar?

SUSANNA, COUNTESS, FIGARO
They have come to ruin me what solution
can I find?

CONTE
Son venuti a vendicarmi, io mi sento a
consolar.

COUNT
They have come to avenge me. I'm beginning to feel better.

FIGARO
Son tre stolidi, tre pazzi, cosa mai vengono
da far?

FIGARO
They are all three stupid fools, whatever
they have come to do?

CONTE
Pian pianin senza schiamazzi, dica ognun
quel che gli par.

COUNT
Softly now, without this clamour, let everyone speak his mind.

MARCELLINA
Un impegno nuziale ha costui con me contratto, e pretendo ch'il contratto deva meco
effettuar.

MARCELLINA
That man has signed a contract binding
him to marry me, and I contend that the
contract must be carried out.

SUSANNA, CONTESSA, FIGARO
Come? Come?

SUSANNA, COUNTESS, FIGARO
What, what?

CONTE
Olà! Silenzio! Io son qui per giudicar.

COUNT
Hey, be silent! I am here to render judgment.

BARTOLO
Io da lei scelto avvocato vengo a far le sue
difese, le legittime pretese io vi vengo a
palesar.

SUSANNA, CONTESSA, FIGARO
È un birbante!

CONTE
Olà! Silenzio! *ecc.*

BASILIO
Io com' uomo al mondo cognito, vengo
qui per testimonio del promesso matrimonio con prestanza di danar.

SUSANNA, CONTESSA, FIGARO
Son tre matti, *ecc.*

CONTE
Olà! Silenzio! Lo vedremo, il contratto leg-
geremo, tutto in ordin deve andar.

SUSANNA, CONTESSA, FIGARO
Son confusa(o), son stordita(o)
disperata(o), sbalordita(o)! Certo un diavol
dell'inferno qui li/ci ha fatti capitar!

**MARCELLINA, BASILIO, BARTOLO,
CONTE**
Che bel colpo! Che bel caso! È cresciuto a
tutti il naso; qualche nume a noi propizio,
qui ci/li ha fatti capitar!

BARTOLO
Appointed as her lawyer I am here in her
defense, to publish to the world her legiti-
mate reasons.

SUSANNA, COUNTESS, FIGARO
He is a rogue!

COUNT
Hey, be silent! *etc.*

BASILIO
Know as a man of the world, I come here
as a witness of his promise of marriage
when she loaned him some money.

SUSANNA, COUNTESS, FIGARO
They are all mad, *etc.*

COUNT
Hey, be silent; we'll see about that. We will
read the contract and proceed in due order.

SUSANNA, COUNTESS, FIGARO
I am confused, stupefied, hopeless, dis-
mayed! Surely some devil from Hell has
brought them/us here!

**MARCELLINA, BASILIO, BARTOLO,
COUNT**
A telling blow, a lucky chance! Victory is
right before our noses; some propitious
power has surely brought them/us here!

Act 3

A salon in the castle

(The salon is decorated for a wedding feast. The Count is alone, pacing up and down.)

RECITATIVE

DISC NO. 2/TRACK 1
The act opens with a quiet internal dialogue as the Count tries to sort out his thoughts, meanwhile giving us a glimpse into his own inner workings.

CONTE
Che imbarazzo è mai questo! Un foglio anonimo… la cameriera in gabinetto chiusa… la padrona confusa… un uom che salta dal balcone in giardino, un altro appresso, che dice esser quel desso… Non so cosa pensar, potrebbe forse qualcun de' miei vassalli… a simil razza è comune l'ardir, ma la Contessa… ah che un dubbio l'offende! Ella rispetta troppo sè stessa, e l'onor mio… l'onore… dove diamin l'ha posto umano errore!

COUNT
Why, what kind of embarrassing situation is this? An anonymous letter, the maid shut up in the closet, her mistress, confused, a man who jumps from balcony to garden, then another who says it was he who jumped. I don't know what to think. It could be that one of my vassals…people of their class often grow bold…But the Countess? Ah, how suspicion offends her! She has too high respect for herself and for my honour…honour…where the devil has human error placed it!

(The Countess and Susanna appear at the back.)

CONTESSA
Via! Fatti core, digli che ti attenda in giardino.

COUNTESS
Go ahead: take heart, and tell him that you'll wait for him in the garden.

CONTE
Saprò se Cherubino era giunto a Siviglia, a tale oggetto ho mandato Basilio.

COUNT
I'll find out whether Cherubino reached Seville; for that purpose I've sent Basilio.

SUSANNA
O cielo! E Figaro?

CONTESSA
A lui non dei dir nulla, in vece tua voglio
andarci io medesma.

CONTE
Avanti sera dovrebbe ritornar.

SUSANNA
Oh Dio! Non oso.

CONTESSA
Pensa ch'è in tua mano il mio riposo.

(She leaves.)

CONTE
E Susanna? Chi sa, ch'ella tradito abbia il
segreto mio… oh, se ha parlato, gli fo'
sposar la vecchia.

SUSANNA
(Marcellina…)
Signor!

CONTE
Cosa bramate?

SUSANNA
Mi par che siate in collera!

CONTE
Volete qualche cosa?

SUSANNA
Signor, la vostra sposa ha i soliti vapori, e vi
chiede il fiaschetto degli odori.

SUSANNA
Heavens! What about Figaro?

COUNTESS
Say nothing to him. I'll go to see him
myself.

COUNT
He should return this evening.

SUSANNA
O God! I dare not.

COUNTESS
Consider that in your hands lies my peace.

COUNT
And Susanna? Who knows, perhaps she
betrayed my secret; oh, if she has told, I'll
make him marry the old woman.

SUSANNA
(Marcellina…)
Sir!

COUNT
What do you want?

SUSANNA
It seems to me you're angry.

COUNT
Do you desire something?

SUSANNA
Sir, your wife is having her vapours, and
asks you for her little smelling bottle.

CONTE
Prendete.

SUSANNA
Or vel riporto.

CONTE
Ah no; potete ritenerlo per voi.

SUSANNA
Per me? Questi non son mali da donne
triviali.

CONTE
Un' amante che perde il caro sposo sul
punto d'ottenerlo?

SUSANNA
Pagando Marcellina colla dote che voi mi
prometteste…

CONTE
Ch'io vi promisi! Quando?

SUSANNA
Credea d'averlo inteso…

CONTE
Sì, se voluto aveste intendermi voi stessa.

SUSANNA
È mio dovere, e quel di Sua Eccellenza è il
mio volere.

COUNT
Take it.

SUSANNA
I'll bring it back.

COUNT
Ah no, you may keep it for yourself.

SUSANNA
For myself? That is no affliction for women
of my class.

COUNT
Not even for a lover who loses her dear
husband on the verge of getting him?

SUSANNA
By paying Marcellina with the dowry that
you promised me…

COUNT
That I promised you? When?

SUSANNA
I believe that it was understood.

COUNT
Yes, if you had been disposed to understand me yourself.

SUSANNA
Such is my duty, and my wish is that of
Your Excellency.

DISC NO. 2/TRACK 2

No. 16: Duetto **In this "duetto," the Count nervously asks Susanna if she'll meet him in the garden that evening, and she assures him—letting us know that she's lying—that she will. The rhythm and highly expressive, if simple, vocal lines find the Count practically begging—how his lust has brought him down!!—and Susanna playing with him exquisitely, here and in the final recitative (track 3).**

CONTE
Crudel! Perchè finora farmi languir così?

COUNT
Heartless! Why until now did you leave me to languish?

SUSANNA
Signor, la donna ognora tempo ha di dir di sì.

SUSANNA
Sir, every lady has her time to say yes.

CONTE
Dunque in giardin verrai?

COUNT
Then you'll come to the garden?

SUSANNA
Se piace a voi, verrò.

SUSANNA
If it pleases you, I'll come.

CONTE
E non mi mancherai?

COUNT
And you won't fail me?

SUSANNA
No, non vi mancherò.

SUSANNA
No, I won't fail you.

CONTE
Verrai?

COUNT
You'll come?

SUSANNA
Sì.

SUSANNA
Yes.

CONTE
Non mancherai?

COUNT
You won't fail me?

SUSANNA
No.

SUSANNA
No.

CONTE Non mancherai?	**COUNT** You won't fail me?
SUSANNA No, non vi mancherò.	**SUSANNA** No, I won't fail you.
CONTE Mi sento dal contento pieno di gioia il cor!	**COUNT** My contented heart now feels full of joy!
SUSANNA Scusatemi se mento, voi ch'intendete amor!	**SUSANNA** Forgive me if I am lying all you who understand love's ways!
CONTE Dunque in giardin verrai?	**COUNT** Then you'll come to the garden?
SUSANNA Se piace a voi, verrò.	**SUSANNA** If it pleases you, I'll come.
CONTE E non mi mancherai?	**COUNT** And you won't fail me?
SUSANNA No, non vi mancherò.	**SUSANNA** No, I won't fail you.
CONTE Verrai?	**COUNT** You'll come?
SUSANNA Sì.	**SUSANNA** Yes.
CONTE Non mancherai?	**COUNT** You won't fail me?
SUSANNA No.	**SUSANNA** No.
CONTE Dunque verrai?	**COUNT** So you'll come?

SUSANNA
No!

CONTE
No?

SUSANNA
Sì, se piace a voi, verrò.

CONTE
Non mancherai?

SUSANNA
No!

CONTE
Dunque verrai?

SUSANNA
Sì!

CONTE
Non mancherai?

SUSANNA
Sì!

CONTE
Sì?

SUSANNA
No, non vi macherò.

CONTE
Mi sento dal contento, *ecc.*

SUSANNA
Scusatemi se mento, *ecc.*

SUSANNA
No!

COUNT
No?

SUSANNA
I mean, yes, if you wish it.

COUNT
You'll not fail me?

SUSANNA
No!

COUNT
So you'll come?

SUSANNA
Yes!

COUNT
You'll not fail me?

SUSANNA
Yes!

COUNT
Yes?

SUSANNA
I mean, no, I'll not fail you.

COUNT
My contented heart, *etc.*

SUSANNA
Forgive me if I am lying, *etc.*

RECITATIVE

CONTE
E perchè fosti meco stamattina si austera?

COUNT
And why were you so austere with me this morning?

SUSANNA
Col paggio ch'ivi c'era.

SUSANNA
Because the page was with us.

CONTE
Ed a Basilio, che per me ti parlò?

COUNT
And with Basilio, who spoke with you for me?

SUSANNA
Ma qual bisogno abbiam noi, che un Basilio…

SUSANNA
Why, what need have we of a Basilio?

CONTE
È vero, è vero, e mi prometti poi… se tu manchi, oh cor mio… ma la Contessa attenderà il vasetto.

COUNT
That's true, true; so you promise me then… if you fail me, my heart…But the Countess must be waiting for the little bottle.

SUSANNA
Eh, fu un pretesto, parlato io non avrei senza di questo.

SUSANNA
Oh, that was only an excuse, I wouldn't have dared to speak without one.

CONTE
Carissima!

COUNT
Dearest!

SUSANNA
Vien gente.

SUSANNA
Someone's coming.

CONTE *(tra sé)*
È mia senz'altro.

COUNT *(aside)*
She's mine, for sure.

SUSANNA *(tra sé)*
Forbitevi la bocca, o signor scaltro.

SUSANNA *(to herself)*
Sharpen up your tongue, crafty sir.

(Enter Figaro.)

FIGARO
Ehi, Susanna, ove vai?

FIGARO
Hey, Susanna, where are you going?

SUSANNA
Taci: senza avvocato hai già vinta la causa.

SUSANNA
Hush! Without a lawyer our case is won already!

FIGARO
Cos'è nato?

FIGARO
What's happened?

(They go out together.)

DISC NO. 2/TRACK 4

No. 17: Recitative and Aria **It is here that the Count finally realizes that he has lost control of the goings-on in his palace, and his rage is palpable. The recitative is written in short phrases since so much is going through the Count's mind, and Mozart lets us feel how disjointed it is to the Count by not giving us a melody to latch on to. It is not surprising that the aria proper is so difficult to sing—with octave leaps, drastic dynamic changes, maddening coloratura and a devilish trill—the Count is mad with fury. All decorum is lost—this man is hanging on by a thread.**

CONTE
Hai già vinta la causa! Cosa sento! In qual laccio cadea? Perfidi. Io voglio... io voglio di tal modo punirvi, a piacer mio la sentenza sarà... Ma se pagasse le vecchia pretendente? Pagarla! In qual maniera? E poi v'è Antonio che all'incognito Figaro ricusa di dare una nipote in matrimonio. Coltivando l'orgoglio di questo mentecatto... tutto giova a un raggiro... il colpo è fatto. Vedrò, mentr'io sospiro, felice un servo mio! E un ben che invan desio, ei posseder dovrà? Vedrò per man d'amore unita a un vile oggetto chi in me destò un affetto che per me poi non ha? Vedrò mentr'io sospiro, *ecc.* Ah no, lasciarti in pace, non vo questo contento, tu non nascesti, audace, per dare

COUNT
Their case is won! What's that! What trap have I fallen into? Tricksters! I'm going to...I'm going to punish you in such a way...the punishment shall be what I choose...But what if he should pay the old suitor? Pay her! With what? And then there is Antonio, who will refuse to give his niece in marriage to the upstart Figaro. By flattering the pride of that half-wit...Everything's falling into my scheme...I'll strike while the iron's hot. Shall I live to see a servant of mine happy and enjoying pleasure that I desire in vain? Shall I see the hand of love unite a lowly person to one who arouses feelings in me she does not feel herself? Shall I live to see, *etc.* Ah no! I shall

a me tormento, e forse ancor per ridere, di mia infelicità! Già la speranza sola delle vendette mie quest'anima consola, e giubilar mi fa! Ah, che lasciarti in pace, *ecc.*

not leave that carefree creature in peace; you were not born, bold fellow, to give me torment or perhaps to laugh at my unhappiness. Now only hope of my revenge consoles my soul and makes me rejoice! Ah. I shall not leave, *etc.*

(enter Marcellina, Don Curzio, Figaro, Bartolo)

RECITATIVE

DISC NO. 2/TRACK 5

As the plot becomes more convoluted, we meet Don Curzio, a lawyer whose stammering only complicates matters further.

CURZIO
E' decisa la lite. O pagarla, o sposarla. Ora ammutite.

CURZIO
The case is settled. Either pay her, or marry her. Now be silent.

MARCELLINA
Io respiro.

MARCELLINA
I breathe again.

FIGARO
Ed io moro.

FIGARO
And I die.

MARCELLINA *(tra sé)*
Alfin sposa sarò d'un uom ch'adoro.

MARCELLINA *(to herself)*
At last I shall marry the man I adore.

FIGARO
Eccellenza! M'appello...

FIGARO
Your Excellency! I appeal...

CONTE
È giusta la sentenza, o pagar, o sposar— bravo, Don Curzio.

COUNT
The sentence is just. Either pay or marry— bravo, Don Curzio!

CURZIO
Bontà di Sua Eccellenza.

CURZIO
Your Excellency is too good!

BARTOLO
Che superba sentenza!

FIGARO
In che superba?

BARTOLO
Siam tutti vendicatti...

FIGARO
Io non la sposerò.

BARTOLO
La sposerai.

CURZIO
O pagarla, o sposarla.

MARCELLINA
Io t'ho prestati due mila pezzi duri.

FIGARO
Son gentiluomo, e senza l'assenso de' miei
nobili parenti...

CONTE
Dove sono? Chi sono?

FIGARO
Lasciate ancor cercarli: dopo dieci anni io
spero di trovarli.

BARTOLO
Qualche bambin trovato?

FIGARO
No, perduto, dottor, anzi rubato.

BARTOLO
What a perfect sentence!

FIGARO
How do you mean, perfect?

BARTOLO
We are all avenged...

FIGARO
I won't marry her.

BARTOLO
You will marry her.

CURZIO
Either pay her or marry her.

MARCELLINA
I lent you two thousand silver crowns.

FIGARO
I am a gentleman, and without the consent
of my noble parents...

COUNT
Where are they? Who are they?

FIGARO
Let them be searched for again; for ten
years I've been trying to find them.

BARTOLO
A foundling child?

FIGARO
No a lost child, doctor, or rather, kidnapped...

CONTE Come?	**COUNT** How's that?
MARCELLINA Cosa?	**MARCELLINA** What?
BARTOLO La prova?	**BARTOLO** Your proof?
CURZIO Il testimonio?	**CURZIO** Your witnesses?
FIGARO L'oro, le gemme e i ricamati panni, che ne' più teneri anni mi ritrovaron addosso i masnadieri, sono gl'indizi veri di mia nascita illustre, e soprattutto questo al mio braccio impresso geroglifico.	**FIGARO** The gold, gems and embroidered clothes that the robbers found me wearing even at that tender age are the true indications of my high birth, and especially this hieroglyphic on my arm.
MARCELLINA Una spatola impressa al braccio destro?	**MARCELLINA** A spatula birthmark on your right arm?
FIGARO E a voi ch'il disse?	**FIGARO** And who was it told you?
MARCELLINA Oh Dio! È desso!	**MARCELLINA** Oh God! It is he!
FIGARO È ver, son io.	**FIGARO** Of course, I am he.
CURZIO Chi?	**CURZIO** Who?
CONTE Chi?	**COUNT** Who?
BARTOLO Chi?	**BARTOLO** Who?

MARCELLINA	**MARCELLINA**
Raffaello!	Little Raphael!
BARTOLO	**BARTOLO**
E i ladri ti rapìr?	And the thieves stole you?
FIGARO	**FIGARO**
Presso un castello.	Near a castle.
BARTOLO	**BARTOLO**
Ecco tua madre!	There is your mother!
FIGARO	**FIGARO**
Balia...	My nursemaid?
BARTOLO	**BARTOLO**
No, tua madre.	No, your mother.
CURZIO, CONTE	**CURZIO, COUNT**
Sua madre?	His mother?
FIGARO	**FIGARO**
Cosa sento!	What's this I hear?
MARCELLINA	**MARCELLINA**
Ecco tuo padre!	There is your father!

DISC NO. 2/TRACK 6

No. 18: Textet If ever comic relief were needed, it is here, and Mozart and da Ponte do not disappoint. With the sudden insight that Figaro is really Marcellina's long-lost son, and even more bizzare—that Bartolo is his father, one entire plot problem (Figaro definitely won't have to marry Marcellina!) is solved and for once, everyone is amazed at the same time. The sudden warmth the three feel towards one another is not allowed any sentimentality—the seemingly endless repitition of "sua madre" and "suo padre" is just too eccentric. This is one of the few moments in all of comic opera which always gets a laugh—both situation and musical treatment are genuinely funny.

(embracing Figaro)

Riconosci in quest'amplesso una madre, amato figlio!	Recognise in this embrace your mother, beloved son.

FIGARO *(a Bartolo)*
Padre mio, fate lo stesso, non mi fate più arrossir.

FIGARO *(to Bartolo)*
My father, do the same, and let me no longer be ashamed.

BARTOLO *(abbracciando Figaro)*
Resistenza, la coscienza far non lascia al tuo desir.

BARTOLO *(embracing Figaro)*
Resistance, my conscience no longer lets you rule.

(Figaro embraces his parents.)

CURZIO
Ei suo padre? Ella sua madre? L'imeneo non può seguir.

CURZIO
He's his father? She's his mother? It's too late for the wedding now.

CONTE
Son smarrito, son stordito, meglio è assai di qua partir.

COUNT
I'm astounded, I'm abashed, I'd better get out of here.

MARCELLINA, BARTOLO
Figlio amato!

MARCELLINA, BARTOLO
Beloved son!

FIGARO
Parenti amati!

FIGARO
Beloved parents!

(Susanna enters.)

SUSANNA
Alto! Alto! Signor Conte, mille doppie son qui pronte, a pagar vengo per Figaro, ed a porlo in libertà.

SUSANNA
Stop, stop, noble sir, I have a thousand double crowns right here. I come to pay for Figaro and to set him at liberty.

MARCELLINA, BARTOLO
Figlio amato!

MARCELLINA, BARTOLO
Beloved son!

CURZIO, CONTE
Non sappiam com'è la cosa, osservate un poco là.

FIGARO
Parenti amati!

SUSANNA *(vede Figaro che abbraccia Marcellina)*
Già d'accordo colla sposa, giusti Dei, che infedeltà.

(She wants to leave but Figaro detains her.)

Lascia, iniquo!

FIGARO
No, t'arresta! Senti, oh cara, senti!

SUSANNA *(dandogli uno schiaffo)*
Senti questa!

MARCELLINA, BARTOLO, FIGARO
E un effetto di buon core tutto amore è quel che fa, *ecc.*

SUSANNA *(a parte)*
Fremo, smanio dal furore, una vecchia me la fa, *ecc.*

CONTE, CURZIO
Freme/o, e smania/o dal furore, il destino me la/gliela fa, *ecc.*

MARCELLINA *(a Susanna)*
Lo sdegno calmate, mia cara figliuola, sua madre abbracciate che or vostra sarà, *ecc.*

CURZIO, COUNT
We're not sure what's taking place. Look over there a moment.

FIGARO
Beloved parents!

SUSANNA *(seeing Figaro hugging Marcellina)*
So he's reconciled with his bride; ye gods, what infidelity!

Leave her, villain!

FIGARO
No, wait! Listen, darling

SUSANNA *(boxing Figaro's ears)*
Listen to this!

MARCELLINA, BARTOLO, FIGARO
A natural action of a good heart, pure love is demonstrated here, *etc.*

SUSANNA *(aside)*
I'm boiling, I'm raging with fury; an old woman has done this to me, *etc.*

COUNT, CURZIO
He's/I'm boiling, he's/I'm raging with fury; destiny has done this to me/him. *etc.*

MARCELLINA *(to Susanna)*
Calm your anger, my dear daughter, embrace his mother, and yours as well, now.

SUSANNA *(a Bartolo)* Sua madre?	**SUSANNA** *(to Bartolo)* His mother?
BARTOLO Sua madre!	**BARTOLO** His mother.
SUSANNA *(al Conte)* Sua madre?	**SUSANNA** *(to the Count)* His mother?
CONTE Sua madre!	**COUNT** His mother.
SUSANNA *(a Curzio)* Sua madre?	**SUSANNA** *(to Curzio)* His mother?
CURZIO Sua madre!	**CURZIO** His mother.
SUSANNA *(a Marcellina)* Sua madre?	**SUSANNA** *(to Marcellina)* His mother?
MARCELLINA Sua madre!	**MARCELLINA** His mother.
MARCELLINA, CURZIO, CONTE, **BARTOLO** Sua madre!	**MARCELLINA, CURZIO, COUNT,** **BARTOLO** His mother!
SUSANNA *(a Figaro)* Tua madre?	**SUSANNA** *(to Figaro)* Your mother?
FIGARO E quello è mio padre che a te lo dirà.	**FIGARO** And that is my father, he'll say so himself.
SUSANNA *(a Bartolo)* Suo padre?	**SUSANNA** *(to Bartolo)* His father?
BARTOLO Suo padre!	**BARTOLO** His father.

SUSANNA *(al Conte)*
Suo padre?

CONTE
Suo padre!

SUSANNA *(a Curzio)*
Suo padre?

CURZIO
Suo padre!

SUSANNA *(a Marcellina)*
Suo padre?

MARCELLINA
Suo padre!

MARCELLINA, CURZIO, CONTE, BARTOLO
Suo padre!

SUSANNA *(a Figaro)*
Tuo padre?

FIGARO
E quella è mia madre, che a te lo dirà, *ecc.*

CURZIO, CONTE
Al fiero tormento di questo momento
quest'anima appena resister or sa.

SUSANNA, MARCELLINA, BARTOLO, FIGARO
Al dolce contento di questo momento
quest'anima appena resister or sa.

(The Count leaves with Curzio.)

SUSANNA *(to the Count)*
His father?

COUNT
His father.

SUSANNA *(to Curzio)*
His father?

CURZIO
His father.

SUSANNA *(to Marcellina)*
His father?

MARCELLINA
His father.

MARCELLINA, CURZIO, COUNT, BARTOLO
His father!

SUSANNA *(to Figaro)*
Your father?

FIGARO
And that is my mother, who'll say so herself, *etc.*

CURZIO, COUNT
My soul can barely resist any longer the
fierce torture of this moment.

SUSANNA, MARCELLINA, BARTOLO, FIGARO
My soul can barely resist any longer the
sweet delight of this moment.

Marcellina and Bartolo have been literally transformed into different people than who everyone (including we in the audience) thought they were. Their voices reflect this new turn of events as they become comical and non-threatening (01:09). Points of view and even identities change like the wind in this dizzy household.

RECITATIVE

MARCELLINA
Eccovi, o caro amico, il dolce frutto dell'antico amor nostro.

MARCELLINA
Here you see, dear friend, the sweet fruit of our ancient love.

BARTOLO
Or non parliamo di fatti sì rimoti, egli è mio figlio, mia consorte voi siete, e le nozze farem quando volete.

BARTOLO
Let us speak no more of such ancient events; he is my son, you are my wife; we shall be married whenever you wish.

MARCELLINA
Oggi, e doppie saranno;

MARCELLINA
Today, and let it be a double ceremony.

(to Figaro)

prendi, questo e il biglietto del denar che a me devi, ed è tua dote.

Take this, which is the note for the money you owed me, and your dowry.

SUSANNA
Prendi ancor questa borsa.

SUSANNA
Take this purse, too.

BARTOLO
E questa ancora.

BARTOLO
And this as well.

FIGARO
Bravi, gittate pur, ch'io piglio ognora.

FIGARO
Wonderful; throw them as long as I can catch them.

SUSANNA
Voliamo ad informar d'ogni avventura Madama e nostro zio. Chi al par di me contenta!

SUSANNA
I must go and tell Madame and my uncle of all that's happened; who is as happy as I am?

FIGARO
Io!

BARTOLO
Io!

MARCELLINA
Io!

SUSANNA, MARCELLINA, BARTOLO, FIGARO
E schiatti il signor Conte al gusto mio.

(All go out arm in arm. Enter Barbarina and Cherubino.)

BARBARINA
Andiam, andiam, bel paggio, in casa mia tutte ritroverai le più belle ragazze del castello, di tutte sarai tu certo il più bello.

CHERUBINO
Ah! Se il Conte mi trova! Misero me! Tu sai che partito ei mi crede per Siviglia.

BARBARINA
Oh ve' che maraviglia! E se ti trova, non sarà cosa nuova. Odi! Vogliamo vestirti come noi, tutte insiem andrem poi a presentar de' fiori a Madamina. Fidati, o Cherubin, di Barbarina.

(They go out. The Countess enters.)

FIGARO
I am!

BARTOLO
I am!

MARCELLINA
I am!

SUSANNA, MARCELLINA, BARTOLO, FIGARO
Let the Count burst for my happiness!

BARBARINA
Come, come, handsome page, at my cottage you will find all the prettiest girls in the castle, and you will be the fairest of all.

CHERUBINO
Ah! If the Count should find me! Unhappy I! You know that he believes I've left for Seville.

BARBARINA
So what of it? If he finds you, that will be nothing new. Listen! I want to dress you like us, and all together we'll go to present flowers to Madame. Have faith, O Cherubino, in Barbarina.

No. 19: Recitative and Aria **But we are brought back, just as quickly and just as potently to the more serious matter at hand: the Countess's unhappiness. This is an interior monologue—the Countess is thinking about how terribly sad her situation has become, what she has had to accept—and she recalls, in the aria (at 01:55) happier days, and she even wishes she were able to expunge them from her memory. But (at 04:35), with an abrupt tempo change, the aria takes a turn towards a ray of hope—the Countess realizes that if her love is strong enough to survive, perhaps the Count's affections will return to her. Here is the Countess in all her glory.**

CONTESSA	COUNTESS
E Susanna non vien! Sono ansiosa di saper come il Conte accolse la proposta. Alquanto ardito il progetto mi par, e ad uno sposo sì vivace e geloso! Ma che mal c'è? Cangiando i miei vestiti con quelli de Susanna, e i suoi coi miei a favor della notte. Oh cielo! A qual'umil stato fatale io son ridotta da un consorte crudel! Che dopo avermi con un misto inaudito d'infedeltà, di gelosia, di sdegno—prima amata, indi offesa, e alfin tradita—fammi or cercar da una mia serva aita! Dove sono i bei momenti di dolcezza e di piacer, dove andaron i giuramenti di quel labbro menzogner! Perché mai, se in pianti e in pene per me tutto si cangiò, la memoria di quel bene dal mio sen non trapassò? Dove sono i bei momenti, *ecc.* Ah! Se almen la mia costanza nel languire amando ognor mi portasse una speranza di cangiar l'ingrato cor. Ah! Se almen la mia costanza, *ecc.*	Still Susanna does not come! I am anxious to know how the Count received the proposal. The scheme appears rather daring, with a husband so forceful and jealous! But what's the harm in it? Changing my clothes for those of Susanna, and she for mine, under cover of night. Heavens! To what humble and dangerous state I am reduced by a cruel husband, who, after having with an unheard-of-combination of infidelity, jealousy and disdain—having first loved me, then abused and finally betrayed me— now forces me to seek the help of a servant! Where are the golden moments of tranquility and pleasure; what became of the oaths of that deceitful tongue? Why did not, when my life changed into tears and pain, the memory of that joy disappear from my breast? Where are the golden moments, *etc.* Ah! If then my constancy still loves through its sorrow, the hope yet remains of changing that ungrateful heart. Ah! If then my constancy, *etc.*

(She goes out. The Count comes in with Antonio.)

The Countess's musings are contrasted with the actions of the motivators of the action, the Count and Susanna, in this brief section.

ANTONIO

Io vi dico signor, che Cherubino è ancora nel castello, e vedete per prova il suo cappello.

ANTONIO

I tell you, sir, that Cherubino is still inside the castle, and you can see his cap here as proof.

CONTE

Ma come se a quest'ora esser giunto a Siviglia egli dovria?

COUNT

But how can this be if he is already at Seville?

ANTONIO

Scusate, oggi Siviglia è a casa mia. Là vestissi da donna e là lasciati ha gl'altri abiti suoi.

ANTONIO

Pardon, but today Seville is at my house; he dressed as a woman there and left behind some of his clothes.

CONTE

Perfidi!

COUNT

Villains!

ANTONIO

Andiam, e li vedrete voi.

ANTONIO

Come on, and you'll see for yourself.

(They go out. The Countess and Susanna come in.)

CONTESSA

Cosa mi narri? E che ne disse il Conte?

COUNTESS

You don't say! And what was the Count's answer?

SUSANNA

Gli si leggeva in fronte il dispetto e la rabbia.

SUSANNA

Anyone could see the spite and anger in his face.

CONTESSA	COUNTESS
Piano, che meglio or lo porremo in gabbia! Dov'è l'appuntamento, che tu gli proponesti?	Keep your voice down, so we can get him in our trap. Where is the meeting you promised him supposed to take place?
SUSANNA	SUSANNA
In giardino.	In the garden.
CONTESSA	COUNTESS
Fissiamogli un loco. Scrivi.	Give him a definite place. Write to him.
SUSANNA	SUSANNA
Ch'io scriva, ma, signora…	I would write, but, my lady…
CONTESSA	COUNTESS
Eh scrivi, dico, e tutto io prendo su me stessa.	Come on and write, I say; I'll take the responsibility myself.

DISC NO. 2/TRACK 10

No. 20: Duettino Here the Countess and Susanna hatch the plot in its final form, and since the rendezvous is to take place in the garden, amid the pines and gentle breezes, the duettino is pastoral and quiet. The women are pleased with their own ingenuity and this moment of peace is a real joy.

(dictating)

Canzonetta sull'aria…	"A little tune on the breeze."
SUSANNA *(Scrivendo)*	SUSANNA *(writing)*
Sull'aria…	"…On the breeze."
CONTESSA	COUNTESS
Che soave zeffiretto—	"What a gentle zephyr—"
SUSANNA	SUSANNA
Zeffiretto -	"zephyr—"

CONTESSA
questa sera spirerà -

SUSANNA
questa sera spirerà -

CONTESSA
sotto i pini del boschetto -

SUSANNA
sotto i pini?

CONTESSA
sotto i pini del boschetto -

SUSANNA
sotto i pini del boschetto -

CONTESSA
ei già il resto capirà,

SUSANNA
certo, certo il capirà.

CONTESSA
ei già il resto capirà.

CONTESSA
Canzonetto sull'aria, *ecc.*

SUSANNA
Che soave zeffiretto, *ecc.*

COUNTESS
"will sigh this evening—"

SUSANNA
"this evening—"

COUNTESS
"beneath the pines in the thicket..."

SUSANNA
beneath the pines?

COUNTESS
"Beneath the pines in the thicket."

SUSANNA
"Beneath the pines in the thicket."

COUNTESS
He will understand the rest.

SUSANNA
Certainly, he'll understand.

COUNTESS
He will understand the rest.

COUNTESS
"Little tune on the breeze." *etc.*

SUSANNA
"What a gentle zephyr." *etc.*

RECITATIVE

Piegato è foglio; or come si sigilla?

I've folded the sheet, now how shall I seal it?

CONTESSA
Ecco... prendi una spilla, servirà di sigillo;

COUNTESS
Here, take a pin. It will serve as a seal.

attendi, scrivi sul riverso del foglio: riman-date il sigillo.	Wait: write on the back of the sheet. "Send back the seal."

SUSANNA	**SUSANNA**
È più bizzarro di quel della patente.	A cleverer stroke than the business of the commission.

CONTESSA	**COUNTESS**
Presto nascondi: io sento venir gente.	Quickly, hide; I hear someone coming.

(Susanna puts the letter in her bosom. Barbarina comes in with a group of peasant girls, and Cherubino also dressed like a peasant girl. They have bunches of flowers.)

NO. 21: CHORUS

DISC NO. 2/TRACK 11
The peasant girls sing a lovely and simple tune to the Countess. It is individuals, rather than groups, who are complicated and problematic in this opera. Shortly, (02:17) the Count will be disarmed by a bit of refreshing youthful candor from Barbarina, although Figaro's re-emergence will set the Count back to his plots.

CORO	**CHORUS**
Ricevete, o padroncina queste rose e questi fior, che abbiam colte stamattina, per mostrarvi il nostro amor. Siamo tante contadine, e siam tutte poverine, ma quel poco che rechiamo ve lo diamo di buon cor.	Receive, beloved protectress, these roses and violets we gathered this morning to prove our love for you. We are only peasant girls and we are all poor, but what little we possess we give you with a good heart.

RECITATIVE

BARBARINA	**BARBARINA**
Queste sono, Madama, le ragazze del loco che il poco ch'han vi vengono ad offrire, e vi chiedon perdon del loro ardire.	Madame, these girls are maids of the countryside; what little they have they offer you, and beg pardon for their presumption.

CONTESSA	**COUNTESS**
Oh brave! Vi ringrazio.	Wonderful! I thank you.

SUSANNA

Come sono vezzose.

CONTESSA

E chi è, narratemi, quell'amabil fanciulla ch'ha l'aria sì modesta?

(points to Cherubino)

BARBARINA

Ell' è una mia cugina e per le nozze è venuta ier sera.

CONTESSA

Onoriamo la bella forestiera; venite qui, datemi i vostri fiori. Come arrossì! Susanna, e non ti pare... che somigli ad alcuno?

SUSANNA

Al naturale...

(Enter the Count and Antonio, who pulls off Cherubino's head-dress and plants his soldier's cap in its place.)

ANTONIO

Eh cospettaccio! È questi l'uffiziale.

CONTESSA

Oh stelle!

SUSANNA

Malandrino.

CONTE

Ebben, Madama!

CONTESSA

Io sono, signor mio, irritata e sorpresa al par di voi.

SUSANNA

How pretty they are!

COUNTESS

And tell me, who is that lovable girl with such a modest air?

BARBARINA

She is a cousin of mine, and arrived yesterday evening for the wedding.

COUNTESS

Let us honour the beautiful girl; come here and give me your flowers. How she blushed! Susanna, doesn't she seem to resemble someone?

SUSANNA

She certainly does.

ANTONIO

By God's Body! There's your officer.

COUNTESS

Heavens!

SUSANNA

Scoundrel.

COUNT

Well, Madame...

COUNTESS

My lord, I am as angry and surprised as you.

CONTE
Ma stamane?

CONTE
But this morning?

CONTESSA
Stamane… per l'odierna festa volevam travestirlo al modo stesso che l'han vestito adesso.

COUNTESS
This morning…we planned to dress him for the day's festivity in the fashion in which he has dressed himself.

CONTE
E perchè non partisti?

COUNT
And why did you not leave?

CHERUBINO
Signor…

CHERUBINO
Sir…

CONTE
Saprò punire la tua disubbidienza.

COUNT
Your disobedience shall be punished.

BARBARINA
Eccellenza! Eccellenza! Voi mi dite sì spesso qualvolta m'abbracciate, e mi baciate: Barbarina, se m'ami, ti darò quel che brami…

BARBARINA
Your Excellency, Your Excellency! You told me yourself, that time when you hugged and kissed me, "Barbarina, if you'll love me, I'll give you whatever you want."

CONTE
Io dissi questo?

COUNT
I said that?

BARBARINA
Voi! Or datemi, padrone, in sposo Cherubino, e v'amerò, com'amo il mio gattino.

BARBARINA
You did. So, my lord, give me Cherubino as husband, and I'll love you as I love my kitten.

CONTESSA
Ebbene, or tocca a voi.

COUNTESS
Well, it's up to you.

ANTONIO
Brava figliuola! Hai buon maestro, che ti fa la scuola.

ANTONIO
Well spoken, my daughter! You have been taught by a good teacher.

CONTE *(tra sé)*
Non so qual uom, qual demone, qual dio
rivolga tutto quanto a torto mio.

(Enter Figaro.)

FIGARO
Signor, se trattenete tutte queste ragazze,
addio feste, addio danza.

CONTE
E che? Vorresti ballar col piè stravolto?

FIGARO
Eh non mi duol più molto. Andiam belle
fanciulle.

CONTE
Per buona sorte i vasi eran di creta.

FIGARO
Senza fallo. Andiamo dunque, andiamo.

ANTONIO
E intanto a cavallo di galoppo a Siviglia
andava il paggio.

FIGARO
Di galoppo, o di passo, buon viaggio! Venite o belle giovani.

CONTE
E a te la sua patente era in tasca rimasta.

FIGARO
Certamente.
(Che razza di domande!)

COUNT *(aside)*
I know not what man, what demon or god
has turned all these wrongs on me.

FIGARO
Sir, if you detain all of these girls then
goodbye to the feasting and dancing.

COUNT
What! Would you dance with a sprained
ankle?

FIGARO
Oh, it doesn't hurt much any longer. Come
on, pretty maidens.

COUNT
Lucky that the pots were made of clay.

FIGARO
How true. Well, come on, come on.

ANTONIO
And meanwhile the page was galloping
toward Seville.

FIGARO
At a gallop or a walk, prosperous journey!
Come, my fine girls.

COUNT
And his commission stayed behind inside
your pocket.

FIGARO
Certainly.
(These are funny questions!)

ANTONIO *(a Susanna che fa dei moti a Figaro)*
Via, non gli far più moti, ei non t'intende.

ANTONIO *(to Susanna, who is making signs to Figaro)* Hey, stop making signs, he doesn't understand you.

(taking Cherubino by the hand and presenting him to Figaro)

Ed ecco chi pretende che sia un bugiardo il mio signor nipote.

And here is the man who claims that my good nephew is a liar.

FIGARO
Cherubino!

FIGARO
Cherubino!

ANTONIO
Or ci sei.

ANTONIO
Now you know.

FIGARO *(al Conte)*
Che diamin canta?

FIGARO *(to the Count)*
What the devil is his tune?

CONTE
Non canta, no, mia dice, ch'egli saltò sta-mane in sui garofani.

COUNT
No tune; he's saying that the boy jumped out on his carnations this morning.

FIGARO
Ei lo dice! Sarà… se ho saltato io, si può dare ch'anch'esso abbia fatto lo stesso.

FIGARO
So he says!…But perhaps…if I jumped he, too, could have done the same thing.

CONTE
Anch'esso?

COUNT
He, too?

FIGARO
Perché no? Io non impugno mai quel che non so.

FIGARO
Why not? I never deny matters of which I know nothing.

NO. 22: FINALE

DISC NO. 2/TRACK 12

The wedding march can be heard approaching while the Count and Countess are stil muttering at each other — a subtle comment on the pretences of wedded bliss. The march itself takes over (00:43), and at first seems to be a magnificent and stately paean to this moment of peace — but listen to it again! Little dissonances in the orchestra (curious screw-turns in the strings, for example) make it clear that beneath all the elegance, something is seriously wrong here.

(The wedding march begins.)

Ecco la marcia, andiamo! Ai vostri posti, oh belle, ai vostri posti! Susanna dammi il braccio!

There's the march, let's go! To your posts, my beauties, to your posts. Susanna, give me your arm.

SUSANNA *(Figaro prende Susanna pel braccio)*
Eccolo.

SUSANNA *(giving her arm)*
Here it is.

(They all go out, leaving the Countess and the Count.)

CONTE
Temerari!

COUNT
Shameless!

CONTESSA
Io son di ghiaccio!

COUNTESS
I feel made of ice!

CONTE
Contessa!

COUNT
Countess!

CONTESSA
Or non parliamo. Ecco qui le due nozze, riceverle dobbiam, alfin si tratta d'una vostra protetta. Seggiamo.

COUNTESS
Don't speak now. Here are the two couples; we must receive them. In the end the question involves your protégée. Let us be seated.

CONTE
Seggiamo. *(E meditiam vendetta!)*

COUNT
Let us be seated *(and meditate on revenge).*

(They sit. Enter hunters with guns slung over their shoulders. Village folk, peasant boys and girls. Two young girls carry in the bridal veil and hat of white feathers; two others the gloves and bunch of flowers. Figaro is with Marcellina. Other girls carry a similar hat for Susanna. Bartolo is with Susanna; he leads her to the Count. She kneels and receives from him the hat, etc. Figaro takes Marcellina to the Countess who performs a similar function.)

DUO RAGAZZE

Amanti costanti, seguaci d'onor, cantate, lodate sì saggio signor. A un dritto cedendo che oltraggia, che offende, ei caste vi rende ai vostri amator.

TWO GIRLS

Faithful lovers, Zealous in honour, sing the praises of such a wise master. Renouncing a right that insults and offends, he renders you spotless to your beloved.

CORO

Cantiamo, lodiamo sì saggio signor!

CHORUS

Sing the praises of such a wise master!

(While kneeling before the Count Susanna tugs at his robe and shows him a letter; she raises her hand to her head and the Count under the pretence of adjusting her hat takes the letter and hides it. Susanna pays her respects and rises. Figaro goes to receive her. Fandango. Marcellina rises presently and Bartolo steps up to receive her from the Countess.)

CONTE *(cava il biglietto e fa l'atto d'un uom che rimase punto al dito: lo scuote, lo preme, lo succhia e vedendo il biglietto sigillato colla spilla dice, gittando la spilla a terra)* Eh, la solita usanza, le donne ficcan gli aghi in ogni loco… ah, capisco il gioco!

COUNT *(takes out the letter and reacts as if he has pricked his finger: shakes it, presses it, sucks it, and seeing that the letter was sealed with a pin, throws the pin on the floor, saying:)* Hmm, as usual…women have pins sticking out everywhere. Ah! Ah! I get the idea!

FIGARO *(a Susanna)*

Un biglietto amoroso che gli diè nel passar qualche galante, ed era sigillato d'una spilla, ond'egli si punse il dito, il Narciso or la cerca, oh che stordito!

FIGARO *(to Susanna)*

That was a love letter that someone gave him in passing, and it was sealed with a pin, on which he hurt his finger. The Narcissus is looking for it. Oh, what foolishness!

CONTE

Andate amici! E sia per questa sera disposto l'apparato nuziale, colla più ricca pompa, io vo' che sia magnifica la festa, e canti, e fochi, e gran cena, e gran ballo; e ognuno

COUNT

Come, my friends, and for this evening let all the trappings of marriage be made ready with richest magnificence. I want the feast to be a grand one: songs, torches, a grand

impari com'io tratto color che a me son cari.

feast and a ball. And all shall see how I treat those who are dear to me.

CORO
Amanti costanti, *ecc.*

CHORUS
Faithful lovers, *etc.*

Act 4

The castle garden

(There is an arbour to the right and one to the left. Night. Barbarina enters, searching for something on the ground.)

NO. 23: CAVATINA

DISC NO. 2/TRACK 13
The curtain rises on Barbarina alone in the dark. She sings a gorgeously sad little solo about her lost pin — or is that really what she is lamenting?

BARBARINA
L'ho perduta, me meschina! Ah chi sa dove sarà? Non la trovo. L'ho perduta! Meschinella! *ecc.* E mia cugina? E il padron, cosa dirà?

BARBARINA
I have lost it, unhappy me! Ah, who knows where it is? I cannot find it, I have lost it, unhappy me, *etc.* And my cousin, and my lord—what will he say?

(Figaro and Marcellina appear.)

RECITATIVE

DISC 2/TRACK 14
Figaro begins to give way to his jealousy in this exchange with Barbarina. It is as if life in a corrupt world is poisoning him as well. The complete change in his relationship with Marcellina is comically highlighted in few words when she appears (01:03).

FIGARO
Barbarina, cos'hai?

FIGARO
Barbarina, what's the matter?

BARBARINA
L'ho perduta, cugino.

BARBARINA
I have lost it, cousin.

FIGARO
Cosa?

FIGARO
What?

MARCELLINA
Cosa?

MARCELLINA
What?

BARBARINA
La spilla, che a me diede il padrone per recar a Susanna.

BARBARINA
The pin that His Lordship gave me to return to Susanna.

FIGARO
A Susanna, la spilla? E così, tenerella, il mestiere già sai di far tutto sì ben quel che tu fai?

FIGARO
To Susanna? The pin? At such a tender age you already know how to ply your trade so well?

BARBARINA
Cos' è? Vai meco in collera?

BARBARINA
What's the matter? Are you angry with me?

FIGARO
E non vedi ch'io scherzo? Osserva:

FIGARO
Don't you see I'm joking? Look:

(He takes a pin from Marcellina's dress.)

questa è la spilla che il Conte da recare ti diede alla Susanna, e servia di sigillo a un bigliettino; vedi s'io sono istrutto.

this is the pin that the Count told you to return to Susanna, and it was used to seal a little letter. You see, I know all about it.

BARBARINA
E perché il chiedi a me quando sai tutto?

FIGARO
Avea gusto d'udir come il padrone ti diè la commissione.

BARBARINA
Che miracoli! "Tieni, fanciulla, reca questa spilla alla bella Susanna, e dille: questo è il sigillo de' pini!"

FIGARO
Ah! ah! De' pini.

BARBARINA
È ver ch'ei mi soggiunse: guarda che alcun non veda; ma tu già tacerai.

FIGARO
Sicuramente.

BARBARINA
A te già niente preme.

FIGARO
Oh niente, niente.

BARBARINA
Addio, mio bel cugino; vo' da Susanna, e poi da Cherubino.

(She leaves hurriedly.)

FIGARO
Madre!

MARCELLINA
Figlio!

BARBARINA
Then why do you ask me if you know?

FIGARO
I wanted to hear how our patron gave you your instructions.

BARBARINA
It's funny! "Here, my girl, take this pin back to the beautiful Susanna, and tell her: this is the seal of the pines."

FIGARO
Ah, ah! Of the pines!

BARBARINA
And then he warned me, "Be careful that no one sees it." But you won't tell.

FIGARO
Absolutely not.

BARBARINA
It's no concern of yours.

FIGARO
Oh, none at all.

BARBARINA
Goodbye, dear cousin, I'll go and find Susanna and then Cherubino.

FIGARO
Mother!

MARCELLINA
My son!

FIGARO
Son morto!

MARCELLINA
Calmati, figlio mio!

FIGARO
Son morto, dico.

MARCELLINA
Flemma, flemma, e poi flemma: il fatto è
serio, e pensar ci convien! Ma guarda un
poco, che ancor non sai di chi si prenda
giuoco.

FIGARO
Ah, quella spilla, o madre, è quella stessa
che poc'anzi ei raccolse.

MARCELLINA
È ver, ma questo al più ti porge un dritto ai
stare in guardia e vivere in sospetto; ma
non sai se in effetto...

FIGARO
All'erta dunque! Il loco del congresso so
dov'è stabilito.

MARCELLINA
Dove vai, figlio mio?

FIGARO
A vendicar tutt' i mariti. Addio!

(He goes out.) Recitative

FIGARO
I am finished!

MARCELLINA
Calm yourself, my son.

FIGARO
I'm finished, I tell you!

MARCELLINA
Phlegm, phlegm; be calm. The matter is
serious and bears consideration! But wait a
while, you still don't know who's the object
of the joke.

FIGARO
Ah, that "pin," mother, is the same on the
Count lately renounced.

MARCELLINA
That's true, but at most this warrants keeping on your guard, and being suspicious;
but you don't know for certain...

FIGARO
On guard, then! I know where they have
agreed to meet.

MARCELLINA
Where are you going, my son?

FIGARO
To avenge all husbands. Farewell!

Barbarina begins plots of her own, while Figaro attempts — unwisely — in his own machinations without the sage advice of his more clever wife.

BARBARINA
Nel padiglione a manca, ei così disse: è questo, è questo! E poi se non venisse?

BARBARINA
In the left-hand lodge, he said: yes, this is it! What if he doesn't come!

(She rushes into the hunting-lodge on the left.)

FIGARO
È Barbarina! Chi va là?

FIGARO
That was Barbarina. Who goes there?

(Basilio and Bartolo appear with a group of peasants and servants.)

BASILIO
Son quelli che invitasti a venir.

BASILIO
Those whom you invited to come here.

BARTOLO
Che brutto ceffo! Sembri un cospirator!
Che diamin sono quegli infausti apparati?

BARTOLO
What a scowl! You look like a conspirator!
Why the devil all these strange preparations?

FIGARO
Lo vedrete fra poco. In questo stesso loco celebrerem la festa della mia sposa onesta e del feudal signor.

FIGARO
You will soon see. On this spot we celebrate the rites of my honourable wife and the lord of the manor.

BASILIO
Ah buono, buono, capisco come egli è.
Accordati si son senza di me.

BASILIO
Ah, good, good, I begin to understand.
They have reached agreement without me.

FIGARO *(a truppo di contadini e servi)*
Voi da questi contorni non vi scostate, e a un fischio mio correte tutti quanti.

FIGARO *(to the peasants and servants)*
Stay in the area and don't go far off. When I give the signal, come running, all of you.

(Figaro leaves with the peasants and servants.)

BAZILE
Il a le diable au corps!

BASILIO
He's bedeviled!

BARTHOLO

Mais qu'y a-t-il donc?

BAZILE

Rien: Suzanne plaît au Comte;
ell a convenu de lui donne un rendz-vous
qui déplaît à Figaro.

BARTHOLO

Eh, quoi! Faudrait-il qu'il le souffre sans
rien dire?

BAZILE

Il ne pourrait pas souffrir, lui, ce que
souffrent tant d'hommes? Et puis, écoutez
à quoi cela lui servira-t-il?, Ici-bas, mon ami,
ill a toujours été dangereux de se heurter
aux grands; ils vous donnent quatre-vingt
dix pour cent et ils ont quand même raison!

(Figaro returns alone.)

BARTOLO

But what has happened?

BASILIO

Nothing: the Count likes Suzanna; she has
agreed to give him an assignation and Figaro
does not like it.

BARTOLO

What then, should he bear it in silence?

BASILIO

Why shouldn't he bear what so many other
have to bear. Besides listen, what good will it
do him? in this world, my friend, it has always
been dangerous to clash with nobility: they
give you ninety for a hundred and they are in
the right!

DISC NO. 2/TRACK 17

No. 26: Recitative and Aria Figaro here foolishly believes that Susanna is about to give in to
the Count. He's anxious and hurt at first, but in the aria (01:35) he offers a warning, speaking directly to the men in the audience, during which he manages to work himself into a frenzy,
singing as many words in a short space of time as be can. By the end, when he has said all he
can about them, he sings "The rest I won't say, because everyone knows it already." And what
is it that he won't say, that we all know?

FIGARO

Tutto è disposto: l'ora dovrebbe esser vicina; io sento gente… è dessa! Non è alcun;
buia è la notte… ed io comincio omai a fare
il scimunito mestiere di marito… Ingrata!
Nel momento della mia cerimonia ei gode-

FIGARO

Everything is ready: the hour must be near,
I hear them coming; it's she; no it's no
one. The night is dark, and I'm already
beginning to ply the foolish trade of cuck-
olded husband. Ungrateful! At the moment

va leggendo: e nel verderlo io rideva di me senza saperlo. Oh Susanna! Susanna! Quanta pena mi costi! Con quell'ingenua faccia, con quegli occhi innocenti, chi creduto l'avria? Ah! Che il fidarsi a donna, è ognor follia. Aprite un po' quegli occhi, uomini incauti e sciocchi, guardate queste femmine, guardate cosa son! Queste chiamate dee dagli ingannati sensi, a cui tributa incensi la debole ragion, *ecc.* Son streghe che incantano per farci penar, sirene che cantano per farci affogar, civette che allettano per trarci le piume, comete che brillano per toglierci il lume. Son rose spinose son volpi vezzose; son orse benigne, colombe maligne, maestre d'inganni, amiche d'affanni, che fingono, mentono, amore non senton, non senton pietà. No, no, no, no, no! Il resto nol dico, già ognuno lo sa. Aprite un po' quegli occhi, *ecc.*

of my wedding ceremony he enjoyed her through a letter, and seeing him laughed at myself without knowing it. Oh, Susanna, Susanna, how many pains have you cost me! With that artless face, with those innocent eyes, who would have believed it! Ah, it's always madness to trust a woman! Open your eyes for a moment, rash and foolish men, look at these women, look at what they are. You call them goddesses, with your befuddled senses, and pay them tribute with your weakened minds. They are witches who work spells to make you miserable, sirens who sing to make you drown, screech-owls that lure you to pluck out your feathers, comets that flash to take away your light. They are thorny roses, cunning vixen, hugging bears, spiteful doves, masters of deceit, friends of trouble, who pretend, lie, feel no love, feel no pity, no, no, no, no no! The rest I won't say, because everyone knows it already. Open your eyes for a moment, *etc.*

(He hides in the trees. Susanna and the Countess appear dressed in each other's clothes. After, Marcellina)

DISC NO. 2/TRACK 18
Recitative **Susanna, with the Countess's collusion, here begins multiple layers of deception for her husband's benefit. It is a case of a very smart person "lying the truth."**

SUSANNA
Signora! ella mi disse che Figaro verravi.

SUSANNA
Madame, she told me that Figaro would come here.

MARCELLINA
Anzi è venuto. Abbassa un po' la voce.

MARCELLINA
Truly, he's already here. Lower your voice a bit.

SUSANNA
Dunque un ci ascolta, e l'altro dee venir a cercarmi. Incominciam.

MARCELLINA
Io voglio qui celarmi.

(She enters the left-hand arbour.)

SUSANNA
Madama, voi tremate. Avreste freddo?

CONTESSA
Parmi umida la notte; io mi ritiro.

FIGARO
Eccoci della crisi al grande istante.

SUSANNA
Io sotto queste piante, se Madama il permette, resto a prendere il fresco una mezz'ora.

FIGARO
Il fresco, il fresco!

CONTESSA
Restaci in buon'ora.

(She hides.)

SUSANNA
Il birbo è in sentinella. Divertiamci anche noi, diamogli la mercè de' dubbi suoi.

SUSANNA
So one man eavesdrops and the other will come to look for me. Let's start.

MARCELLINA
I'll hide in here.

SUSANNA
Madame, you're trembling; are you cold?

COUNTESS
The night seems humid; I'll withdraw.

FIGARO
Here we are at the moment of crisis.

SUSANNA
Within this grove, if Madame permits it, I shall stay and take the fresh air for half an hour.

FIGARO
Fresh air, fresh air!

COUNTESS
Stay as long as you wish.

SUSANNA
The rogue is watching. I, too, shall have my little sport, I'll pay him for his suspicions.

No. 27: Recitative and Aria There's irony in the text of Susanna's great solo because she is supposedly punishing Figaro for his doubting her, but rarely has a lovelier, more sincere song been sung. In the simple recitative (track 19) Figaro might just believe that Susanna is waiting for another man, but for the fact that he is not as swept away by the aria (track 20), which is, essentially, an ode to the pleasures of love and nature. The orchestra comments: strings whisper smoothly, like the murmuring of the water and the gentle breeze, and the woodwinds supply the smile of the grass and cool feel of the grass beneath Susanna's feet. This aria is an island of joy—an extension of Susanna's duettino with the Countess in Act III, but more personal.

Giunse alfin il momento, che godrò senza affanno in braccio all'idol mio! Timide cure! Uscite dal mio petto, a turbar non venite il mio diletto! Oh come par che all'amoroso foco l'amenità del loco, la terra e il ciel risponda, come la notte i furti miei seconda! Deh vieni non tardar, o gioia bella, vieni ove amore per goder t'appella, finché non splende in ciel notturna face; finché l'aria è ancor bruna, e il mondo tace. Qui mormora il ruscel, qui scherza l'aura, che col dolce sussurro il cor restaura, qui ridono i fioretti e l'erba è fresca, ai piaceri d'amor qui tutto adesca. Vieni, ben mio, tra queste piante ascose. Vieni, vieni! Ti vo' la fronte incoronar di rose!	At last the moment is near when carefree I shall exult in the embrace of him I worship. Timid care, be banished from my heart, and come not to disturb my joy. Oh, how the beauties of this place, of heaven and earth, respond to the fire of my love. How night furthers my designs! Come now, delay not, lovely joy, come where love calls you to pleasure. The nocturnal torch shines not yet in heaven; the air is still murky, and the earth silent. Here the brook murmurs, the breezes play and with gentle sighing refresh the heart. Here the flowers are laughing, and the grass is cool; all things beckon to love's delights. Come, my soul, within this hidden grove. Come! I would crown your brow with roses!

(She hides in the trees on the opposite side from Figaro.)

Recitative The action and the music gather pace from here to the very end, with frequent interruptions as the characters catch up to the latest revelations.

FIGARO	**FIGARO**
Perfida! E in quella forma meco mentia? Non so s'io veglio, o dormo.	Deceiver! So you lied to me with such skill! I don't know whether I'm awake or sleeping.

CHERUBINO *(entrando)*
La la la la la la la lera! Io sento gente, entriamo ove entrò Barbarina. Oh, vedo qui una donna.

CHERUBINO *(entering)*
La la la la la la lera! I hear someone, so I'll go in where Barbarina went. Oh, I see a woman in there.

CONTESSA
Ahimè, meschina!

COUNTESS
Ah, miserable me!

CHERUBINO
M'inganno! A quel cappello che nell'ombra vegg'io parmi Susanna.

CHERUBINO
I was deceived! In that cap under a shadow it looks like Susanna.

CONTESSA
E se il Conte ora vien, sorte tiranna!

COUNTESS
And if the Count comes now, cruel fate!

NO. 28: FINALE

CHERUBINO
Pian pianin, le andrò più presso, tempo perso non sarà.

CHERUBINO
Softly now I'll come closer to you, we shall not waste any time.

CONTESSA
Ah, se il Conte arriva adesso qualche imbroglio accaderà!

COUNTESS
Ah, if the Count comes along what a fight there will be!

CHERUBINO
Susannetta! Non risponde, colla mano il volto asconde, or la burlo in verità.

CHERUBINO
Dearest Susanna! She doesn't answer, but hides her face with her hand; now I shall really tease her.

CONTESSA *(cercando di andarsene)*
Arditello, sfacciatello, ite presto via di qua, *ecc.*

COUNTESS *(trying to get away)*
Presumptuous, impudent boy, go away from here immediately, *etc.*

CHERUBINO
Smorfiosa, maliziosa, io già so perché sei qua, *ecc.*

CHERUBINO
Mincing, malicious woman, I already know why you're here, *etc.*

CONTE *(da lontano)*
Ecco qui la mia Susanna!

SUSANNA, FIGARO
Ecco qui 'uccellatore!

CHERUBINO
Non far meco la tiranna!

SUSANNA, CONTE, FIGARO
Ah! Nel sen mi batte il core!

CONTESSA
Via partite, o chiamo gente!

SUSANNA, CONTE, FIGARO
Un'altr'uom con lei si sta;

CHERUBINO
Dammi un bacio, o non fai niente;

SUSANNA, CONTE, FIGARO
Alla voce, è quegli il paggio.

CONTESSA
Anche un bacio! Che coraggio!

CHERUBINO
E perché far io non posso quel che il Conte ognor farà?

SUSANNA, CONTESSA, CONTE, FIGARO
Temerario!

CHERUBINO
Oh ve' che smorfie! Sai ch'io fui dietro il sofà.

COUNT *(from a distance)*
That must be my Susanna!

SUSANNA, FIGARO
Here comes the fowler!

CHERUBINO
Don't try to play the tyrant with me!

SUSANNA, COUNT, FIGARO
Ah, my heart is pounding in my breast!

COUNTESS
Quickly, go, or I'll call for help!

SUSANNA, COUNT, FIGARO
There is another man with her.

CHERUBINO
Give me a kiss, or you'll do nothing.

SUSANNA, COUNT, FIGARO
By his voice, that must be the page.

COUNTESS
A kiss, you say! What temerity!

CHERUBINO
And why can't I do what the Count always does?

SUSANNA, COUNTESS, COUNT, FIGARO
Rash boy!

CHERUBINO
Why make a face? You know that I was behind the chair!

SUSANNA, CONTESSA, CONTE, FIGARO
Se il ribaldo ancor sta saldo, la faccenda
guasterà.

SUSANNA, COUNTESS, COUNT, FIGARO
If the rake stays much longer he'll ruin
everything.

CHERUBINO *(le vuol dare un bacio)*
Prendi intanto!

CHERUBINO *(trying to kiss the Countess)*
I'll take it anyway!

(The Count steps between them and receives the kiss himself.)

CONTESSA, POI CHERUBINO
O cielo! Il Conte!

COUNTESS, THEN CHERUBINO
Heavens! The Count!

(Cherubino runs to hide in the left-hand arbour.)

FIGARO
Vo' veder cosa fan là.

FIGARO
I want to see what they're doing.

(The Count makes a swipe at Cherubino but strikes Figaro instead.)

CONTE
Perché voi non ripetete ricevete questo qua!

COUNT
So that you won't repeat the offence, take
that!

FIGARO, CONTESSA, CONTE, SUSANNA
Ah! Ci ho/ha fatto un bel guadagno colla
mia curiosità/sua temerità, *ecc.*

FIGARO, COUNTESS, COUNT, SUSANNA
Ah, I have/he has made quite a gain
through my curiosity/his temerity, *etc.*

(Figaro and Susanna go off in opposite directions.)

CONTE
Partito è alfin l'audace, accostati, ben mio!

COUNT
At last the rogue has gone, come nearer, my
dearest.

CONTESSA
Giacché così vi piace, eccomi qui, signor.

COUNTESS
If it please you thus, here I am, sir.

FIGARO
Che compiacente femmina! Che sposa di
buon cor!

FIGARO
What a complaisant woman! What a good-
hearted wife!

CONTE
Porgimi la manina!

CONTESSA
Io ve la do.

CONTE
Carina!

FIGARO
Carina?

CONTE
Che dita tenerelle! Che delicata pelle! Mi pizzica, mi stuzzica, m'empie d'un nuovo ardor! *ecc.*

SUSANNA, CONTESSA, FIGARO
La cieca prevenzione delude la ragione inganna i sensi ognor, *ecc.*

CONTE
Oltre la dote, oh cara! ricevi anco un brillante che a te porge un amante in pegno del suo amor.

(He gives her a ring.)

CONTESSA
Tutto Susanna piglia dal suo benefattor.

SUSANNA, CONTE, FIGARO
Va tutto a maraviglia, ma il meglio manca ancor.

CONTESSA
Signor, d'accese fiaccole io veggio il balenar.

COUNT
Give me your hand.

COUNTESS
I give it to you.

COUNT
Dearest!

FIGARO
Dearest?

COUNT
What dainty fingers! What delicate skin! I'm tingling, I'm feverish, I'm filled with new ardour, *etc.*

SUSANNA, COUNTESS, FIGARO
Blind precipitousness deludes reason and always tricks the senses, *etc.*

COUNT
Besides your dowry, beloved, receive this jewel, offered by a lover in pledge of his love.

COUNTESS
Susanna owes everything to her benefactor.

SUSANNA, COUNT, FIGARO
Everything is going perfectly! But the best is coming yet.

COUNTESS
Sir, I can see the light from bright torches.

CONTE Entriam, mia bella Venere, andiamoci a celar, *ecc.*	**COUNT** Let us enter, my fair Venus, let us go in and hide, *etc.*
SUSANNA, FIGARO Mariti scimuniti, venite ad imparar.	**SUSANNA, FIGARO** All you deceived husbands, come and learn your lessons.
CONTESSA Al buio, signor mio?	**COUNTESS** In the dark, my lord?
CONTE È quello che vogl'io: tu sai che là per leggere, io non desio d'entrar.	**COUNT** It is my wish: you know that I don't want to go inside and read.
FIGARO La perfida lo seguita, è vano il dubitar.	**FIGARO** The betrayer is following him; doubts are foolish now.
SUSANNA, CONTESSA I furbi sono in trappola, comincia ben l'affar.	**SUSANNA, COUNTESS** The rogues are in the trap, the affair is beginning well.
CONTE Chi passa?	**COUNT** Who goes there?
FIGARO Passa gente!	**FIGARO** None of your business!
CONTESSA È Figaro! Men vo!	**COUNTESS** It's Figaro! I'm going!
CONTE Andate, andate! Io poi verrò.	**COUNT** Go on. I'll find you soon.

(The Count disappears in the bushes. The Countess goes out to the right.)

FIGARO
Tutto è tranquillo e placido, entrò la bella
Venere: col vago Marte prendere, nuovo
Vulcan del secolo, in rete la potrò.

FIGARO
All is peaceful and silent: The beautiful
Venus has gone to the embrace of her fond
Mars, but a modern Vulcan will soon have
her in his net.

SUSANNA *(imitando la voce della* Contessa*)*
Ehi, Figaro! Tacete!

SUSANNA *(in a feigned voice)*
Hey, Figaro, keep your voice down!

FIGARO
Oh, questa è la Contessa. A tempo qui
guingete, vedrete là voi stessa il Conte e la
mia sposa. Di propria man la cosa toccar io
vi farò.

FIGARO
Oh, there is the Countess. You come at a
perfect moment to see for yourself the
Count with my wife. You'll be able to
touch them with your very own hand.

SUSANNA *(dimenticando di cangiare la voce)*
Parlate un po' più basso: di qua non muovo
il passo, ma vendicar mi vo'.

SUSANNA *(forgetting to alter her voice)*
Speak a little lower: from the spot I shall
not move until I am avenged.

FIGARO
(Susanna!) Vendicarsi!

FIGARO
(Susanna!) Avenged?

SUSANNA
Sì.

SUSANNA
Yes.

FIGARO
Come potria farsi? La volpe vuol sorpren-
dermi, e secondarla vo', *ecc.*

FIGARO
How can that be done? The vixen is trying
to catch me, and I'm going to help her, *etc.*

SUSANNA
L'iniquo io vo' sorprendere, poi so quel che
farò, *ecc.*

SUSANNA
I'm going to catch the villain, and I know
how to go about it, *etc.*

FIGARO *(con finta premura)*
Ah, se Madama il vuole!

FIGARO *(with comic affectation)*
Ah, if it please Madame!

SUSANNA
Su via, manco parole!

SUSANNA
Get up, not a word!

FIGARO
Ah, Madama!

SUSANNA
Su via, manco parole!

FIGARO
Eccomi a vostri piedi, ho pieno il cor di foco. Esaminate il loco, pensate al traditor!

SUSANNA
Come la man mi pizzica!

FIGARO
Come il polmon mi si altera!

SUSANNA
Che smania! Che furor! *ecc.*

FIGARO
Che smania! Che calor! *ecc.*

SUSANNA
E senz'alcun affetto?

FIGARO
Suppliscavi il rispetto. Non perdiam tempo invano; datemi un po' la mano…

SUSANNA *(dandogli uno schiaffo)*
Servitevi, signor.

FIGARO
Che schiaffo!

SUSANNA
Che schiaffo! E questo, e ancora questo, e questo, e poi quest'altro.

FIGARO
Ah, Madame!

SUSANNA
Get up, not a word!

FIGARO
Here I am at your feet, with my heart full of fire. Look around you, and remember the betrayer!

SUSANNA
How my hand is itching!

FIGARO
I can hardly breathe!

SUSANNA
What madness! What fury! *etc.*

FIGARO
What madness! What fever! *etc.*

SUSANNA
But there is no affection between us?

FIGARO
Let respect be enough. We must not let time pass in vain, give me your hand a moment.

SUSANNA *(in her natural voice, boxing his ears)*
Help yourself, sir.

FIGARO
You slapped me!

SUSANNA
You slapped me! Here's another, and another and still another.

FIGARO
Non batter così presto!

SUSANNA
E questo, signor scaltro, e questo, e poi
quest'altro ancor.

FIGARO
Oh schiaffi graziosissimi. Oh, mio felice
amor! *ecc.*

SUSANNA
Impara, impara, o perfido, a fare il sedut-
tor, *ecc.*

FIGARO
Pace, pace, mio dolce tesoro: io conobbi la
voce che adoro, e che impressa ognor serbo
nel cor.

SUSANNA
La mia voce?

FIGARO
La voce che adoro.

SUSANNA, FIGARO
Pace, pace, mio dolce tesoro! pace, pace,
mio tenero amor.

(The Count returns.)

CONTE
Non la trovo, e girai tutto il bosco.

SUSANNA, FIGARO
Questi è il Conte, alla voce il conosco.

FIGARO
Don't beat me so furiously!

SUSANNA
And another, you sharper, and then still
one more!

FIGARO
Oh, most gracious blows! Oh, perfect love!
etc.

SUSANNA
I'll teach you, deceitful man, to play the
seducer, *etc.*

FIGARO
Peace, peace, my sweet treasure: I recog-
nised the voice which I adore and carry
engraved in my heart.

SUSANNA
My voice?

FIGARO
The voice I adore.

SUSANNA, FIGARO
Peace, peace, my sweet treasure, peace,
peace, my gentle beloved.

COUNT
I cannot find her, and I've combed the forest.

SUSANNA, FIGARO
That's the Count, I recognise his voice.

CONTE
Ehi, Susanna! Sei sorda, sei muta?

SUSANNA
Bella, bella! Non l'ha conosciuta!

FIGARO
Chi?

SUSANNA
Madama.

FIGARO
Madama?

SUSANNA
Madama!

SUSANNA, FIGARO
La commedia, idol mio, terminiamo, consoliamo il bizzaro amator, *ecc.*

(Figaro throws himself at her feet.)

FIGARO
Sì, Madama, vio siete il ben mio.

CONTE
La mia sposa! Ah, senz'arme son io!

FIGARO
Un ristoro al mio cor concedete?

SUSANNA
Io son qui fate quel che volete.

CONTE
Ah, ribaldi, ribaldi!

COUNT
Hey, Susanna, are you deaf or dumb?

SUSANNA
Wonderful! He didn't recognise her!

FIGARO
Whom?

SUSANNA
Madame.

FIGARO
Madame?

SUSANNA
Madame!

SUSANNA, FIGARO
Let's terminate this farce, my beloved, and console this capricious lover, *etc.*

FIGARO
Yes, Madame, you are the light of my life.

COUNT
My wife? Ah, I have no weapons!

FIGARO
Will you grant a cure for my heart?

SUSANNA
Here I am, I'll do as you wish.

COUNT
Ah, scandalous, scandalous!

SUSANNA, FIGARO	**SUSANNA, FIGARO**
Ah, corriamo, corriamo mio bene e le pene compensi il piacer.	Ah, let us make haste, beloved, and exchange pain for pleasure.

(They move towards the arbour on the left. The Count grasps Figaro.)

DISC NO. 2/TRACK 26

After fifteen minutes of confusion, face-slapping, humiliation, playfulness and not-so-playfulness, and the loving reconciliation of Susanna and Figaro, the Count, in all his mania, takes over, making one mistake after another, and refusing to pardon the wrongdoers. But when the Countess reveals herself (01:06) it is left only for the Count to apologize to her (01:30). He does so with such simplicity and beauty that the Countess melts at once, commenting that she is kinder than he, and so forgives more easily. Everyone is exhausted after this day of intense plotting and turmoil and joins in a quick chorus (04:10) in which they all agree to celebrate what appears like the restoration of order, as the curtain falls.

CONTE	**COUNT**
Gente, gente, all'armi, all'armi!	Help, help, weapons, weapons!
FIGARO *(con finto spavento)*	**FIGARO** *(feigning great fright)*
Il padrone!	The master!
CONTE	**COUNT**
Gente, gente, aiuto, aiuto!	My men, help, help!

(enter Antonio, Basilio, Bartolo, Don Curzio and servants)

FIGARO	**FIGARO**
Son perduto!	I'm lost!
BASILIO, CURZIO, ANTONIO, BARTOLO	**BASILIO, CURZIO, ANTONIO, BARTOLO**
Cos'avvenne? Cos'avvenne?	What happened?
CONTE	**COUNT**
Il scellerato m'ha tradito, m'ha infamato, e con chi state a veder.	The villain has betrayed me, has defamed me, and you shall see with whom.

BASILIO, CURZIO, ANTONIO, BARTOLO
Son stordito, sbalordito, non mi par che ciò sia ver!

BASILIO, CURZIO, ANTONIO, BARTOLO
I'm amazed, confounded, I can't believe it's true!

FIGARO
Son storditi, sbalorditi, oh che scena, che piacer!

FIGARO
They're amazed, confounded, oh, what a scene, what fun!

(Going to the arbour the Count hands out, in turn, Cherubino, Barbarina, Marcellina and Susanna.)

CONTE
Invan resistete, uscite, Madama; il premio ora avrete di vostra onestà … Il paggio!

COUNT
In vain you resist, come out Madame; now you shall be rewarded for your honesty…
The page!

ANTONIO
Mia figlia!

ANTONIO
My daughter!

FIGARO
Mia madre!

FIGARO
My mother!

BASILIO, CURZIO, ANTONIO, BARTOLO
Madama!

BASILIO, CURZIO, ANTONIO, BARTOLO
Madame!

CONTE
Scoperta è la trama la perfida è qua!

COUNT
The plot is revealed, and there is the deceiver.

SUSANNA *(inginocchiandosi)*
Perdono, perdono!

SUSANNA *(kneeling)*
Pardon, pardon.

CONTE
No, no! Non sperarlo!

COUNT
No, no, do not expect it!

FIGARO *(inginocchiandosi)*
Perdono, perdono!

FIGARO *(kneeling)*
Pardon, pardon!

CONTE	**COUNT**
No, no, non vo' darlo!	No, no, I will not!

TUTTI SLAVO IL CONTE	**ALL EXCEPT THE COUNT** *(kneeling)*
(inginocchiandosi) Perdono! *ecc.*	Pardon! *etc.*

CONTE	**COUNT**
No!	No!

(The Countess emerges from the right-hand arbour.)

CONTESSA	**COUNTESS**
Almeno io per loro perdono otterrò.	At least I may obtain their pardon.

BASILIO, CURZIO, CONTE, ANTONIO, BARTOLO	**BASILIO, CURZIO, COUNT, ANTONIO, BARTOLO**
Oh cielo! Che veggio! Deliro! Vaneggio! Che creder non so.	Heaven! What do I see? I'm raving! Going crazy! I don't know what to believe.

CONTE *(inginocchiandosi)*	**COUNT** *(kneeling)*
Contessa perdono! Perdono, perdono!	Countess, your pardon! Pardon!

CONTESSA	**COUNTESS**
Più docile io sono, e dico di sì.	I am more clement, and answer, yes.

TUTTI	**ALL**
Ah! Tutti contenti saremo così. Questo giorno di tormenti, di capricci e di follia, incontenti e in allegria solo amor può terminar. Sposi, amici, al ballo, al gioco, alle mine date foco! Ed a suon di lieta marciacorriam tutti a festeggiar, *ecc.*	Ah! All shall be made happy thereby. Only love can resolve this day of torments, caprice and folly, into joy and happiness. Spouses and sweethearts, to dancing and fun, and let's have some fireworks! And to the sound of a gay march hurry off to celebrate, *etc.*

END	**END**

THE MARRIAGE OF FIGARO

Wolfgang Amadeus Mozart

COMPACT DISC ONE 76.46

OVERTURE ACT ONE		4:21
1	Cinque, dieci, venti *Figaro/Susanna*	2:48
2	Se a caso Madama *Figaro/Susanna*	2:28
3	Bravo, signor padrone—Se vuol ballare *Figaro*	3:18
4	La vendetta, oh, la vendetta *Bartolo*	3:10
5	Via, resti servita *Susanna/Marcellina*	2:16
6	Non so più cosa son, cosa faccio *Cherubino*	2:35
7	Cosa sento! *Count/Basilio/Susanna*	4:45
8	Non più andrai farfallone amoroso *Figaro*	3:35

ACT TWO

9	Porgi amor	4:15
	Countess	
10	Vieni, cara Susanna	4:17
	Countess/Susanna/Cherubino	
11	Voi, che sapete	2:46
	Cherubino	
12	Bravo! Che bella voce!	1:03
	Countess/Susanna/Cherubino	
13	Venite, inginocchiatevi	3:20
	Susanna	
14	Quante buffonerie!	3:24
	Countess/Susanna/Cherubino/Count	
15	Susanna, or via sortite	3:09
	Count/Countess/Susanna	
16	Dunque voi non aprite?	0:52
	Count/Countess	
17	Aprite, presto, aprite	0:57
	Susanna/Cherubino	
18	Oh guarda il demonietto	1:39
	Susanna/Cherubino	
19	Esci ormai, garzon mainato	2:44
	Count/Countess	
20	Susanna! Susanna!	5:26
	Count/Countess/Susanna	
21	Signori, di fuori!	3:30
	Figaro/Count/Susanna/Countess	
22	Ah! Signor, signor!	6:03
	Antonio/Count/Susanna/Countess/Figaro	
23	Voi Signor, che giusto siete	3:54
	Marcellina/Basilio/Bartolo/Susanna/Countess/Figaro/Count	

ACT THREE

1	Che imbarazzo è mai questo	2:17
	Count/Countess/Susanna	
2	Crudel! Perche finora farmi languir così?	2:44
	Count/Susanna	
3	E perchè fosti meco	0:41
	Count/Susanna/Figaro	
4	Hai già vinta la causa— Vedrò mentr'io sospiro	4:51
	Count	
5	E decisa la lite	1:46
	Don Curzio/Marcellina/Figaro/Count/Bartolo	
6	Riconosci in questíamplesso	4:56
	Marcellino/Figaro/Bartolo/Don Curzio/Count/Susanna	
7	Eccovi, o caro amico	1:47
	Marcellina/Bartolo/Susanna/Figaro/Barbarina/Cherubino	
8	E Susanna non vien!...Dove sono	6:22
	Countess	
9	Io vi dico, signor	0:52
	Antonio/Count/Countess/Susanna	
10	Canzonetta sull'aria...	3:06
	Countess/Susanna	
11	Ricevete, o padroncina	4:00
	Chorus/Barbarina/Countess/Susanna/Antonio/Count/Cherubino/Figaro	
12	Ecco la marcia	6:44
	Figaro/Susanna/Count/Countess/Young men/Chorus	

ACT FOUR

13	L'ho perduta, me meschina!	1:50
	Barbarina	
14	Barbarina, cos'hai?	2:10
	Figaro/Barbarina/Marcellina	
15	Nel padiglione a manca	1:13
	Barbarina/Figaro/Basilio/Bartolo	

16	Ha I diavoli nel corpo!...In quegli anni	4:37
	Basilio/Bartolo	
17	Tutto è disposto... Aprite un po'quegli occhi	4:22
	Figaro	
18	Signora, ella mi disse...	0:44
	Susanna/Marcellina/Countess/Figaro	
19	Giunse alfin il momento	1:17
	Susanna	
20	Deh vieni, non tardar	3:19
	Susanna	
21	Perfida! E in quella forma meco mentia?	0:34
	Figaro/Cherubino/Countess	
22	Pian, pianin...	3:24
	Cherubino/Countess/Count/Susanna/Figaro	
23	Partito è alfin l'audace	2:46
	Count/Countess/Figaro/Susanna	
24	Tutto è tranquillo e placido	4:05
	Figaro/Susanna	
25	Pace, pace mio dolce tesoro	2:09
	Figaro/Susanna/Count	
26	Ecco la marcia	5:17
	All	

LA BOHÈME

LA BOHÈME

Giacomo Puccini

TEXT BY DAVID FOIL

Additional commentary by William Berger

BLACK DOG
& LEVENTHAL
PUBLISHERS
NEW YORK

The enclosed compact discs ℗ 1964 EMI Records Ltd.
Digital Remastering ℗ 1990 by EMI Records Ltd.
Product of EMI-Capitol Music Special Markets, 1750 North Vine Street, Los Angeles, California 90028.

Libretto by Meilhac & Halévy. Reproduced courtesy of Angel/EMI Classics.

Published by
Black Dog & Leventhal Publishers, Inc.
151 West 19th Street
New York, NY 10011

Distributed by
Workman Publishing Company
225 Varick Street
New York, NY 10014

Manufactured in China

Cover and interior design by Elizabeth Driesbach

ISBN-13: 978-1-57912-509-7

h g f e d c b a

Library of Congress Cataloging-in-Publication Data available on file.

*T*here is no better place to begin exploring opera than with *La Bohème*. It tells an irresistible story that is charming, sexy, and, ultimately, heartrending. The action is breathtaking. And, from the opening bars, Puccini's music is unforgettable in its infectious energy, its expressive beauty, and its wealth of melody. It is an experience to cherish, to relive again and again.

You will hear the entire opera on the two compact discs included on the inside front and back covers of this book. As you explore the book, you will discover the story behind the opera and its creation, the background of the composer, biographies of the principal singers and conductor, and the opera's text, or libretto, both in the original Italian and in an English translation. Special commentary has been included throughout the libretto to aid in your appreciation and to highlight key moments in the action and the score.

Enjoy this book and enjoy the music.

LA BOHÈME

$\mathscr{I}$n the hundred years since its premiere, Giacomo Puccini's *La Bohème* has become the most consistently popular opera of the twentieth century. It might even be argued that *La Bohème* is the opera that defines opera for modern audiences. That hardly seemed possible the morning after its first performance.

The eagerly awaited premiere of *La Bohème* took place in Turin's Teatro Regio on February 1, 1896, with Arturo Toscanini conducting. Nothing less than a blockbuster was expected

Left: A heartbroken Placido Domingo as Rodolfo clutches Mimì's bonnet.
Above: Giacomo Puccini (1858–1924)

from the promising composer whose opera *Manon Lescaut* had premiered exactly three years earlier, to the day, in the same theater. The first performance of *La Bohème* actually went rather well, with its handpicked cast performing up to the exacting standards that were the hallmarks of any Toscanini performance. The audience seemed to like at least parts of what it was seeing and hearing. Yet there was nothing infectious about its response—in short, no buzz—and a vague sense of disappointment materialized, like a hangover, when the performance ended. The intermission chatter, most of the next morning's reviews, the gossip that would quickly spread through Italy's musical circles—none of it was encouraging.

Most of the critics found *La Bohème* to be inconsequential, vulgar, and lightweight, and unlikely to hold the interest of audiences even through the current season. Carlo Bersenzio typified the critics's reaction with his conclusion in *La stampa*, writing that "*Bohème*, just as it makes little impression on the emotions of the listener, will leave few traces in the history of our lyric theater." That dismissive tone would be echoed by critics at the opera's premieres in London in 1897 and New

York in 1900. That once consummate crank among New York music critics, Henry Krehbiel, began his review of the Metropolitan Opera's premiere of the opera by saying, "*La Bohème* is foul in subject, and fulminant but futile in its music." The apathy of these reactions devastated Puccini, despite the fitful bursts of appreciation from that first audience and Toscanini's passionate assurances that the opera would prevail.

In the midst of all this soul-killing blather, though, something else was happening. *La Bohème* was developing into the best kind of hit there is—a word-of-mouth hit—one that, as a Hollywood observer later said of a smash movie hated by critics and industry insiders, "nobody liked much except the

La Bohème is set in the Paris of Victor Hugo and Honoré de Balzac.

people in the audience." As a matter of fact, *La Bohème* played twenty-four additional performances in Turin to sold-out houses during the remainder of the month of February 1896, when only eight performances had been originally scheduled. Though Puccini was to endure still more indifference from the cognoscenti after the Rome and Naples premieres, he had only to wait until April to taste absolute triumph, when he traveled to Palermo for the first Sicilian production, after which he took repeated bows to thunderous ovations. So enthusiastic was *that* opening-night audience that the singers had to be called back to the stage in their street clothes to repeat the finale, even though half of the orchestra members had gone home. Within a year, *La Bohème* would be enthusiastically applauded in Buenos Aires, Alexandria, Moscow, Lisbon, Manchester, Berlin, Rio de Janeiro, Mexico City, London, Vienna, Los Angeles, and the Hague. In a sense, the applause has never stopped.

Why is *La Bohème* considered the quintessential opera? There are obvious reasons. For one thing, the opera tells an indelibly touching story with universal appeal, a story heightened and ennobled by the deft melodic expression of Puccini's score. For another, it is a tightly focused musical drama, divided into four acts that are short, accessible, and highly watchable, none of them lasting a second longer than necessary. The opera's allure lies as well in its setting—a rollicking "scene" of dashing young artists, dreamers, and "wannabes" in the Paris of Victor Hugo and Honoré de Balzac, living, loving, and dying in the raw splendor of the moment—a milieu which Puccini knew something of from his own student days in Milan. The

LA VIE DE BOHÊME

DRAME EN CINQ ACTES

PAR

THÉODORE BARRIÈRE ET HENRY MURGER

REPRÉSENTÉ POUR LA PREMIÈRE FOIS, A PARIS, SUR LE THÉATRE DES VARIÉTÉS, LE 22 NOVEMBRE 1849
ET REPRIS SUR LE THÉATRE DE L'ODÉON, LE 9 MAI 1873

DISTRIBUTION DE LA PIÈCE

	VARIÉTÉS.	ODÉON.		VARIÉTÉS.	ODÉON.
DURANDIN, homme d'affaires.....	MM. DUSSERT.	MM. NOEL MARTIN.	UN MONSIEUR............	MM. CHASLER.	MM. FRÉVILLE.
RODOLPHE, son neveu, poëte.....	P. LARA.	P. BERTON.	UN MÉDECIN............	RHÉAL.	VALBEL.
MARCEL, peintre.............	DANFERNY.	POREL.	CÉSARINE DE ROUVRE, jeune veuve..	Mme MARQUET.	Mme DEFARENNES.
SCHAUNARD, musicien..........	CH. PÉREY.	G. RICHARD.	MIMI................	TOUILLIER.	E. BROISAT.
GUSTAVE COLLINE, philosophe....	MEYER.	CLERH.	MUSETTE..............	PAGE.	L. LEBLANC.
M. BENOIT, maître d'hôtel.......	BARDOU jeune	RICHARD.	PHÉMIE..............	P. FOTEL.	FAUST.
BAPTISTE, domestique..........	KOPP.	FRANÇOIS.	UNE DAME.............	WILHEM.	NOÉMIE.
UN GARÇON DE CAISSE.........	GALLIN.	ERNEST.	UN COMMISSIONNAIRE. — DOMESTIQUES DE CÉSARINE. — INVITÉS.		

— Droits de reproduction, de traduction et de représentation réservés —

Playbill for Théodore Barrière's 1873 adaptation of Henri Murger's novel,
Scènes de la vie de Bohème, on which Giuseppe Giacosa and Luigi Illica
based their libretto.

romantic plot is virtually unequaled in its ability to generate immediate empathy in an audience, *any* audience, anywhere in the world.

More intriguing, though, are the reasons for the curious hesitation on the part of the first audiences and critics, the very reasons the opera has enjoyed enduring success.

In Turin, in the last weeks of 1895, audiences heard for the first time Richard Wagner's *Götterdämmerung*, with Toscanini conducting—an experience that left them thrilled but overwhelmed, struggling to grasp its lofty ideals and follow the new direction in which it seemed to be leading opera. And then, out of the blue, came *La Bohème*—a finely crafted opera, to be sure, but one devoid of spectacle or intellectual pretension. Short, fleetfooted, and to-the-point, full of raucous humor and emotional hairpin turns, almost shocking in its sexual candor, and populated with life-size characters who might have wandered in off the streets—could this opera be a part of the same elevated medium as Wagner's or, indeed, Verdi's?

The answer is yes. Building on what he had learned from both composers, Puccini was determined to create a fluid and energetic musical drama that would realize Henri Murger's modest episodic novel, *Scènes de la vie de bohème*, in subtle and sensitive detail. Those first, privileged audiences who heard *La Bohème* probably were nonplused that the opera, compelling and sophisticated as it seemed to be, was about something so . . . well, *ordinary*. Puccini may have been alone

The award-winning musical *Rent* was inspired by *La Bohème*.

in appreciating the fact that ordinary did not have to mean banal, that it could, in fact, be disarming in its eloquence. Other operas in the then-popular style of realism called verismo dealt with ordinary people. Ruggero Leoncavallo's *I pagliacci* and Mascagni's *Cavalleria rusticana* shocked and delighted audiences in the early 1890s with their tales of lust and revenge among the poor and downtrodden, but they were essentially as melodramatic, bloody, and frenzied as the most typical Italian opera of the nineteenth century. *La Bohème* would be very different: an opera that took its character and scale from the small, inconsequential details that make everyday life, in retrospect, a provocative, touching, and occasionally heartrending common experience.

La Bohème casts a spell that has yet to be broken. Almost a century to the day, after the opera's world premiere, the New York theater world was entranced by the first performance of an inventive new musical called *Rent,* inspired by and based on *La Bohème.* Now set on New York's Lower East Side, Murger's characters and Puccini's score have been transformed in a modern age of relative freedom that is clouded with the threat of AIDS. *Rent* was the work of composer-lyricist-librettist Jonathan Larson, a perfectionist in search of a new expressive style who died suddenly just before his show opened off-off-Broadway. As if to echo the backstage story of *La Bohème,* the success of *Rent* took the New York cognoscenti completely by surprise. Within three months it had moved to Broadway with huge fanfare and record advance ticket sales and won Larson a posthumous Pulitzer Prize in drama.

An early advertising poster for *La Bohème.*

Puccini's success in *La Bohème* was so unique—and it was *his* success, for he drove his librettists Giuseppe Giacosa and Luigi Illica to the point of mutiny to get precisely what he wanted—that it might even be seen as a prototype for another phenomenon that was only a few years in the future. In *La Bohème*, Puccini had created the first great feature-length film.

Of course, there were no feature-length sound movies when Puccini, Giacosa, and Illica were writing *La Bohème.* That kind of technical sophistication was some forty years in the future. (There was, however, a beautiful silent film of *La Bohème* made in 1926, with Lillian Gish as the heroine Mimì.) But their realization of the story is best described as cinematic in its impact. They synthesized plot, dialogue, music, pace, atmosphere, and visual detail into an unusually lean, well-integrated, and propulsive narrative. Puccini the composer acts as the director, so to speak, with his score serving to adjust the perspective, intensify the mood, isolate the details, and link them to the action. He moves the "camera," choosing the close-ups and staging the master shots, controlling the dynamic range and flow of energy in the story. Though it seems quaint and even friendly

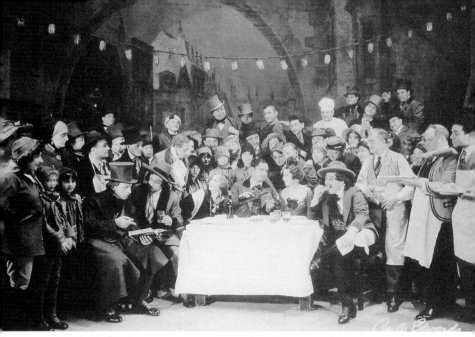

Inside Cafè Momus in a 1930 Metropolitan Opera production.

now, *La Bohème* unnerved its first audiences because it dared to be genuine, unvarnished, unpretentious—in short, real in a way that few operatic love stories had ever been.

Puccini's is not the only opera called *La Bohème*. Sometime in early 1893, Ruggero Leoncavallo (1857–1919) had apparently decided to base an opera on the French writer Murger's celebrated novel and the popular play that Théodore Barrière had adapted from it. Though Puccini had recently enjoyed his first solid success with the debut of his third opera *Manon Lescaut*, Leoncavallo was a much bigger name in Italian opera at that time. His *I pagliacci* had taken the world by storm the year before, and Leoncavallo was seriously considered, if only briefly, the most likely candidate to assume the mantle of Italian opera's undisputed master, the aging Giuseppe Verdi. Puccini and Leoncavallo were friends from their conservatory days in Milan, and Leoncavallo was one of a succession of people who had tried to bring some order to the troublesome libretto for Puccini's *Manon Lescaut.*

In a casual encounter in Milan in March of 1893, Puccini told Leoncavallo that he intended to write an opera based on the Murger novel and the Barrière play. Leoncavallo was first shocked and then furious. Not only was he already at work on such an opera but he insisted that it was *he* who had first mentioned the property to Puccini. Other sources indicate that Giacosa and Illica—both who had finally whipped the *Manon Lescaut* libretto into shape and would become Puccini's finest librettists—had decided to write a libretto for *La Bohème* even before the *Manon Lescaut* premiere. But history is unclear on who actually had the idea first. Since Leoncavallo did not premiere his version of *La Bohème* until 1897, he could not have had much of a headstart when he learned of Puccini's

Ruggero Leoncavallo (1858–1919) was enraged when Pucini decided to develop *La Bohème*, an opera he had already begun working on.

A manuscript page from *La Bohème* shows Puccini's corrections and marginal drawings.

plans in the winter of 1893. Still, his publisher Sonzogno mounted a publicity campaign to convince the public that the idea for such an opera belonged exclusively to Leoncavallo.

In an interview in the Milan newspaper *Corriere della Sera*, Puccini stated that he did not know of his friend Leoncavallo's intentions until their fateful meeting, and that now, of course, it was "too late" for him to drop his plans. He added, in a challenge that must have enraged Leoncavallo, that the public should ultimately decide who had written the better opera.

The public did decide. Puccini and his librettists worked relentlessly for three years on *La Bohème* and beat Leoncavallo to the stage by well over a year. Despite the hesitant reaction of its first audience, the opera quickly became a runaway hit. Leoncavallo proved to be something of a one–trick pony, never able to equal the enduring success of *I pagliacci*, despite the popularity of several of his operas in his lifetime. His version of *La Bohème*—quite different in plot and structure from Puccini's—contained some lovely passages and, though not a failure, the polite praise it received seemed to damn it, as the entire world appeared to go mad for Puccini's opera. Leoncavallo's anger over what he considered betrayal by Puccini turned into profound bitterness, and ended their friendship. As his star began to fall, Puccini's rose.

Did Puccini steal the idea from Leoncavallo? It is possible. He had the nerve, after all, to make an opera of Abbé Prevost's novel *Manon Lescaut* less than a decade after the debut of French composer Jules Massenet's hugely successful *Manon*. And, in choosing to follow *La Bohème* with *Tosca*, Puccini had to wrest the exclusive rights to Victorien Sardou's play *La Tosca* away from another celebrated Italian composer of the day, Alberto Franchetti. Puccini's behavior in these matters could be callous, cruel, and breathtakingly arrogant, but he had the one quality that, in an artist, can forgive the rest—genius.

Giacomo Puccini was born in the Italian town of Lucca on December 22, 1858. He represented the fifth generation of a dynasty of musicians who had dominated the city's musical life for over a century. Puccini was only five when his father Michele died, and it was his mother Albina who saw to it that the eldest son carried on the family tradition. The boy was hardly enthusiastic. Far more interested in fun and games, he was a poor student who showed no inclination at all for the rigors of musical study. Only when he was sent to Lucca's Instituto Musicale Pacini, to be taught by a former student of his father's, did Puccini discover that he was interested in music. That interest quickly turned into a passion. The teenager became a passably good pianist and organist who still had a fondness for trickery; as an inside joke, while serving as a church organist in Lucca, he was known to weave popular secular songs into the music he played for the services. He began composing when he was seventeen but the turning point in his development came the following year, when he saw a performance of *Aida* in Pisa. It convinced him that his future lay in writing for the theater.

In 1880, after graduating from the Lucca conservatory, Puccini received a stipend that allowed him to move to Milan to study composition at that city's conservatory with Antonio Bazzini and Amilcare Ponchielli, the young, respected composer of *La Gioconda*. Puccini's three years as a student in Milan shaped him as a composer, and his threadbare existence as a

poor student appears to have made him particularly sympathetic to the characters and situations he would encounter in Murger's *Scènes de la vie de bohème*. His graduation exercise, an orchestral work called *Capriccio sinfonico*, won him warm praise and it, too, would play an important role in *La Bohème*—the vigorous orchestral openings to the opera's first and last acts were lifted from that student work.

It was Ponchielli who brought Puccini together with his first librettist, Ferdinando Fontana. Together they wrote *Le villi* (1884), a short opera that failed to win a prize but that did attract favorable notice and the attention of Giulio Ricordi, the head of the formidable Ricordi publishing empire, which published all of Verdi's operas and was a dominant force in Italian opera throughout the nineteenth and twentieth centuries. Ricordi commissioned an opera from Puccini, and, after five years, Puccini and Fontana came up with *Edgar*, a turgid three-act drama that contains a great deal of beautiful music. Reaction to the 1889 premiere at La Scala, Milan, was lukewarm, convincing the supremely confident Puccini that even he could not prevail against a weak or inept libretto.

When he set to work on *Manon Lescaut,* he was determined to fight for the libretto he needed. Writers came and went until he found a productive relationship through Giulio Ricordi with Giuseppe Giacosa (1847–1906) and Luigi Illica (1857–1919). They methodically went about their work in a way that impressed Puccini. Generally, Illica dealt with the mechanics of plot and narrative, while Giacosa concentrated on writing the actual text, though their tasks in the partnership frequently varied. Their efficient and compelling work spoke for itself. *Manon Lescaut* was a triumph, and the composer and librettists decided to continue their collaboration with *La Bohème.*

Puccini was a master of musical drama, as seen in the setting of *La Bohème* at the Lyric Opera of Chicago.

The creation of *La Bohème* was an arduous and combative process. Puccini drove Giacosa and Illica to distraction with his fanatical insistence on a tightly woven plot and precise articulation of the text. They fought bitterly, but when the librettists heard the score Puccini had written—with its subtle, reflexive, and infinitely sensitive handling of mood and emotion—they understood why he pushed so relentlessly. He was right when he exhorted them, "Simplify, simplify." Puccini understood that text and plot could only go so far in opera, that music would seal the drama, and that the ideal libretto provided the composer with the necessary foundation for what, in the end, was a *musical* drama.

The overwhelming international success of *Manon Lescaut* and *La Bohème* made Puccini a very wealthy man, a celebrity, and the leader of a generation of composers that, in addition to the wounded Leoncavallo, included Pietro Mascagni (*Cavalleria rusticana*), Umberto Giordano (*Andrea Chénier*), and Francesco Cilea (*Adriana Lecouvreur*). His next opera, *Tosca* (1900), was another success, as was *Madama Butterfly* (1904), both written in collaboration with Giacosa and Illica. Incidentally, the La Scala premiere of *Madama Butterfly* was an out-and-out disaster. The audience, provoked by a group jealous of Puccini's success, jeered the opera and subjected the composer to his first humiliation in the theater. Furious, Puccini withdrew the score and attacked the problems the opera seemed to have in its premiere; the revised version that reached the stage three months later was a revelation, and *Madama Butterfly* joined his earlier successes as an international hit.

In the remaining twenty years of his life, Puccini never quite matched the astonishing run he achieved with those four successive hits, though several of his later operas—especially *La fanciulla del West*, the original "spaghetti Western," written for the Metropolitan Opera in 1910; the wicked and dazzling one-act comedy *Gianni Schicchi*; and the epic *Turandot*, left unfinished at his death—are eminently worthy of comparison. The depth of Puccini's talent is reflected in the painstaking study and

An EMI recording session of *La Bohème*. Seated in foreground are Nicolai Gedda on left and Thomas Schippers in center; in background, Mario Sereni leaning over table and Mirella Freni seated at far right.

effort he lavished on the task of composing *Turandot*, even though he began to work on it when he was in his sixties and suffering from the cancer that would kill him in 1924. Yet for all the sophistication and invention as a composer that he displayed in his later years, Puccini never again portrayed human passion as perceptively as he did in *La Bohème*. The brilliant stage managing of *Tosca* and the deft manipulation of *Madama Butterfly* remind us, from time to time, that we are in the hands of a shrewd master craftsman, instinctive entertainer, and consummate musical dramatist. In *La Bohème*, the artifice is invisible. Each turn of phrase seems as inevitable as breathing. The result, for once, is not opera. It is poetry.

THE STORY OF THE OPERA

Act 1

On Christmas Eve, in the year 1830, two passionate young bohemian artists—a poet named Rodolfo and a painter named Marcello—busy themselves with work in their studio apartment in the garret of a house in the Latin quarter of Paris. Neither is really getting much done, but the effort at least takes their minds off the bitter cold and the fact that they don't have any fuel for their stove. Rodolfo finally decides to burn his manuscript to provide some heat. Their friend, a philosopher named Colline, arrives just in time to savor the warmth, but the fire does not last long, and when it dies out, Colline and Marcello boo its author.

At that moment, two boys burst in bearing abundant gifts that seem too good to be true—food, wine, and fuel for the stove. The source of this bounty is the musician Schaunard, the fourth member of this quartet of hapless idealists, who

Marcello and Rodolfo in their tiny garret.

bursts in with a wild tale about how he wound up with a pocketful of money, which he tosses on the table. While his friends are happy for him, they are more interested in eating, drinking, and building a hearty fire than in hearing his story. Realizing that his good will has upstaged his own story, Schaunard suggests that they go out to eat, since it is Christmas Eve and he is—for the moment, anyway—flush with money.

Their departure is delayed by the unexpected arrival of the old landlord Benoit. The rent, which they don't have, is due. Marcello invites Benoit into the apartment, letting him see the money Schaunard has left on the table, and offers him a drink. All four of the bohemians play up to Benoit, making him feel like "one of the boys" and manage to convince him to tell outrageous stories of his way with women. The landlord lets it slip that he is married, at which point the bohemians turn on him in a show of fake indignation that he takes so seriously that he flees the garret without giving another thought to the rent.

Rodolfo sends the others ahead to wait for him downstairs so he can finish an article he is writing. Once he is alone, though, he realizes that he is in no mood to write. A knock at the door stirs him. It is his neighbor, the frail and consumptive Mimì, who asks him to light her candle. When she enters the garret, Mimì almost collapses, dropping both the candle and the key to her room. Alarmed, Rodolfo relights her candle. Mimì is about to leave when she realizes that her key is missing. A sudden draft of cold air once again extinguishes her candle and, seeing his opportunity, Rodolfo quietly blows his out as well. In the darkness, they search for the key, which Rodolfo soon finds and pockets. A moment later, he touches Mimì's chilled hand,

Renata Tebaldi, the Italian soprano discovered by Toscanini, as Mimì.

which he offers to warm. He introduces himself and admits that she has stolen his heart. She, in turn, reveals herself to Rodolfo: her real name is Lucia, she makes artificial flowers, and she hungers for the arrival of spring. Time seems to stand still. When the bohemians shout up to the garret from the street, Rodolfo tells them to go ahead to the Café Momus, where he will join them. As he turns back from the window, he sees Mimì standing in a shaft of moonlight, appearing indescribably beautiful to him. Both are overcome by the realization that they are in love, and she suggests they leave to join the bohemians. Rodolfo asks Mimì about what might happen later, after dinner, and she teasingly tells him to wait and see. They leave, arm in arm, enraptured . . . and, at last, oblivious to the cold.

Act 2

The street outside the Café Momus is thronged with shoppers, diners, and street vendors. On their way to dinner, Rodolfo has bought a pink bonnet for Mimì in a millinery shop. When the couple arrives at the café, the bohemians greet Mimì with deep bows and mock gallantry, making her laugh and feel

Dance at Bougival by Pierre Auguste Renoir.

immediately welcome. All this good will curdles with the arrival of Musetta, a dazzling girl who has recently broken Marcello's heart by dumping him for a rich, older man, Alcindoro. Musetta sweeps in, trailed by the frantic Alcindoro, and takes a table near the bohemians. This is no coincidence: Musetta, realizing that Marcello is nearby, begins to taunt him mercilessly by making a show of herself, which mortifies Alcindoro and makes Marcello seethe. The other bohemians fill Mimì in on the details of that romance, which amuse her and remind her suddenly of how deeply she loves Rodolfo. Desperate to get rid of Alcindoro, Musetta screams as if her foot were in pain. The old man leaps about to mollify her, finally running off to the cobbler with her offending shoe as she falls into the arms of the utterly beguiled Marcello. When the bill comes, the bohemians realize they have spent all of Schaunard's money and cannot pay for dinner. Suddenly, a military parade marches in. In the frenzy, the bohemians tag along and march off, leaving the bill, which is presented to Alcindoro when he returns to the empty café.

Act 3

A couple of months pass, and Paris is buried in the depths of winter. On a freezing February morning, Mimì turns up at an inn near the Barrière d'Enfer, one of the gates of the city of Paris. Marcello and Musetta are living at a nearby inn, and Mimì—whose poor health is becoming ever more apparent—has come to ask Marcello for advice about Rodolfo. Their passionate love affair has become turbulent, and Rodolfo's jealousy is threatening their future. Marcello tells Mimì she should leave him and reveals that Rodolfo is actually asleep inside the inn, having turned up earlier that morning. When Rodolfo emerges, Mimì hides. He explains to Marcello that he has been jealous because Mimì is a coquette, but finally admits that Mimì is seriously, perhaps fatally ill, and his heart is breaking at the thought of losing her. In the shadows, Mimì is seized with a fit of coughing and the devastated Rodolfo rushes to her side. From inside the inn's tavern, a scream from Musetta distracts Marcello, who rushes in to deal with her. When they are alone, Mimì quietly tells Rodolfo that she is

The street outside Cafè Momus in a Metropolitan Opera production.

leaving him. She tells him to gather her possessions, but they later agree to stay together until the spring, reaching an understanding just as Marcello and Musetta burst out of the tavern, their vigorous fighting providing an ironic counterpoint to the sorrow of Mimì and Rodolfo.

Musetta's ploy as depicted in a 1993 production at the Santa Fe opera.

Act 4

With the arrival of spring, Marcello and Rodolfo are back in their Parisian garret, once more struggling to look busy. Newly single, they are trying to avoid thinking about the women they have loved and lost. Idle talk about their work turns to gossip about Mimì and Musetta and wondering what has become of them. Colline and Schaunard turn up with the makings of a modest supper. The distraction is so welcome that the joking turns into a wild improvised melodrama, complete with cross dressing and a duel fought with loaves of bread.

In the midst of the commotion, the door flies open to reveal Musetta, who is frantic. She has left Mimì waiting downstairs and tells

Enrico Caruso as Rodolfo.

them that Mimì is now so frail that she cannot even climb the steps, that she knew of nowhere else to go. Rodolfo rushes out to find Mimì and carry her upstairs while the others create a place for her to rest. They have nothing to offer her, so Musetta sends Marcello off with her earrings to pay for food, a doctor, and some medicine. She decides to join him, so she can buy a muff to warm Mimì's hands. Colline decides to pawn his beloved overcoat, and he urges Schaunard to come along so Rodolfo and Mimì can have some time alone. The lovers savor their moment together, recalling their first meeting and how suddenly and completely they fell in love. One by one, the others return from their missions. Rodolfo busies himself arranging the drapes, and the exhausted Mimì falls asleep. Musetta alone knows how sick Mimì is, and she kneels in fervent prayer. But it is too late. When Colline returns and asks about Mimì, none of the others can even form the words to answer him. When Rodolfo attempts to offer an optimistic answer, he realizes what the awful silence and his friends' stricken faces mean. Mimì is dead. Marcello embraces Rodolfo and tells him to be courageous, but the poet is shattered, collapsing over Mimì's lifeless body and crying out her name as the others watch in sorrow.

Mimì (Angela Gheorghiu) and Rodolfo (Roberto Alagna) savor their last moments together in 1996 production at the Metropolitan Opera.

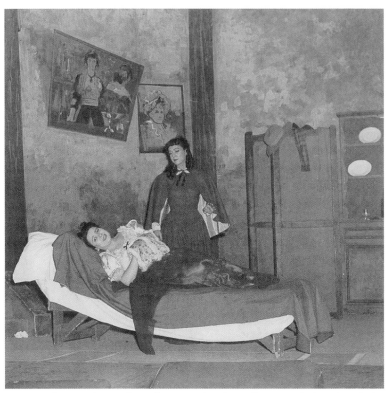

Musetta (Patrice Munsel) comforts an ailing Mimì (Victoria de Los Angeles) in the 1951 Metropolitan Opera production of *La Bohème*.

THE PERFORMERS

Nicolai Gedda (Rodolfo) has become the model of the modern tenor, equally at home on opera, recital, and concert stages, a sophisticated singer equipped with a firm but flexible technique that has allowed him to perform a repertoire almost unprecedented in its breadth. He was born in Stockholm in 1925 to a Swedish mother and a Russian father (who was a bass in the Don Cossack Choir) and spent part of his childhood in Leipzig. His gift for languages was a key factor in his early success. Gedda made his professional debut in Stockholm in 1952 in the title role of Adolphe Adam's *Le Postillon de Longjumeau.* Walter Legge of EMI Records happened to hear Gedda during a Stockholm visit that year and, noting his linguistic skill as well as his brilliant lyric tenor voice, immediately signed him for an upcoming recording of *Boris Godunov.* Major European debuts followed quickly, as Gedda established himself with a succession of important recordings for EMI. In addition to opera, he was recognized as a distinguished *lieder* singer and oratorio soloist. In the year following

Nicolai Gedda as Rodolfo.

his 1957 Metropolitan Opera debut, he created the title role in the company's world premiere of Samuel Barber's *Vanessa*. For the next thirty years, Gedda sang operatic roles as diverse as the boyish Nemorino in *L'Elisir d'amore* and the heroic title part in Wagner's *Lohengrin*. Later in his career, he took on Russian roles and explored unusual areas of the song repertoire, with occasional forays into novelty, singing, for instance, on composer-conductor Leonard Bernstein's definitive recording of the musical *Candide*.

MIRELLA FRENI (Mimì) was born in 1935 in Modena, a few months earlier than the city's most famous son, Luciano Pavarotti. As infants, the two singers-to-be—who would later become affectionate colleagues—shared the same wet nurse, and their mothers worked in the same cigarette factory. Freni began studying voice with her uncle, making her first public

Mirella Freni as Mimì in her 1965 Metropolitan Opera debut.

appearance at the age of eleven with another prodigy, the pianist Leone Magiera, who would become her first husband. She made her opera debut in 1955 in Modena as Micaëla in *Carmen*, inaugurating what would be a stellar international stage and recording career of extraordinary range and longevity. After singing several seasons with provincial Italian houses, Freni made strong impressions in debuts with the Amsterdam Opera (1959), London's Covent Garden (1961), and Milan's La Scala (1962), quickly becoming one of Europe's most sought-after lyric sopranos. The role of Mimì became her calling card, especially after her performance in the successful 1963 film of Franco Zeffirelli's La Scala production, conducted by Herbert von Karajan. Freni sang Mimì in her debuts at Moscow's Bolshoi Opera (1964) and New York's Metropolitan Opera (1965). She also excelled in such roles as Susanna in *Le nozze di Figaro*, Violetta in *La traviata*, Zerlina in *Don Giovanni*, Marguerite in *Faust*, and Juliette in *Roméo et Juliette*. In the 1970s, when Freni decided to sing heavier roles—a dangerous choice for a lyric soprano—many critics predicted that it would ruin her voice. Bolstered by a steady technique and the sensitive support of conductors such as von Karajan and Riccardo Muti, she was instead acclaimed for bringing a distinctive lyrical warmth to performances and recordings of the title role in *Aida*, Cio-Cio-San in *Madama Butterfly*, Elisabetta in *Don Carlo*, and Leonora in *La forza del destino*. In 1981, she married the Bulgarian bass Nicolai Ghiaurov, a colleague who virtually became her professional partner, notably after

Freni began singing Russian roles such as Tatyana in *Eugene Onegin*. In the 1990s, she has been noted for her performances in the demanding prima donna roles of such verismo warhorses as *Adriana Lecouvreur* and *Fedora*.

Mario Sereni as Marcello.

MARIO SERENI (Marcello) enjoyed great popularity in the 1950s and 1960s in the important baritone roles of the Italian repertoire, both in major international houses and on recordings. Born in Perugia, Italy, in 1928, Sereni attended Rome's Accademia de Santa Cecilia and the Accademia Chigiana in Siena, where he was the student of Mario Basiola. His professional career began in 1953 on an unusually high level—at the Maggio Musicale Fiorentino (Florence May Festival)—and within four years, he had made his Metropolitan Opera debut as Gérard in *Andrea Chénier* and had also sung at Buenos Aires's Teatro Colón. Sereni enjoyed a long and steady career at the Metropolitan Opera, London's Covent Garden, Milan's La Scala, the Vienna Staatsoper, and other companies around the world. Despite his success, Sereni remained in the shadow of the more charismatic baritones of his time—principally Leonard Warren, Tito Gobbi, Robert Merrill, Ettore Bastianini, Piero Cappuccilli, and Rolando Panerai—and critics of the time frequently dismissed his singing. Yet his many recordings (he can be heard on the legendary *Lisbon Traviata* recording of 1958 with Maria Callas and Alfredo Kraus) reveal a singer and musician of considerable distinction, with a handsome voice, a durable technique, and a fine sense of style.

THOMAS SCHIPPERS (1930–1977) was a prodigiously gifted American conductor whose professional career began only a few days after his twentieth birthday, when he led the New York premiere of Gian Carlo Menotti's *The Consul*. Born in Kalamazoo, Michigan, Schippers made his public debut as a pianist

at the age of six and became a church organist when he was fourteen. He attended the Curtis Institute of Music and Yale University, where he took composition lessons from Paul Hindemith. At the age of eighteen, he won second prize in a conducting competition sponsored by the Philadelphia Orchestra. Schippers's career really took off, though, through his work with Menotti; in addition to *The Consul* premiere, he conducted the 1951 television premiere of Menotti's *Amahl and the Night Visitors* and, a year later, made his New York City Opera debut at the helm of Menotti's *The Old Maid and the Thief.* He remained at New York City Opera until 1954, then made his New York Philharmonic debut in 1955. That same year he made his Metropolitan Opera debut, the beginning of an association that would last the rest of his life. (It was Schippers who was conducting the 1960 performance of Verdi's *La forza del destino* during which baritone Leonard Warren died onstage.) Rich, young, matinee-idol handsome, well-spoken, and a superb musician, Schippers became the quintessential celebrity conductor in a media-driven age. He joined Leonard Bernstein for the New York Philharmonic's historic visit to the

Gedda and Freni at an EMI recording session of La Bohème.

U.S.S.R. in 1959, conducted the world premiere of Manuel de Falla's *Atlántida* at La Scala in 1962 and, two years later, became one of the youngest conductors in the history of the Bayreuth Festival. In the fall of 1966, Schippers led the world premiere of Samuel Barber's *Antony and Cleopatra*, which officially opened the Metropolitan Opera's new home at Lincoln Center, where he later led the company's first performances of Modest Mussorgsky's original version of *Boris Godunov* and Gioacchino Rossini's *The Siege of Corinth*, which provided Beverly Sills with her Met debut. From 1958 until 1976, the year before his death, he maintained close ties to Menotti's Festival of Two Worlds in Spoleto, Italy. In 1970, Schippers was named conductor of the Cincinnati Symphony Orchestra and later joined the faculty of the city's college conservatory of music. For all his success, Schippers's life ended in suffering: his wife died of cancer in 1973 and he died of the same disease four years later. Unable to continue as conductor of the Cincinnati Symphony Orchestra, Schippers was named its conductor laureate and, in turn, he bequeathed the orchestra five million dollars.

The Libretto

Act 1

A GARRET A large window through which an expanse of snow-covered roofs is seen. At right, a stove. A table, a bed, four chairs, a painter's easel with half-finished canvas books everywhere, manuscripts. Rodolfo is thoughtful, looking out the window. Marcello works at his painting "The Crossing of the Red Sea," his hands stiff with cold; he tries to warm them by blowing on them now and again.

DISC NO. 1/TRACK 1

Questo Mar Rosse **The opera begins with a vigorous melodic subject that Puccini created for his Capriccio sinfonico, written when he was a conservatory student. A whiplash from the orchestra, it plunges the listener immediately into the action. The first act is then off to a gallop, a concentrated whirlwind of activity lasting around twenty minutes that does not stop until the bohemians decide to adjourn the Café Momus. The score responds so articulately to the action (and is just as sensitively orchestrated) that matters of tempo and pace vary from bar to bar, and it must be experienced moment by moment.**

MARCELLO

Questo "Mar Rosso" mi ammollisce
e assidera come se addosso
mi piovesse in stille.
Per vendicarmi affogo un Faraone.

to Rodolfo

Che fai?

MARCELLO

This "Red Sea" of mine
makes me feel cold and numb
as if it were pouring over me.
I'll drown a Pharaoh in revenge.

What are you doing?

RODOLFO

Nei cieli bigi
guardo fumar dai mille
comignoli Parigi,

RODOLFO

I'm looking at Paris,
seeing the skies grey with smoke
from a thousand chimneys,

e penso a quel poltrone
d'un vecchio caminetto ingannatore
che vive in ozio come un gran signor.

MARCELLO
Le sue rendite oneste
da un pezzo non riceve.

RODOLFO
Quelle sciocche foreste
che fan sotto la neve?

MARCELLO
Rodolfo, io voglio dirti
un mio pensier profondo
ho un freddo cane.

RODOLFO
Ed io, Marcel, non ti nascondo
che non credo al sudor della fronte.

and I think of that no-good,
hateful stove of ours that lives
a gentleman's life of idleness.

MARCELLO
It's been a long time
since he received his just income.

RODOLFO
What are those stupid forests
doing, all covered with snow?

MARCELLO
Rodolfo, I want to tell you
a profound thought I've had
I'm cold as hell.

RODOLFO
As for me, Marcello, I'll be frank
I'm not exactly sweating.

Act II of *La Bohème* in a 1993 production at the Santa Fe Opera.

MARCELLO

Ho ghiacciate le dita
quasi ancora le tenessi immollate
giù in quella gran ghiacciaia
che è il cuore di Musetta.

A sigh escapes him, and he leaves off painting.

RODOLFO

L'amore è un caminetto che sciupa
troppo…

MARCELLO

E in fretta!

RODOLFO

Dove l'uomo è fascina.

MARCELLO

E la donna è l'alare…

RODOLFO

L'uno brucia in un soffio…

MARCELLO

E l'altro a guardare…

RODOLFO

Ma intanto que si gela…

MARCELLO

E si muore d'inedia…

RODOLFO

Fuoco ci vuole…

MARCELLO

And my fingers are frozen—
as if I still were holding them
in that enormous glacier,
Musetta's heart.

RODOLFO

Love is a stove that burns too much…

MARCELLO

Too fast!

RODOLFO

Where the man is the fuel…

MARCELLO

And woman the spark…

RODOLFO

He burns in a moment…

MARCELLO

And she stands by, watching!

RODOLFO

Meanwhile, we're freezing in here!

MARCELLO

And dying from lack of food!

RODOLFO

We must have a fire…

MARCELLO *(afferrando una sedia)*
Aspetta...sacrifichiam la sedia

MARCELLO *(seizing a chair)*
Wait...we'll sacrifice the chair!

Rodolfo keeps Marcello from breaking the chair. Suddenly he shouts with joy.

RODOLFO
Eureka!

RODOLFO
Eureka!

MARCELLO
Trovasti?

MARCELLO
You've found it?

RODOLFO
Sì. Aguzza l'ingegno.
L'idea vampi in fiamma.

RODOLFO
Yes. Sharpen your wits.
Let Thought burst into flame.

MARCELLO *(additando il suo quadro)*
Bruciamo il "Mar Rosso"?

MARCELLO *(pointing to his picture)*
Shall we burn the "Red Sea"?

RODOLFO
No. Puzza la tela dipinta.
Il mio dramma...
L'ardente mio dramma ci scaldi.

RODOLFO
No. Painted canvas smells.
My play...
My burning drama will warm us.

MARCELLO
Vuoi leggerlo forse? Mi geli.

MARCELLO
You mean to read it? I'll freeze.

RODOLFO
No, in cener la carta si sfaldi
e l'estro rivoli ai suoi cieli.
Al secol gran danno minaccia...
Ma Roma è in periglio...

RODOLFO
No, the paper will unfold in ash
and genius soar back to its heaven.
A serious loss to the age...
but Rome is in danger...

MARCELLO
Gran cor!

MARCELLO
What a noble heart!

RODOLFO

A te l'atto primo!

MARCELLO

Qua.

RODOLFO

Straccia.

MARCELLO

Accendi.

Rodolfo lights the part of the manuscript thrown in the fire. Then the two friends draw up chairs and sit down, voluptuously warming themselves.

RODOLFO E MARCELLO

Che lieto baglior

The door opens and Colline enters, frozen, stamping his feet. He throws some books on the table.

COLLINE

Già dell'Apocalisse appariscono i segni.
In giorno di Vigilia non si accettano
pegni!

surprised

Una fiammata!

RODOLFO

Zitto, si dà il mio dramma…

MARCELLO

…al fuoco.

RODOLFO

Here, take the first act!

MARCELLO

Here.

RODOLFO

Tear it up.

MARCELLO

Light it.

RODOLFO AND MARCELLO

What blissful heat!

COLLINE

Signs of the Apocalypse begin to appear.
No pawning allowed on Christmas Eve.

A fire!

RODOLFO

Quiet, my play's being given…

MARCELLO

…to the stove.

COLLINE	**COLLINE**
Lo trovo scintillante.	I find it full of fire.
RODOLFO	**RODOLFO**
Vivo.	Brilliant.
MARCELLO	**MARCELLO**
Ma dura poco.	But brief.
RODOLFO	**RODOLFO**
La brevità, gran pregio.	Brevity, its great merit.
COLLINE	**COLLINE**
Autore, a me la sedia.	Your chair, please, Mr. Author.
MARCELLO	**MARCELLO**
Questi intermezzi	These intermissions
fan morir d'inedia.	kill you with boredom.
Presto!	Get on with it!
RODOLFO	**RODOLFO**
Atto secondo.	Act two.
MARCELLO	**MARCELLO**
Non far sussurro.	No whispering.

DISC NO. 1/TRACK 2

The imposing Colline joins the friends in the garret, and engages in the mock-heroic banter that is the hallmark of this arty crowd. The orchestra imitates the sounds of fire while the friends watch Rodolfo's play burn in the stove, typical of the attention and importance given to life's details throughout this score.

COLLINE	**COLLINE**
Pensier profondo!	What profundity!

MARCELLO
Giusto color!

MARCELLO
How colorful!

RODOLFO
In quell'azzurro guizzo languente
sfuma un'ardente scena d'amor.

RODOLFO
In that dying blue flame
an ardent love-scene dies.

COLLINE
Scoppietta un foglio.

COLLINE
See that page crackle.

MARCELLO
Là c'eran baci!

MARCELLO
There were the kisses!

RODOLFO
Tre atti or voglio d'un colpo udir.

RODOLFO
I want to hear three acts at once.

He throws the rest of the manuscript on the fire.

COLLINE
Tal degli audaci l'idea s'integra.

COLLINE
And so unified is your bold conception.

TUTTI
Bello in allegra vampa svanir.

ALL
Beautiful death on the joyful flame.

They applaud. Then the flame dies.

MARCELLO
Oh! Dio…già s'abbassa la fiamma.

MARCELLO
Oh Lord! The flame is dying.

COLLINE
Che vano, che fragile dramma!

COLLINE
So useless, so fragile a drama!

MARCELLO
Già scricchiola, increspasi, muor.

MARCELLO
Already curling up to die.

COLLINE E MARCELLO	COLLINE AND MARCELLO
Abbasso, abbasso l'autore.	Down with the author!

Two porters come in, one carrying food, bottles of wine and cigars; the other has a bundle of wood. At the sound, the three men in front of the fire turn around and with shouts of amazement fall upon the provisions.

DISC NO. 1/TRACK 3

The appearance of Schaunard and his bounty lifts the friends's spirits, marked by faster tempi in the score. Schaunard's description of the pleasures of the Latin Quarter (02:51) will become a motif heard at key moments throughout the opera.

RODOLFO	RODOLFO
Legna!	Wood!

MARCELLO	MARCELLO
Sigari!	Cigars!

COLLINE	COLLINE
Bordò!	Bordeaux!

RODOLFO	RODOLFO
Legna!	Firewood!

MARCELLO	MARCELLO
Bordò!	Bordeaux!

TUTTI	ALL THREE
Le dovizie d'una fiera	Destiny provides us
il destin ci destinò…	with a feast of plenty!

The porters leave. Schaunard enters triumphantly, throwing some coins on the floor.

SCHAUNARD
La Banca di Francia
per voi si sbilancia.

COLLINE (*raccattando gli scudi insieme agli altri*)
Raccatta, raccatta!

MARCELLO
Son pezzi di latta!…

SCHAUNARD
Sei sordo?…sei lippo?

showing a crown

Quest'uomo chi è?

RODOLFO
Luigi Filippo!
M'inchino al mio Re!

TUTTI
Sta Luigi Filippo ai nostri piè!

Schaunard wants to tell his adventure, but the others won't listen to him. They set the provisions on the table and put wood in the stove.

SCHAUNARD
Or vi dirò questo'oro,
o meglio, argento
ha la sua brava istoria…

RODOLFO
Riscaldiamo il camino!

SCHAUNARD
The Bank of France
has gone broke just for you.

COLLINE (*gathering up coins, with the others*)
Pick them up!

MARCELLO
They must be made of tin!…

SCHAUNARD
Are you deaf? or blind?

Who is this man?

RODOLFO
Louis Philippe!
I bow to my King!

ALL
Louis Philippe is at our feet!

SCHAUNARD
Now I'll tell you this gold,
this silver, rather
has a noble history…

RODOLFO
Let's fire the stove!

COLLINE
Tanto freddo ha sofferto

SCHAUNARD
Un inglese...un signor...lord
o milord che sia, volea un musicista...

MARCELLO
Via! Prepariamo la tavola!

SCHAUNARD
Io? Volo!...

RODOLFO
L'esca dov'è

COLLINE
Là.

MARCELLO
Qua.

SCHAUNARD
...e mi presento.
M'accetta, gli domando...

COLLINE
Arrosto freddo.

MARCELLO
Pasticcio dolce.

SCHAUNARD
...A quando le lezioni?
Mi presento, m'accetta,

COLLINE
It's hard to endure so much cold!

SCHAUNARD
An Englishman...a gentleman...
A lord...was looking for a musician...

MARCELLO
Come! Let's set the table!

SCHAUNARD
And I? I flew to him...

RODOLFO
Where are the matches?

COLLINE
There.

MARCELLO
Here.

SCHAUNARD
...I introduce myself.
He hires me. I ask him...

COLLINE
Cold roast beef.

MARCELLO
Sweet pastry.

SCHAUNARD
When do the lessons begin?...
I introduce myself, he hires me.

gli domando A quando le lezioni?
Risponde "Incominciam…
guardare!" e un pappagallo
m'addita al primo pian.
Poi soggiunge "Voi suonare
finché quello morire!"

RODOLFO
Fulgida folgori la sala splendida!

MARCELLO
Ora le candele.

SCHAUNARD
E fu così
suonai tre lunghi dì…
Allora usai l'incanto
di mia presenza bella…
Affascinai l'ancella…
Gli propinai prezzemolo…

MARCELLO
Mangiar senza tovaglia?

RODOLFO
No un'idea!

He takes a newspaper from his pocket.

MARCELLO E COLLINE
Il Costituzional!

RODOLFO
Ottima carta…
Si mangia e si divora un'appendice!

I ask When do the lessons begin?
He replies "Let's start…
look!" and points to a parrot
on the first floor.
Then adds; "You play
until that bird dies!"

RODOLFO
The dining room's brilliant!

MARCELLO
Now the candles.

SCHAUNARD
And so it went
I played for three long days…
Then I used my charm,
my handsome figure…
I won the serving-girl over…
We poisoned a little parsley…

MARCELLO
Eat without a tablecloth?

RODOLFO
No! I've an idea.

MARCELLO AND COLLINE
The Constitutional!

RODOLFO
Excellent paper…
You eat and devour the news!

SCHAUNARD

Lorito allargò l'ali,
Lorito il becco aprì,
un poco di prezzemolo;
da Socrate morì!

COLLINE *(a Schaunard)*
Chi? …

SCHAUNARD

Il diavolo vi porti tutti quanti…
Ed or che fate?
No! queste cibarie
sono la salmeria
pei dì futuri
tenebrosi e oscuri.
Pranzare in casa il dì della Vigilia
mentre il Quartier Latino le sue vie
addobba di salsiccie e leccornie?
Quando un olezzo di frittelle imbalsama le
vecchie strade?
Là le ragazze cantano contente…

TUTTI
La vigilia di Natal!

SCHAUNARD

Ed han per eco, ognuna uno studente!
Un po' di religione, o miei signori
si beva in casa, ma si pranzi fuor…

They pour the wine. A knock at the door.

SCHAUNARD

Lorito spread his wings,
Lorito opened his beak,
took a peck of parsley,
and died like Socrates!

COLLINE *(to Schaunard)*
Who?

SCHAUNARD

Go to the devil, all of you…
Now what are you doing?
No! These delicacies
are the provender
for the dark and gloomy
days in the future.
Dine at home on Christmas Eve
when the Latin Quarter
has decked its streets with eatables?
When the perfume of fritters
is wafted through the ancient streets?
There the girls sing happily…

ALL
It's Christmas Eve!

SCHAUNARD

And each has a student echoing her!
Have some religion, gentlemen
we drink at home, but we dine out.

This comical interlude with the fussy old landlord and his blunt request, "Rent!" shows us the bohemians in action: rhetorical fourishes mix with the risqué (02:14), while they remain sharp-witted and able to survive.

BENOIT *(di fuori)*
Si può?

BENOIT *(outside)*
May I come in?

MARCELLO
Chi è là?

MARCELLO
Who's there?

BENOIT
Benoit.

BENOIT
Benoit.

MARCELLO
Il padrone di casa!

MARCELLO
The landlord!

SCHAUNARD
Uscio sul muso.

SCHAUNARD
Bolt the door.

COLLINE
Non c'è nessuno.

COLLINE
Nobody's home.

SCHAUNARD
È chiuso.

SCHAUNARD
It's locked.

BENOIT
Una parola.

BENOIT
Just one word.

SCHAUNARD *(dopo essersi consultato cogli altri, va ad aprire)*
Sola!

SCHAUNARD *(after consulting the others, opens the door)*
Just one!

Benoit enters.

BENOIT *(mostrando una carta)*
Affitto.

MARCELLO
Olà! Date una sedia.

RODOLFO
Presto.

BENOIT
Non occorre, lo vorrei…

SCHAUNARD
Segga.

MARCELLO
Vuol bere?

BENOIT
Grazie.

RODOLFO E COLLINE
Tocchiamo.

SCHAUNARD
Beva.

Benoit sets down his glass and shows the paper to Marcello.

BENOIT
Questo
è l'ultimo trimestre…

MARCELLO
E n'ho piacere…

BENOIT *(showing a paper)*
Rent.

MARCELLO
Here! Give him a chair.

RODOLFO
At once.

BENOIT
Don't bother, I'd like…

SCHAUNARD
Be seated.

MARCELLO
Something to drink?

BENOIT
Thank you.

RODOLFO AND COLLINE
A toast.

SCHAUNARD
Drink.

BENOIT
This is the bill
for three month's rent…

MARCELLO
That's fine…

BENOIT
E quindi…

SCHAUNARD
Ancora un sorso.

BENOIT
Grazie.

I QUATTRO
Tocchiam. Alla sua salute!

BENOIT *(riprendendo con Marcello)*
A lei ne vengo
perché il trimestre scorso
mi promise…

MARCELLO
Promisi ed or mantengo.

He points to the money on the table.

RODOLFO *(piano a Marcello)*
Che fai?

SCHAUNARD
Sei pazzo?

MARCELLO *(a Benoit, senza guardare gli altri)*
Ha visto? Or via,
resti un momento in nostra compagnia.
Dica quant'anni ha,
caro Signor Benoit?

BENOIT
Therefore

SCHAUNARD
Another drop.

BENOIT
Thank you.

THE FOUR
A toast. To your health!

BENOIT *(to Marcello again)*
I come to you
because last quarter
you promised me…

MARCELLO
I promised and I'll pay.

RODOLFO *(aside to Marcello)*
What are you doing?

SCHAUNARD
Are you crazy?

MARCELLO *(to Benoit, ignoring the others)*
You see? Now then
stay with us a moment.
Tell me how old are you,
dear M. Benoit?

BENOIT Gli anni…Per carità!	**BENOIT** My age?…Spare me!
RODOLFO Su e giù la nostra età.	**RODOLFO** Our age, more or less, I'd say.
BENOIT Di più, molto di più.	**BENOIT** More, much more.

They refill his glass.

COLLINE Ha detto su e giù.	**COLLINE** He said more or less.
MARCELLO L'altra sera al Mabil l'han colto in peccato d'amor.	**MARCELLO** The other evening at the Mabille they caught him making love.
BENOIT Io?	**BENOIT** Me?
MARCELLO Al Mabil l'altra sera l'han colto… Neghi?	**MARCELLO** They caught him at the Mabille the other evening… Deny it, then.
BENOIT Un caso.	**BENOIT** An accident.
MARCELLO Bella donna!	**MARCELLO** A lovely woman!
BENOIT *(mezzo brillo)* Ah! Molto!	**BENOIT** *(half-drunk)* Ah! Very!
SCHAUNARD POI RODOLFO Briccone!	**SCHAUNARD, THEN RODOLFO** You rascal!

COLLINE

Seduttore!

Una quercia…un cannone!

RODOLFO

L'uomo ha buon gusto.

MARCELLO

Il crin ricciuto e fulvo.

Ei gongolava arzillo e pettoruto.

BENOIT

Son vecchio ma robusto.

COLLINE, SCHAUNARD E RODOLFO

Ei gongolava arzuto e pettorillo.

MARCELLO

A lui cedea

la femminil virtù.

BENOIT

Timido in giovertù,

ora me ne ripago.

Si sa, è uno svago

qualche donnetta allegra…e…un po'…

non dico una balena

o un mappamondo

o un viso tondo da luna piena.

Ma magra, proprio magra, no, poi no!

Le donne magre son grattacapi

e spesso…sopracapi…

e son piene di doglie…

per esempio, mia moglie…

COLLINE

Seducer!

He's an oak, a ball of fire!

RODOLFO

He's a man of taste.

MARCELLO

With that curly, tawny hair.

How he swaggered, proud and happy!

BENOIT

I'm old but strong.

COLLINE, SCHAUNARD AND RODOLFO

How he swaggered, proud and happy!

MARCELLO

Feminine virtue

gave in to him.

BENOIT

I'm paying myself back now

for my shy youth…

my pastime, you know,

a lively woman…a bit…

well, not a whale exactly

or a relief-map of the world

or a face like a full moon,

but not thin, really thin. No!

Thin women are worrisome

and often…a nuisance…

always full of complaints,

for example—my wife! …

Marcello rises, feigning moral indignation. The others do the same.

MARCELLO

Quest'uomo ha moglie

e sconcie voglie ha nel cor!

GLI ALTRI

Orror!

RODOLFO

E ammorba, e appesta

la nostra onesta magion.

GLI ALTRI

Fuor!

MARCELLO

Si abbruci dello zucchero!

COLLINE

Si discacci il reprobo.

SCHAUNARD

È la morale offesa che vi scaccia!

BENOIT

Io di…io di…

GLI ALTRI

Silenzio!

BENOIT

Miei signori…

GLI ALTRI

Silenzio…via signore…

Via di qua! E buona sera

a vostra signoria! Ah! Ah! Ah!

MARCELLO

This man has a wife

and foul desires in his heart!

THE OTHERS

Horrors!

RODOLFO

He corrupts and pollutes

our respectable home.

THE OTHERS

Out with him!

MARCELLO

Burn some incense!

COLLINE

Throw out the scoundrel!

SCHAUNARD

Our offended morality expels you!

BENOIT

I say…I…

THE OTHERS

Silence!

BENOIT

My dear sirs…

THE OTHERS

Silence…Out, sir…

away with you! And good evening

to your worship! Ha! Ha! Ha!

Benoit is thrown out. Marcello shuts the door.

MARCELLO
Ho pagato il trimestre.

MARCELLO
I've paid the rent.

SCHAUNARD
Al Quartiere Latin ci attende Momus.

SCHAUNARD
In the Latin Quarter Momus awaits us.

MARCELLO
Viva chi spende!

MARCELLO
Long life to him who pays!

SCHAUNARD
Dividiamo il bottin!

SCHAUNARD
We'll divide my loot!

GLI ALTRI
Dividiam!

THE OTHERS
Let's divide!
They share the coins.

They share the coins.

MARCELLO (*presentando uno specchio a Colline*)
Là ci son beltà scese dal cielo.
Or che sei ricco, bada alla decenza!
Orso, ravviati il pelo.

MARCELLO (*giving Colline a mirror*)
Beauties are there, come from above.
Now you're rich, you must look presentable. You bear!
Trim your fur.

COLLINE
Farò la conoscenza
la prima volta d'un barbitonsore.
Guidatemi ai ridicolo
oltraggio d'un rasoio.

COLLINE
I'll make my first acquaintance
of a beard-barber.
Lead me to the absurd,
outrageous razor.

TUTTI
Andiam.

ALL
Let's go.

The violin plays a languid recollection of the theme we heard at the beginning of the opera, when it represented Rodolfo and his boisterous nature. Now it sounds as if the same man needs to be alone and find inspirations. Colline's fall down the stairs (00:37) draws our attention offstage, an area that will shortly assume new importance.

RODOLFO	**RODOLFO**
Io resto per terminar	I must stay to finish
l'articolo di fondo	my article for the paper,
del Castoro.	*The Beaver.*
MARCELLO	**MARCELLO**
Fa presto.	Hurry, then!
RODOLFO	**RODOLFO**
Cinque minuti. Conosco il mestier.	Five minutes. I know my trade.
COLLINE	**COLLINE**
T'aspetterem dabbasso dal portier.	We'll wait for you downstairs.
MARCELLO	**MARCELLO**
Se tardi udrai che coro.	You'll hear us if you dawdle.
RODOLFO	**RODOLFO**
Cinque minuti.	Five minutes.
SCHAUNARD	**SCHAUNARD**
Taglia corta la coda al tuo Castoro.	Cut that *Beaver's* tail short.

Rodolfo takes a light and opens the door. The others start down the stairs.

MARCELLO (*di fuori*)	**MARCELLO** (*outside*)
Occhio alla scala	Watch the stairs.
Tieni alla ringhiera	Hold on to the railing.

RODOLFO *(alzando il lume)*	**RODOLFO** *(raising the light)*
Adagio.	Careful.
COLLINE	**COLLINE**
È buio pesto.	It's pitch dark.
SCHAUNARD	**SCHAUNARD**
Maledetto portier!	That damn janitor!
COLLINE	**COLLINE**
Accidenti!	Hell!
RODOLFO	**RODOLFO**
Colline, sei morto?	Colline, are you killed?
COLLINE *(dal basso)*	**COLLINE** *(from below)*
Non ancor.	Not yet.
MARCELLO	**MARCELLO**
Vien presto.	Come soon.

Rodolfo closes the door, sets his light on the table, and tries to write. But he tears up the paper and throws the pen down.

RODOLFO	**RODOLFO**
Non sono in vena.	I'm not in the mood.

There's a timid knock at the door.

DISC NO. 1/TRACK 6

Mimì is heard before she is seen, a device Puccini uses in other operas as well for his heroines. It is an instruction to the audience, inviting us to "see" her primarily through our ears. The rest of this first section of their meetings is all short, broken phrases. The unspoken text is what counts in this initial encounter.

Chi è là?

MIMÌ *(di fuori)*
Scusi.

RODOLFO
Una donna!

MIMÌ
Di grazia, mi si è spento
il lume.

RODOLFO *(aprendo)*
Ecco.

MIMÌ *(sull'uscio, con un lume spento in
mano ed una chiave)*
Vorrebbe…?

RODOLFO
S'accomodi un momento.

MIMÌ
Non occorre.

RODOLFO
La prego, entri.

Mimì enters, and has a fit of coughing.

Si sente male?

MIMÌ
No…nulla.

Who's there?

MIMÌ *(outside)*
Excuse me.

RODOLFO
A woman!

MIMÌ
I'm sorry…my light
has gone out.

RODOLFO *(opening the door)*
Here.

MIMÌ *(in the doorway, holding a candlestick
and key)*
Would you…?

RODOLFO
Come in for a moment.

MIMÌ
There's no need.

RODOLFO
Please…come in.

You're not well?

MIMÌ
No…it's nothing.

RODOLFO

Impallidisce!

MIMÌ

È il respir…quelle scale…

She faints, and Rodolfo is just in time to support her and help her to a chair. The key and the candlestick fall from her hands.

RODOLFO

Ed ora come faccio?

He gets some water and sprinkles her face.

Così.
Che viso d'ammalata!

Mimì comes to.

Si sente meglio?

MIMÌ

Sì.

RODOLFO

Qui c'è tanto freddo
Segga vicino al fuoco.

He helps her to a chair by the stove.

Aspetti…un po'di vino.

MIMÌ

Grazie.

RODOLFO

You're pale!

MIMÌ

I'm out of breath…the stairs…

RODOLFO

Now what shall I do?

So.
How ill she looks!

Are you better now?

MIMÌ

Yes.

RODOLFO

It's so cold here. Come and sit
by the fire.

Wait…some wine.

MIMÌ

Thank you.

RODOLFO
A lei.

MIMÌ
Poco, poco.

RODOLFO
Così.

MIMÌ
Grazie.

RODOLFO
(Che bella bambina!)

MIMÌ *(alzandosi)*
Ora permetta
che accenda il lume.
Tutto è passato.

RODOLFO
Tanta fretta!

MIMÌ
Sì.

Rodolfo lights her candle for her.

Grazie. Buona sera.

RODOLFO
Buona sera.

Mimì goes out, then reappears at the door.

RODOLFO
Here.

MIMÌ
Just a little.

RODOLFO
There.

MIMÌ
Thank you.

RODOLFO
(What a lovely creature!)

MIMÌ *(rising)*
Now, please,
relight my candle.
I'm better now.

RODOLFO
Such a hurry!

MIMÌ
Yes.

Thank you. Good evening.

RODOLFO
Good evening.

Mimì returs to the music of Rodolfo's theme. Perhaps she is "in" on a type of game she is playing with Rodolfo, or perhaps we are to understand that he has found his inspiration at last.

MIMÌ
Oh! sventata, sventata!
la chiave della stanza
dove l'ho lasciata?

MIMÌ
Oh! foolish me!
Where have I left the key to my room?

RODOLFO
Non stia sull'uscio
il lume vacillá al vento.

RODOLFO
Don't stand in the door
the wind makes your light flicker.

Her candle goes out.

MIMÌ
Oh Dio! Torni ad accenderlo.

MIMÌ
Heavens! Will you relight it?

Rodolfo hastens to her with his light, but when he reaches the door, his candle goes out, too. The room is dark.

RODOLFO
Oh Dio! Anche il mio s'è spento.

RODOLFO
There…Now mine's out, too.

MIMÌ
Ah! E la chiave ove sarà?

MIMÌ
Ah! And where can my key be?

RODOLFO
Buio pesto!

RODOLFO
Pitch dark!

MIMÌ
Disgraziata!

MIMÌ
Unlucky me!

RODOLFO
Ove sarà?

RODOLFO
Where can it be?

MIMÌ

Importuna è la vicina…

RODOLFO

Ma le pare!

MIMÌ

Importuna è la vicina…

RODOLFO

Cosa dice? ma le pare!

MIMÌ

Cerchi.

RODOLFO

Cerco.

They hunt, touching the floor with their hands.

MIMÌ

Ove sarà?

RODOLFO

Ah!

He finds the key and pockets it.

MIMÌ

L'ha trovata?

RODOLFO

No.

MIMÌ

Mi parve…

MIMÌ

You've a bothersome neighbor…

RODOLFO

Not at all.

MIMÌ

You've a bothersome neighbor…

RODOLFO

What do you mean? Not at all!

MIMÌ

Search.

RODOLFO

I'm searching.

MIMÌ

Where can it be?

RODOLFO

Ah!

MIMÌ

Did you find it?

RODOLFO

No.

MIMÌ

I thought…

RODOLFO	**RODOLFO**
In verità!	Truthfully!
MIMÌ	**MIMÌ**
Cerca?	Are you hunting?
RODOLFO	**RODOLFO**
Cerco.	I'm hunting for it.

Guided by her voice, Rodolfo pretends to search as he draws closer to her. Then his hand meets hers, and he holds it.

MIMÌ *(sopresa)*	**MIMÌ** *(surprised)*
Ah!	Ah!

They rise. Rodolfo continues to hold Mimì's hand.

Rodolfo (Richard Tucker) and Mimì (Nadine Conner) discover they have fallen in love at first sight.

Che gelida manina The first aria is sung when Rodolfo and Mimì are alone and he conspires to touch her hand. A shiver of delight that sets off a chain of extraordinary musical
events, it is well worth the wait. Rodolfo's aria is possibly the most charming seduction
in all of opera. After his transparent ploy to persuade Mimì to stay, he tells her in an
expansive and swaggering turn of melody (01:24) that he is a poet richer than a million-
aire because of his passion. But he also admits, in a more ardent melody (02:24), that he
is already madly in love with her. He describes this rush of feeling as being like the dawn
and giving him the sweetest hope. At this point, the tenor must rise to a high C. Many
tenors routinely transpose the aria down a half tone, and Puccini himself reluctantly
endorsed the idea when no less than Caruso (always wary of his high C) begged him to.

RODOLFO

Che gelida manina!

Se la lasci riscaldar.

Cercar che giova?

Al buio non si trova.

Ma per fortuna

è una notte di luna,

e qui la luna l'abbiamo vicina.

Aspetti, signorina,

le dirò con due parole chi son,

chi son, e che faccio, come vivo.

Vuole?

Mimì is silent.

Chi son? Chi son? Son un poeta.

Che cosa faccio? Scrivo.

E come vivo? Vivo.

In povertà mia lieta

scialo da gran signore

rime ed inni d'amore.

Per sogni e per chimere

e per castelli in aria

RODOLFO

How cold your little hand is!

Let me warm it for you.

What's the use of searching?

We'll never find it in the dark.

But luckily

there's a moon,

and she's our neighbor here.

Just wait, my dear young lady,

and meanwhile I'll tell you

in a word who and what I am.

Shall I?

Who am I? I'm a poet.

My business? Writing.

How do I live? I live.

In my happy poverty

I squander like a prince

my poems and songs of love.

In hopes and dreams

and castles-in-air,

l'anima ho milionaria.	I'm a millionaire in spirit.
Talor dal mio forziere	But sometimes my strong-box
ruban tutti i gioielli	is robbed of all its jewels
due ladri gli occhi belli.	by two thieves; a pair of pretty eyes.
V'entrar con voi pur ora	They came in now with you
ed i miei sogni usati,	and all my lovely dreams,
ed i bei sogni miei	my dreams of the past,
tosto si dileguar!	were soon stolen away.
Ma il furto non m'accora	But the theft doesn't upset me,
poichè, poichè v'ha preso stanza	since the empty place was filled
la speranza.	with hope.
Or che mi conoscete	Now that you know me,
parlate voi. Deh parlate.	it's your turn to speak.
Chi siete? Vi piaccia dir?	Who are you? Will you tell me?

DISC NO. 1/TRACK 9

Sì. Mi chiamono Mimì Mimì's response is as multifaceted as Rodolfo's. She begins halt-
ingly, describing her humble existence in a melody of touching vulnerability. She is so
modest that she asks Rodolfo if he is listening; he is, of course, hanging on her every
word (01:42). When she resumes, she has a bit more confidence, detailing her day-to-day

Linda Ronstadt as Mimì and Gary Morris as
Rodolfo in a New York Shakespeare Festival
production of *La Bohème*.

life in the winter with a sprightly tune that changes only when she savors the image of spring. Suddenly, unable to contain her passion, Mimì extols the beauties of spring and its promise of love in an expansive, soaring melody (02:42) that reveals a robust soul quite different from the tubercular girl who knocked on the door and now, almost apologetically, emerges from her sudden reverie (04:40), apologizing for the intrusion.

MIMÌ
Sì.
Mi chiamano Mimì,
ma il mio nome è Lucia.
La storia mia è breve.
A tela o a seta
ricamo in casa e fuori.
Son tranquilla e lieta,
ed è mio svago
far gigli e rose.
Mi piaccion quelle cose
che han sì dolce malia,
che parlano d'amor, di primavere,
che parlano di sogni e di chimere,
quelle cose che han nome poesia…
Lei m'intende?

RODOLFO
Sì.

MIMÌ
Mi chiamano Mimì.
Il perchè non so.
Sola, mi fo il pranzo
da me stessa.
Non vado sempre a messa,
ma prego assai il Signor.
Vivo sola, soletta,
là in una bianca cameretta;

MIMÌ
Yes.
They call me Mimì,
but my real name's Lucia.
My story is brief.
I embroider silk and satin
at home or outside.
I'm tranquil and happy
and my pastime
is making lilies and roses.
I love all things
that have gentle magic,
that talk of love, of spring,
that talk of dreams and fancies—
the things called poetry…
do you understand me?

RODOLFO
Yes.

MIMÌ
They call me Mimì,
I don't know why.
I live by myself
and I eat alone.
I don't often go to church,
but I like to pray.
I stay all alone
in my tiny white room,

guardo sui tetti e in cielo.	I look at the roofs and the sky.
Ma quando vien lo sgelo	But when spring comes
il primo sole è mio,	the sun's first rays are mine.
il primo bacio dell'aprile è mio!	April's first kiss is mine, is mine!
Il primo sole è mio.	The sun's first rays are mine!
Germoglia in un vaso una rosa,	A rose blossoms in my vase,
foglia a foglia l'aspiro.	I breathe its perfume, petal by petal.
Così gentil è il profumo d'un fior.	So sweet is the flower's perfume.
Ma i fior ch'io faccio, ahimè,	But the flowers I make, alas,
i fior ch'io faccio,	the flowers I make, alas,
ahimè non hanno odore.	alas, have no scent.
Altro di me non le saprei narrare.	What else can I say?
Sono la sua vicina	I'm your neighbor, disturbing you
che la vien fuori d'ora a importunate.	at this impossible hour.

DISC NO. 1/TRACK 10

Puccini cleverly has the voices of the friends appear offstage, as if on the street below, creating an ensemble that informs the rest of the scene with additional melody, despite the distinctly intimate nature of the moment.

SCHAUNARD *(dal cortile)*	**SCHAUNARD** *(from below)*
Ehi! Rodolfo!	Hey! Rodolfo!
COLLINE	**COLLINE**
Rodolfo!	Rodolfo!
MARCELLO	**MARCELLO**
Olà! Non senti?	Hey! Can't you hear?
Lumaca!	You slow-coach!
COLLINE	**COLLINE**
Poetucolo!	You scribbler!

SCHAUNARD

Accidenti al pigro!

Rodolfo, impatient, goes to the window to answer. When the window is opened, the moonlight comes in, lighting up the room.

RODOLFO

Scrivo ancora tre righi a volo.

MIMÌ

Chi sono?

RODOLFO

Amici.

SCHAUNARD

Sentirai le tue.

MARCELLO

Che te ne fai lì solo?

RODOLFO

Non son solo. Siamo in due.
Andate da Momus, tenete il posto.
Ci saremo tosto.

**MARCELLO, SCHAUNARD
E COLLINE**

Momus, Momus, Momus,
zitti e discreti andiamocene via.
Momus, Momus.
Trovò la poesia.

SCHAUNARD

To hell with that lazy one!

RODOLFO

I've a few more words to write.

MIMÌ

Who are they?

RODOLFO

Friends.

SCHAUNARD

You'll hear about this.

MARCELLO

What are you doing there alone?

RODOLFO

I'm not alone. There's two of us.
Go to Momus and get a table.
We'll be there soon.

**MARCELLO, SCHAUNARD
AND COLLINE**

Momus, Momus, Momus.
Quietly, discreetly, we're off.
Momus, Momus.
He's found his poem at last.

Turning, Rodolfo sees Mimì wrapped in a halo of moonlight. He contemplates her, in ecstasy.

Café Momus in Rolf Gerard's stageset for a 1952-53 production at the Metropolitan Opera.

DISC NO. 1/TRACK 11

O soave fanciulla This rapturous duet captures the infatuation Rodolfo feels for Mimì—just seeing her standing in a shaft of moonlight mesmerizes him. Her feelings are the same. The duet climaxes quickly (00:39), but it is the afterglow that is so charming, as they banter about what might happen when they return from the Café Momus (02:36). Puccini sends them out into the night (03:19), deliriously happy, singing of love as their voices fade into the cold Christmas Eve air.

RODOLFO

O soave fanciulia, o dolce viso,
di mite circonfuso alba lunar,
in te ravviso il sogno
ch'io vorrei sempre sognar!

RODOLFO

Oh! lovely girl! Oh, sweet face
bathed in the soft moonlight.
I see in you the dream
I'd dream forever!

MIMÌ
(Ah, tu sol comandi, amor!…)

RODOLFO
Fremon già nell'anima
le dolcezze estreme.

MIMÌ
(Tu sol comandi, amore!)

RODOLFO
Fremon nell'anima
dolcezze estreme, ecc.
Nel bacio freme amor!

MIMÌ
(Oh! come dolci scendono
le sue lusinghe al core…
Tu sol comandi, amor!)

Rodolfo kisses her.

No, per pietà!

RODOLFO
Sei mia!

MIMÌ
V'aspettan gli amici…

RODOLFO
Già mi mandi via?

MIMÌ
Vorrei dir…ma non oso.

MIMÌ
(Ah! Love, you rule alone!…)

RODOLFO
Already I taste in spirit
the heights of tenderness!

MIMÌ
(You rule alone, o Love!)

RODOLFO
Already I taste in spirit
the heights of tenderness!
Love trembles in our kiss!

MIMÌ
(How sweet his praises
enter my heart…
Love, you alone rule!)

No, please!

RODOLFO
You're mine!

MIMÌ
Your friends are waiting.

RODOLFO
You send me away already?

MIMÌ
I daren't say what I'd like…

RODOLFO

Di'.

MIMÌ

Se venissi con voi?

RODOLFO

Che? Mimì!

Sarebbe cosi dolce restar qui.

C'è freddo fuori.

MIMÌ

Vi starò vicina!

RODOLFO

E al ritorno?

MIMÌ

Curioso!

RODOLFO

Dammi il braccio, o mia piccina…

MIMÌ

Obbedisco, signor!

RODOLFO

Che m'ami…di'…

MIMÌ

Io t'amo.

RODOLFO E MIMÌ *(mentre escono)*

Amor! Amor! Amor!

RODOLFO

Tell me.

MIMÌ

If I came with you?

RODOLFO

What? Mimì!

It would be so fine to stay here.

Outside it's cold.

MIMÌ

I'd be near you!

RODOLFO

And when we come back?

MIMÌ

Who knows?

RODOLFO

Give me your arm, my dear…

MIMÌ

Your servant, sir…

RODOLFO

Tell me you love me!

MIMÌ

I love you.

RODOLFO AND MIMÌ *(as they go out)*

Beloved! My love! My love!

Act 2

IN THE LATIN QUARTER A square with shops of all kinds. On one side is the Café Momus. Mimì and Rodolfo move about with the crowd. Colline is nearby at a rag-woman's stand. Schaunard is buying a pipe and a trumpet. Marcello is pushed here and there by the throng. It is evening. Christmas Eve.

DISC NO. 1/TRACK 12

Even the librettists tried to persuade Puccini that it would be illogical for the bohemians to spend the evening outdoors after they complained of the cold, but Puccini stood fast. The result was this magnificent view of the crowd dynamics, so detailed and complex that the initial audiences were completely baffled by it. Paris itself becomes an important character in the opera, yet we never lose the melodic thread of the principals in this most intimate of stories.

I VENDITORI	HAWKERS
Aranci, datteri!	Oranges, dates!
Caldi i marroni.	Hot roasted chestnuts!
Ninnoli, croci.	Crosses, knick-knacks!
Torroni e caramelle.	Cookies and candies!
Fiori alle belle.	Flowers for the ladies!
Oh! la crostata.	Pies for sale!
Panna montata.	With whipped cream!
Fringuelli, passeri.	Finches and larks!
Datteri! Trote!	Dates! Fresh fish!
Latte di cocco! Giubbe!	Coconut milk! Skirts!
Carote!	Carrots!

LA FOLLA	THE CROWD
Quanta folla! Che chiasso!	What a throng! Such noise!
Stringiti a me, corriamo.	Hold tight! Let's run!
Lisa! Emma!	Lisa! Emma!
Date il passo.	Make way there!
Emma, quando ti chiamo!	Emma, I'm calling you!
Ancora un altro giro…	Once more around…
Pigliam via Mazzarino.	We'll take Rue Mazarin,
Qui mi manca il respiro!…	I can't breathe here…
Vedi? Il Caffè è vicino.	See? The café's right here.
Oh! stupendi gioielli!	What wonderful jewels!
Son gli occhi assai più belli!	Your eyes are more wonderful!
Pericolosi esempi	This crowd tonight
la folla oggi ci dà!	sets a dangerous example!
Era meglio ai miei tempi!	Things were better in my day!
Viva la libertà!	Long live freedom!

At the Café

Andiam. Qua, camerier!	Let's go. Here, waiter!
Presto. Corri.	Hurry. On the run.
Vien qua. A me.	Come here. My turn.
Birra! Un bicchier!	Beer! A glass!
Vaniglia. Ratafià.	Vanilla. Liqueur!
Dunque? Presto!	Well? Hurry.
Da ber! Un caffè…	Drinks! Coffee…
Presto. Olà…	Quickly. Hey, there…

SCHAUNARD   **SCHAUNARD**

blowing on the trumpet, producing odd sounds

Falso questio Re!	This D is out of tune.
Pipa e corno quant'è?	How much for the horn and pipe?

COLLINE

at the rag-woman's, who is sewing up an enormous overcoat he has just bought

È un poco usato…

RODOLFO
Andiam.

MIMÌ
Andiam per la cuffietta?

COLLINE
Ma è serio e a buon mercato…

RODOLFO
Tienti al mio braccio stretta…

MIMÌ
A te mi stringo.

MIMÌ, RODOLFO
Andiam!

They go into the milliner's.

MARCELLO
Io pur mi sento in vena di grida:
Chi vuol, donnine allegre, un po' d'amor?

VENDITORI
Datteri! Trote! Prugne di Tours!

MARCELLO
Facciamo insieme a vendere e comprar:
Io do ad un soldo il vergine mio cuor.

COLLINE

It's a little worn…

RODOLFO
Let's go.

MIMÌ
Are we going to buy the bonnet?

COLLINE
…But it's cheap and dignified.

RODOLFO
Hold tight to my arm.

MIMÌ
I'll hold you tight.

MIMÌ, RODOLFO
Let's go!

MARCELLO
I, too, feel like shouting:
which of you happy girls wants love?

HAWKERS
Dates! Trout! Plums from Tours!

MARCELLO
Let us make a bargain together—
for a penny I'll sell my virgin heart.

SCHAUNARD
Fra spintoni e pestate accorrendo,
affretta la folla e si diletta
nel provar voglie matte—
insoddisfatte.

VENDITORI
Ninnoli, spillette! *ecc.*

COLLINE *(mostrando un libro)*
Copia rara, anzi unica
la grammatica Runica.

SCHAUNARD
(Uomo onesto!)

MARCELLO
A cena!

SCHAUNARD E COLLINE
Rodolfo?

MARCELLO
Entrò da una modista.

Rodolfo and Mimì come out of the shop.

RODOLFO
Vieni, gli amici aspettano.

MIMÌ
Mi sta ben questa cuffietta rosa?

VENDITORI
Panna montata! Latte di cocco!
Oh! la crostata! Panna montata!

SCHAUNARD
Pushing and shoving and running, the
crowd hastens to its joys,
feeling insane desires—
unappeased.

HAWKERS
Trinkets! Brooches! *etc.*

COLLINE *(showing a book)*
A rare find, truly unique
a Runic grammar.

SCHAUNARD
(What an honest fellow!)

MARCELLO
Let's eat!

SCHAUNARD AND COLLINE
And Rodolfo?

MARCELLO
He went into the milliner's.

RODOLFO
Come, my friends are waiting.

MIMÌ
Is my pink bonnet becoming?

HAWKERS
Whipped cream! Coconut milk!
Pies! Whipped cream!

AL CAFFÈ	**CAFÈ CUSTOMERS**
Camerier! Un bicchier!	Waiter! A glass!
Presto Olà…Ratafia.	Quick. Hey there…Liqueur.
RODOLFO	**RODOLFO**
Sei bruna	You're dark,
e quel color ti dona.	that colour suits you.
MIMÌ (*guardando verso la bottega*)	**MIMÌ** (*looking back at the shop*)
Bel vezzo di corallo.	That lovely coral necklace.
RODOLFO	**RODOLFO**
Ho uno zio milionario.	I've a millionaire uncle.
Se fa senno il buon Dio	If God acts wisely
voglio comprarti un vezzo	I'll buy you a necklace
assai più bel!…	much more beautiful…
MONELLI, SARTINE, STUDENTI	**URCHINS, MIDINETTES, STUDENTS**
Ah! ah! ah! ah! *ecc.*	Ah! ah! ah! *etc.*
BORGHESI	**TOWNSPEOPLE**
Facciam coda alla gente!	Let's follow these people!
Ragazze, state attente!	Girls, watch out!
Che chiasso! quanta folla!	Such noise! What a throng!
Pigliam via Mazzarino!	We'll take the Rue Mazarin!
Io soffoco, partiamo!	I'm stifling, let's go!
Vedi il caffè è vicin!	See, the café's right here!
Andiam là, da Momus!	Let's go there, to Momus!
Ah!…	Ah!…
VENDITORI	**HAWKERS**
Oh! la crostata! Panna montata!	Pies for sale! Whipped cream!
Fiori alle belle!	Flowers for the ladies!
Ninnoli, datteri, caldi i marron!	Knick-knacks, dates, hot roasted chestnuts!
Fringuelli, passeri,	Finches, larks!
panna, torron!	Cream cakes!

The friends interact with each other and with the crowd in ever more intriguing ways in this section. Note the overlap of the bohemians ordering expensive dishes at the café as the children whine for more toys (02:19). It's a sly comment that could only be made in opera, and only in the best operas.

RODOLFO
Chi guardi?

RODOLFO
Whom are you looking at?

COLLINE
Odio il profano volgo al par d'Orazio.

COLLINE
I hate the vulgar herd as Horace did.

MIMÌ
Sei geloso?

MIMÌ
Are you jealous?

RODOLFO
All'uom felice sta il sospetto
accanto.

RODOLFO
The man who's happy must be
suspicious too.

SCHAUNARD
Ed io quando mi sazio
vo' abbondanza di spazio.

SCHAUNARD
And when I'm stuffing myself
I want plenty of room about me.

MIMÌ
Sei felice?

MIMÌ
Are you happy then?

MARCELLO *(al cameriere)*
Vogliamo una cena prelibata.

MARCELLO *(to the waiter)*
We want a prize dinner.

RODOLFO
Ah, si. Tanto.

RODOLFO
Oh yes. Very.

MARCELLO
Lesto.

MARCELLO
Quickly.

SCHAUNARD	**SCHAUNARD**
Per molti.	And bring plenty.
RODOLFO	**RODOLFO**
E tu?	And you?
MIMÌ	**MIMÌ**
Si, tanto.	Very.

Marcello, Schaunard, and Colline sit at a table in front of the café.

STUDENTI	**STUDENTS**
Là, da Momus!	There, to Momus!
SARTINE	**MIDINETTES**
Andiam! Andiam!	Let's go! Let's go!
MARCELLO, COLLINE, SCHAUNARD	**MARCELLO, COLLINE, SCHAUNARD**
Lesto.	Quickly!
VOCE DI PARPIGNOL *(in lontananza)*	**VOICE OF PARPIGNOL** *(in the distance)*
Ecco i giocattoli di Parpignol!	Here are the toys of Parpignol!
RODOLFO	**RODOLFO**
Due posti!	Two places.
COLLINE	**COLLINE**
Finalmente, eccoci qui!	Here they are at last!
RODOLFO	**RODOLFO**
Questa è Mimì, gaia fioraia.	This is Mimì, happy flower-girl.
Il suo venir completa	Her presence alone
la bella compagnia.	makes our company complete.
Perché…perché son io il poeta;	For…for I am a poet;

essa la poesia.
Dal mio cervel sbocciano i canti,
dalle sue dita sbocciano i fior—
dall'anime esultanti
sboccia l'amor.

MARCELLO
Dio che concetti rari!

COLLINE
Digna est intrari.

SCHAUNARD
Ingrediat si necessit.

COLLINE
Io non do che un accessit.

VOCE DI PARPIGNOL *(più vicino)*
Ecco i giocattoli di Parpignol!

COLLINE
Salame…

MARCELLO
What rare imagery!

COLLINE
Digna es intrari.

SCHAUNARD
Ingrediat si necessit.

COLLINE
I grant only one accessit.

VOICE OF PARPIGNOL *(closer)*
Here are the toys of Parpignol!

COLLINE
Salami…

Parpignol arrives in the square, pushing a barrow covered with frills and flowers.

RAGAZZI E BAMBINE
Parpignol! Parpignol! Parpignol!…
Ecco Parpignol! Parpignol!
Col carretto tutto fior!
Ecco Parpignol!
Voglio la tromba, il cavallin!
Il tambur, tamburel…
Voglio il cannon, voglio il frustin,
dei soldati i drappel.

CHILDREN
Parpignol! Parpignol! Parpignol!
Here is Parpignol!
With his cart all decked with flowers!
Here is Parpignol!
I want the horn, the toy horse!
The drum! The tambourine!
I want the cannon; I want the whip,
I want the troop of soldiers.

SCHAUNARD
Cervo arrosto.

MARCELLO
Un tacchino.

SCHAUNARD
Vin del Reno!

COLLINE
Vin da tavola!

SCHAUNARD
Aragosta senza crosta!

MAMME
Ah! che razza di furfanti indemoniati,
che ci venite a fare in questo loco?
A casa, a letto! Via, brutti sguaiati,
gli scappellotti vi parranno poco!…
A casa! A letto,
razza di furfanti, a letto!

UN RAGAZZO
Vo' la tromba, il cavallin…

RODOLFO
E tu Mimì, che vuoi?

MIMÌ
La crema.

SCHAUNARD
E gran sfarzo.
C'è una dama.

SCHAUNARD
Roast venison.

MARCELLO
A turkey.

SCHAUNARD
Rhine wine!

COLLINE
Table wine!

SCHAUNARD
Shelled lobster!

MOTHERS
What a bunch of naughty rascals!
What are you doing here now?
Go home to bed, you noisy things.
Slaps will be the least you'll get…
Go home to bed,
you bunch of rascals, to bed!

A BOY
I want the horn, the toy horse.…

RODOLFO
What will you have, Mimì?

MIMÌ
Some custard.

SCHAUNARD
The best.
A lady's with us.

RAGAZZI E BAMBINE	CHILDREN
Viva Parpignol!	Bravo Parpignol!
Il tambur, tamburel…	The drums! The tambourine!
Dei soldati il drappel.	A troop of soldiers!

DISC NO. 1/TRACK 14

The crowd fades into the backgroud as the friends concentrate on each other at the dinner table. Their intimacy is shortly invaded by the shrieking laughter of Musetta (02:09), bringing the crowd back into the score with her.

They run off, following Parpignol.

MARCELLO	MARCELLO
Signorina Mimì, che dono raro	Tell me, Mimì, what rare gift
le ha fatto il suo Rodolfo?	has Rodolfo given you?

MIMÌ	MIMÌ
Una cuffietta a pizzi tutta rosa	An embroidered pink bonnet, all
ricamata. Coi miei capelli bruni	with lace. It goes well
ben si fonde.	with my dark hair.
Da tanto tempo tal cuffietta	I've longed for such a bonnet
è cosa desiata…ed egli ha letto	for months.…and he read
quel che il core asconde…	what was hidden in my heart…
Ora colui che legge dentro a un core	Anyone who can read the heart's secret
sa l'amore…ed è lettore.	knows love…he's such a reader.

SCHAUNARD	SCHAUNARD
Esperto professore…	He's a professor in the subject.

COLLINE	COLLINE
Che ha già diplomi e non son armi	With diplomas, and his verses
primele sue rime…	are not a beginner's…

SCHAUNARD

Tanto che sembra ver
ciò che egli esprime!

MARCELLO

O bella età d'inganni e d'utopie!
Si crede, spera, e tutto bello appare.

RODOLFO

La più divina delle poesie
è quella, amico, che c'insegna ad amare

MIMÌ

Amare è dolce ancora più del miele!

MARCELLO

Secondo il palato è miele o fiele!

MIMÌ

O Dio, l'ho offeso!

RODOLFO

È in lutto, o mia Mimì.

SCHAUNARD E COLLINE

Allegri! e un toast.

MARCELLO

Qua del liquor!

TUTTI

E via i pensier,
alti i bicchier. Beviam.

SCHAUNARD

That's why what he says
seems to be true!

MARCELLO

Oh, sweet age of false utopias!
You hope and believe, and all seems
beautiful.

RODOLFO

The poem most divine, my friend,
is what teaches us to love!

MIMÌ

Love is sweet, sweeter than honey.

MARCELLO

That depends it's honey or gali!

MIMÌ

Heavens! I've offended him!

RODOLFO

He's mourning, Mimì.

SCHAUNARD AND COLLINE

Cheer up! A toast!

MARCELLO

Something to drink!

ALL

Away with brooding,
raise you glass. We'll drink.

MARCELLO (*vedendo Musetta che entra, ridendo*)
Ch'io beva del tossico!

MARCELLO (*seeing Musetta enter, laughing*)
I'll drink some poison!

SCHAUNARD, COLLINE E RODOLFO
Oh! Musetta!

SCHAUNARD, COLLINE E RODOLFO
Oh! Musetta!

MARCELLO
Essa!

MARCELLO
Her!

LE BOTTEGAIE
To'! Lei! Sì! To'! Lei!
Musetta!
Siamo in auge! Che toeletta!

THE SHOPWOMEN
What! Her! Yes! Well! Her!
Musetta!
She's made it. What a dress!

Musetta stops, accompanied by the old and pompous Alcindoro. She sits at another table in front of the café.

ALCINDORO
Come un facchino
correr di qua…di là…
No, no, non ci sta…

ALCINDORO
Running like a porter
back and forth…
No, it's not proper.

MUSETTA (*chiamando Alcindoro come si chiama un cane*)
Vien, Lulù!

MUSETTA (*calling Alcindoro as if he were a dog*)
Here, Lulu!

ALCINDORO
Non ne posso più.

ALCINDORO
I can't take any more.

MUSETTA
Vien, Lulù.

MUSETTA
Come, Lulu.

SCHAUNARD
Quel brutto coso mi par che sudi!

SCHAUNARD
That ugly old fool all in a lather!

ALCINDORO
Come? qui fuori? qui?

MUSETTA
Siedi. Lulù.

ALCINDORO
Tali nomignoli,
prego, serbateli
al tu per tu.

MUSETTA
Non farmi il Barbablù!

COLLINE
È il vizio contegnoso…

MARCELLO
Colla casta Susanna.

MIMÌ
Essa è pur ben vestita.

RODOLFO
Gli angeli vanno nudi.

MIMÌ
La conosci? Chi è?

ALCINDORO
What? Outside? Here?

MUSETTA
Sit, Lulu.

ALCINDORO
Please, save these
little nicknames of yours
for when we're alone.

MUSETTA
Don't act like Bluebeard!

COLLINE
He's evil behind that front!

MARCELLO
With the chaste Susanna.

MIMÌ
But she's beautifully dressed.

RODOLFO
Angels go naked.

MIMÌ
You know her? Who is she?

DISC NO. 1/TRACK 15
Marcello decries the crimes of Musetta while she decides to win him back in what must
be opera's most curious instance of a dyfunctional love duet. The comments of the
others overlap and evanesce in a miracle of organic construction.

MARCELLO

Domandatelo a me.
Il suo nome è Musetta…
Cognome — Tentazione!
Per sua vocazione
fa la rosa dei venti;
gira e muta soventi
d'amanti e d'amore…
E come la civetta
è uccello sanguinario;
il suo cibo ordinario
è il cuore…mangia il cuore!
Per questo io non ne ho più.

MUSETTA

(Marcello è là…mi vide…
E non mi guarda il vile!
Quel Schaunard che ride!
Mi fan tutti una bile!
Se potessi picchiar,
se potessi graffiar!
Ma non ho sotto man
che questo pellican.
Aspetta!)
Ehi! Camerier!

MARCELLO (*nascondendo la commozione*)
Passatemi il ragù.

MUSETTA

Ehi! Camerier! questo piatto
ha una puzza di rifritto!

throwing the plate on the ground

MARCELLO

Ask me that question.
Her first name's Musetta.
Her last name's Temptation.
Her occupation is being
a leaf in the wind…
Always turning, changing
her lovers and her loves…
Like the screech-owl
she's a bird of prey.
Her favourite food
is the heart…she devours them!
And so I have no heart.

MUSETTA

(Marcello's there…he saw me…
But the coward won't look at me.
And that Schaunard's laughing!
They all make me livid!
If I could just hit them!
Scratch their eyes out!
But I've got this old
pelican on my hands.
Just wait!)
Waiter!

MARCELLO (*hiding his emotion*)
Pass me the stew.

MUSETTA

Hey! Waiter! This plate
smells dirty to me!

ALCINDORO
No, Musetta, zitto, zitto!

MUSETTA
(Non si volta.)

ALCINDORO
Zitto. Zitto. Modi. Garbo.

MUSETTA
(Ah! Non si volta.)

ALCINDORO
A chi parli?

COLLINE
Questo pollo è un poema!

MUSETTA
(Ora lo batto, lo batto!)

ALCINDORO
Con chi parli?

MUSETTA
Al cameriere. Non seccar!

SCHAUNARD
Il vino è prelibato!

MUSETTA
Voglio fare il mio piacere…

ALCINDORO
Parla pian!

ALCINDORO
No, Musetta! Quiet, now!

MUSETTA
(He won't look.)

ALCINDORO
Quiet, now. Manners! Please!

MUSETTA
(He won't look.)

ALCINDORO
To whom are you speaking?

COLLINE
This chicken is a poem!

MUSETTA
(Now I'll hit him, I'll hit him!)

ALCINDORO
Who are you talking to?

MUSETTA
To the waiter. Don't be a bore!

SCHAUNARD
The wine is excellent.

MUSETTA
I want my own way!

ALCINDORO
Lower your voice!

MUSETTA
Vo' far quel che mi pare!

ALCINDORO
Parla pian, parla pian!

MUSETTA
Non secc-a-a-ar!

SARTINE E STUDENTI
Guarda, guarda, chi si vede,
proprio lei, Musetta!
Con quel vecchio che balbetta,
proprio lei, Musetta!
Ah! ah! ah! ah!

MUSETTA
(Che sia geloso di questa mummia?)

ALCINDORO
La convenienza…il grado…la virtù!

MUSETTA
(Vediamo se mi resta
tanto poter su lui
da farlo cedere.)

SCHAUNARD
La commedia è stupenda!

MUSETTA *(guardando Marcello)*
Tu non mi guardi.

ALCINDORO
Vedi bene che ordino?

MUSETTA
I'll do as I please!

ALCINDORO
Lower your voice!

MUSETTA
Don't be a bore!

MIDINETTES AND STUDENTS
Look, look who it is,
Musetta herself!
With that stuttering old man,
it's Musetta herself!
Ha ha ha ha ha!

MUSETTA
(But could he be jealous of this mummy?)

ALCINDORO
Decorum…my rank…my reputation!

MUSETTA
(Let's see if I still
have enough power over him
to make him give in.)

SCHAUNARD
The play is stupendous!

MUSETTA *(looking at Marcello)*
You aren't looking at me.

ALCINDORO
Can't you see I'm ordering?

SCHAUNARD
La commedia è stupenda!

COLLINE
Stupenda!

RODOLFO (a Mimì)
Sappi per tuo governo
che non darei perdono in sempiterno.

SCHAUNARD
Essa all'un parla perché l'altro intenda.

MIMÌ (a Rodolfo)
Io t'amo tanto, e sono
tutta tua…
Che mi parli di perdono?

COLLINE (a Schaunard)
E l'altro invan crudel
finge di non capir,
ma sugge miel.

MUSETTA
Ma il tuo cuore martella.

ALCINDORO
Parla piano.

MUSETTA
Ma il tuo cuore martella.

ALCINDORO
Piano, piano!

SCHAUNARD
The play is stupendous!

COLLINE
Stupendous!

RODOLFO (to Mimì)
Let me tell you now
I'd never be forgiving.

SCHAUNARD
She speaks to one for the other to hear.

MIMÌ (to Rodolfo)
I love you so, and I'm
all yours…
Why speak of forgiveness?

COLLINE (to Schaunard)
And the other, cruel, in vain
pretends he is deaf,
but enjoys it all.

MUSETTA
But your heart's like a hammer.

ALCINDORO
Lower your voice.

MUSETTA
But your heart's like a hammer.

ALCINDORO
Lower your voice.

Quando men' vo The most famous melody from the score occurs in Act II. It is a teasing waltz melody sung by the self-absorbed Musetta, who marvels at the effect she has on people. The song seems to be aimed directly at Marcello who was once her lover. The tension between them becomes unbearable in the ensuing ensemble (02:20), and, when Musetta finally conspires to be with him, Marcello joyously reprises the melody of the waltz (03:43) as he waits to embrace her amid the madness of the moment.

MUSETTA
Quando men' vo soletta
per la via,
la gente sosta e mira,
e la bellezza mia
tutta ricerca in me,
ricerca in me da capo a piè.

MARCELLO
Legatemi alla seggiola!

ALCINDORO
Quella gente che dirà?

MUSETTA
Ed assaporo allor la bramosia
sottil che dagli occhi traspira
e dai palesi vezzi intender sa
alle occulte beltà.
Così l'effluvio del desio
tutta m'aggira.
Felice mi fa, felice mi fa.

ALCINDORO
(Quel canto scurrile
mi muove la bile!)

MUSETTA
As I walk alone
through the streets,
the people stop to look
and inspect my beauty,
examining me
from head to toe.

MARCELLO
Tie me to the chair!

ALCINDORO
What will people say?

MUSETTA
And then I savour the subtle
longing in their eyes
when, from my visible charms,
they guess at the beauty concealed.
This onrush of desire
surrounds me.
It delights me, it delights me.

ALCINDORO
(This scurrilous song
infuriates me!)

Frances Greer as Musetta in a 1944 production.

MUSETTA

E tu che sai, che memori e ti struggi,
da me tanto rifuggi?
So ben le angoscie tue
non le vuoi dir,
ma ti senti morir.

MIMÌ

Io vedo ben che quella poveretta
tutta invaghita di Marcello ell'è!

ALCINDORO

Quella gente che dirà?

MUSETTA

And you know, who remember and suffer,
how can you escape?
I know you won't admit
that you're in torment,
but it's killing you.

MIMÌ

I can tell that the poor girl
is head over heels in love with Marcello.

ALCINDORO

What will people say?

RODOLFO
Marcello un dì l'amò…

SCHAUNARD
Ah! Marcello cederà!

RODOLFO
…La fraschetta l'abbandonò…

COLLINE
Chi sa mai quel che avverrà!

RODOLFO
…per poi darsi
a miglior vita.

SCHAUNARD
Trovan dolce a pari il laccio
chi lo tende e chi ci dà.

COLLINE
Santi numi! in simil briga
mai Colline intopperà!

MUSETTA
(Ah! Marcello smania…
Marcello è vinto!)

ALCINDORO
Parla piano…Zitto, zitto!

MIMÌ
Quell'infelice mi muove a pietà.

RODOLFO
Marcello loved her once…

SCHAUNARD
Ah! Marcello will give in!

RODOLFO
…the flirt ran off…

COLLINE
Who knows what'll happen!

RODOLFO
…to find
a better life.

SCHAUNARD
The snare is equally sweet
to hunter and hunted.

COLLINE
Gods above! I'd never land myself
in such a situation!

MUSETTA
(Ah! Marcello's going mad!
Marcello is vanquished!)

ALCINDORO
Lower your voice! Be quiet!

MIMÌ
I feel so sorry for the poor girl.

COLLINE
Essa è bella — non son cieco…

MIMÌ *(stringendosi a Rodolfo)*
T'amo!

SCHAUNARD
(Quel bravaccio a momenti cederà!
Stupenda è la commedia!
Marcello cederà.)

to Colline

Se una tal vaga persona
ti trattasse a tu per tu,
la tua scienza brontolona
manderesti a Belzebù.

RODOLFO
Mimì!
È fiacco amore
quel che le offese vendicar no sa.
Spento amor non risorge, *ecc.*

MIMÌ
Quell'infelice mi muove a pietà.
L'amor ingeneroso è tristo amor!
Quell'infelice, *ecc.*

COLLINE
…ma piaccionmi assai più
una pipa e un testo greco.
Essa è bella, non son cieco, *ecc.*

ALCINDORO
Modi, garbo! Zitto, zitto!

COLLINE
She's lovely—I'm not blind…

MIMÌ *(nestling close to Rodolfo)*
I love you!

SCHAUNARD
(The braggart is about to yield!
The play is stupendous!
Marcello will give in!)

If such a pretty creature
stopped and talked to you,
you'd gladly send to the devil
all your bearish philosophy.

RODOLFO
Mimì!
Love is weak
when it leaves wrongs unavenged.
Love, once dead, cannot be revived, *etc.*

MIMÌ
I feel so sorry for the poor girl.
Love is sad when it's unforgiving.
I feel so sorry, *etc.*

COLLINE
…but I'm much happier
with my pipe and a Greek text.
She's beautiful, I'm not blind, *etc.*

ALCINDORO
Mind your manners! Be quiet!

MUSETTA

So ben le angoscie tue non le vuoi dir.
Ah! ma ti senti morir.

to Alcindoro

Io voglio fare il mio piacere,
voglio far quel che mi par.
Non seccar, non seccar, non seccar!
(Or conviene liberarsi del vecchio.)

pretending a pain

Ahi!

ALCINDORO

Che c'è?

MUSETTA

Qual dolore, qual bruciore!

ALCINDORO

Dove?

MUSETTA

Al piè!

MARCELLO

(Gioventù mia, tu non sei morta,
né di te è morto il sovvenir…
Se tu battessi alla mia porta
t'andrebbe il mio core ad aprir!)

MUSETTA

Sciogli! slaccia! rompi! straccia!
Te ne imploro.

MUSETTA

I know you won't admit your torment.
Ah! but you feel like dying!

I'll do as I please!
I'll do as I like,
don't be a bore, a bore, a bore!
(Now to get rid of the old man.)

Ouch!

ALCINDORO

What is it?

MUSETTA

The pain! The pain!

ALCINDORO

Where?

MUSETTA

My foot!

MARCELLO

(My youth, you're still alive,
your memory's not dead…
If you came to my door,
my heart would open it!)

MUSETTA

Loosen it! Untie it! Break it! Tear it!
Please!

Laggiù c'è un calzolaio.	There's a shoemaker nearby.
Corri presto! ne voglio un altro paio.	Run quickly! I want another pair!
Ahi! che fitta, maledetta scarpa stretta!	Ah, how it pinches, this damn tight shoe!
Or la levo…eccola qua.	I'll take it off…here it is.
Corri, va, corri! Presto, va, va!	Run, go on, run! Hurry, hurry!

MIMÌ
(Io vedo ben ell'è invaghita di Marcello.)

MIMÌ
(I can see she's madly in love with Marcello.)

RODOLFO
(Io vedo ben la commedia è stupenda!)

RODOLFO
(I can see the play's stupendous!)

ALCINDORO
Imprudente!
Quella gente che dirà?
Ma il mio grado!
Vuoi ch'io comprometta?
Aspetta! Musetta! Vo'!

ALCINDORO
How unwise!
What will people say?
My reputation!
Do you want to ruin it?
Wait! Musetta! I'm going!

He hurries off.

COLLINE E SCHAUNARD
(La commedia è stupenda!)

COLLINE AND SCHAUNARD
(The play is stupendous!)

MUSETTA
Marcello!

MUSETTA
Marcello!

MARCELLO
Sirena!

MARCELLO
Siren!

They embrace passionately.

SCHAUNARD
Siamo all'ultima scena!

SCHAUNARD
Here's the finale!

The waiter brings the bill.

TUTTI	ALL
Il conto!	The bill!

SCHAUNARD	SCHAUNARD
Così presto?	So soon?

COLLINE	COLLINE
Chi l'ha richiesto?	Who asked for it?

SCHAUNARD	SCHAUNARD
Vediam.	Let's see.

DISC NO. 1/TRACK 17

At the end of the act, the friends's whispering concerns about who will pay the bill are juxtaposed with the distant sounds of the marching band, which shortly overtakes all other music in the score. The friends literally "get lost" in the crowd around the band (01:22) as all Paris seems to celebrate the unions of the lovers.

COLLINE E RODOLFO	COLLINE AND RODOLFO
Caro!	It's high!

Drums are heard approaching.

RODOLFO, SCHAUNARD, COLLINE	RODOLFO, SCHAUNARD, COLLINE
Fuori il danaro!	Out with the money!

SCHAUNARD	SCHAUNARD
Colline, Rodolfo e tu, Marcel?	Colline, Rodolfo and you, Marcello?

MONELLI	CHILDREN
La Ritirata!	The Tattoo!

MARCELLO	MARCELLO
Siamo all'asciutto!	We're broke!

SCHAUNARD
Come?

SCHAUNARD
What?

SARTINE, STUDENTI
La Ritirata!

MIDINETTES, STUDENTS
The Tattoo!

RODOLFO
Ho trenta soldi in tutto!

RODOLFO
I've only got thirty sous.

BORGHESI
La Ritirata!

TOWNSPEOPLE
The Tattoo!

MARCELLO, SCHAUNARD, COLLINE
Come? Non ce n'è più?

MARCELLO, SCHAUNARD, COLLINE
What? No more money?

SCHAUNARD
Ma il mio tesoro ov'è?

SCHAUNARD
Where's my wealth?

MONELLI
S'avvicinan per di qua?

URCHINS
Are they coming this way?

MUSETTA *(al cameriere)*
Il mio conto date a me.

MUSETTA *(to the waiter)*
Bring me my bill.

SARTINE, STUDENTI
No! Di là!

MIDINETTES, STUDENTS
No! That way!

MONELLI
S'avvicinan per di là!

URCHINS
They're coming this way!

SARTINI, STUDENTI
Vien di qua!

MIDINETTES, STUDENTS
They're coming that way!

MONELLI
No! vien di là!

URCHINS
No, that way!

MUSETTA
Bene!

BORGHESI, VENDITORI
Largo! largo!

RAGAZZI
Voglio veder! voglio sentir!

MUSETTA
Presto, sommate quello con questo!…
Paga il signor che stava qui con me.

MAMME
Lisetta, vuoi tacere?
Tonio, la vuoi finire?

FANCIULLE
Mamma, voglio vedere!
Papà, voglio sentire!

**RODOLFO, MARCELLO,
SCHAUNARD, COLLINE**
Paga il signor!

RAGAZZI
Vuò veder la Ritirata!

MAMME
Vuoi tacer, la vuoi finir!

SARTINE
S'avvicinano di qua!

BORGHESI
S'avvicinano di là!

MUSETTA
Good!

TOWNSPEOPLE
Make way! Make way!

CHILDREN
I want to see! I want to hear!

MUSETTA
Quick, add these two bills together…
The gentleman who was with me will pay.

MOTHERS
Lisetta, please be quiet.
Tonio, stop that at once!

GIRLS
Mama, I want to see.
Papa, I want to hear.

**RODOLFO, MARCELLO,
SCHAUNARD, COLLINE**
The gentleman will pay!

CHILDREN
I want to see the Tattoo!

MOTHERS
Please be quiet! Stop that at once!

MIDINETTES
They're coming this way!

TOWNSPEOPLE
They're coming that way!

BORGHESI, STUDENTI, VENDITORI
Sì, di qua!

MONELLI
Come sarà arrivata,
la seguiremo al passo.

COLLINE, SCHAUNARD, MARCELLO
Paga il signor!

MUSETTA
E dove s'è seduto,
ritrovi il mio saluto!

putting the bill on the chair

BORGHESI
In quel rullìo tu senti
la patria maestà.

**RODOLFO, COLLINE,
SCHAUNARD, MARCELLO**
E dove s'è seduto,
ritrovi il suo saluto!

LA FOLLA
Largo, largo, eccoli qua!

MONELLI
Ohè attenti, eccoli qua!

MARCELLO
Giunge la Ritirata!

LA FOLLA
In fila!

TOWNSPEOPLE, STUDENTS, HAWKERS
Yes, this way!

URCHINS
When it comes by,
we'll march with it!

COLLINE, SCHAUNARD, MARCELLO
The gentleman will pay!

MUSETTA
And here, at his place,
he'll find my farewell!
putting the bill on the chair

TOWNSPEOPLE
That drum-roll expresses
our country's glory.

**RODOLFO, COLLINE,
SCHAUNARD, MARCELLO**
And here, at this place,
he'll find her farewell!

THE CROWD
Make way, make way, here they come!

URCHINS
Hey! Look out, here they are!

MARCELLO
Now the Guard is coming!

THE CROWD
All in line!

COLLINE, MARCELLO

Che il vecchio non ci veda
fuggir colla sua preda.

RODOLFO

Giunge la Ritirata!

MARCELLO, SCHAUNARD, COLLINE

Quella folla serrata
il nascondiglio appresti!

LA FOLLA

Ecco il tambur maggiore, più fiero
d'un antico guerriero! Il tambur maggior!

**MIMÌ, MUSETTA, RODOLFO,
MARCELLO, SCHAUNARD, COLLINE**

Lesti! lesti! lesti!

LA FOLLA

I Zappatori! i Zappatori, olà!
Ecco il tambur maggior!
Pare un general!
La Ritirata è qua!
Eccola là Il bel tambur maggior!
La canna d'or, tutto splendor!
Che guarda, passa, va!

**RODOLFO, MARCELLO,
SCHAUNARD, COLLINE**

Viva Musetta! Cuor biricchin!
Gloria ed onor, onor e gloria
del Quartier Latin!

COLLINE, MARCELLO

Don't let the old fool see us
make off with his prize.

RODOLFO

The Guard is coming!

MARCELLO, SCHAUNARD, COLLINE

That crowded throng
will be our hiding-place.

THE CROWD

Here's the drum-major! Produer
than an ancient warrior! The drum-major!

**MIMÌ, MUSETTA, RODOLFO,
MARCELLO, SCHAUNARD, COLLINE**

Hurry! Let's run off!

THE CROWD

The Sappers! The Sappers, hooray!
Here's the drum-major!
Like a general!
The Tattoo is here!
Here he is, the handsome drum-major!
The golden baton, all a-glitter!
See, he looks at us as he goes past!

**RODOLFO, MARCELLO,
SCHAUNARD, COLLINE**

Bravo Musetta! Artful minx!
Glory and honour, the glory and honour
of the Latin Quarter!

LA FOLLA	THE CROWD
Tutto splendor!	All a-glitter!
Di Francia è il più bell'uom!	The handsomest man in France,
Il bel tambur maggior!	the drum-major!
Eccola là Che guarda, passa, va!	Here he is! See, he looks at us as he goes past!

Since Musetta cannot walk with only one shoe, Marcello and Colline carry her on their shoulders. They all follow the guards and disappear. Alcindoro comes back with a new pair of shoes, and the waiter hands him the bill. When he sees the amount and sees nobody around, Alcindoro falls, bewildered, onto a chair.

Act II in a 1991 production by the Houston Grand Opera.

Act 3

THE BARRIÈRE D'ENFER Beyond the tollgate is the main highway. At left, a tavern. A small square flanked by plane trees. Some customs officers are asleep around a brazier. Shouts and laughter issue from the cabaret. Dawn. February. The snow is everywhere. Some street-sweepers are beyond the gate, stamping their feet in the cold.

DISC NO. 2/TRACKS 1 & 2

The brash exuberance of Act 2 now devolves into the pathos of this sad, snowbound act. The contrast is explicit in the very melancholy orchestral introduction of falling chords, a superb musical analogy of the frozen landscape. Listen again: it's actually the theme Schaunard had sung when describing the joys of the Latin Quarter, which was played in its fullest form at the beginning of Act 2. Here, it is three times as slow as it had been previously, like the painful recollection of a happy time while in misery.

SPAZZINI

Ohè là, le guardie…Aprite!
Quelli di Gentilly! Siam gli spazzini,
Fiocca la neve. Ohè, là! Qui s'agghiaccia.

SWEEPERS

Hey, there! Guards! Open up!
We're the sweepers from Gentilly.
It's snowing. Hey! We're freezing here.

UN DOGANIERE *(sbadigliando)*

Vengo.

CUSTOMS OFFICER *(yawning)*

I'm coming.

VOCI DAL CABARET

Chi nel ber trovò il piacer
nel suo bicchier,
d'una bocca nell'ardor
trovò l'amor.

VOICES FROM THE TAVERN

Some find pleasure
in their cups.
On ardent lips
some find love.

VOCE DI MUSETTA	**VOICE OF MUSETTA**
Ah! Se nel bicchier sta il piacer,	Ah! Pleasure is in the glass!
il giovin bocca sta l'amor	Love lies on your lips.

VOCI DAL CABARET	**VOICES FROM THE TAVERN**
Trallerallè	Tar la la la
Eva e Noè.	Eve and Noah.

VOCI DAL BOULEVARD	**VOICES FROM THE HIGHWAY**
Hopp-là! Hopp-là!	Houp-la! Giddap!

DOGANIERE	**CUSTOMS OFFICER**
Son già le lattivendole!	Here come the milkmaids!

He opens the gate. The milkmaids enter together with a string of peasants' carts.

LE LATTIVENDOLE	**MILKMAIDS**
Buon giorno!	Good morning!

LE CONTADINE	**PEASANT WOMEN**
Burro e cacio!	Butter and cheese!
Polli ed ova!	Chickens and eggs!
Voi da che parte andate?	Which way are you going?
A San Michele.	To Saint Michel!
Chi troverem più tardi?	Shall we meet later?
A mezzodì.	Yes, at noon.

They go off. Enter Mimì. When she reaches the first tree, she has a fit of coughing. Then recovering herself, she says to the sergeant

MIMÌ	**MIMÌ**
Sa dirmi, scusi, qual è	Excuse me, where's the tavern
l'osteria dove un pittor lavora?	where a painter is working?

SERGENTE	**SERGEANT**
Eccola.	There it is.

MIMÌ	MIMÌ
Grazie.	Thank you.

A waitress comes out of the tavern. Mimì approaches her.

O buona donna, mi fate il favore	Oh, good woman, please…
di cercarmi il pittore	Be good enough to find me
Marcello? Ho da parlargli.	Marcello, the painter.
Ho tanta fretta.	I must see him quickly.
Ditegli, piano, che Mimì l'aspetta.	Tell him Mimì's waiting.

SERGENTE *(ad uno che passa)*	**SERGEANT** *(to someone coming in)*
Ehi, quel paniere!	Hey! That basket!

DOGANIERE	**CUSTOMS OFFICER**
Vuoto!	Empty!

SERGENTE	**SERGEANT**
Passi.	Let him through.

Marcello comes out of the tavern.

DISC NO. 2/TRACK 3

Mimì, though almost breathless when she arrives, pours out her emotions to Marcello, doubled by the orchestra (00:53). This is a technique used by "verismo" composers to tell us of a character's unadorned, unedited sincerity.

MARCELLO	**MARCELLO**
Mimì?!	Mimì?!

MIMÌ	MIMÌ
Speravo di trovarvi qui.	I hoped I'd find you here.

MARCELLO

È ver, siam qui da un mese
di quell'oste alle spese.
Musetta insegna il canto
ai passeggieri.
Io pingo quei guerrieri
sulla facciata.
È freddo. Entrate.

MIMÌ

C'è Rodolfo?

MARCELLO

Sì.

MIMÌ

Non posso entrar.
No! No!

MARCELLO

Perché?

MIMÌ

O buon Marcello, aiuto! Aiuto!

MARCELLO

Cos'è avvenuto?

MIMÌ

Rodolfo m'ama e mi fugge
Rodolfo si strugge per gelosia.
Un passo, un detto, un vezzo,
un fior lo mettono in sospetto…
Onde corrucci ed ire.
Talor la notte fingo di dormire

MARCELLO

That's right. We've been here
a month, at the host's expense.
Musetta teaches
the guests singing.
And I paint those warriors
by the door there.
It's cold. Come inside.

MIMÌ

Is Rodolfo there?

MARCELLO

Yes.

MIMÌ

I can't go in.
No, no!

MARCELLO

Why not?

MIMÌ

Oh! help me, good Marcello! Help me!

MARCELLO

What's happened?

MIMÌ

Rodolfo—he loves me
but flees from me, torn
by jealousy. A glance, a gesture,
a smile, a flower arouses
his suspicions, then anger, rage…
Sometimes at night I pretend

e in me lo sento fisso
spiarmi i sogni in viso.
Mi grida ad ogni istante
non fai per me, ti prendi
un altro amante,
non fai per me. Ahimè!
In lui parla il rovello, lo so;
ma che rispondergli, Marcello?

MARCELLO
Quando s'è come voi
non si vive in compagnia.

MIMÌ
Dite bene. Lasciarci conviene.
Aiutateci, aiutateci voi.
Noi s'è provato
più volte, ma invano.

MARCELLO
Son lieve a Musetta,
ella è lieve a me,
perché ci amiamo in allegria.
Canti e risa, ecco il fior
d'invariabile amor!

MIMÌ
Dite bene, dite bene.
Lasciarci conviene.
Fate voi per il meglio.

MARCELLO
Sta ben. Ora lo sveglio.

MIMÌ
Dorme?

to sleep, and I feel his eyes
trying to spy on my dreams.
He shouts at me all the time
"You're not for me.
Find another.
You're not for me." Alas!
I know it's his jealousy speaking,
but what can I answer, Marcello?

MARCELLO
When two people are like you two,
they can't live together.

MIMÌ
You're right. We should separate.
Help us, Marcello, help us.
We've tried
again and again, but in vain.

MARCELLO
I take Musetta lightly,
and she behaves like me.
We love light-heartedly.
Laughter and song—that's the secret
of a lasting love.

MIMÌ
You're right, you're right.
We should separate.
Do your best for us.

MARCELLO
All right. I'll wake him up.

MIMÌ
Is he sleeping?

MARCELLO
È piombato qui
un'ora avanti l'alba.
S'assopì sopra una panca.
Guardate.

Mimì coughs.

Che tosse!

MIMÌ
Da ieri ho l'ossa rotte.
Fuggì da me stanotte
dicendomi è finita.
A giorno sono uscita
e me ne venni a questa volta.

MARCELLO *(osservando Rodolfo
nell'interno)*
Si desta…s'alza.
Mi cerca. Viene.

MIMÌ
Ch'ei non mi veda.

MARCELLO
Or rincasate, Mimì.
Per carità, non fate scene qua!

Mimì hides behind a tree, Rodolfo hastens out of the tavern.

MARCELLO
He stumbled in here
an hour before dawn
and fell asleep on a bench.
Look at him…

What a cough!

MIMÌ
I've been aching all over since
yesterday. He fled during the night, saying
"It's all over." I set out
at dawn and came here to find you.

MARCELLO *(watching Rodolfo through
the window)*
He's waking up. He's looking
for me…Here he comes.

MIMÌ
He mustn't see me.

MARCELLO
Go home now, Mimì.
For God's sake, no scenes here.

Rodolfo hides his true emotions in macho posturing, which is something tenors convey better than anyone. Marcello, of course, see through it all.

RODOLFO
Marcello. Finalmente.
Qui niun ci sente.
Io voglio separarmi da Mimì.

MARCELLO
Sei volubil così?

RODOLFO
Già un'altra volta credetti
morto il mio cor.
Ma di quegli occhi azzurri
allo splendor esso è risorto.
Ora il tedio l'assale…

MARCELLO
E gli vuoi rinnovare il funeral?

RODOLFO
Per sempre!

MARCELLO
Cambia metro.
Dei pazzi è l'amor tetro
che lacrime distilla
Se non ride e sfavilla,
l'amore è fiacco e roco.
Tu sei geloso.

RODOLFO
Un poco.

RODOLFO
Marcello. At last!
No one can hear us here.
I've got to leave Mimì.

MARCELLO
Are you as fickle as that?

RODOLFO
Already once before I thought
my heart was dead.
But it revived at the gleam
of her blue eyes.
Now boredom assails it…

MARCELLO
And you'll bury it again?

RODOLFO
Forever!

MARCELLO
Change your ways!
Gloomy love is madness
and brews only tears.
If it doesn't laugh and glow
love has no strength or voice.
You're jealous.

RODOLFO
A little.

MARCELLO

Collerico, lunatico,
imbevuto di pregiudizi,
noioso, cocciuto!

MARCELLO

You're raving mad,
a mass of suspicions,
a boor, a mule!

MIMÌ

(Or lo fa incollerire!
Me poveretta!)

MIMÌ

(He'll make him angry.
Poor me!)

RODOLFO

Mimì è una civetta
che frascheggia con tutti.
Un moscardino di Viscontino
le fa l'occhio di triglia.
Ella sgonnella e scopre la caviglia
con un far promettente e lusinghier.

RODOLFO

Mimì's just a flirt
toying with them all.
A foppish Viscount eyes her
with longing. She shows him
her ankles, promising,
luring him on.

MARCELLO

Lo devo dir?
Che non mi sembri sincer.

MARCELLO

Must I tell you?
You aren't being honest.

RODOLFO

Ebbene, no. Non lo son.
Invan, invan nascondo
la mia vera tortura.
Amo Mimì sovra ogni cosa
al mondo. Io l'amo! Ma ho paura.

RODOLFO

All right, then, I'm not.
I try in vain to hide
what really torments me.
I love Mimì more than the world.
I love her! But I'm afraid…

DISC NO. 2/TRACK 6

This celebrated trio reveals Rodolfo's true motivations at last as Mimì confronts the reality of her situation. The melody (00:22) seems like the musical analog of repressed sobs.

Mimì è tanto malata!
Ogni dì più declina.
La povera piccina
è condannata…

Mimì is terribly ill,
weaker every day.
The poor little thing
is doomed…

MARCELLO

Mimì?

MIMÌ

(Che vuoi dire?)

RODOLFO

Una terribil tosse

l'esil petto le scuote.

Già la smunte gote

di sangue ha rosse…

MARCELLO

Povera Mimì!

MIMÌ

(Ahimè, morire?)

RODOLFO

La mia stanza è una tana

squallida. Il fuoco è spento.

V'entra e l'aggira il vento

di tramontana.

Essa canta e sorride

e il rimorso m'assale.

Me, cagion del fatale

mal che l'uccide.

MARCELLO

Che far dunque?

MIMÌ

(O mia vita! È finita!

Ahimè! morir! *ecc.*)

MARCELLO

Mimì?

MIMÌ

(What does he mean?)

RODOLFO

A horrible coughing

racks her fragile chest…

Her pale cheeks

are flushed…

MARCELLO

Poor Mimì!

MIMÌ

(Am I dying? Alas!)

RODOLFO

My room's like a cave.

The fire has gone out.

The wind, the winter wind

roars through it.

She laughs and sings;

I'm seized with remorse.

I'm the cause of the illness

that's killing her.

MARCELLO

What's to be done?

MIMÌ

(Oh! my life! It's over!

Alas! To die! *etc.*)

RODOLFO

Mimì di serra è fiore.
Povertà l'ha sfiorita,
per richiamarla in vita
non basta amore.

MARCELLO

Poveretta. Povera Mimì! Povera Mimì!

Mimì sobs and coughs.

RODOLFO

Che! Mimì! Tu qui!
M'hai sentito?

MARCELLO

Ella dunque ascoltava.

RODOLFO

Facile alla paura,
per nulla io m'arrovello.
Vien là nel tepore.

He tries to lead her inside.

MIMÌ

No, quel tanfo mi soffoca.

Musetta's laughter comes from inside.

RODOLFO

Ah! Mimì!

MARCELLO

È Musetta che ride.

RODOLFO

Mimì's a hothouse flower,
blighted by poverty.
To bring her back to life
love's not enough.

MARCELLO

Poor thing. Poor Mimì!

RODOLFO

What, Mimì? You here!
You heard me?

MARCELLO

She was listening then.

RODOLFO

I'm easily frightened,
worked up over nothing.
Come inside where it's warm.

MIMÌ

No. It's so close. I'd suffocate.

RODOLFO

Ah, Mimì!

MARCELLO

That's Musetta laughing.

| Con chi ride? | And with whom? |
| Ah la civetta! Imparerai. | The flirt! I'll teach her. |

Marcello runs into the tavern.

DISC NO. 2/TRACK 7

Addio … D'onde lieta uscì al tuo grido **Mimì's aria of farewell comes after she, from a hiding place, has overheard Rodolfo telling Marcello that she is mortally ill, and that his jealousy and frustration are driven by the idea that he might lose her. A coughing fit reveals to the men that she has been listening, and when Rodolfo tries to explain himself she tells him she must leave him. She bids him farewell in a lyrical moment equal to her first-act aria. Beginning with a halting tenderness and gathering the strength that blossoms into melody (02:23), she says she will have someone pick up her things, though he might want to keep the little bonnet he bought her the night they met.**

Beniamino Gigli
(1890-1957) as Rodolfo.

MIMÌ *(a Rodolfo)*
Addio.

RODOLFO
Che! Vai?

MIMÌ
D'onde lieta uscì al tuo grido
d'amore torna sola Mimì.
Al solitario nido
ritorna un'altra volta
a intesser finti fior.
Addio senza rancor.
— Ascolta, ascolta.
Le poche robe aduna che lasciai
sparse. Nel mio cassetto
stan chiusi quel cerchietto
d'or e il libro di preghiere.
Involgi tutto quanto in un grembiale
e manderò il portiere…
— Bada, sotto il guanciale
c'è la cuffietta rosa.
Se vuoi…serbarla a ricordo d'amor…
Addio, senza rancor.

MIMÌ *(to Rodolfo)*
Good-bye.

RODOLFO
What? You're going?

MIMÌ
Back to the place I left
at the call of your love.
I'm going back alone
to my lonely nest
to make false flowers.
Good-bye…no hard feelings.
But listen.
Please gather up the few things
I've left behind. In the trunk
there's the little bracelet
and my prayer book. Wrap them…
in an apron and I'll send
someone for them…
wait! Under my pillow
there's my pink bonnet.
If you want…keep it in memory
of our love. Good-bye, no hard feelings.

DISC NO. 2/TRACK 8

Dunque è proprio finita Immediately following Mimì's farewell, this scene, which emerges
as a quartet, proves the third act is the heart and soul of La Bohème. It fills out superbly
the characters of Mimì, Rodolfo, Musetta, and Marcello, with Puccini's wonderfully
reflexive writing catching the tensions and transforming them into expressive melody
(01:05). The tragic mood and the sweetness of the music is contrasted by the amusing
bickering of Musetta and Marcello (01:57), reminding the listener that life rattles on
for most people, even as Mimì and Rodolfo contemplate a different future.

Jussi Björling (1911-1960) as Rodolfo.

RODOLFO
Dunque è proprio finita.
Te ne vai, la mia piccina?
Addio, sogni d'amor!

MIMÌ
Addio dolce svegliare alla mattina.

RODOLFO
Addio sognante vita!

MIMÌ
Addio rabuffi e gelosie…

RODOLFO
…Che un tuo sorriso acqueta.

MIMÌ
Addio sospetti…

RODOLFO
So it's really over.
You're leaving, my little one?
Good-bye to our dreams of love.

MIMÌ
Good-bye to our sweet wakening.

RODOLFO
Good-bye, life in a dream.

MIMÌ
Good-bye, doubts and jealousies…

RODOLFO
That one smile of yours could dispel.

MIMÌ
Good-bye, suspicions…

RODOLFO
Baci.

MIMÌ
...Pungenti amarezze...

RODOLFO
...Ch'io da vero poeta
rimavo con carezze.

RODOLFO E MIMÌ
Soli, l'inverno è cosa da morire!

MIMÌ
Soli...

RODOLFO E MIMÌ
Mentre a primavera
c'è compagno il sol.

MIMÌ
C'è compagno il sol.

Marcello and Musetta come out, quarreling.

MARCELLO
Che facevi? Che dicevi?
Presso il foco a quel signore?

MUSETTA
Che vuoi dir? Che vuoi dir?

MIMÌ
Niuno è solo l'april.

RODOLFO
Kisses...

MIMÌ
...Poignant bitterness...

RODOLFO
...That, like a poet,
I made rhyme with caress.

RODOLFO AND MIMÌ
To be alone in winter is death!

MIMÌ
Alone...

RODOLFO AND MIMÌ
But when spring comes
the sun is our companion.

MIMÌ
The sun is our companion.

MARCELLO
What were you doing and saying
by the fire with that man?

MUSETTA
What do you mean? What do you mean?

MIMÌ
Nobody's lonely in April.

MARCELLO
Al mio venire
hai mutato di colore.

MUSETTA
Quel signore mi diceva…
"Ama il ballo, signorina?"

RODOLFO
Si parla coi gigli e le rose.

MIMÌ
Esce dai nidi un cinguettìo gentile.

MARCELLO
Vana, frivola civetta!

MUSETTA
Arrossendo io rispendevo
"Ballerei sera e mattina."

MARCELLO
Quel discorso asconde mire
disoneste.

MUSETTA
Voglio piena libertà.

MARCELLO
Io t'acconcio per le feste…

RODOLFO E MIMÌ
Al fiorir di primavera
c'è compagno il sol.

MARCELLO
When I came in
you blushed suddenly.

MUSETTA
The man was asking me…
"Do you like dancing, Miss?"

RODOLFO
One can speak to roses with lilies.

MIMÌ
Birds twitter softly in their nests.

MARCELLO
Vain, empty-headed flirt!

MUSETTA
I blushed and answered
"I could dance day and night!"

MARCELLO
That speech conceals
infamous desires.

MUSETTA
I want complete freedom.

MARCELLO
I'll teach you a thing or two…

RODOLFO AND MIMÌ
With the coming of spring,
the sun is our companion!

MUSETTA

Che mi canti?
Che mi gridi? Che mi canti?
All'altar non siamo uniti.

MARCELLO

...Se ti colgo a incivettire!
Bada, sotto il mio cappello
non ci stan certi ornamenti.

MUSETTA

Io detesto quegli amanti
che la fanno da mariti.

RODOLFO E MIMÌ

Chiacchieran le fontane,
la brezza della sera balsami
stende sulle doglie umane.

MARCELLO

Io non faccio da zimbello
ai novizi intraprendenti.
Vana, frivola civetta!
Ve ne andate? Vi ringrazio,
or son ricco divenuto.

MUSETTA

Fo all'amor chi mi piace.
Non ti garba?
Fo all'amor con chi mi piace.
Musetta se ne va.

MARCELLO E MUSETTA

Vi saluto.

MUSETTA

What do you think
you're saying?
We're not married, after all.

MARCELLO

...If I catch you flirting!
Keep in mind, no horns
will grow under my hat.

MUSETTA

I can't stand lovers
who act just like husbands.

RODOLFO AND MIMÌ

The fountains whisper,
the evening breeze heals the pain
of human creatures...

MARCELLO

I won't be laughed at
by some young upstart.
Vain, empty-headed flirt!
You're leaving? I thank you,
I'll be a rich man then.

MUSETTA

I'll flirt with whom I please.
You don't like it?
I'll flirt with whom I please.
Musetta goes her way.

MARCELLO AND MUSETTA

Good-bye.

RODOLFO E MIMÌ

Vuoi che aspettiam
la primavera ancor?

MUSETTA

Signor, addio
vi dico con piacer!

MARCELLO

Son servo e me ne vo!

MUSETTA *(mentre ella se ne va)*

Pittore da bottega!

MARCELLO

Vipera!

MUSETTA

Rospo!

MARCELLO *(ritornando nella taverna)*

Strega!

MIMÌ

Sempre tua…per la vita.

RODOLFO E MIMÌ

Ci lasceremo alla stagion dei fior!

MIMÌ

Vorrei che eterno
durasse il verno!

RODOLFO E MIMÌ

Ci lascierem alla stagion dei fior!

RODOLFO AND MIMÌ

Shall we wait
until spring comes again?

MUSETTA

I bid you, sir,
farewell—with pleasure!

MARCELLO

Your servant, and I'm off!

MUSETTA *(leaving)*

You house-painter!

MARCELLO

Viper!

MUSETTA

Toad!

MARCELLO *(re-entering the tavern)*

Witch!

MIMÌ

Always yours….all my life.

RODOLFO AND MIMÌ

We'll part when the flowers bloom!

MIMÌ

I wish that winter
would last forever!

RODOLFO AND MIMÌ

We'll part when flowers bloom!

Act 4

THE GARRET Marcello once more at his easel; Rodolfo at his table. They try to work, but instead they are talking.

DISC NO. 2/TRACK 9

In un coupè? **The fourth act begins just as the first act did, with the theme of the bohemians Puccini borrowed from his *Capriccio sinfonico*. It is slightly altered, suggesting change and the passage of time, and it lands the listener squarely in the middle of an idle conversation in which Rodolfo recounts to Marcello how and where he had seen Musetta recently.**

MARCELLO	**MARCELLO**
In un coupè?	In a coupé?
RODOLFO	**RODOLFO**
Con pariglia e livree.	With footmen and horses.
Mi salutò ridendo.	She greeted me, laughing.
Tò Musetta — le dissi —	"So, Musetta," I said,
e il cuor?	"your heart?
"Non batte o non lo sento	It doesn't beat—at least I don't feel it.
grazie al velluto che il copre."	Thanks to the velvet that covers it."
MARCELLO	**MARCELLO**
Ci ho gusto davver.	I'm glad, really glad.
RODOLFO	**RODOLFO**
(Loiola va. Ti rodi e ridi.)	(Faker, go on! You're laughing
	and fretting inside.)

MARCELLO
Non batte? Bene.
Io pur vidi…

RODOLFO
Musetta?

MARCELLO
Mimì.

RODOLFO
L'hai vista?

with pretended unconcern

Oh guarda!

MARCELLO
Era in carrozza
vestita come una regina.

RODOLFO
Evviva. Ne son contento.

MARCELLO
(Bugiardo. Si strugge d'amor.)

RODOLFO
Lavoriam.

MARCELLO
Lavoriam.

MARCELLO
Not beating? Good.
I also saw…

RODOLFO
Musetta?

MARCELLO
Mimì.

RODOLFO
You saw her?

Really?

MARCELLO
She was in a carriage
dressed like a queen.

RODOLFO
That's fine. I'm delighted.

MARCELLO
(The liar! Love's consuming him.)

RODOLFO
Let's get to work.

MARCELLO
Yes, to work.

They start working, but quickly throw down brush and pen.

RODOLFO

Che penna infame!

RODOLFO

This pen is terrible!

MARCELLO

Che infame pennello!

MARCELLO

So is this brush!

DISC NO. 2/TRACK 10

Ah, Mimì, tu più non torni The idle gossip makes both men wistful, and each longs to see his beloved again. The duet they sing is richly sentimental, full of regret tinged with a little hope (01:41). But after a bit of swagger from both singers, they are left with nothing else to say (or sing), and—as they ponder their memories (02:28)—it is up to the orchestra to finish the melody.

RODOLFO

(O Mimì, tu più non torni.
O giorni belli,
piccole mani, odorosi capelli,
collo di neve! Ah! Mimì,
mia breve gioventù.)

RODOLFO

(O Mimì, you won't return!
O lovely days! Those tiny hands,
those sweet-smelling locks,
that snowy neck! Ah! Mimì!
My short-lived youth.)

MARCELLO

(Io non so come sia
che il mio pennello lavori
e impasti colori contro voglia mia.
Se pingere mi piace
o cielo o terre
o inverni o primavere,
egli mi traccia due pupille nere
e una bocca procace,
e n'esce di Musetta il viso ancor...

MARCELLO

(I don't understand how my brush
works and mixes colours
to spite me.
Whether I want to paint
earth or sky, spring
or winter, the brush
outlines two dark eyes
and inviting lips,
and Musetta's face comes out...)

RODOLFO

(E tu, cuffietta lieve,
che sotto il guancial partendo

RODOLFO

(And you, little pink bonnet
that she hid under the pillow

ascose, tutta sai
la nostra felicità,
vien sul mio cor,
sul mio cor morto,
poiché è morto amor.)

as she left, you know
all of our joy.
Come to my heart,
my heart that's dead
with our dead love.)

MARCELLO
(E n'esce di Musetta il viso
tutto vezzi e tutto frode.
Musetta intanto gode
e il mio cuor vile
la chiama ed aspetta.)

MARCELLO
(Her face comes forward then,
so lovely and so false.
Meanwhile Musetta is happy
and my cowardly heart
calls her, and waits for her.)

DISC NO. 2/TRACKS 11 & 12

This final act is in many ways a reflection of the first act, except that everything has changed for the friends. Schaunard returns to the garret with only a herring, and the subsequent gaiety has a forced quality that was absent from the first act. Even a silly minuet in cheap drag abruptly turns into a mock-fight (track 12, 00:46).

RODOLFO
Che ora sia?

RODOLFO
What time is it?

MARCELLO
L'ora del pranzo…
Di ieri.

MARCELLO
It's time for dinner…
yesterday's dinner.

RODOLFO
E Schaunard non torna.

RODOLFO
And Schaunard's not back.

Schaunard comes in and sets four rolls on the table. Colline is with him.

SCHAUNARD
Eccoci.

SCHAUNARD
Here we are.

RODOLFO E MARCELLO
Ebbene?

MARCELLO
Del pan?

COLLINE
È un piatto degno di Demostene
un'aringa…

SCHAUNARD
…salata.

COLLINE
Il pranzo è in tavola. (Si seggono.)

MARCELLO
Questa è cuccagna
da Berlingaccio.

SCHAUNARD (Mette la bottiglia
d'acqua nel cappello di Colline)
Ora lo sciampagna
mettiamo in ghiaccio.

RODOLFO
Scelga, o Barone,
trota o salmone?

MARCELLO
Duca, una lingua
di pappagallo?

SCHAUNARD
Grazie, m'impingua,
stasera ho un ballo.

RODOLFO AND MARCELLO
Well?

MARCELLO
Just bread?

COLLINE
A dish worthy of Demosthenes
A herring…

SCHAUNARD
…salted.

COLLINE
Dinner's on the table. (They sit down.)

MARCELLO
This is like a feast day
in wonderland.

SCHAUNARD (puts the water-bottle in
Colline's hat)
Now let's put
the champagne on ice.

RODOLFO
Which do you choose, Baron,
salmon or trout?

MARCELLO
Well, Duke, how about
some parrot-tongue?

SCHAUNARD
Thanks, but it's fattening.
I must dance this evening.

Colline gets up.

RODOLFO
Già sazio?

RODOLFO
Full already?

COLLINE
Ho fretta.
Il Re m'aspetta.

COLLINE
I'm in a hurry.
The King is waiting for me.

MARCELLO
C'è qualche trama?

MARCELLO
Is there some plot?

**RODOLFO, MARCELLO,
SCHAUNARD**
Qualche mister?

**RODOLFO, MARCELLO,
SCHAUNARD**
Some mystery?

COLLINE
Il Re mi chiama
al minister.

COLLINE
The King has asked me
to join his cabinet.

**MARCELLO, RODOLFO,
SCHAUNARD**
Bene!

**MARCELLO, RODOLFO,
SCHAUNARD**
Fine!

COLLINE
Però vedrò…Guizot!

COLLINE
So…I'll see Guizot!

SCHAUNARD
Porgimi il nappo.

SCHAUNARD
Pass me the goblet.

MARCELLO
Sì. Bevi. Io pappo.

MARCELLO
Here. Drink. I'll eat.

SCHAUNARD
Mi sia permesso…
al nobile consesso…

SCHAUNARD
By the leave…
of this noble company…

RODOLFO
Basta.

MARCELLO
Fiacco!

COLLINE
Che decotto!

MARCELLO
Leva il tacco.

COLLINE
Dammi il gotto.

SCHAUNARD
M'ispira irresistibile
l'estro della romanza…

GLI ALTRI
No!

SCHAUNARD
Azione coreografica allora?

GLI ALTRI
Sì.

SCHAUNARD
La danza con musica vocale!

COLLINE
Si sgombrino le sale.
Gavotta.

RODOLFO
Enough!

MARCELLO
Weakling!

COLLINE
What a concoction!

MARCELLO
Get out of here!

COLLINE
The goblet, please.

SCHAUNARD
I'm irresistibly inspired
by the Muse of poetry…

THE OTHERS
No!

SCHAUNARD
Something choreographic then?

THE OTHERS
Yes.

SCHAUNARD
Dance with vocal accompaniment!

COLLINE
Let the hall be cleared.
A gavotte.

MARCELLO
Minuetto.

RODOLFO
Pavanella.

SCHAUNARD
Fandango.

COLLINE
Propongo la quadriglia.

RODOLFO
Mano alle dame.

COLLINE
Io detto.

SCHAUNARD
La lera la lera la!

RODOLFO *(galante a Marcello)*
Vezzosa damigella…

MARCELLO
Rispetti la modestia.
La prego.

COLLINE
Balancez.

SCHAUNARD
Prima c'è il Rond.

MARCELLO
Minuet.

RODOLFO
Pavane.

SCHAUNARD
Fandango.

COLLINE
I suggest the quadrille.

RODOLFO
Take your lady's arm.

COLLINE
I'll call the figures.

SCHAUNARD
La lera la lera la!

RODOLFO *(gallantly, to Marcello)*
Lovely maiden…

MARCELLO
Please, sir,
respect my modesty.

COLLINE
Balancez.

SCHAUNARD
The Rond comes first.

COLLINE	**COLLINE**
No, bestia.	No, damn it.
SCHAUNARD	**SCHAUNARD**
Che modi da lacchè!	What boorish manners!
COLLINE	**COLLINE**
Se non erro lei m'oltraggia.	You provoke me, I believe.
Snudi il ferro.	Draw your sword.
SCHAUNARD	**SCHAUNARD**
Pronti. Assaggia.	Ready. Lay on.
Il tuo sangue voglio ber.	I'll drink your blood.

Colline takes the fire-tongs and Schaunard the poker. They fight as the others sing.

COLLINE	**COLLINE**
Un di noi si sbudella.	One of us will be run through!
SCHAUNARD	**SCHAUNARD**
Apprestate una barella.	Have a stretcher ready!
COLLINE	**COLLINE**
Apprestate un cimiter.	And a graveyard too!
RODOLFO E MARCELLO	**RODOLFO AND MARCELLO**
Mentre incalza la tenzone	While the battle rages,
gira e balza Rigodone.	the dancers circle and leap.

Musetta enters

MARCELLO	**MARCELLO**
Musetta!	Musetta!

C'è Mimì … c'è Mimì The cavorting of the young men stops suddenly, sickeningly, when Musetta arrives with the news that she has the desperately ill Mimì downstairs with nowhere else to turn. The household suddenly mobilizes on her behalf. As demonstrated in the first act, Puccini is unparalleled in his ability to capture this kind of activity, down to the smallest detail, in a smooth flow of musical ideas.

MUSETTA
C'è Mimì…c'è Mimì
che mi segue e che sta male.

MUSETTA
Mimì's here…she's coming
and she's ill.

RODOLFO
Ov'è?

RODOLFO
Where is she?

MUSETTA
Nel far le scale
più non si resse.

MUSETTA
She couldn't find strength
to climb all the stairs.

Rodolfo hastens out to Mimì, who is seated on the last step. Then they carry her into the room and place her on the bed.

RODOLFO
Ah!

RODOLFO
Ah!

SCHAUNARD
Noi accostiamo quel lettuccio.

SCHAUNARD
We'll move the bed closer.

RODOLFO
Là. Da bere.

RODOLFO
Here. Something to drink.

MIMÌ
Rodolfo.

MIMÌ
Rodolfo.

RODOLFO
Zitta. Risposa.

RODOLFO
Rest now. Don't speak.

MIMÌ

O mio Rodolfo,
mi vuoi qui con te?

RODOLFO

Ah, mia Mimì!
Sempre, sempre!

MUSETTA *(agli altri, piano)*

Intesi dire che Mimì, fuggita
dal Viscontino, era in fin di vita.
Dove stia? Cerca, cerca…la veggo
passar per via,
trascinandosi a stento
Mi dice, "Più non reggo…
Muoio, lo sento…
Voglio morir con lui…
Forse m'aspetta…"

MARCELLO

Sst!

MIMÌ

Mi sento assai meglio…

MUSETTA

"…M'accompagni, Musetta?"

MIMÌ

Lascia ch'io guardi intorno.
Ah, come si sta bene qui.
Si rinasce, si rinasce…
Ancor sento la vita qui…
No, tu non mi lasci più…

MIMÌ

O my Rodolfo!
You want me here with you?

RODOLFO

Ah! My Mimì!
Always, always!

MUSETTA *(aside, to the others)*

I heard Mimì had fled
from the Viscount and was dying.
Where was she? I sought her…
Just now I saw her in the street
stumbling along. She said,
"I can't last long.
I know I'm dying…
but I want to die with him…
Perhaps he's waiting for me.."

MARCELLO

Sh!

MIMÌ

I feel much better…

MUSETTA

"…Please take me, Musetta?"

MIMÌ

Let me look around.
How wonderful it is here.
I'll recover… I will…
I feel life here again.
You won't leave me ever…

RODOLFO
Benedetta bocca,
tu ancor mi parli.

MUSETTA
Che ci avete in casa?

MARCELLO
Nulla.

MUSETTA
Non caffè? Non vino?

MARCELLO
Nulla. Ah! Miseria.

SCHAUNARD
Fra mezz'ora è morta!

MIMÌ
Ho tanto freddo.
Se avessi un manicotto!
Queste mie mani riscaldare
non si potranno mai?

RODOLFO
Qui. Nelle mie, Taci.
Il parlar ti stanca.

MIMÌ
Ho un po' di tosse.
Ci sono avvezza.
Buon giorno, Marcello,
Schaunard, Colline, buon giorno.
Tutti qui, tutti qui
sorridenti a Mimì.

RODOLFO
Beloved lips,
you speak to me again.

MUSETTA
What is there in the house?

MARCELLO
Nothing.

MUSETTA
No coffee? No wine?

MARCELLO
Nothing. Poverty!

SCHAUNARD
She can't last an hour!

MIMÌ
I'm so cold.
If I had a muff!
Won't these hands of mine
ever be warm?

RODOLFO
Here. In mine. Don't speak.
You'll tire yourself.

MIMÌ
It's just a little cough.
I'm used to it.
Hello, Marcello,
Schaunard, Colline…
All of you are here,
smiling at Mimì.

RODOLFO
Non parlar, non parlar.

MIMÌ
Parlo pian. Non temere.
Marcello date retta
è assai buona Musetta.

MARCELLO *(porge la mano a Musetta)*
Lo so. Lo so.

MUSETTA *(dà gli orecchini a Marcello)*
A te, vendi, riporta
qualche cordial.
Manda un dottore!

RODOLFO
Riposa.

MIMÌ
Tu non mi lasci?

RODOLFO
No, no!

MUSETTA
Ascolta!
Forse è l'ultima volta che ha espresso
un desiderio,
poveretta! Pel manicotto
io vo. Con te verrò.

MARCELLO
Sei buona, o mia Musetta.

Marcello and Musetta go out.

RODOLFO
Don't speak, don't…

MIMÌ
I'll speak softly. Don't fear.
Marcello, believe me—
Musetta is so good.

MARCELLO *(holds Musetta's hand)*
I know. I know.

MUSETTA *(gives her earrings to Marcello)*
Here. Sell them. Bring
back some cordial
and send the doctor!

RODOLFO
Rest now!

MIMÌ
You wont leave me?

RODOLFO
No, no!

MUSETTA
Listen!
Perhaps it's the poor thing's
last request.
I'll get the muff.
I'm coming with you.

MARCELLO
How good you are, Musetta.

Vecchia zimarra The philosopher Colline resolves to sell his coat in order to buy items to make Mimì comfortable, and he bids the garment farewell in a brief, touching aria. The tenor Enrico Caruso once sang this aria in a Metropolitan Opera performance of La Bohème in Philadelphia. The bass had lost his voice and so—with no other alternative available since the act moves so swiftly that no one onstage would have time to leave and come back—Caruso, who was singing Rodolfo, turned his back to the audience and sang the aria while the bass mimed it.

COLLINE *(levandosi il pastrano)*	**COLLINE** *(taking off his greatcoat)*
Vecchia zimarra, senti,	Listen, my venerable coat,
io resto al pian, tu ascendere	I'm staying behind, you'll
il sacro monte or devi.	go on to greater heights.
Le mie grazie ricevi.	I give you my thanks.
Mai non curvasti il logoro	You never bowed your worn back
dorso ai ricchi ed ai potenti.	to the rich or powerful.
Passar nelle tue tasche	You held in your pockets
come in antri tranquilli	poets and philosophers
filosofi e poeti.	as if in tranquil grottoes…
Ora che i giorni lieti	Now that those happy times
fuggir, ti dico addio,	have fled, I bid you farewell,
fedele amico mio. Addio.	faithful old friend. Farewell.

He puts the bundle under his arm, then whispers to Schaunard.

Schaunard, ognuno per diversa via	Schaunard, each separately,
mettiamo insieme due atti di pietà;	let's combine two kindly acts;
io…questo!…E tu…	mine is this…and you…
lasciali soli là…	leave the two of them alone.

SCHAUNARD	**SCHAUNARD**
Filosofo, ragioni!	Philosopher, you're right!
È ver… Vo via!	I'll go along.

They leave.

Sono andati? **Alone together at last, while the others run errands to fetch things to relieve Mimì's discomfort, Mimì and Rodolfo recall their happier days in a nostalgic duet that ends with Mimì fainting as she recalls the words Rodolfo sang when he first touched her hand (04:03).**

MIMÌ	MIMÌ
Sono andati? Fingevo di dormire	Have they gone? I pretended to sleep
perché volli con te sola restare.	because I wanted to be alone with you.
Ho tante cose che ti voglio dire,	I've so many things to tell you,
o una sola ma grande come il mare,	or one thing—huge as the sea,
come il mare profonda ed infinita…	deep and infinite as the sea…
Sei il mio amor…e tutta la mia vita.	I love you…you're all my life.

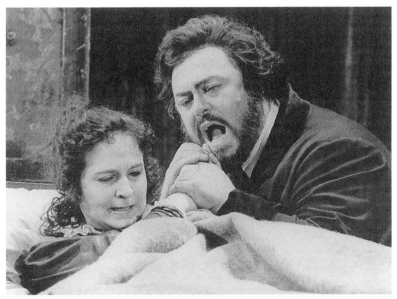

Luciano Pavarotti as Rodolfo and Fiamma Izzo D'Amico as Mimì in Peking's Tian Qiao Theatre's 1986 production of *La Bohème*.

RODOLFO

Ah Mimì, mia bella Mimì!

MIMÌ

Son bella ancora?

RODOLFO

Bella come un'aurora.

MIMÌ

Hai sbagliato il raffronto.
Volevi dir bella
come un tramonto
"Mi chiamano Mimì…
il perché non so"

RODOLFO

Tornò al nido la rondine
e cinguetta.

He takes the bonnet from its place over his heart.

MIMÌ

La mia cuffietta!
La mia cuffietta!
Ah! te lo rammenti
quando sono entrata
la prima volta là?

RODOLFO

Se lo rammento!

MIMÌ

Il lume s'era spento.

RODOLFO

Ah! my beautiful Mimì!

MIMÌ

Am I beautiful still?

RODOLFO

Beautiful as the dawn.

MIMÌ

You've mistaken the image
you should have said,
beautiful as the sunset.
"They call me Mimì…
but I don't know why."

RODOLFO

The swallow comes back to her nest to
twitter.

MIMÌ

My bonnet!
My bonnet!
Ah! do you remember
when I came in here
the first time?

RODOLFO

Do I remember!

MIMÌ

The light had gone out.

RODOLFO

Eri tanto turbata.

Poi smarristi la chiave…

MIMÌ

E a cercarla tastoni ti sei messo!

RODOLFO

E cerca, cerca…

MIMÌ

Mio bel signorino,

posso ben dirlo adesso,

lei la trovò assai presto.

RODOLFO

Aiutavo il destino.

MIMÌ

Era buio e il mio rossor

non si vedeva…

"Che gelida manina…

Se la lasci riscaldar…"

Era buio e la man

tu mi prendevi…

Mimì has another spasm, a fit of choking.

RODOLFO

Oh Dio! Mimì!

Schaunard enters at that moment.

SCHAUNARD

Che avvien?

RODOLFO

You were so upset.

Then you lost your key…

MIMÌ

And you knelt to hunt for it!

RODOLFO

I searched and searched…

MIMÌ

My dear sir,

now I can tell you

you found it quick enough.

RODOLFO

I was helping Fate.

MIMÌ

It was dark. You couldn't

see me blushing.

"How cold your little hand is…

Let me warm it for you…"

It was dark. You took

my hand in yours…

RODOLFO

Good God! Mimì!

SCHAUNARD

What's wrong?

MIMÌ	MIMÌ
Nulla. Sto bene.	Nothing. I'm fine.

RODOLFO	RODOLFO
Zitta. Per carità.	Please...don't talk.

MIMÌ	MIMÌ
Si, si, perdona.	Yes, yes forgive me.
Or sarò buona.	Now I'll be good.

Marcello and Musetta come back, then Colline. Musetta sets a candle on the table.

DISC NO. 2/TRACK 16

Dorme? ... Riposa **Matters worsen. Mimì lays dying. Musetta prays for her soul, but Schaunard realizes that Mimì has, in fact, died (03:07). Rodolfo is the last to realize it, and he is at first unwilling to accept it. As Marcello tells him to have courage, the orchestra speaks first, the French horns wailing in sorrow (03:45). As Rodolfo cries Mimì's name, a tragic phrase from her third-act farewell aria brings the opera to an end.**

MUSETTA	MUSETTA
Dorme?	Is she sleeping?

RODOLFO	RODOLFO
Riposa.	She's resting.

MARCELLO	MARCELLO
Ho veduto il dottore.	I saw the doctor.
Verrà. Gli ho fatto fretta.	He's coming. I made him hurry.
Ecco il cordial.	Here's the cordial.

MIMÌ	MIMÌ
Chi parla?	Who's speaking?

MUSETTA *(porgendo il manicotto)*	**MUSETTA** *(handing her the muff)*
Io, Musetta.	Me. Musetta.

The final scene in a 1991 production by the Houston Grand Opera.

MIMÌ

O come è bello e morbido!
Non più, non più, le mani
allividite. Il tepore le abbellirà.

to Rodolfo

Sei tu che me lo doni?

MUSETTA

Sì.

MIMÌ

Tu! Spensierato!
Grazie. Ma costerà
Piangi? Sto bene.
Pianger così perché?
Qui…amor…sempre con te!
Le mani…al caldo…e dormire.

Silence

MIMÌ

Oh, how lovely and soft it is.
No more, no more…my hands all
ugly and cold…the warmth will heal them.

Did you give it to me?

MUSETTA

Yes, he did.

MIMÌ

You spendthrift!
Thank you…but the cost…
You're crying? I'm well.
Why are you crying like this?
Here…beloved…with you always!
My hands…the warmth…to sleep.

RODOLFO
Che ha detto il medico?

MARCELLO
Verrà.

MUSETTA *(pregando)*
Madonna benedetta,
fate la grazia a questa poveretta
che non debba morire.

breaking off, to Marcello

Qui ci vuole un riparo
perché la fiamma sventola.

Marcello sets a book on the table which acts as a shade.

Così.
E che possa guarire.
Madonna santa, io sono
indegna di perdono,
mentre invece Mimì
è un angelo del cielo.

RODOLFO
Io spero ancora. Vi pare
che sia grave?

MUSETTA
Non credo.

Schaunard approaches the bed.

SCHAUNARD *(piano a Marcello)*
Marcello, è spirata.

RODOLFO
What did the doctor say?

MARCELLO
He's coming.

MUSETTA *(praying)*
Oh blessed Mother,
be merciful to this poor child
who doesn't deserve to die.

We need a shade here;
the candle's flickering.

So.
Let her get well,
Holy Mother, I know
I'm unworthy of forgiveness,
but Mimì is an angel
come down from heaven.

RODOLFO
I still have hope.
You think it's serious?

MUSETTA
I don't think so.

SCHAUNARD *(softly to Marcello)*
Marcello, she's dead.

COLLINE *(entra e dàdel danaro*
a Musetta)
Musetta, a voi.
Come va?

COLLINE *(enters, and gives money*
to Musetta)
Here, Musetta.
How is she?

RODOLFO
Vedi, è tranquilla.

RODOLFO
You see, she's resting.

Rodolfo becomes aware of the strange expression of the others.

Che vuol dire?
Quell'andare e venire…
Quel guardarmi così?…

What does this mean?
This going back and forth?
Why are you looking at me like this?

MARCELLO
Coraggio.

MARCELLO
Courage.

Rodolfo runs over to the bed.

RODOLFO
Mimì!…Mimì!…

RODOLFO
Mimì!…Mimì!…

THE END

PHOTO CREDITS

All photographs are copyrighted by the photographers and in some instances by the lending institutions.

Jim Caldwell/Houston Grand Opera: 117, 153; Corbis-Bettmann: 10, 13, 17, 20, 49, 128; Dover Publications, Inc.: 9, 19, 23, 31; Hans Fahrmeyer/Santa Fe Opera: 38, 55; Winnie Klotz/Metropolitan Opera: 8, 36–37, 41; Joan Marcus: 14; Metropolitan Opera Archives: 18, 39, 42, 44, 45, 47, 80, 86, 107, 130; Ferrucio Nuzzo/EMI Ltd.: 26, 50; Picture Fund coutesy, Museum of Fine Arts, Boston: 32, 53; Dan Rest/Lyric Opera of Chicago: 24–25; Reuters/Corbis-Bettmann: 149; Marty Sohl/San Francisco Opera: 30; Underwood Photo Archives: 11; UPI/Corbis-Bettmann: 82.

LA BOHÈME

Giacomo Puccini

COMPACT DISC ONE

ATTO PRIMO/ACT ONE/ERSTER AKT/PREMIER ACTE

1	Questo Mar Rosso	4:14
2	Pensier profondo!	1:18
	Marcello/Rodolfo/Colline	
3	Legna!…Sigari!	3:41
	Rodolfo/Marcello/Colline/Schaunard	
4	Si può?…Chi è là?	5:09
	Benoit/Marcello/Schaunard/Colline/Rodolfo	
5	Io resto per terminar	0:54
	Rodolfo/Marcello/Colline/Schaunard	
6	Non sono in vena…Scusi	2:24
7	Oh! sventata, sventata!	1:37
	Rodolfo/Mimì	
8	Che gelida manima!	4:27
	Rodolfo	
9	Sì. Mi chiamano Mimì	4:54
	Mimì/Rodolfo	
10	Ehi! Rodolfo!	0:40
	Schaunard/Colline/Marcello/Rodolfo/Mimì	
11	O soave fanciulla	3:57
	Rodolfo/Mimì	

ATTO SECONDO/ACT TWO/ZWEITER AKT/DEUXIÈME ACTE

12	Aranci, datteri!	2:42
	Coro/Schaunard/Colline/Rodolfo/Mimì/Marcello	
13	Chi guardi?	2:59
	Rodolfo/Colline/Mimì/Schaunard/Marcello/Parpignol/Coro	
14	Viva Parpignol!	2:50
15	Domandatelo a me	2:30
	Coro/Marcello/Mimì/Schaunard/Colline/Rodolfo/Alcindoro/Musetta	
16	Quando men'vo	5:00
	Musetta/Marcello/Alcindoro/Mimì/Rodolfo/Schaunard/Colline	
17	Caro!…Fuori il danaro!	2:07
	Colline/Rodolfo/Schaunard/Coro/Marcello/Musetta/Mimì	

COMPACT DISC TWO

ATTO TERZO/ACT THREE/DRITTER AKT/TROISIÈME ACTE

1	Ohè, là, le guardie…Aprite!	3:54
	Coro/Un doganiere/Musetta	
2	Sa dirmi, scusi, qual'è l'osteria	1:04
	Mimì/Sergente/Un doganiere	
3	Mimì?!…Speravo di trovarvi qui	4:55
	Marcello/Mimì	
4	Marcello. Finalmente	1:07
	Rodolfo/Marcello/Mimì	
5	Mimì è una civetta	1:14
	Rodolfo/Marcello	
6	Mimì è tanto malata!	2:46
	Rodolfo/Marcello/Mimì	
7	Addio…D'onde lieta usci al tuo grido	3:19
	Mimì	

8   Dunque è proprio finita   5:33
         Rodolfo/Mimì/Marcello/Musetta

ATTO QUARTO/ACT FOUR/VIERTER AKT/QUATRIÈME ACTE

9   In un coupè?   1:21
10   O Mimì, tu più non torni   2:58
         Marcello/Rodolfo
11   Che ora sia?   2:23
12   Gavotta…Minuetto   1:44
         Rodolfo/Marcello/Schaunard/Colline
13   C'è Mimì…c'è Mimì   5:28
         Musetta/Rodolfo/Schaunard/Mimì/Marcello
14   Vecchia zimarra   3:21
         Colline/Schaunard
15   Sono andati?   5:05
         Mimì/Rodolfo/Schaunard
16   Dorme?…Riposa   4:58
         Musetta/Rodolfo/Marcello/Mimì/Schaunard/Colline

LA TRAVIATA

LA TRAVIATA

Giuseppi Verdi

TEXT BY DANIEL S. BRINK

Additional commentary by William Berger

BLACK DOG
& LEVENTHAL
PUBLISHERS
NEW YORK

Published by
Black Dog & Leventhal Publishers, Inc.
151 West 19th Street
New York, NY 10011

Distributed by
Workman Publishing Company
225 Varick Street
New York, NY 10014

Manufactured in China

Cover and interior design by Elizabeth Driesbach

ISBN-13: 978-1-57912-507-3

h g f e d c b a

Library of Congress Cataloging-in-Publication Data available on file.

La Traviata—one of the greatest works from the most celebrated opera composers in history—is one of the mainstays of the operatic stage. Verdi achieved a magical and delicate balance between a tragic love story, a socially and politically courageous plot and some of the most powerful and heartbreaking music ever written.

You will hear the entire opera on the two compact discs included on the inside front and back covers of this book. As you explore the book, you will discover the story behind the opera and its creation, the life of the composer, biographies of the principal singers and conductor, and the opera's text, or libretto, both in Italian and English. Expert commentary has been added to the libretto to aid in your appreciation and to highlight key moments in the score.

Enjoy this book and enjoy the music.

ABOUT THE AUTHOR

*D*aniel S. Brink is the Artistic Advisor and Principal Coach/Accompanist for the Colorado Opera Festival, Artistic Director for the Company Singers, a development program for young operatic hopefuls and Artistic Director/Conductor of the Colorado Springs Choral Society small ensemble, MOSI-AC. Mr. Brink is a lecturer in Music and principal accompanist at The Colorado College, and has performed extensively in the United States and Europe. He is a highly regarded director, recitalist, teacher, adjudicator and writer.

ACKNOWLEDGEMENTS

I would like to thank Annette Megneys of the Colorado College Music Library and Jan Boothroyd, Executive Director of the Colorado Opera Festival for their invaluable assistance in researching this project. I would also like to thank my editor, Jessica MacMurray, whose influence afforded me the opportunity to write about these beloved works.

LA TRAVIATA

*G*iuseppe Verdi—the name has been synonymous with opera for a century and a half. He was born into an Italy divided under French and Austrian rule, and his work would eventually play a part in Italy's unification. His voice gave Italy a musical identity when the whole artistic world was proclaiming Richard Wagner the wave of the future. Over a sixty-year career, he gave the world 32 operas, including rewrites, which were extensive. He wrote countless other works, the most famous of which is his *Requiem*, written on the death of Alesandro Manzoni, an Italian author whose work had inspired Verdi in his youth.

He was born on October 10, 1813, in the small village of Le Roncole in northern Italy. His father, Carlo Verdi, a poor

Giuseppe Verdi (1813–1901)

peasant, ran the local combination shop (an inn and tavern) and farmed a small plot of land. Verdi had only one sibling, a younger sister who was retarded and who died in her teenage years. As a child, he showed an early interest in music. It is said that he used to follow an itinerant fiddle player all around the village, and that he would be transfixed by the organ music at church on Sundays, sometimes forgetting his duties as acolyte. And sometime before his eighth birthday, Verdi's father gave him an old spinet—a small harpsichord—whose popularity had already long since been supplanted by the piano.

Carlo Verdi had dealings with Antonio Barezzi, a leading businessman in the larger town of Busseto three miles away. Barezzi owned the city's department store and was the president of the local Philharmonic Society, an amateur group which performed at local events and played concerts throughout the region. When Giuseppe was ten years old, his father and Barezzi arranged for him to go and board with a cobbler in Busseto, so that his general education could be taken over by Don Pietro Seletti, a priest at the local cathedral, and his musical education could be formalized under Ferdinando Provesi, music director at the cathedral.

The young Verdi proved himself a diligent worker, though he was more successful in his musical studies than in his other subjects. And every Sunday he walked the three miles to Le Roncole to play the organ at the village church. As Verdi's skills advanced, he composed marches and overtures for the Philharmonic Society and occasionally served as its conductor. At age 16, he moved into Barezzi's home and helped him both conduct his business affairs and coordinate his musical leadership in the city.

In 1832, it was decided that Giuseppe's talent warranted sending him to the Milan Conservatory. Milan was the musical capital of Italy and the home of La Scala, Italy's leading

Act II, Her Majesty's Theatre, London, 1856

opera house. At age 19, with the financial backing of Barezzi and a local charitable foundation, Verdi moved to Milan. However, he was not accepted at the Conservatory, and the reasons why were never given. He was sent instead to study privately with Vincenzo Lavigna, a respected conductor at La Scala, under whose tutelage Verdi thrived. Years later, when a desire was expressed to change the name of the Milan conservatory to the Verdi Conservatory, Verdi refused to grant permission, saying, "They didn't want me when I was young, they can't have me now that I'm old."

In the summer of 1833, Verdi's former mentor, Provesi, died, leaving the music director's post in Busseto open. Barezzi and the Philharmonic Society wanted Verdi for the job, while the leadership at the cathedral backed another candidate. This conflict divided the town into two camps and eventually required government intervention. In the end, Verdi won the position. The dispute had lasted three years, by which time Verdi's studies with Lavigna were completed. And his time in Milan had exposed him to the triumphs of the leading opera composers of the era—the sparkling comedies of Rossini, the masterful melodic gift of Bellini, and the seductive charm of Donizetti. He had also been presented with a libretto, *Oberto, Conte di San Bonifacio*, and had already begun work on it before he returned to Busseto to begin his new job.

With his education complete and a paying position in Busseto, he married Barezzi's eldest daughter, Margherita, with

Joan Cross as Violetta; Sadlers Wells Opera, 1941

whom he had fallen in love over the years of his close association with her father. He settled into his new job and family life, but continued to work on his opera and court the appropriate connections in Milan to see it produced. Verdi was introduced to Bartolomeo Merelli, the new impresario at La Scala, and after a long period of alternating promise and disappointment, he was granted a production of *Oberto* in the fall of 1839. The opera was a huge success and prompted Merelli to commission three more operas from Verdi. His new professional course appeared to be set, so Verdi resigned his position in Busseto and moved to Milan.

While success was the order of the day in his work, Verdi's personal life was unraveling tragically. Since their marriage, Margherita had borne Verdi two children, a daughter, Virginia, born in March of 1837, and a son, Icilio, born in July of 1838. One month and a day after Icilio's birth, Virginia suddenly died of an unidentified illness. Fourteen months later, in October of 1839, Icilio died.

Again, the cause was unknown. The young parents were horrified. Then, on June 18, 1840, Margherita died of encephalitis. Alone and devastated, Verdi pressed on through the premiere of his second opera, *Un Giorno di Regno*, the only comedy he would attempt until his final opera, *Falstaff*, debuted in 1893. *Un Giorno* was a dismal failure.

Professionally and personally defeated, Verdi wanted to stop composing and canceled his contract with Merelli, becoming a near recluse. Several months later, Verdi ran into Merelli on the street, and the impresario encouraged him to resume

his work. Gradually, Verdi
responded, and his next
effort, *Nabucco*, a biblical
epic on the Babylonian cap-
tivity of the Jews, was the
overwhelmingly successful
result. A particular chorus
from the opera, *Va, pensiero,
sull'ali dorate* (Fly, thought,
on golden wings), is sung
by the captive Hebrews as
they recall the beauty of
their homeland and long
for freedom. The Milanese
public, under oppressive
Austrian rule, identified

with the chorus's sentiment, and from the first performance
it became the anthem for an Italian nation longing for independence. Many years later, at Verdi's funeral, the thousands
who lined the streets began singing this chorus spontaneous-
ly as his body was carried by.

With the success of *Nabucco*, Verdi's financial worries were
over. Between 1843 and 1850, he produced 13 new operas,
most of which were warmly accepted by the public and critics
alike. While not all of these remain in the popular repertoire
today, they represent a steady growth in Verdi's musical style

and dramatic ideals. The construction of these operas owes much to Verdi's predecessors. They are made up of a series of "set numbers"—arias which reveal the inner thoughts of the characters and recitatives and ensembles that advance the dramatic action. Like Rossini, Bellini and Donizetti, the kings

Metropolitan Opera production of *La Traviata*, 1989

of the bel canto era, Verdi's primary musical tool was a gift for melody, where the orchestra plays a secondary role to the voice. (In contrast, in Wagner's music dramas, the orchestra almost becomes another character, and its contribution is essential to the dramatic flow.)

Of these early Verdi works, *Ernani*, *Macbeth* and perhaps *Luisa Miller* are the most frequently performed today, although all of them have received periodic revivals and even complete recordings in the past few decades. These three, however, best represent Verdi's capacity for emotional intensity and the vital, earthy quality that distinguishes his best work. Most of the operas of this period take place against the backdrop of political intrigue, and during these years Verdi had many run-ins with the Austrian censors. In the minds of the Italian people, Verdi was increasingly becoming a political figure, and lines from his operas became bywords for the resistance to Austrian occupation. In his opera, *Attila*, for example, we hear the line "*Avrai tu L'universo, resti l'Italia a me*" (You may have the rest of the world, leave Italy to me). This became the motto of the *Risorgamento*, the movement to unite Italy under one native ruler. In his *La Battaglia di Legnano*, there is a scene in which an imprisoned officer of the resistance throws himself into the river below, distraught at his inability to join his fellows in the march on the oppressor. At a performance of this opera in 1849, a soldier in the audience was so caught up in the passion of the moment that he threw himself out of the gallery and into the orchestra pit. Miraculously, no one was hurt.

Also during this period, to the annoyance of the Austrian police, the walls of most major cities in Italy were covered with graffiti saying "*Viva Verdi*." This cry of the underground had a double meaning: First, it was for many an acknowledgment of Giuseppe Verdi as a voice for the unification movement; it was also an acrostic for "*Viva Vittorio Emmanuele, Re D'Italia*"

(Long live Victor Emmanuel, King of Italy). Vittorio Emmanuele was then king of Piedmont, the northwestern region of the peninsula, and he was thought to be a sympathetic ruler. He would eventually become king of a mostly united Italy, and reign from 1861 to 1878. For himself, Verdi remained an unwilling political hero, saying throughout his life that he knew nothing of politics. He was even pressed into service for a time as a representative from Busseto and its district to the first Italian Parliament, but thought of himself as an ill-informed and ineffectual legislator.

The intervening years also saw important developments in Verdi's personal life. Giuseppina Strepponi was a leading soprano of the time, and she had known and worked with Verdi since the beginnings of his career. Her influence was instrumental in ensuring that his first opera, *Oberto*, was staged, and she had created the leading role of Abigaille in his triumphant *Nabucco*. They had remained good friends, but sometime during the middle of the 1840s, friendship blossomed into

Alexander Dumas (1824–1895)

Act III, Metropolitan Opera, 1981

love. She had retired from the stage and was teaching in Paris, where their affair probably began. By the end of the decade, she was living with Verdi in Busseto, much to the consternation of his father-in-law and mentor, Antonio Barrezzi, his parents, and the rest of the populace of his hometown, who shunned them both. Their relationship was idyllic, however, and after an inexplicable wait of over ten years, they were married in 1859. She remained his indispensable lover, helpmate and confidante for the rest of their lives. She died in 1897, a year and a half before Verdi's death.

In 1848, Verdi purchased his sprawling estate at Sant'Agata. This was to be his home and haven for the rest of his life.

Over the years, he had become a shrewd businessman, carefully overseeing the contracts for performances of all his works. Now he applied those same skills to the occupation of his ancestors, running a large and very successful farm in what was, at first glance, a flat and forbidding landscape. He studied modern farming techniques to improve the yield of the soil, and he contributed much to the area's depressed economy by employing many of the local peasants with whom he dealt generously. Through the years, farming proved to be an even greater passion for Verdi than music, and it contributed greatly to his wealth. He always thought of himself as a simple man from the country, and it was in this environment that his creative energies were most acute.

The years from 1850 to 1853 saw the creation of three of Verdi's most enduring works, *Rigoletto, Il Trovatore* and *La Traviata*. Until these operas, the characters to whom Verdi was attracted were mainly historical and monochromatic. A character was either all good or all bad, and Verdi's capacity to represent that in musical terms had developed well. Now, however, he actively sought enigmatic characters, ones who were both hostile and loving, hero and outcast. As a result, the way in which Verdi structured his operas underwent a change. Where his basic unit of construction had always been the aria, now it became the scene, and the result was heightened dramatic effect.

Rigoletto was based on Victor Hugo's *Le Roi S'Amuse (The King Amuses Himself)*. During its preparation, Verdi had no end of troubles with the censors, who initially banned the

libretto altogether. They no doubt thought the corrupt king in the story could all too easily be equated in the public mind with any number of the current Italian leaders placed in power by Austria. Through lengthy negotiation, Verdi was able to gain approval for the libretto, after changing the characters's names and the time and locale of the action, But he then had only 40 days to complete the score prior to its scheduled premiere.

Rigoletto is the story of a deformed jester whose beloved daughter is seduced by the libertine duke in whose court the jester entertains. Seeking revenge, he hires an assassin to kill the duke. Instead, the jester's daughter is accidentally killed as she attempts to save the duke who has loved her and left her. This work was an exceptionally lurid tale for the Italian stage at that time. Rigoletto, the hunchback jester, is both a loving father and an attempted murderer. Gilda, his daughter (who was raped), sacrifices her life for her rapist, and the decadent duke gets off scot-free. There are no unqualified heroes or completely innocent victims here, and it was a challenge to the moral sensibilities of the day. Still, the public was enthralled, though the critics dutifully objected to the subject matter.

Verdi's next endeavor was to set *El Trovador*, a Spanish drama by Gutierrez. It is a dark and complex story centered on the gypsy, Azucena. She is driven both by her vendetta against the Count di Luna and by her all-consuming love for her son, Manrico. This dual nature and moral ambiguity, as in the character of Rigoletto, was attractive to Verdi. He was very keen on maintaining the intensity of the Spanish version and rejected the work of his librettists several times during the creative

process. What resulted was a taut little drama with a wealth of deeply passionate music, though much of the real action of the story takes place offstage. The opera, *Il Trovatore*, opened in Rome on January 19, 1853, and was an unqualified success. It immediately began to be produced all over the operatic world.

Nicolai Gedda as Alfredo

In the winter of 1851–52, while he was working on *Il Trovatore* for its Roman debut, Verdi and Strepponi went to Paris. There, he saw "La Dame aux Camélias," a new play by Alexandre Dumas fils, based on the author's 1848 novel, *Camille.* Verdi may have been familiar with the widely read novel, as well as with the play, which was the rage in Paris. It was the character of Camille—called Violetta in the opera—that piqued Verdi's interest. Like the hunchback, Rigoletto, and the Gypsy, Azucena, the courtesan Violetta was a figure that would be shunned by polite society. Yet she is ennobled by her capacity for loving self-sacrifice. Verdi immediately commissioned a libretto from Francesco Maria Piave, who had contributed the verses for six of his previous operas including the highly esteemed *Macbeth* and *Rigoletto.* The opera, *La Traviata,* would be produced on March 6, 1853, at the Teatro La Fenice in Venice, only seven weeks after the world was first introduced to *Il Trovatore* in Rome.

Verdi spent the bulk of 1852 working on *Il Trovatore* and *La Traviata* concurrently. After his stay in Rome for the preparation and premiere of *Il Trovatore,* he returned to Busseto. There he received disturbing news from a friend in Venice. Fanny Salvini-Donatelli, the soprano who he had hired to create the role of Violetta, had been giving some substandard performances, and Verdi was warned that her work might mar the premiere of *La Traviata.* Writing quickly to Venice,

Act II, Scene II, guests masquerading at Flora's party.
Glyndebourne Festival Opera

Verdi requested the role be recast, but the soprano he preferred was unavailable, and it was contractually too late to search for another.

Verdi arrived in Venice only 13 days prior to the premiere. It had been his custom to arrive several weeks before an opening and meticulously oversee every facet of rehearsal and production. He also usually spent these final weeks orchestrating the new work, never promising the orchestral parts in the contract until the day before the final rehearsal. It is possible, in this case, that these last 13 days were actually spent feverishly orchestrating the score, and Verdi had no time to attend rehearsals. There is no correspondence from the time that recorded how he spent his time or what his reactions were to the preparation of his new work.

The premiere was a complete fiasco. The audience, polite at first, was increasingly cool as the opera progressed, and during the final act, in which Violetta is dying of consumption, there was continuous laughter. It seems that Salvini-Donatelli was not only the picture of health but rather plump, and her persistent cough became a source of comic relief rather than pathos. The critics acknowledged that the singers were most of the problem. The tenor singing the role of Violetta's lover, Alfredo, was losing his voice, and the baritone, in the role of Alfredo's father, Germont, put nothing into his performance. He had been the creator of the plum role of *Rigoletto* and was a well-known interpreter of the title role in Verdi's *Macbeth*, so the smaller, less pivotal role of Germont seem to him too inconsequential to warrant his careful attention.

Verdi, never one to be swayed by public opinion, was unusually cavalier about the opera's failure. The day after the opening, he dashed off a series of short notes to friends and associates. His note to a former student, Emanuele Muzio, typifies his demeanor; "Dear Emanuele: "*Traviata* last night—a fiasco. Was it my fault or the singers's? . . . Time will tell."

There is an atypical lack of correspondence from Verdi about the whole matter. The opera, originally written as a contemporary drama, was set in early 1700s for the Venice production—an alteration that Verdi would usually not have tolerated. Also, he had never been complacent about casting problems before, vehemently fighting for his rights to cast the first performances of works and even cancelling them if his wishes were not followed.

Whatever the reasons for his casual approach, *La Traviata* was simply shelved for a year, until Verdi was approached by a Signor Gallo, a violinist from Venice whose family owned a respected theatre there, the Teatro San Benedetto. He had enjoyed the opera and wanted to stage a revival at the smaller theater. On May 6, 1854, 14 months after its disastrous premiere, *La Traviata* took stage again to tremendous acclaim. Verdi mused that it was the same opera heard by the same public, and there was no accounting for the radical shift in their response. Like so many of its predecessors, it overcame a nightmarish premiere, was soon heard in all the world's major opera houses, and has remained an indispensable part of the standard repertoire to this day.

Perhaps both the opera's initial failure and ultimate success are due in part to the scandalous subject matter. Violetta, a beautiful young courtesan, abandons her lavish Parisian lifestyle for the true love of Alfredo, a penniless young man from Provence. They are blissfully happy until his father intervenes, demanding that Violetta break off the relationship, because the fiancé of the young man's sister will not marry

Dress Rehearsal, Glyndebourne Festival Opera

her while her brother's illicit union continues. Violetta agrees and sacrifices the idyllic relationship, telling Alfredo she no longer loves him. She returns to her empty life in Paris. In the end, alone and dying of tuberculosis, Violetta awaits Alfredo's return. His father tells him about her noble gesture, and

Alfredo comes to be reunited with her. His appearance gives her the hope of recovery, but it is too late, and she dies in his arms.

The Italian operatic audience was accustomed to seeing human tribulation padded by the trappings of historical distance. The immediacy of presenting a modern French courtesan as a sympathetic character, whose nobility of spirit made her sacrifice her only chance at real happiness for the sake of her lover's family, was seen as an affront to the social mores of the time. Yet this same scenario was seen as vindication by those ostracized because of their lifestyles, and they rallied around the work. Verdi, who at this time was still "living in sin" with Strepponi, was one of them.

The great Giuseppe Verdi, who had for many years subtly reflected the political injustices of his homeland in his operas, now appeared to be taking on the whole social order of his time.

THE STORY OF THE OPERA

Christine Nilsson as Violetta

Act 1

Violetta Valéry, a young and beautiful courtesan, is receiving guests at a lavish party at her beautiful Paris home. She warmly greets her dearest friend, Flora and her escort, the Marquis, who express concern about her capacity to host such a party, as she has recently been quite ill. Violetta responds with her personal philosophy, saying that she gives her life over to pleasure, and that pleasure is the best medicine for her ills.

Another friend, Viscount Gaston de Letorieres, enters with a friend, Alfredo Germont, a young man from Provence.

Alfredo Germont (Beniamino Prior) during the infamous *Drinking Song*, San Francisco Opera, 1980

Gaston introduces Alfredo to Violetta, telling her that the young man has long been an admirer. Violetta greets him warmly. After asking a servant if dinner is prepared, she calls on all to be seated and join in a toast. Gaston tells Violetta that during her recent illness Alfredo came to her home daily to inquire about her well-being. She is incredulous, but Gaston assures her it is true. She seeks verification from Alfredo, who admits it is true. She then teases her escort, the Baron Douphal, saying that he was nowhere near as attentive. The Baron replies that he has only known her a year, and Flora chides him for his response. The Baron then confides to Flora that he is developing a dislike for Alfredo.

Gaston invites the Baron to propose a toast, but he silently refuses. Everyone then begins coaxing Alfredo to propose a toast. He shyly asks Violetta if it would please her, and she responds that it would. Alfredo then begins a lively waltz song in praise of wine and pleasure, but especially in praise of love and the irresistible beauty of Violetta. She, in turn, sings that all, including love, is folly and that life's meaning is found in seeking pleasure.

They drink, and music is heard from an adjoining room. Violetta than invites her guests to go to the ballroom and dance. As they begin to leave the room Violetta rises to join them, but suddenly feels faint. Everyone gathers around her expressing concern, but she assures them that it is nothing and sends them in to dance, saying she will join them in a moment. All leave except Alfredo. Unaware that he is there, Violetta looks in a mirror and remarks at how pale she is. Alfredo chides her for her frivolous lifestyle, telling her she must take care of herself and that if she were his, he would take care of her. She responds that there is no one to care for her. Alfredo declares his love, but she dismisses it with a laugh. He is hurt by her response, and gradually she begins to understand that he is serious. They join in a duet in which Alfredo recounts the day he first saw her and how he has been in love with her ever since. She gently responds that she cannot love him or accept his love, that she can only offer him friendship and that he must find another love. She asks him to speak no more of love, and he replies that he will obey. She tenderly gives him a flower from her bosom, asking him to return it when it has

Chorus members of the San Francisco Opera celebrate a festive evening, Act I.

withered. "Tomorrow?" he asks. "Yes," she replies. They gently say good-bye, and Alfredo kisses her hand and leaves.

The guests reenter, noting that dawn is breaking and they must go. They all thank Violetta for her hospitality and gradually leave the house.

Alone, Violetta reflects on the profound affect Alfredo's declaration of love has had on her. Could this be what she has always longed for? Could she really escape her lonely and meaningless existence? But her pensive and hopeful mood changes abruptly. She declares that a meaningful love for her is folly, and she must continue to follow her frantic pursuit of pleasure until she dies. She stops short as she hears

Alfredo's voice from under her balcony, repeating his ardent love for her. She momentarily reconsiders his sincerity, but quickly returns to her assertion that she must be always free and ends the Act in a florid affirmation of the lifestyle she has chosen.

Act 2

SCENE ONE

We are in the drawing room of the country home where Alfredo and Violetta have come to live together. Alfredo enters in hunting attire and pauses to reflect on the wonderful life he and Violetta have shared since she left the whirlwind of her social life in Paris three months before. Together, and unmindful of the world, they have created the perfect haven of love.

Their maid, Annina, enters, dressed for travel and clearly having just returned from a trip. Alfredo asks where she has been. Reluctantly, she tells him that Violetta sent her to Paris to arrange for the sale of her belongings to support their new life together. Filled with shame at his naiveté, Alfredo vows to go to Paris and secure the funds necessary to pay their mounting debts. He departs.

Violetta enters and asks Alfredo's whereabouts. Annina simply replies that he has gone to Paris and will return by evening. Another servant enters and delivers an invitation from Flora to a dance that evening. Violetta remarks that Flora will wait for her in vain.

The servant reenters to announce that a gentleman has arrived to see Violetta. She asks the servant to show the visitor in, and the servant presents Giorgio Germont, Alfredo's father. She is startled, but graciously offers him a seat. After he sits, he rudely exclaims that his son's life is being ruined because of her. She responds indignantly and asks him to leave, but he tells her that his son plans to give her all his possessions. She tells him that can't be true and shows him the contract

Alfredo (Beniamino Prior) & Violetta (Valerie Masterson)

for the sale of all her goods. His brusque tone abates, and he asks how a woman capable of such nobility could have such a negative reputation. She replies that she loves Alfredo and has found happiness with him. She has made peace with her past, has repented and has been forgiven.

Verdi, 1867

The elder Germont then tells her the reason for his visit. He tells her of Alfredo's sister and her impending marriage. Her fiancé, however, will not marry her unless Alfredo abandons his illicit affair and returns to his family. Violetta responds that to leave Alfredo for a time will be difficult, but she will do it. A brief separation, however, is not what Germont is requesting—he must ask her to give him up forever. Horrified, Violetta tells him that she cannot give Alfredo up, that she has no friends or family, and has given up everything for his love. She also confides that she has a deadly disease and hasn't long to live. Germont suggests that young men like his son are fickle, and he may not always love her as he does now; since the union is not blessed by God, she may be left alone. Violetta reflects that her past sins will forever haunt her. Resigned, she tearfully tells Germont she will sacrifice the one precious thing in her life for his family's happiness. Germont comforts her, acknowledging her noble gesture and the quality of love she holds for Alfredo. He asks her if there is anything he can do for her,

and she in turn asks that after her death Alfredo may know of the sacrifice she made for love of him. They bid each other farewell, and Germont retires to the garden outside.

Violetta sits down, writes a farewell letter to her lover and seals it. Alfredo enters and startles her, asking to whom she is writing. She admits it was to him, but says he must read it later. He asks her if his father has come, telling her that he received a stern letter from him, but assuring her that the elder Germont will love her at first sight. She lies, telling Alfredo that his father has not come and that she should not be there when he does. Alfredo should calm him first. Weeping, Violetta declares her love for Alfredo and begs him to

Alfredo & Giorgio Germont at Flora's party, Act II

express his love in return. Bidding him farewell, she leaves through the garden.

Confused by her demeanor, Alfredo absentmindedly reads a few lines from a book and then notices a man in the garden. A servant enters, telling him that Violetta has left with Annina. Shortly after, a messenger enters to deliver Violetta's farewell letter. Alfredo begins to read it and with a cry of despair, he turns to find his father at the door and throws himself into his arms. Germont tries to comfort him with a tender aria recalling the beauty of Provence, where the young man was raised. Germont implores Alfredo to return to his home and be a source of pride to his family again. Alfredo, who has been sitting with his face buried in his hands, suddenly looks up in a rage. He concludes it was Baron Douphol who stole Violetta from him and promises revenge. His father begs him to abandon this madness and return home. Alfredo sees the invitation from Flora on the table and is sure he will find Violetta there. In spite of his father's efforts to stop him, he storms from the room, determined to go to Paris and retrieve Violetta.

Act 2

In the lavish salon of Flora's Paris home, she is entertaining guests. She tells the Marquis that Alfredo and Violetta are coming, but he informs her they are separated and that Violetta will be coming with Baron Douphol. Dr. Grenvil expresses his surprise, as he had seen them only yesterday and they appeared happy. A brilliant entertainment ensues in which masked guests perform as gypsies and matadors. Flora and the Marquis tease one another about imagined infidelities, and all join in the good-natured banter.

Alfredo arrives, and the guests inquire as to Violetta's whereabouts. He non-chalantly responds that he doesn't know where she is. They then invite him to play cards, and he goes to the gaming table with Gaston and other guests to play.

Violetta enters on Baron Douphol's arm. He sees Alfredo, and taking Violetta aside, demands that she not say a single word to him. Disturbed by the tense scene, Violetta is taken aside by Flora and the Doctor who quietly ask what has happened.

Meanwhile, Alfredo is winning at cards. He loudly boasts that one unlucky in love is lucky at cards, and that his winnings

Alfredo (Beniamino Prior) sings of his broken heart

will allow him to return to the country with the one who left him. The Baron challenges him to a game. Alfredo wins the first hand. Angrily, the Baron doubles the stakes. Alfredo wins again. The tension is broken by a servant announcing that dinner is served. Alfredo offers to continue the play, but the Baron answers that they will continue later. They all exit to the dining room.

Violetta quickly returns. She has asked Alfredo to come back to the salon so she can warn him against angering the Baron further. Alfredo enters the salon and disdainfully asks what Violetta wants. She tells him that she fears a duel, and if Alfredo should be killed, she would die. He arrogantly says he would cut the Baron down, and he asks her why she should care what happens to him. She begs him to leave. He responds that he will go only if she will follow. She confesses she has taken an oath not to stay with him. Alfredo demands to know who would make her take such an oath. Was it Douphol? Lying, Violetta answers, "Yes." Alfredo asks if she loves Douphol. Again, she lies, "Yes."

Infuriated, Alfredo runs to the door, calling all the guests back into the salon. They rush into the room, and Alfredo imperiously asks if they know this woman, who was once willing to sell all she had for love of him. He then declares that he will clear himself of the stain of this dishonor and repay what he owes her in full. He hurls his winnings at her feet. Humiliated, Violetta faints in Flora's arms.

The guests, horrified at Alfredo's actions, deride his insensitivity and demand that he leave at once. His father has arrived to witness the scene and expresses his contempt for his son's actions. Suddenly aware of what he has done, Alfredo comes to his senses and timidly expresses his remorse, arguing that he was driven to madness by the loss of his love. In a moving ensemble, all present express their various feelings: the Baron reviling Alfredo for his actions; the guests sympathizing with Violetta; and Germont, in an aside, reflecting on Violetta's virtue and faithfulness, about which only he truly knows. Violetta's voice soars above the ensemble as she expresses the hope that some day Alfredo will know the depth and breadth of her love for him. The Baron challenges Alfredo to a duel, and the remorseful young man is led away by his father.

Act 3

Violetta lies dying in her semi-darkened bedroom. Annina sits sleeping in a chair near her mistress's bed. Violetta awakens and requests some water, which Annina brings her. She then asks Annina to open the shutters. As she does, she sees Dr. Grenvil arriving in the street below. Violetta comments on what a faithful friend he has been and asks Annina's help in getting up to receive him. With difficulty, Annina helps Violetta to a nearby sofa, and upon entering, the doctor helps to make her comfortable.

He asks how she is feeling, and she responds that though she is suffering, she is at peace. The priest has been there to visit her, and he was most comforting. The doctor assures her that she will be feeling better soon. As he leaves, Annina asks about Violetta's condition, and the doctor tells her that she has only hours to live.

Annina returns to Violetta, offering encouragement. Violetta inquires if it is a holiday, and Annina tells her it is Carnival, and all of Paris is going mad. She then asks the maid how much money is left, and Annina replies they have 20 louis.

Violetta (Marie McLaughlin) in her final moments

46

Violetta instructs her to give ten to the poor, and when Annina suggests that won't leave them with much, Violetta assures her that it will be enough. She asks for her letters, then sends Annina away to make the donation.

Violetta opens a letter from Alfredo's father which she reads aloud. He tells her that the Baron was wounded in the duel, but is recovering. He also relates that Alfredo is abroad, but that he has been told of her sacrifice and is coming with his father to beg her forgiveness. The letter closes with his wishes for her happy future. It is, however, too late.

Violetta waits for Alfredo and his father, but they don't come. She looks in a mirror and sees how her disease has ravaged her. She mourns the loss of her happy love and says that her grave will be unmarked and unadorned by flowers or tears. She prays for God's forgiveness and desperately asks that she may come to Him.

As her soliloquy ends, Violetta hears the sound of revelers in the street. Annina enters and tries to keep her calm as she tells her that Alfredo is coming. He enters and they embrace ecstatically. He reaffirms his love and begs her forgiveness. She responds that there is nothing to forgive. Now they are together and nothing will separate them again. Alfredo paints an ideal picture of their future together. They will leave Paris for the country, they will make up for all their heartaches, her health will return and they will live together always in perfect bliss. In a euphoric trance, Violetta repeats his vision.

Strengthened by her joy, Violetta rises to her feet, saying they must go to church and give thanks for their reunion, but she

Violetta & Alfredo,
reunited

falters and collapses into a chair. Alarmed, Alfredo supports her, but she attempts to rally again, asking Annina to bring her dress. Unable even to dress herself, Violetta falls back in defeat, cursing her weakness. In a panic, Alfredo sends Annina for the doctor and Violetta repeats the command, telling Annina to inform the doctor that her love has returned, and she must live again.

The maid leaves, and Violetta tells Alfredo that if his return cannot make her live, nothing can. As Alfredo attempts to calm her, she bewails the loss of her young life and all her hopes for happiness. Then Alfredo's father enters, and Violetta greets him warmly. He tells her he has come to welcome her as his daughter. But with a gentle embrace, she tells him it is too late. The doctor enters, and Violetta tells him she is dying in the presence of those she loves. Realizing that her death is imminent, Germont is stricken with remorse for having caused the separation of the two lovers.

Violetta then takes a small medallion from a drawer. It is a portrait of herself which she gives to Alfredo so that he may remember her. She tells him that he will love again, and when he does, he should give the medallion to his love and tell her that it is a portrait of one who is in heaven, praying for their happiness. As Violetta repeats these sentiments, all present pour out their grief over her impending death. Suddenly, there is a change in her demeanor. She rises and says the pain is gone, that she is reviving. She is overcome with joy. Then just as suddenly, she falls lifeless on the sofa. Dr. Grenvil rushes to check her condition and confirms that she is gone while Alfredo, Germont and Annina cry out in despair.

LA TRAVIATA

Giuseppe Verdi

1813 - 1901

Violetta Valéry . . . . Beverly Sills
Alfredo Germont . . . . Nicolai Gedda
Giorgio Germont . . . . Rolando Panerai
Flora Bervoix . . . . Delia Wallis
Annina . . . . Mirella Fiorentini
Gastone . . . . Keith Erwen
Barone Douphol . . . . Terence Sharpe
Marchese d'Obigny . . . . Richard Van Allan
Dottore Grenvil . . . . Robert Lloyd
Giuseppe/Servant . . . . Mario Carlin
Commissionario . . . . William Elvin

Conducted by Aldo Ceccato
Royal Philharmonic Orchestra
The John Alldis Choir
Chorus Master: John Alldis

51

THE PERFORMERS

BEVERLY SILLS (Violetta Valèry) is one of the most amazing personalities ever to grace the operatic stage. For 50 years her presence has been felt throughout the world of opera and beyond. Born Belle Silverman in Brooklyn, she was a child star by the age of three and a fixture on New York radio until the age of twelve, when she "retired" to focus on her studies. These included Italian, French, and piano lessons, and voice lessons with the esteemed vocal pedagogue, Estelle Liebling. At the age of sixteen, Sills toured in operetta with the Schubert Opera Company, and a year later debuted with the Philadelphia Civic Opera and the esteemed San Francisco Opera Company.

In 1955 Sills joined the New York City Opera, achieving an early triumph in the New York premiere of Douglas Moore's *The Ballad of Baby Doe*. She continued with the company in leading roles, including all three heroines in Offenbach's *The Tales of Hoffman* in 1965. In 1966 she portrayed Cleopatra in Handel's *Giulio Cesare* to such unprecedented acclaim that it launched her international career.

Beverly Sills and her daughter, who is deaf.

In short order Sills conquered the operatic capitals of Europe, singing Mozart's "Queen of the Night" in *The Magic Flute* in Vienna, Pamira in Rossini's *The Siege of Corinth* at Milan's La Scala and the title role in Donizetti's *Lucia di Lammermoor* at Covent Garden. In the early 1970s, she sang all three of Donizetti's Tudor queens—*Maria Stuarda, Anna Bolena,* and *Elisabeth I* in *Roberto Deveraux* for her home company. These established her as one of the undisputed queens of bel canto in this century, and in 1975 she debuted at the Metropolitan Opera House as Pamira in Rossini's *The Siege of Corinth.*

Sills's repertoire encompasses more than 50 roles, from the Baroque rarity of Rameau's *Hippolyte et Aricie* to the twelve-tone intricacies of Nono's *Intolleranza*—and everything in between. One of her most famous portrayals was as Massenet's *Manon*, a work somewhat outside the mainstream of her standard fare. During her singing career she also did much to advance the cause of opera in America with her appearances on popular TV talk shows and in television specials, one of the most memorable of which paired her with the musical theater artist, Julie Andrews.

After retiring from the stage, Sills became General Director of the New York City Opera which she ran with distinction from 1979–89. Today she presides over the Board of Directors of Lincoln Center in New York, the premiere performing arts center in the nation. In 1980 she received the Presidential Medal of Freedom, and in 1985, a Kennedy Center Honor.

The role of Violetta holds a special place in Beverly Sills's heart. It was her first leading role as an aspiring young artist, one she performed countless times on tour, and it was also the vehicle for her successful debuts in Naples, Berlin and Venice. Early in life, she acquired the nickname "Bubbles," a name which reflects her ingratiating personality and a vocal quality which is so evident in this portrayal. Her unparalleled coloratura is dazzling in her first-act aria, *Sempre libera*, and the warmth of her second-act self-denial is heartrending. Her incredible acting skill is apparent in the careful handling of her third-act decline, in which the aria *Addio del passato* is particularly moving. In this recording we are treated to the broad vocal and dramatic range of one of the greatest ladies of the operatic stage.

NICOLAI GEDDA (Alfredo Germont) is widely regarded as having one of the most beautiful tenor voices of the century. He is frequently pointed to as the best possible model for young singers, who learn by listening to the integrity of his pitch, the beauty of his vocal lines and the ease of his technique. Also one of the most intelligent operatic artists of the century, he speaks and sings fluently in seven languages.

Gedda was born in Stockholm, the son of a Swedish mother and a Russian father. After leaving school he began a career in banking, but with the help of a client was able to begin vocal studies with the Swedish tenor, Carl Martin Oehman. After winning the Christine Nilsson Award, Gedda studied at the Royal Conservatory of Music in Stockholm.

He made his operatic debut in 1952 in *Le Postillon de Lonjumeau* at the Royal Opera House in Stockholm. Only months later, Gedda was hired to record the role of Dmitri the Pretender in Mussorgsky's *Boris Godunov*, and his future was secured. In 1953 he debuted at La Scala as Don Ottavio in Mozart's *Don Giovanni* and was chosen by Carl Orff to create the role of the groom in his *Il Trionfo di Afrodite*. Over the next two years he debuted at the Paris Opera and Covent Garden, and in 1957 he made his Metropolitan Opera debut, creating the role of Anatol in Samuel Barber's *Vanessa* in his first year there, and singing there regularly for over twenty years.

In 1964 he created the leading tenor role in the American premiere of Menotti's *The Last Savage*, and in 1965 he was given the title Court Singer to the Royal Court of Sweden, an honor conferred on fewer than 12 artists in 200 years. The scope of Gedda's repertoire is unsurpassed, including over 200 works in the concert and operatic repertoire. He is equally at home as Lensky in Tchaikovsky's *Eugene Onegin* or singing an English folk song. His extensive discography includes almost 40 complete opera recordings in six languages, encompassing both lyric and dramatic roles and affording him the honor of being the most recorded tenor alive. He remains active today, mainly as a recitalist and in concert, and his recording career has continued into the 1990s.

The role of Alfredo is perfectly suited to Gedda's voice, and he is at his lyric best in this recording, handling the intimacy of *De miei bollenti spiriti* and the bravado of the frequently omitted second-act cabaletta with equal aplomb.

ROLANDO PANERAI (Giorgio Germont) was born in the small town of Campi Bisenzio near Florence. He pursued his vocal studies in Florence and Milan and made his debut in 1946 in Florence as Enrico Ashton in Donizetti's *Lucia di Lammermoor*. Over the following two years he appeared regularly in Naples where he debuted as Pharoah in Rossini's *Mosé in Egitto*. In 1951 he made his La Scala debut as the high priest in Saint-Saëns's *Samson et Dalila*. He appeared there regularly for a

Swedish tenor Nicolai Gedda

number of years, singing such diverse roles as Appolo in Gluck's *Alceste* and the husband in Menotti's comedy, *Amelia al Ballo*. In 1957 he sang the title role in the Italian premiere of Hindemith's *Mathis der Maler* at La Scala, and in 1962 he created the title role in Turchi's *Il Buon Soldato Svejk* there.

Panerai's international career began in 1955 when he created the role of Ruprecht in Prokofiev's *The Fiery Angel* in Aix-en-Provence, where he also portrayed Mozart's Figaro. He debuted in Salzburg in 1957 as Ford in Verdi's *Falstaff*, and his American debut was with the San Francisco Opera in 1958, where he sang both the Rossini and Mozart Figaros and Marcello in Puccini's *La Bohème*. His career has included all the major houses in Italy, Great Britain, France, Germany and the United States, including the Metropolitan Opera in New York. He remains active today; two of his latest specialties are the title roles in Verdi's *Falstaff* and Puccini's *Gianni Schicchi*.

Panerai's extensive discography includes over twenty complete operas, ranging from Mozart to Wagner in the German repertoire and from Rossini to Puccini in the Italian repertoire. Panerai's Germont is an intimate paternal figure which he portrays with a consistent richness of sound and intelligent characterization. He is the perfect father to Gedda's delicate and vital Alfredo, and with the elegance of Sills's Violetta, he masterfully rounds out an ideal cast for Verdi's masterpiece.

ALDO CECCATO (the conductor), is a native of Milan who began his musical career as a successful young pianist, equally comfortable in the classical and jazz genres. He studied at the

Milan Conservatory and at Berlin's Hochschule fur Musik, where he conducted a student performance of Verdi's *Otello*. It was the concert in Milan where he conducted seven Vivaldi concerti that commanded the attention of the European musical establishment. He made his professional debut with *Don Giovanni* at Milan's Teatro Nuovo in 1964, and in 1966 he conducted the Italian premiere of Busoni's *Die Brautwahl* in Florence to critical acclaim. His early association with the famous Italian conductor-composer, Victor de Sabata, who admired the young conductor's interpretation of his tone poem *Juventu*, helped to establish demand for Ceccato's work.

His growing fame in Italy soon led to engagements in Germany, France, Britain and South America, and in 1969 Ceccato made his American debut at the Chicago Lyric Opera conducting Bellini's *I Puritani*. In 1970 he made his debut with the New York Philharmonic and went on to guest conduct all the major American orchestras. He also conquered all the major opera houses in Europe, guest conducting at Covent Garden, the Glyndebourne Festival and the Paris Opera, to name just a few. Since 1975, he has confined his activity primarily to Germany.

This *Traviata* is one of only two opera recordings under Ceccato's baton. He recorded Donizetti's *Maria Stuarda* also in 1971 and also with Beverly Sills. Known for his powerful leadership and attention to detail, Ceccato delivers an expansive reading of *La Traviata*, imbuing the genteel French setting with an unmistakably Verdian soul.

The Libretto

Act 1

PRELUDE

A drawing room in Violetta's home. In the background a door, opening to another room. There are two other lateral doors; to the left, a fireplace with a mirror over the mantel. In the centre of the room, a huge table richly laden. (Violetta is seated on a sofa, talking with Dr Grenvil and other friends. Some of her friends go to greet various guests as they arrive. Among them, the Baron and Flora, escorted by the Marquis.)

DISC NO. 1/TRACK 1

The Prelude begins with a somber theme which represents the tragedy of Violetta's illness and early death. It is a theme we will hear again at the beginning of act III. This motive gives way to the theme of Violetta's farewell to Alfredo at the end of act II, scene 1. Here it is a sad and elegant encapsulation of the heroine herself. The melody is first stated by violins and cellos (01:47), then repeated by the cellos (02:50) with a violin obbligato or countermelody above it.

DISC NO. 1/TRACK 2

The first scene opens with a lively theme that underscores the whole scene. This is real party music, reminiscent of the first scene of Verdi's previous opera, *Rigoletto*. The chorus speaks as one character throughout the opera, responding as one to the progressing action.

CORO I
Dell'invito trascorsa è già l'ora.
Voi tardaste.

CHORUS I
You were invited for an earlier hour.
You have come late.

CORO II
Giocammo da Flora, e giocando quell'ore volar.

CHORUS II
We were playing cards at Flora's,
and the time passed quickly.

VIOLETTA *(va loro incontro)*
Flora, amici, la notte che resta d'altre gioie
qui fate brillar. Fra le tazze più viva è la
festa.

VIOLETTA *(going to greet them)*
Flora, my friends, the rest of the evening
will be gayer because you are here. Surely
the evening is livelier with good food and
drink?

FLORA, MARCHESE
E goder voi potrete?

FLORA, MARQUIS
And can you be lively?

VIOLETTA
Lo voglio; al piacere m'affido, ed io soglio
con tal farmaco i mali sopir.

VIOLETTA
I must be.
I give myself to pleasure, since pleasure
is the best medicine for my ills.

TUTTI
Sì, la vita s'addoppia al gioir.

ALL
Indeed, life is doubly heightened by pleasure.

(The Viscount Gastone de Letorières enters with Alfredo Germont. Servants are busily engaged at the table.)

GASTONE
In Alfredo Germont, o signora, ecco un
altro che molto v'onora; pochi amici a lui
simili sono.

GASTONE
My dear Madam, in Alfredo Germont
I present a man who greatly admires you;
few friends are so fine as he.

VIOLETTA
(Violetta dà la mano ad Alfredo, che gliela bacia.)
Mio Visconte, mercé di tal dono.

VIOLETTA
(She offers her hand to Alfredo, who kisses it.)
My dear Viscount, thank you for this gift.

MARCHESE
Caro Alfredo -

MARQUIS
My dear Alfredo -

ALFREDO
Marchese -

ALFREDO
Marquis -

(They shake hands.)

GASTONE *(ad Alfredo)*	**GASTONE** *(to Alfredo)*
T'ho detto:	As I told you,
l'amistà qui s'intreccia al diletto.	here friendship joins with pleasure.

(Meanwhile the servants have finished setting the table.)

VIOLETTA	**VIOLETTA**
Pronto è il tutto?	Is everything ready?
(Un servo fa cenno di sì.)	*(A servant nods in affirmation.)*
Miei cari, sedete:	Please be seated:
è al convito che s'apre ogni cor.	it is at table that the heart is gayest.

TUTTI	**ALL**
Ben diceste - le cure segrete fuga sempre	Well spoken - secret cares fly before that
l'amico licor.	great friend, wine.

(They take their places at the table. Violetta is seated between Alfredo and Gastone. Facing her Flora takes her place between the Marquis and the Baron. The remaining guests take their various places around the table. A moment of silence as the food is served. Violetta and Gastone are whispering to each other.)

È al convito che s'apre ogni cor.	It is at table that the heart is gayest.

GASTONE	**GASTONE**
Sempre Alfredo a voi pensa.	Alfredo thinks of you always.

VIOLETTA	**VIOLETTA**
Scherzate?	You are joking?

GASTONE	**GASTONE**
Egra foste, e ogni dì con affanno qui volò,	While you were ill, every day he called
di voi chiese.	to ask about you.

VIOLETTA	**VIOLETTA**
Cessate. Nulla son io per lui.	Don't talk like that. I am nothing to him.

GASTONE Non v'inganno.	**GASTONE** I do not deceive you.
VIOLETTA Vero è dunque? Onde ciò? Nol comprendo.	**VIOLETTA** It is true then? But why? I don't understand.
ALFREDO Sì, egli è ver.	**ALFREDO** Yes, it is true.
VIOLETTA Le mie grazie vi rendo. Voi, barone, non faceste altrettanto.	**VIOLETTA** I thank you. You, Baron, were less attentive.
BARONE Vi conosco da un anno soltanto.	**BARON** I have only known you for a year.
VIOLETTA Ed ei solo da qualche minuto.	**VIOLETTA** And he for just a few minutes.
FLORA *(sottovoce al Barone)* Meglio fora se aveste taciuto.	**FLORA** *(in a low voice, to the Baron)* It would have been better to say nothing.
BARONE *(piano a Flora)* M'è increscioso quel giovin.	**BARON** *(softly, to Flora)* I don't like this young man.
FLORA Perché? A me invece simpatico egli è.	**FLORA** Why not? I think he's very pleasant.
GASTONE *(ad Alfredo)* E tu dunque non apri più bocca?	**GASTONE** *(to Alfredo)* And you have nothing more to say?
MARCHESE *(a Violetta)* È a madama che scuoterlo tocca.	**MARQUIS** *(to Violetta)* It's up to you to make him talk.

VIOLETTA
Sarò l'Ebe che versa.

ALFREDO
E ch'io bramo immortal come quella.

TUTTI
Beviamo.

GASTONE
O barone, né un verso, né un viva
troverete in quest'ora giuliva?

(The Baron shakes his head.)

Dunque a te -

(nodding to Alfredo)

TUTTI
Sì, sì, un brindisi.

ALFREDO
L'estro non m'arride.

GASTONE
E non sei tu maestro?

ALFREDO *(a Violetta)*
Vi fia grato?

VIOLETTA
Sì.

ALFREDO *(s'alza)*
Sì? L'ho già in cor.

VIOLETTA
I shall be Hebe, the cup-bearer.

ALFREDO
And, like her, immortal, I hope.

ALL
Let us drink.

GASTONE
Baron - can't you find a toast for this happy
occasion?

Then it's up to you -

ALL
Yes, yes, a toast.

ALFREDO
Inspiration fails me.

GASTONE
But aren't you a master?

ALFREDO *(to Violetta)*
Would it please you?

VIOLETTA
Yes.

ALFREDO *(rising)*
Yes? I have it already in my heart.

MARCHESE	MARQUIS
Dunque attenti!	Then - attention!

TUTTI	ALL
Sì, attenti al cantor.	Yes, to the poet.

DISC NO. 1/TRACK 3

Libiamo is one of the most famous "drinking songs" in the operatic repertoire. Its lusty waltz rhythm is a favorite of opera lovers, and it is frequently extracted and performed outside the opera. Within the drama, the swirling melody perfectly describes the giddy social rounds of the Parisian party circuit.

ALFREDO	ALFREDO
Libiamo, ne' lieti calici	Drink from the joyful glass,
che la bellezza infiora,	resplendent with beauty,
e la fuggevol ora	drink to the spirit of pleasure
s'inebrii a voluttà.	which enchants the fleeting moment.
Libiam ne' dolci fremiti	Drink to the thrilling sweetness
che suscita l'amore,	brought to us by love,
poiché quell'occhio al core	for these fair eyes, irresistibly,
(indicando Violetta)	(indicating Violetta)
onnipotente va.	pierce us to the heart.
Libiamo amore, amor fra i calici	Drink - for wine
più caldi baci avrà.	will warm the kisses of love.

TUTTI	ALL
Ah! Libiam, amor fra i calici	Drink - for wine
più caldi baci avrà.	will warm the kisses of love.

VIOLETTA *(s'alza)*	VIOLETTA *(rising)*
Tra voi saprò dividere	I shall divide my gaiety
il tempo mio giocondo;	among you all;
tutto è follia nel mondo	Everything in life is folly,
ciò che non è piacer.	except for pleasure.
Godiam, fugace e rapido	Let us be joyful, for love

è il gaudio dell'amore,
è un fior che nasce e muore,
né più si può goder.
Godiam, c'invita un fervido
accento lusinghier.

is a fleeting and short-lived joy.
A flower which blossoms and fades,
whose beauty is soon lost forever.
Be joyful - a caressing voice
invites us warmly to joy.

TUTTI
Ah! godiamo, la tazza e il cantico
la notte abbella e il riso;
in questo paradiso
ne scopra il nuovo dì.

ALL
Ah! Be carefree - for wine and song
with laughter, embellish the night.
The new day breaking will find us still
in this happy paradise.

VIOLETTA *(ad Alfredo)*
La vita è nel tripudio.

VIOLETTA *(to Alfredo)*
Life is only pleasure.

ALFREDO *(a Violetta)*
Quando non s'ami ancora.

ALFREDO *(to Violetta)*
For those who don't know love.

VIOLETTA
Nol dite a chi l'ignora.

VIOLETTA
Speak not of love to one who knows not
what it is.

ALFREDO
È il mio destin così.

ALFREDO
Such is my destiny.

TUTTI
Godiamo, la tazza e il cantico
la notte abbella e il riso;
in questo paradiso
ne scopra il nuovo dì.

ALL
Be carefree - for wine and song
with laughter, embellish the night.
The next day breaking will find us still
in this happy paradise.

(The sound of music is heard, coming from an adjoining room.)

Reknowned soprano Mirella Freni, as Violetta

In this section, Violetta's and Alfredo's exchanges are heard in relief against the background dance music. She is keeping up a brave front at this point, both about her illness and her vulnerability to true love.

Che è ciò?	What is that?
VIOLETTA	**VIOLETTA**
Non gradireste ora le danze?	Wouldn't you like to dance now?
TUTTI	**ALL**
Oh, il gentil pensier! Tutti accettiamo.	How kind of you! We accept with pleasure.
VIOLETTA	**VIOLETTA**
Usciamo dunque.	Let us go, then.

(As they are going out through the centre door, Violetta suddenly turns pale.)

Ohimè!	Oh!
TUTTI	**ALL**
Che avete?	What is the matter?
VIOLETTA	**VIOLETTA**
Nulla, nulla.	Nothing, it is nothing.
TUTTI	**ALL**
Che mai v'arresta?	Why have you stopped here?
VIOLETTA	**VIOLETTA**
Usciamo.	Let us go out.

(She takes a few steps, but then is forced to stop again and to sit down.)

Oh Dio!	Oh God!

TUTTI Ancora!	**ALL** Again!
ALFREDO Voi soffrite?	**ALFREDO** Are you ill?
TUTTI Oh ciel! Ch'è questo?	**ALL** Heavens, what can it be?
VIOLETTA Un tremito che provo. Or là passate.	**VIOLETTA** It's just a chill. Go on - please - there.

(She points towards the other room.)

Fra poco anch'io sarò.	In just a few minutes I shall come -
TUTTI Come bramate.	**ALL** As you wish.

(All except Alfredo go into the other room.)

VIOLETTA *(Si alza e va a guardarsi allo specchio.)* Oh, qual pallor!	**VIOLETTA** *(looking into a mirror)* How pale I am!

(turning she sees Alfredo)

Voi qui.	You are here!
ALFREDO Cessata è l'ansia che vi turbò?	**ALFREDO** Are you feeling better now?
VIOLETTA Sto meglio.	**VIOLETTA** Yes, better, thank you.

Violetta & Alfredo (Beniamino Prior & Valerie Masterson)

ALFREDO
Ah, in cotal guisa v'ucciderete - aver v'è
d'uopo cura dell'esser vostro -

VIOLETTA
E lo potrei?

ALFREDO
Oh, se mia foste,
custode io veglierei pe' vostri soavi dì.

VIOLETTA
Che dite? Ha forse alcuno
cura di me?

ALFREDO *(con passione)*
Perché nessuno al mondo v'ama.

VIOLETTA
Nessun?

ALFREDO
Tranne sol io.

VIOLETTA
Gli è vero. Sì grande amore dimenticato
avea.

ALFREDO
Ridete? E in voi v'ha un core?

VIOLETTA
Un cor? Sì, forse... e a che lo richiedete?

ALFREDO
Ah, se ciò fosse. Non potreste allora celiar.

ALFREDO
Ah, this way you will kill yourself -
you must take care of yourself -

VIOLETTA
But can I?

ALFREDO
If you were mine,
I should watch over you.

VIOLETTA
What are you saying? Is there anyone
to care for me?

ALFREDO *(passionately)*
That's because no one in the world loves you -

VIOLETTA
No one?

ALFREDO
Except me.

VIOLETTA
It's true! I had forgotten this great love.

ALFREDO
You laugh? Have you no heart?

VIOLETTA
A heart? Yes, perhaps - but why do you ask?

ALFREDO
Ah, if that were so, then you couldn't laugh
at me.

| **VIOLETTA** | **VIOLETTA** |
| Dite davvero? | Are you serious? |

| **ALFREDO** | **ALFREDO** |
| Io non v'inganno. | I do not deceive you. |

| **VIOLETTA** | **VIOLETTA** |
| Da molto è che mi amate? | Have you been in love with me for long? |

DISC NO.1/TRACK 5

Un dì felice, eterea. **In this intimate duet, Alfredo recalls his sight of Violetta and rhapsodizes about his love for her. Soon (00:39) his halting, self-conscious phrases expand into a lush melody that comes to represent their love and which reappears throughout the opera.**

ALFREDO	**ALFREDO**
Ah, sì; da un anno.	Yes, for a year.
Un dì felice, eterea,	One day you passed before me,
mi balenaste innante,	happy and light as air,
e da quel dì tremante	and ever since that day,
vissi d'ignoto amor,	even without knowing it, I loved you -
di quell'amor ch'è palpito	with that love which is the very breath
dell'universo intero,	of the universe itself -
misterioso, altero,	mysterious and noble,
croce e delizia al cor.	both cross and ecstasy of the heart.

VIOLETTA	**VIOLETTA**
Ah, se ciò è ver, fuggitemi.	Ah, if this is true, then leave me -
Solo amistade io v'offro:	I offer you only friendship:
amar non so, nè soffro	I cannot love, nor can I accept
un così eroico amore.	so heroic a love from you.
Io sono franca, ingenua;	I am simple and frank.
altra cercar dovete;	You must find another.
non arduo troverete	It won't be hard, then,
dimenticarmi allor.	for you to forget me.

ALFREDO
Ah, amore misterioso, altero,
croce e delizia al cor.

ALFREDO
Love mysterious and noble,
both cross and ecstasy of the heart.

VIOLETTA
Non arduo troverete dimenticarmi allor.

VIOLETTA
It won't be hard, then, for you to forget me.

DISC NO. 1/TRACK 6

The party and its music literally burst in on Violetta's private moment with Alfredo, as Gastone opens the door. Violetta's dialogue with Alfredo suggests other, more personal, doors are opening as well.

GASTONE (sulla porta di mezzo)
Ebben? Che diavol fate?

GASTONE (in the doorway)
Well, now? What the devil are you doing?

VIOLETTA
Si folleggiava.

VIOLETTA
We were joking.

GASTONE
Ah, ah! Sta ben - restate.

GASTONE
Aha! Good! Please stay.

(He withdraws.)

VIOLETTA
Amor dunque non più.
Vi garba il patto?

VIOLETTA
Then - no more love.
Do you accept the pact?

ALFREDO
Io v'obbedisco. Parto.

ALFREDO
I obey. I shall leave you.

VIOLETTA (si toglie un fiore dal seno)
A tal giungeste?
Prendete questo fiore.

VIOLETTA (taking a flower from her bosom)
It's like that, then?
Take this flower.

ALFREDO
Perché?

ALFREDO
Why?

VIOLETTA
Per riportarlo -

ALFREDO
Quando?

VIOLETTA
Quando sarà appassito.

ALFREDO
Oh! Ciel! Domani -

VIOLETTA
Ebben, domani.

ALFREDO (*prende con trasporto il fiore*)
Io son felice!

VIOLETTA
D'amarmi dite ancora?

ALFREDO (*per partire*)
Oh, quanto v'amo!

VIOLETTA
Partite?

ALFREDO (*torna a lei, le bacia la mano*)
Parto.

VIOLETTA
Addio.

ALFREDO
Di più non bramo.

VIOLETTA
You shall bring it back -

ALFREDO
When?

VIOLETTA
When it has withered.

ALFREDO
Oh Heavens! Tomorrow.

VIOLETTA
Good, tomorrow.

ALFREDO (*joyously accepting the flower*)
I am happy!

VIOLETTA
Do you still think you love me?

ALFREDO (*about to leave*)
Oh, how much I love you!

VIOLETTA
You are leaving?

ALFREDO (*coming near her, kissing her hand*)
I am leaving.

VIOLETTA
Goodbye.

ALFREDO
I desire nothing more.

ALFREDO, VIOLETTA	**ALFREDO, VIOLETTA**
Addio. Addio.	Goodbye. Goodbye.

(Alfredo goes out as the other guests return to the drawing room, flushed from dancing.)

The exhilarating gaiety of the guests's music as they take their leave of Violetta reflects the exhausting relentlessness of the pleasure-seekers's lifestyle.

TUTTI	**ALL**
Si ridesta in ciel l'aurora	Dawn is breaking in the sky
e n'è forza di partire;	and we must leave.
mercé a voi, gentil signora,	Thank you, gentle lady,
di sì splendido gioir.	for this delightful evening.
La città di feste è piena,	The city is filled with parties,
volge il tempo dei piacer;	the season of pleasure is at its height.
nel riposo ancor la lena	We shall sleep now, to regain our strength
si ritempri per goder.	for another night of joy.

(They go out.)

Alone, Violetta muses on Alfredo's expressions of love. This begins a scene lasting twelve and a half minutes—a real tour de force for the solo soprano on stage.

VIOLETTA *(sola)*	**VIOLETTA** *(alone)*
È strano! È strano! In core	How strange! How strange! His words
scolpiti ho quegli accenti!	are burned upon my heart!
Saria per me sventura un serio amore?	Would a real love be a tragedy for me?
Che risolvi, o turbata anima mia?	What decision are you taking, oh my soul?

A dress rehearsal at the Glyndebourne Festival Opera

Null'uomo ancora t'accendeva - O gioia	No man has ever made me fall in love.
ch'io non conobbi, esser amata amando!	What joy, such as I have never known -
E sdegnarla poss'io	loving, being loved!
per l'aride follie del viver mio?	And can I scorn it
	for the arid nonsense of my present life?

DISC NO.1/TRACK 9

Ah, fors'è lui, is a very well-known and masterfully constructed aria. It begins with halting phrases in a minor key as Violetta reflects on her strange reaction to Alfredo's declaration of love. The moment is truly internal, and the music requires a thoroughly different vocal expression than anything Violetta has yet sung. Her reflections eventually include the great love theme Alfredo had sung, sounding here almost like a prayer.

Ah, fors'è lui che l'anima	Ah, perhaps he is the one
solinga ne' tumulti	whom my soul,
godea sovente pingere	lonely in the tumult, loved
de' suoi colori occulti!	to imagine in secrecy!
Lui che modesto e vigile	Watchful though I never knew it,
all'egre soglie ascese,	he came here while I lay sick,
e nuova febbre accese,	awakening a new fever,
destandomi all'amor.	the fever of love,
A quell'amor ch'è palpito	of love which is the very breath
dell'universo intero,	of the universe itself -
misterioso, altero,	Mysterious and noble,
croce e delizia al cor!	both cross and ecstasy of the heart.

DISC NO.1/TRACK 10

Follie! Follie! In a sudden change of mood, Violetta escapes her reverie and reasserts her preference for her gay lifestyle. The orchestra skips along with her as what is mainly a role for lyric soprano becomes a coloratura showpiece.

Follie! follie! Delirio vano è questo!	Folly! All is folly! This is mad delirium!
Povera donna, sola,	A poor woman, alone, lost in this

abbandonata in questo
popoloso deserto
che appellano Parigi. Che spero or più?
Che far degg'io? Gioire,
di voluttà ne' vortici perir.
Gioir, gioir!

crowded desert which is known to men as
Paris. What can I hope for?
What should I do? Revel
in the whirlpool of earthly pleasures.
Revel in joy! Ah!

DISC NO.1/TRACK 11

Sempre libera ("Forever free"). **Violetta defines her creed in this most famous and difficult cabaletta. (The term is derived from the Italian word, cavallo, meaning "horse," and
the music gallops along appropriately.) In an interesting dramatic effect, Alfredo's voice
is heard from outside, declaring again his love for her (00:59), but Violetta will not be
swayed. Her declaration of independence brings the act to a close with a stunning penul-
timate E-flat above high C—a note not written by Verdi, but a modern embellishment
expected by most modern listeners.**

Sempre libera degg'io
folleggiare di gioia in gioia,
vo' che scorra il viver mio
pei sentieri del piacer.
Nasca il giorno, o il giorno muoia,
sempre lieta ne' ritrovi,
a diletti sempre nuovi
dee volare il mio pensier.

Forever free, I must pass
madly from joy to joy.
My life's course shall be
forever in the paths of pleasure.
Whether it be dawn or dusk,
I must always live. Ah!
Gaily in the world's gay places,
ever seeking newer joys.

ALFREDO *(sotto al balcone)*
Amore, amor è palpito...

ALFREDO *(outdoors, under the balcony)*
Love is the very breath...

VIOLETTA
Oh!

VIOLETTA
Oh!

ALFREDO
...dell'universo intero -

ALFREDO
...of the universe itself -

VIOLETTA
Oh amore.

ALFREDO
Misterioso, misterioso, altero,
croce, croce e delizia,
croce e delizia, delizia al cor.

VIOLETTA
Follie! follie! Ah sì! Gioir, gioir!
Sempre libera degg'io
folleggiare di gioia in gioia,
vo' che scorra il viver mio
pei sentieri del piacer.
Nasca il giorno, o il giorno muoia,
sempre lieta ne' ritrovi,
a diletti sempre nuovi,
dee volare il mio pensier.

ALFREDO
Amor è palpito
dell'universo -

VIOLETTA
Ah! Dee volar il mio pensier.
Ah! il mio pensier. Il mio pensier.

VIOLETTA
Love.

ALFREDO
Mysterious and noble,
both cross and ecstasy,
cross and ecstasy of the heart.

VIOLETTA
Folly! Folly! Ah yes! From joy to joy,
forever free, I must pass
madly from joy to joy.
My life's course shall be
forever in the paths of pleasure.
Whether it be dawn or dusk,
I must always live. Ah!
Gaily in the world's gay places,
ever seeking newer joys, etc.

ALFREDO
Love is the very breath
of the universe itself.

VIOLETTA
Oh! My thoughts have to seek new joys.
Oh! My thoughts. My thoughts.

Act 2

SCENE ONE

*A country house near Paris. A drawing room on the ground floor. In the background, facing the audi-
ence, there is a fireplace; on the mantelpiece, a clock and above it a mirror. On either side of the fireplace,
French doors open on a garden. On the floor above, two other doors, facing each other. Chairs, tables,
books, writing materials.*

(Alfredo enters in hunting clothes.)

DISC NO. 1/TRACK 12
**The second act begins in the idyllic setting of Alfredo and Violetta's country hideaway.
The vigorous introduction in the strings describes the joy of the young lovers in their new
life together.**

DISC NO. 1/TRACK 13
De' miei bollenti spiriti **is another famous aria which frequently finds its way to the concert
stage. Accompanied by energetic pizzicato strings, Alfredo pours out his youthful, ardent
euphoria. Verdi did not specify a tempo for this aria, and interpretations vary widely. It is
sometimes performed very quickly, emphasizing Alfredo's impetuosity. In this performance, a statelier rendition convinces us of the sincerity of Alfredo's love.**

ALFREDO *(depone il fucile)*
Lunge da lei per me non v'ha diletto!
Volaron già tre lune
dacché la mia Violetta
agi per me lasciò, dovizie, amori
e le pompose feste ov'agli omaggi avvezza,
vedea schiavo ciascun di sua bellezza.

ALFREDO *(putting down his shotgun)*
I have no joy in life when she is far away!
Three months have passed
since Violetta gave up for me
a life of ease, luxury, love affairs
and the pomp of society, where, surrounded
by adoration, she enslaved all with her

Ed or contenta in questi ameni luoghi
tutto scorda per me. Qui presso
a lei io rinascer mi sento.
E dal soffio d'amor rigenerato
scordo ne' gaudi suoi tutto il passato.
De' miei bollenti spiriti
il giovanile ardore
ella temprò col placido sorriso dell'amor!
Dal dì che disse: Vivere
io voglio a te fedel, ah, sì
dell'universo immemore,
io vivo quasi in ciel.

beauty. Now, happy in this quiet country
home, she has forgotten everything for me.
And here, near her, I feel like a man
reborn; invigorated by the pulse of love,
I have forgotten the past in the joy of being
with her. The violent fire of my youthful
spirits was tempered by the quiet smile of
her love!
Ever since the day when she said:
"I want to live only for you"
I seem to live in heaven,
unmindful of the world.

(Annina enters, dressed for travelling.)

DISC NO.1/TRACK 14

As Alfredo grills Annina regarding the reasons for her trip to Paris, he is accompanied by
agitated figures in the strings. However sincere Alfredo may be in his love, he is still inse-
cure about the relationship.

ALFREDO
Annina, donde vieni?

ALFREDO
Annina, where have you come from?

ANNINA
Da Parigi.

ANNINA
From Paris.

ALFREDO
Chi tel commise?

ALFREDO
Who sent you?

ANNINA
Fu la mia signora.

ANNINA
My mistress.

ALFREDO
Perché?

ALFREDO
Why?

ANNINA	**ANNINA**
Per alienar cavalli, cocchi,	To take the horses, the carriages,
e quanto ancor possiede.	and whatever else is hers.
ALFREDO	**ALFREDO**
Che mai sento!	What is this!
ANNINA	**ANNINA**
Lo spendio è grande a viver qui solinghi.	It is very expensive, living here all alone.
ALFREDO	**ALFREDO**
E tacevi?	What are you hiding from me?
ANNINA	**ANNINA**
Mi fu il silenzio imposto.	I was sworn to silence.
ALFREDO	**ALFREDO**
Imposto? Or v'abbisogna?	Sworn! Tell me, how much is needed?
ANNINA	**ANNINA**
Mille luigi.	A thousand louis.
ALFREDO	**ALFREDO**
Or vanne - andrò a Parigi.	Go now - I shall go to Paris.
Questo colloquio non sappia la signora.	Madam must know nothing of our talk.
Il tutto valgo a riparare ancora.	I can still take care of everything.

DISC NO. 1/TRACK 15

This piece is a cabaletta for tenor, frequently cut by at least half, if not altogether, because
it tends to hold up the dramatic action. In this recording, it is restored in full and ends on
a magnificent high C!

Oh mio rimorso! Oh, infamia!	Oh remorse! Oh infamy!
Io vissi in tale errore.	I have lived in such blind ignorance.

Ma il turpe sonno a frangere,	But this vile torpor has been broken,
Il ver mi balenò!	By the flash of truth!
Per poco in seno acquetaiti,	Lie pacified for a brief time in my breast,
O grido dell'onore;	Oh, cry of honor;
M'avrai securo vindice;	You will have sure vengeance of me;
Quest'onta laverò.	I will wash away this shame.
O mio rossor! Oh infamia!	Oh shame! Oh infamy!
Ah si, quest'onta laverò, *ecc.*	Oh yes, I will wash away this shame, *etc.*
O mio rossor! Oh infamia! *ecc.*	Oh remorse! O infamy! *etc.*

(He leaves. Soon Violetta enters with various papers in her hand. She speaks with Annina.)

DISC NO. 1/TRACK 16

Alfredo's father enters the scene to an ominous theme in the low strings [1:04]. Thus begins the long confrontation scene between Germont and Violetta, in many ways the emotional core of the whole opera. The music will shift at several points as the two negotiate their various claims.

VIOLETTA	**VIOLETTA**
Alfredo?	Alfredo?
ANNINA	**ANNINA**
Per Parigi or or partiva.	He has just left for Paris.
VIOLETTA	**VIOLETTA**
E tornerà?	When will he come back?
ANNINA	**ANNINA**
Pria che tramonti il giorno -	Before evening.
dirvel m'impose -	He asked me to tell you.
VIOLETTA	**VIOLETTA**
È strano!	How strange!
ANNINA *(presentandole una lettera)*	**ANNINA** *(handing her a letter)*
Per voi.	For you.

VIOLETTA *(prendendola)*
Sta ben. In breve
giungerà un uom d'affari -
entri all'istante.

VIOLETTA *(taking it)*
Good. In a few minutes a man is coming
on business.
Show him in immediately.

(Violetta, reading the letter)

Ah, ah! Scopriva Flora il mio ritiro.
E m'invita a danzar per questa sera!
Invan m'aspetterà.

Aha! Flora has found my hideaway! She has
invited me to a dance this evening!
She'll wait for me in vain.

ANNINA
È qui un signore.

ANNINA
A gentleman to see you.

VIOLETTA
Sarà lui che attendo.

VIOLETTA
It must be the man I'm expecting.

(She gestures for Annina to admit him. Giorgio Germont enters.)

GERMONT
Madamigella Valéry?

GERMONT
Mademoiselle Valéry?

VIOLETTA
Son io.

VIOLETTA
Yes.

GERMONT
D'Alfredo il padre in me vedete!

GERMONT
I am Alfredo's father!

VIOLETTA

VIOLETTA

(Surprised, she offers him a chair.)

Voi!

You!

Alfredo (Walter MacNeil), distraught over Violetta's sudden departure

GERMONT

Sì, dell'incauto, che a ruina corre,
ammaliato da voi.

VIOLETTA *(risentita, alzandosi)*

Donna son io, signore, ed in mia casa;
ch'io vi lasci assentite
più per voi che per me.

(She is on the point of going out.)

GERMONT

(Quai modi!) Pure -

VIOLETTA

Tratto in error voi foste.

GERMONT

De' suoi beni egli dono vuol farvi.

VIOLETTA

Non l'osò finora - rifiuterei.

GERMONT *(guardando intorno)*

Pur tanto lusso -

VIOLETTA

A tutti è mistero quest'atto.
A voi nol sia.

(She gives him the paper.)

GERMONT *(Germont scorre le carte.)*

Ciel! Che discopro!
D'ogni vostro avere or volete spogliarvi?
Ah, il passato, perché v'accusa?

GERMONT

Yes, father of this reckless lad, who is
rushing to his ruin because of you.

VIOLETTA *(rising, with resentment)*

I, sir, am a woman and in my own home.
Now please excuse me,
more for your sake than for mine.

GERMONT

(What spirit!) And yet -

VIOLETTA

You have been badly advised.

GERMONT

He wants to give you all his possessions.

VIOLETTA

So far, he hasn't dared - I should refuse.

GERMONT *(looking about him)*

Such luxury -

VIOLETTA

This paper is a secret from everyone.
But it shall not be from you.

GERMONT *(after looking at them briefly)*

Heavens! What is this!
You wish to sell everything you own?
Ah, why does your past accuse you so?

VIOLETTA	VIOLETTA
Più non esiste - or amo Alfredo, e Dio lo cancellò col pentimento mio.	The past does not exist - I love Alfredo now; God wiped out my past with my repentance.

GERMONT	GERMONT
Nobili sensi invero!	These are truly noble sentiments!

VIOLETTA	VIOLETTA
Oh, come dolce mi suona il vostro accento!	Ah, how good to hear these words from you!

GERMONT	GERMONT
Ed a tai sensi un sacrifizio chieggo -	And in the name of these sentiments, I ask a sacrifice -

VIOLETTA (alzandosi)	VIOLETTA (arising)
Ah, no, tacete - terribil cosa chiedereste certo.Il previdi - v'attesi - era felice troppo.	Ah, no, do not say it. Certainly you would ask some frightening thing. I knew it - I expected you - I was too happy.

GERMONT	GERMONT
D'Alfredo il padre la sorte, l'avvenir domanda or qui de' suoi due figli.	Alfredo's father asks you to decide the fate of his two children.

VIOLETTA	VIOLETTA
Di due figli!	His two children!

DISC NO. 1/TRACK 17

Germont begins his entreaty lyrically as he tries to coax Violetta into pitying the difficult position of his lovely and innocent daughter.

GERMONT	GERMONT
Sì! Pura siccome un angelo	Yes. God blessed me with a daughter,

Iddio mi diè una figlia;
se Alfredo nega riedere
in seno alla famiglia,
l'amato e amante giovine
cui sposa andar dovea,
or si ricusa al vincolo
che lieti ne rendeva.
Deh, non mutate in triboli
le rose dell'amor.
A' prieghi miei resistere no, no
non voglia il vostro cor.

VIOLETTA

Ah, comprendo - dovrò per alcun tempo
da Alfredo allontanarmi - doloroso
fora per me - pur -

GERMONT

Non è ciò che chiedo.

VIOLETTA

Cielo, che più cercate?
Offersi assai!

GERMONT

Pur non basta.

VIOLETTA

Volete che per sempre a lui rinunzi?

GERMONT

È d'uopo!

like an angel in her purity;
if Alfredo refuses to return
to the bosom of his family,
the young man in love and beloved in turn,
who was soon to marry my daughter,
would reject this bond
on which our happiness depends.
Ah, do not be the cause of love's roses
changing into thorns.
Do not let your heart refuse
what I so fervently ask of you. No! No!

VIOLETTA

Ah, I understand - I must leave Alfredo
for a time. It will be painful
for me - yet -

GERMONT

That is not what I ask.

VIOLETTA

Heaven, what more can you ask!
I offered much!

GERMONT

But not enough.

VIOLETTA

You want me to give him up forever?

GERMONT

You must!

Violett's phrases become breathy as she begins to realize the exorbitant price of Germont's request.

VIOLETTA

Ah no! - giammai! No, no!

Non sapete quale affetto

vivo, immenso m'arda in petto?

Che né amici, né parenti

io non conto tra' viventi?

E che Alfredo m'ha giurato

che in lui tutto troverò?

Non sapete che colpita

d'atro morbo è la mia vita?

Che già presso il fine vedo?

Ch'io mi separi da Alfredo!

Ah, il supplizio è sì spietato,

che a morir preferirò.

GERMONT

È grave il sacrifizio,

ma pur tranquilla uditemi,

bella voi siete e giovine -

col tempo -

VIOLETTA

Ah, più non dite -

v'intendo - m'è impossibile.

Lui solo amar vogl'io.

GERMONT

Sia pure - ma volubile sovente è l'uom -

VIOLETTA

Gran Dio!

VIOLETTA

No - never! No, no!

Can you not see what tremendous,

burning love I feel for him,

I, who have no friends or family

among the living?

Don't you know that Alfredo swore

that I should find everything in him?

Don't you know that my life

is endangered by a terrible disease,

that I have but a short time to live?

To leave Alfredo forever?

Ah, the anguish would be so cruel

that I should prefer to die.

GERMONT

The sacrifice is great,

but hear me out patiently.

You are still young and beautiful -

in time -

VIOLETTA

Ah, say nothing more.

I understand - I cannot -

I shall never love anyone but him.

GERMONT

That may well be - but men are often fickle.

VIOLETTA

Oh God!

Germont tries a new tack with Violetta, focusing on the fickle nature of men and playing on Violetta's fears of aging. His music becomes extremely sinister and manipulative.

GERMONT

Un dì, quando le veneri
il tempo avra fugate,
fia presto il tedio a sorgere -
che sarà allor? Pensate -
per voi non avran balsamo
i più soavi affetti,
poiché dal ciel non furono
tai nodi benedetti.

GERMONT

Once time has staled
the delights of love,
tedium will follow quickly.
Then what? Think -
Even the deepest feelings
can bring you no balm,
since this bond was never
blessed by heaven.

VIOLETTA

È vero! È vero!

VIOLETTA

It's true! It's true!

GERMONT

Ah, dunque sperdasi tal sogno seduttore.

GERMONT

Ah, then lay aside this beguiling dream.

VIOLETTA

È vero! È vero!

VIOLETTA

It's true! It's true!

GERMONT

Siate di mia famiglia l'angel consolatore
Violetta, deh, pensateci, ne siete in tempo
ancor. È Dio che ispira, o giovine,
tai detti a un genitor.

GERMONT

Be rather the consoling angel
of my family. Violetta. Think -
You still have time. Young lady, it is God
who inspires these words on a father's lips.

VIOLETTA

Così alla misera ch'è un dì caduta,
di più risorgere speranza è muta!
Se pur benefico le indulga Iddio,
l'uomo implacabil per lei sarà.

VIOLETTA

All hope of rising again is forever gone.
For the wretched woman who erred one
day! Even if God grants her mercy
charitably Man will always be implacable.

GERMONT
Siate di mia famiglia l'angiol consolator.

GERMONT
Be rather the consoling angel of my family.

VIOLETTA *(poi, piangendo, a Germont)*
Ah! dite alla giovine sì bella e pura
ch'avvi una vittima della sventura,
cui resta un unico raggio di bene -
che a lei il sacrifica e che morrà!

VIOLETTA *(then, to Germont as she weeps)*
Oh, tell your daughter, so lovely and pure,
that a poor and wretched woman,
who has but one precious thing in life -
will sacrifice it for her - and then will die!

GERMONT
Piangi, piangi, o misera, supremo, il veggo,
è il sacrifizio che ora ti chieggo.
Sento nell'anima già le tue pene;
coraggio e il nobile tuo cor vincerà!

GERMONT
Weep, weep, poor girl. I see now
that the sacrifice I asked could not be
greater. Within my heart I feel what you
must suffer; be brave, your noble heart will
conquer all.

DISC 1/TRACK 20
Violetta's response is in hushed phrases in the haunting key of E flat, suggesting someone who is physically stunned and summoning all her strength to suppress her true emotions. Germont's interjections are sympathetic yet still stern and not consoling.

VIOLETTA
Dite alla giovine sì bella e pura
ch'avvi una vittima della sventura,
cui resta un unico raggio di bene
che a lei il sacrifica e che morrà!

VIOLETTA
Tell your daughter, so lovely and pure,
that a poor and wretched woman,
who has but one precious thing in life -
will sacrifice it for her - and then will die!

GERMONT
Ah supremo, il veggo,
è il sacrificio ch'ora ti chieggo.
Sento nell'anima già le tue pene;
coraggio e il nobile cor vincerà!
Piangi, o misera!

GERMONT
I see now that the sacrifice I asked could,
not be greater, within my heart I feel what
you must suffer, be brave, your noble heart
will conquer all.
Weep, poor girl.

A very quiet tone pervades as Violetta and Germont dare not say that she must tell Alfredo she has left him for another man. The tension, and emotion, builds in the orchestra here, rather than the vocal lines.

VIOLETTA
Imponete.

VIOLETTA
Tell me what I must do.

GERMONT
Non amarlo ditegli.

GERMONT
Tell him you don't love him.

VIOLETTA
Nol crederà.

VIOLETTA
He won't believe me.

GERMONT
Partite.

GERMONT
Go away, then.

VIOLETTA
Seguirammi.

VIOLETTA
He will follow me.

GERMONT
Allor -

GERMONT
Then -

VIOLETTA
Qual figlia m'abbracciate,
forte così sarò.

VIOLETTA
Embrace me as if I were your daughter -
it will give me strength.

(They embrace.)

Tra breve ei vi fia reso.
Ma afflitto oltre ogni dire.

Soon he will be yours again,
but desperately sad.

(pointing to the garden)

A suo conforto di colà volerete.

Out there you will hurry to comfort him.

(Violetta sits down to write.)

GERMONT	**GERMONT**
Che pensate?	What is it?
VIOLETTA	**VIOLETTA**
Sapendo, v'opporreste al pensier mio.	If I told you, you would oppose my wish.
GERMONT	**GERMONT**
Generosa! E per voi che far poss'io?	Generous woman! What can I do for you?
O generosa!	Generous woman!

DISC NO. 1/TRACK 22

Emotions finally burst forth in this section, as Germont tries to encourage Violetta in music reminiscent of people preparing for war. They then exchange sympathetic farewells.

VIOLETTA *(tornando a lui)*
Morrò! La mia memoria non fia ch'ei
maledica, se le mie pene orribili vi sia chi
almen gli dica.

VIOLETTA *(returning near him)*
I shall die! Let him not curse my memory;
when I am dead, let someone tell him of
my suffering.

GERMONT
No, generosa, vivere,
e lieta voi dovrete;
mercè di queste lagrime
dal cielo un giorno avrete.

GERMONT
No, generous woman, you must live,
and live in happiness.
Heaven one day will recompense these
tears.

VIOLETTA
Conosca il sacrifizio
ch'io consumai d'amore -
che sarà suo fin l'ultimo
sospiro del mio cor.

VIOLETTA
Let him know the sacrifice
which I made for love -
for the very last breath of life
will be for him alone.

GERMONT
Premiato il sacrifizio
sarà del vostro core;
d'un'opra così nobile
sarete fiera allor. Sì, sì

VIOLETTA
Conosca il sacrifizio
ch'io consumai d'amore -
che sarà suo fin l'ultimo
sospiro del mio cor.

GERMONT
Sarete fiera allor.
D'un'opra così nobile
sarete fiera allor.
Premiato il sacrifizio
sarà del vostro cor;
d'un'opra così nobil
sarete fiera allor.

VIOLETTA
Qui giunge alcun! Partite!

GERMONT
Oh, grato v'è il cor mio!

VIOLETTA
Partite! Non ci vedrem più forse

(They embrace.)

VIOLETTA, GERMONT
Siate felice!

GERMONT
And your heart's sacrifice
will be rewarded.
Then your heart will be proud
of so noble an act. Yes, yes, yes -

VIOLETTA
Let him know the sacrifice
which I made for love -
For the very last breath of life
will be for him alone.

GERMONT
Of so noble an act
then your heart will be proud
of so noble an act.
And your heart's sacrifice
will be rewarded.
Then your heart will be proud
of so noble an act.

VIOLETTA
Someone is coming…you must leave.

GERMONT
Oh, how grateful I am to you!

VIOLETTA
Leave me. We may never see each other
again.

VIOLETTA, GERMONT
May you be happy.

VIOLETTA
Addio!

GERMONT
Addio!

VIOLETTA
Conosca il sacrifizio,

GERMONT
Sì!

VIOLETTA
...ch'io consumai d'amore -
che sarà suo fin l'ultimo...
Addio!

GERMONT
Addio!

VIOLETTA
che sarà suo fin l'ultimo...
Addio!

VIOLETTA, GERMONT
Felice siate, addio!

(Germont goes out through the garden door.)

VIOLETTA
Goodbye!

GERMONT
Goodbye!

VIOLETTA
Let him know the sacrifice...

GERMONT
Yes.

VIOLETTA
...which I made for love...
...for the very last breath of life.
Goodbye!

GERMONT
Goodbye!

VIOLETTA
...for the very last breath of life.
Goodbye!

VIOLETTA, GERMONT
May you be happy...goodbye!

DISC NO. 1/TRACK 23
Violetta says little while writing Alfredo, and a plaintive clarinet gives voice to her sighs.

VIOLETTA
Dammi tu forza, o cielo!

VIOLETTA
Give me strength, oh Heaven!

(She sits down and writes, then rings for the servant...Annina enters.)

ANNINA
Mi richiedeste?

ANNINA
You rang for me?

VIOLETTA
Sì, reca tu stessa questo foglio.

VIOLETTA
Yes, please deliver this letter yourself.

(Annina reads the address, then looks up in surprise.)

Silenzio - va' all'istante.

Silence - go immediately.

(Annina goes out.)

Ed or si scriva a lui.
Che gli dirò? Chi men darà il coraggio?

And now to write to him.
What can I say? Who will give me courage?

(She writes, then seals the letter.)

DISC NO. 1/TRACK 24

Alfredo enters, and over an agitated figure in the orchestra, he questions Violetta about the letter. The tension continues (00:40) as she asks him to meet his father after she has gone. At the piece's climax (01:40), we hear the expansive theme we heard in the Prelude over tremolo strings. Here, the theme is all raw emotion and a great demand on the lyric soprano, but crucial for the convincing expression of her love.

ALFREDO *(Entra.)*
Che fai?

ALFREDO *(entering)*
What are you doing?

VIOLETTA

VIOLETTA

(concealing the letter)

Nulla.

Nothing.

ALFREDO
Scrivevi?

VIOLETTA
Sì - no

ALFREDO
Qual turbamento! A chi scrivevi?

VIOLETTA
A te -

ALFREDO
Dammi quel foglio.

VIOLETTA
No, per ora.

ALFREDO
Mi perdona - son io preoccupato -

VIOLETTA
Che fu?

ALFREDO
Giunse mio padre -

VIOLETTA
Lo vedesti?

ALFREDO
Ah, no: severo scritto mi lasciava.
Però l'attendo, t'amerà in vederti.

ALFREDO
You were writing?

VIOLETTA
Yes - no -

ALFREDO
But what confusion! To whom were you
writing?

VIOLETTA
To you -

ALFREDO
Give me the letter.

VIOLETTA
No, not now.

ALFREDO
Forgive me - I am concerned about -

VIOLETTA
What has happened?

ALFREDO
My father was here.

VIOLETTA
Did you see him?

ALFREDO
Ah, no. He left a stern letter for me.
But I'm expecting him. He'll love you at
first sight.

VIOLETTA
Ch'ei qui non mi sorprenda,
lascia che m'allontani - tu lo calma -
ai piedi suoi mi getterò -
divisi ei più non ne vorrà -
sarem felici -
perché tu m'ami, Alfredo, non è vero?

VIOLETTA
He must not find me here.
Let me go away - you calm him -
I'll throw myself at his feet - then
he'll not want to separate us. We shall be
happy - because you love me, you love me
Alfredo, you love me, don't you?

ALFREDO
Oh, quanto! Perché piangi?

ALFREDO
So much! Why are you weeping?

VIOLETTA
Di lagrime aveva d'uopo -
or son tranquilla -
lo vedi? Ti sorrido - lo vedi?
Sarò là tra quei fior presso a te sempre.
Amami, Alfredo, quant'io t'amo.
Addio!

VIOLETTA
I needed tears -
now I feel better -
See? I am smiling at you - see?
I shall always be here, near you, among the
flowers.
Love me, Alfredo, love me as much as I
love you.
Goodbye!

(She runs out into the garden.)

DISC NO. 2/TRACK 1

Alfredo's fears are so persistent that he only reads the first few words of Violetta's letter before he breaks down.

ALFREDO
Ah, vive sol quel core all'amor mio!

ALFREDO
Ah, this dear one lives only for my love!

(He sits down, reads a book for a moment. Then he stands up and goes to look at the clock on the mantel.)

È tardi; ed oggi forse
più non verrà mio padre.

It is late: perhaps today
my father will not come.

(Alfredo's father is seen at a distance, crossing the garden.)

Qualcuno è nel giardino!	Someone is in the garden!
Chi è là?	Who is it?

(He is on the point of going out.)

COMMISSIONARIO	**MESSENGER**
Il signor Germont?	Signor Germont?

ALFREDO	**ALFREDO**
Son io.	I am he.

COMMISSIONARIO	**MESSENGER**
Una dama	A lady in a carriage, not far down the road,
da un cocchio, per voi, di qua non lunge,	gave me this letter.
mi diede questo scritto.	

(He gives the letter to Alfredo, who tips him.)

ALFREDO	**ALFREDO**
Di Violetta! Perché son io commosso!	From Violetta! Why am I so upset?
A raggiungerla forse ella m'invita -	Perhaps she wants me to join her -
Io tremo! Oh ciel! Coraggio!	I am trembling. Oh, Heaven! Courage!

(He opens the letter and reads:)

"Alfredo, al giungervi di questo foglio…"	"Alfredo, by the time you receive this letter"

(thunderstruck, he cries out:)

Ah!	Ah!

(Turning, he sees his father, and throws himself into his arms.)

Padre mio!	Father!

GERMONT	GERMONT
Mio figlio!	My son!
Oh, quanto soffri! Oh, tergi il pianto -	Oh, how you are suffering!
ritorna di tuo padre orgoglio e vanto.	Ah, dry your tears - be once again your
	father's pride.

(In despair, Alfredo sits down at the table, his head in his hands.)

Di Provenza il mar il suol is one of the most outstanding baritone arias in the repertoire. The opening theme, played by woodwinds in thirds, has a folk-like quality which describes the rural setting that was Alfredo's childhood home. The aria has the structure of music written a generation before Verdi, and therefore is appropriate to represent the point of view of the older generation as well as having an inherently old-fashioned feel.

Di Provenza il mar, il suol	The sea, the hills of Provence,
chi dal cor ti cancellò?	who effaced them from your heart?
Chi dal cor i cancellò, di Provenza	Who has erased the memory from
il mar, il suol?	your heart?
Al natio fulgente sol qual destino ti furò?	What destiny took you away
Qual destino ti furò al natio fulgene sol?	from the sunny land of your birth?
Oh, rammenta pur nel duol	Oh, what destiny drove you away?
ch'ivi gioia a te brillò;	Oh, remember in your sorrow
E che pace colà sol su te splendere ancor può.	what joy warmed you there;
Dio mi guidò!	and that only there can your soul find
Ah! il tuo vecchio genitor	peace again.
tu non sai quanto soffrì.	God brought me here!
Te lontano, di squallor	Ah! You cannot know how your old father
il suo tetto si coprì.	has suffered.
Il suo tetto si coprì di squallore, di squallor,	With you away his house is clouded with
Ma se alfin ti trovo ancor,	sorrow. In deepest sadness his roof has been
se in me speme non fallì,	shrouded.
se la voce dell'onor	But if at last I have found you,
in te appien non ammutì,	if my hope has not been in vain.

Ma se alfin ti trovo ancor, *ecc.*	If the voice of honour is not wholly stilled
Dio m'esaudì! *ecc.*	in you. But I have found you again, *etc.*
	God has answered my prayer! *etc.*

(embracing him)

Nè rispondi d'un padre all'affetto?	Don't you return your father's love?

DISC NO. 2/TRACKS 3 & 4

No, non udrai rimproveri begins as a stately cabaletta as Germont continues to persuade his son to abandon his love nest. Tension builds (01:54) as he is interrupted by Alfredo, who hasn't heard a word. The scene crashes to a dramatic close (03:24) as Alfredo storms from the house, seeking revenge for his lost love. This exciting aria is rarely heard in live performance.

ALFREDO	**ALFREDO**
Mille serpi divoranmi il petto.	A thousand furies are torturing my breast.
Mi lasciate.	Leave me.

GERMONT	**GERMONT**
Lasciarti!	Leave you!

ALFREDO	**ALFREDO**

(resolute)

(Oh vendetta!)	(Oh, revenge!)

GERMONT	**GERMONT**
Non più indugi; partiamo – t'affretta –	Do not delay; let us go – be quick –

ALFREDO	**ALFREDO**
(Ah, fu Douphol!)	(Ah, it was Douphol!)

GERMONT
M'ascolti tu?

ALFREDO
No!

GERMONT
Dunque invano trovato t'avrò.
No, non udrai rimproveri;
Copriam d'oblio il passato;
L'amor che m'ha guidato
Sa tutto perdonar.
Vieni, i tuoi in giubilo,
Con me rivedi ancora
A chi penò fnora
Tal gioia non negar.
Un padre ed una suora –
T'affretta a consolare.
No, non udrai rimproveri, *ecc.*

ALFREDO
Mille serpi divranmi il petto...

GERMONT
M'ascolti tu?

ALFREDO
No!

GERMONT
Un padre ed una suora -
T'affretta a consolar.
No, non udrai rimroveri, *ecc.*

GERMONT
Will you listen to me?

ALFREDO
No!

GERMONT
Then, have I found you in vain?
No, you shall hear no reproaches;
let us bury the past;
The love which guided me
Can pardon all.
Come, see your loved ones again,
Together with me.
Do not deny this happiness
To one who has suffered greatly.
Your father and your sister –
Hasten to console them.
No, you shall hear no reproaches, *etc.*

ALFREDO
A thousand furies are torturing my breast...

GERMONT
Are you listening?

ALFREDO
No!

GERMONT
Your father and your sister –
Hasten to console them.
No you shall hear no reproaches, *etc.*

ALFREDO

(Suddenly he sees Flora's letter on the table and exclaims:)

	ALFREDO
Ah! ell'è alla festa!	Ah! She is at the party! Let me fly
Volisi l'offesa a vendicar.	to take revenge for this offence.

GERMONT	**GERMONT**
Che dici! Ah, ferma!	What are you saying? Stop!

(Alfredo runs out of the house, followed by his father.)

SCENE TWO

A salon in Flora's home, richly furnished and brightly lighted. A door to the rear, others on either side. To the right, somewhat to the foreground, a gaming table with equipment for play; left, an elaborate table with flowers and refreshments; nearby, sofa and chairs.

(Flora, the Marquis and Dr. Grenvil enter with other guests - all chatting.)

DISC NO. 2/TRACK 5

In contrast to the drama of the previous scene, Verdi first treats us to the same type of party music we heard at the beginning of the opera.

FLORA	**FLORA**
Avrem lieta di maschere la notte:	Later we shall be entertained by masks:
n'è duce il viscontino -	the Viscount is in charge.
Violetta ed Alfredo anco invitai.	I've invited Violetta and Alfredo.

MARCHESE	**MARQUIS**
La novità ignorate?	Haven't you heard the news?
Violetta e Germont sono disgiunti.	Violetta and Germont have separated.

107

DOTTORE, FLORA Fia vero?	**DOCTOR, FLORA** Have they really?
MARCHESE Ella verrà qui col barone.	**MARQUIS** She is coming with the Baron.
DOTTORE Li vidi ieri ancor - parean felici.	**DOCTOR** I saw them only yesterday - they looked happy.

(The sound of laughing voices is heard.)

FLORA Silenzio - udite?	**FLORA** Silence - do you hear?
FLORA, DOTTORE, MARCHESE Giungono gli amici.	**FLORA, DOCTOR, MARQUIS** Our friends are coming.

DISC NO. 2/TRACK 6 & 7

Verdi interrupts the action with these Gypsy and Spanish entertainments. This lively music gives us a rest from the tension in the plot. Many of the ballets Verdi wrote for his other operas were later additions to existing scores, composed as concessions to local tastes in Paris where ballets in opera were de rigueur. Those are rarely performed within the operas today. This choral ballet, however, is always performed, since Verdi conceived it from the start as an important relief to the dramatic tension.

(Ladies disguised as gypsies enter.)

ZINGARE Noi siamo zingarelle venute da lontano; d'ognuno sulla mano leggiamo l'avvenir. Se consultiam le stelle	**GYPSIES** We are gypsies, come from afar; the fortunes of all we can read in their hands. When we call upon the stars,

null'avvi a noi d'oscuro,
e i casi del futuro
possiamo altrui predir.
Vediamo -

nothing is hidden from us,
and we can tell you all
what the future holds in store.
Let us see -

CORO I *(osservando la mano di Flora)*
Voi, signora, rivali alquante avete.

CHORUS I *(examining Flora's palm)*
You, Madam, have many rivals.

CORO II *(osservando la mano del Marchese)*
Marchese, voi non siete model di fedeltà.

CHORUS II *(examining the Marquis's palm)*
Marquis, you are scarcely a model of
fidelity.

FLORA *(al Marchese)*
Fate il galante ancora?
Ben, vo' me la paghiate -

FLORA *(to the Marquis)*
So you still play the gallant?
Fine - I'll make you pay for this.

MARCHESE
Che diamin vi pensate?
L'accusa è falsità.

MARQUIS
What the devil are you thinking?
It's a bare-faced lie.

FLORA
La volpe lascia il pelo,
non abbandona il vizio.
Marchese mio, giudizio,
o vi farò pentir.

FLORA
The fox may lose his brush,
but never abandons his rascality.
Take care, my dear Marquis,
or you'll be sorry, I swear.

TUTTI
Su via, si stenda un velo
sui fatti del passato;
già quel ch'è stato è stato,
badiamo/badate all'avvenir.

ALL
Come, come, whatever's happened
shall be veiled by the past;
what's been has been,
think only of what's to be.

(Flora and the Marquis shake hands. Now from the right, Gastone and other men, dressed as Spanish matadors and picadors, enter.)

GASTONE, MATTADORI
Di Madride noi siam mattadori,
siamo i prodi del circo dei tori,
testé giunti a godere del chiasso
che a Parigi si fa pel Bue grasso;
È una storia se udire vorrete,
quali amanti noi siamo saprete.

GLI ALTRI
Sì, sì, bravi; narrate, narrate:
con piacere l'udremo.

GASTONE, MATTADORI
Ascoltate.
È Piquillo un bel gagliardo
biscaglino mattador:
forte il braccio, fiero il guardo
delle giostre egli è signor.
D'Andalusa giovinetta
follemente innamorò;
ma la bella ritrosetta
così al giovane parlò:
"Cinque tori in un sol giorno
vo' vederti ad atterrar;
e, se vinci, al tuo ritorno
mano e cor ti vo' donar."
Sì, gli disse, e il mattadore,
alle giostre mosse il piè;
cinque tori, vincitore,
sull'arena egli stendé.

GLI ALTRI
Bravo, bravo il mattadore,
ben gagliardo si mostrò,
se alla giovane l'amore
in tal guisa egli provò!

GASTONE, MATADORS
We're matadors, from Madrid,
the champions of the bullring.
We've just arrived to join in the fun
of carnival time in Paris;
if you'll hear our story to the end,
you'll know what great lovers we are.

THE OTHERS
Yes, yes, good! Tell us, tell us:
we'll hear your story with pleasure.

GASTONE, MATADORS
Listen, then.
Piquillo is a strapping young man.
A matador from Biscay:
strong of arm and fierce of eye,
he is the lord of the bullring.
He fell for an Andalusian lass,
madly in love fell he;
but the stubborn little miss
answered him this way:
"Five bulls in a single day -
I'll see you kill them all;
and if you win, when you return,
my heart and hand are yours."
"Yes, yes." said he, and off he went,
to the bullring straight away;
five bulls our conquering hero met,
and killed them all that day.

THE OTHERS
Bravo, bravo, this matador -
he showed himself such a champion,
and, in so doing,
he proved his love!

GASTONE, MATTADORI	GASTONE AND MATADORS
Poi, tra plausi, ritornato	Then, amidst the applause,
alla bella del suo cor,	he went back to his love,
colse il premio desiato	and there received the longed-for prize,
tra le braccia dell'amor.	wrapped in his sweetheart's arms.

GLI ALTRI	THE OTHERS
Con tai prove i mattadori	It is with tests like this that matadors
san le belle conquistar!	sweep lovely women off their feet!

GASTONE, MATTADORI	GASTONE AND MATADORS
Ma qui son più miti i cori;	But here the thing is simpler;
a noi basta folleggiar.	it's enough for us if we can frolic.

TUTTI	ALL
Sì, allegri. Or pria tentiamo	Yes, with carefree gaiety. Now first
della sorte il vario umor;	let's try the humour of Fortune;
la palestra dischiudiamo	we'll open the ring
agli audaci giuocator.	to the dauntless gamblers.

(The men unmask. Some of them walk about, talking together, while the others prepare to play. Alfredo enters.)

DISC NO. 2/TRACK 8

Tension resumes as the card game begins (00:33), and the vocal lines take on a static quality with the exception of Violetta's asides (01:14, 02:26 and 03:20), which soar out over the texture expressing her distress.

TUTTI	ALL
Alfredo! Voi!	Alfredo! You!

ALFREDO	ALFREDO
Sì, amici -	Yes my friends -

FLORA
Violetta?

ALFREDO
Non ne so.

TUTTI
Ben disinvolto! Bravo!
Or via, giuocar si può.

(Gastone cuts the cards. Alfredo and others place their bets. Violetta enters, escorted by the Baron. Flora goes forward to meet her.)

FLORA
Qui desiata giungi.

VIOLETTA
Cessi al cortese invito.

FLORA
Grata vi son, barone, d'averlo pur gradito.

BARONE
Germont è qui! Il vedete?

VIOLETTA
Cielo! Gli è vero. Il vedo.

BARONE
Da voi non un sol detto
si volga a questo Alfredo -
non un detto, non un detto!

VIOLETTA
(Ah, perché venni, incauta!
Pietà, gran Dio, di me!)

FLORA
Violetta?

ALFREDO
I don't know where she is.

ALL
How nonchalant! Bravo!
Come, now we can play.

FLORA
I am so glad you have come.

VIOLETTA
I couldn't refuse your kind invitation.

FLORA
I am grateful to you, too, Baron, for coming.

BARON
Germont is here! Do you see him!

VIOLETTA
Heaven! It's true. I see him.

BARON
You will not say
one word to this Alfredo -
not one word, not one word!

VIOLETTA
(Ah, why was I so rash as to come!
Mercy, oh God!)

FLORA *(fa sedere Violetta presso di sé sul divano)* Meco t'assidi; narrami - quai novità vegg'io?	**FLORA** *(to Violetta, as she invites her to sit next to her on the sofa)* Sit here with me, tell me - what is this I see?

(Dr. Grenvil approaches the two women, who are talking together in a low voice. The Marquis remains to one side with the Baron. Gastone deals the cards while Alfredo and various others bet. Still other guests are talking slowly here and there about the room.)

ALFREDO Un quattro!	**ALFREDO** A four!
GASTONE Ancora hai vinto!	**GASTONE** You win again!
ALFREDO Sfortuna nell'amore fortuna reca al giuoco.	**ALFREDO** Unlucky in love means luck at cards.

(He places his bet and wins again.)

TUTTI È sempre vincitore!	**ALL** He wins every time!
ALFREDO Oh, vincerò stasera: e l'oro guadagnato poscia a goder tra' campi ritornerò beato.	**ALFREDO** Oh, tonight I shall win. And with the gold I shall return happily to the country.
FLORA Solo?	**FLORA** Alone?
ALFREDO No, no, con tale che vi fu meco ancora, poi mi sfuggia -	**ALFREDO** No, no, with one who was with me, but ran away -

VIOLETTA Mio Dio!	**VIOLETTA** Oh, God!
GASTONE	**GASTONE**

(to Alfredo, indicating Violetta)

Pietà di lei!	Take pity on her!
BARONE	**BARON**

(to Alfredo, making a bad job of restraining his anger)

Signor!	Sir!

VIOLETTA *(al Barone)* **VIOLETTA** *(to the Baron)*
Frenatevi, o vi lascio. Restrain yourself, or I shall leave you.

ALFREDO **ALFREDO**
Barone, m'appellaste? Baron, you called me?

BARONE **BARON**
Siete in sì gran fortuna, Your luck is so good
che al giuoco mi tentaste. I'm tempted to play.

ALFREDO *(ironico)* **ALFREDO** *(ironically)*
Sì? La disfida accetto. Yes? I accept your challenge.

VIOLETTA **VIOLETTA**
Che fia? Morir mi sento! What will happen? I shall die!
Pietà, gran Dio, di me! Take pity, dear God, take pity on me!

BARONE *(punta)* **BARON** *(betting)*
Cento luigi a destra. A hundred louis on the right.

ALFREDO *(punta)*	**ALFREDO** *(betting)*
Ed alla manca cento.	On the left - a hundred.
GASTONE	**GASTONE**
Un asso - un fante - hai vinto!	Ace - jack - you win!
BARONE	**BARON**
Il doppio?	Double?
ALFREDO	**ALFREDO**
Il doppio sia.	Good - double.
GASTONE *(tagliando)*	**GASTONE** *(dealing)*
Un quattro, un sette.	Four - seven.
TUTTI	**ALL**
Ancora!	Again!
ALFREDO	**ALFREDO**
Pur la vittoria è mia!	The victory is mine after all!
CORO	**CHORUS**
Bravo davver!	Bravo! Really,
La sorte è tutta per Alfredo!	luck is on Alfredo's side!
FLORA	**FLORA**
Del villeggiar la spesa	The Baron has paid
farà il baron, già il vedo.	for the holiday, I see.
ALFREDO	**ALFREDO**
Seguite pur.	Continue if you wish.
SERVO	**A SERVANT**
La cena è pronta.	Dinner is served.

FLORA
Andiamo.

CORO *(Tutti partono.)*
Andiamo.

VIOLETTA
(Che fia? morir mi sento!
Pietà, gran Dio, di me!)

ALFREDO *(al Barone)*
Se continuar v'aggrada -

BARONE
Per ora nol possiamo:
più tardi la rivincita.

ALFREDO
Al giuoco che vorrete.

BARONE
Seguiam gli amici; poscia -

ALFREDO
Sarò qual bramerete - Andiam.

BARONE
Andiam.

FLORA
Let us go.

CHORUS *(moving towards the table)*
Let us go.

VIOLETTA
(What will happen? I shall die? Take pity,
dear God, take pity on me!)

ALFREDO *(aside, to the Baron)*
If you wish to continue -

BARON
We cannot, for the moment;
we'll play again, later.

ALFREDO
At any game you like.

BARON
Let us follow our friends; later -

ALFREDO
As you wish - let's go.

BARON
Let's go.

(All go out through the centre door; for a moment the scene is deserted. Then Violetta returns, distressed.)

Violetta and Alfredo confront one another over a taut musical accompaniment which reflects his insanely jealous bravado.

VIOLETTA

Invitato a qui seguirmi,
verrà desso? Vorrà udirmi?
Ei verrà, ché l'odio atroce
puote in lui più di mia voce.

ALFREDO

Mi chiamaste? Che bramate?

VIOLETTA

Questi luoghi abbandonate,
un periglio vi sovrasta -

ALFREDO

Ah, comprendo! Basta, basta.
E sì vile mi credete?

VIOLETTA

Ah no, no mai -

ALFREDO

Ma che temete?

VIOLETTA

Tremo sempre del barone.

ALFREDO

È fra noi mortal quistione -
s'ei cadrà per mano mia
un sol colpo vi torria
coll'amante il protettore.
V'atterrisce tal sciagura?

VIOLETTA

I invited him to follow me.
Will he come? Will he listen to me?
He will come, for his bitter hatred
will bring him, if not my voice.

ALFREDO

You called me? What do you want?

VIOLETTA

Please leave here at once.
You are in danger.

ALFREDO

Ah, I understand! Enough -
do you think I am such a coward?

VIOLETTA

Ah, no, no, never -

ALFREDO

What are you afraid of?

VIOLETTA

I am afraid of the Baron.

ALFREDO

There is bad blood between us -
if he falls into my hands,
a single blow will take away
your lover and your protector.
Would such a misfortune frighten you?

VIOLETTA
Ma s'ei fosse l'uccisore?
Ecco l'unica sventura -
ch'io pavento a me fatale!

ALFREDO
La mia morte! Che ven cale?

VIOLETTA
Deh, partite, e sull'istante.

ALFREDO
Partirò, ma giura innante
che dovunque seguirai
i passi miei.

VIOLETTA
Ah, no, giammai.

ALFREDO
No! giammai?

VIOLETTA
Va', sciagurato
scorda un nome ch'è infamato.
Va' - mi lascia sul momento -
di fuggirti un giuramento sacro io feci.

ALFREDO
A chi? dillo - chi potea?

VIOLETTA
A chi dritto pien n'avea.

VIOLETTA
But if he should kill you?
That is the only misfortune
which I fear - for it would kill me too!

ALFREDO
My death! What do you care?

VIOLETTA
Ah, leave, leave this minute!

ALFREDO
I shall leave, but first swear
that you will follow me
wherever I go.

VIOLETTA
Ah, no, never.

ALFREDO
No! Never?

VIOLETTA
Go wretched man!
Forget a name which is dishonoured.
Go - leave me this instant -
I took a sacred oath to leave you.

ALFREDO
But who - who could ask it of you?

VIOLETTA
Someone who had full right.

ALFREDO	**ALFREDO**
Fu Douphol?	Was it Douphol?
VIOLETTA	**VIOLETTA**
Sì.	Yes.
ALFREDO	**ALFREDO**
Dunque l'ami?	You love him, then?
VIOLETTA	**VIOLETTA**
Ebben - l'amo -	Well - I love him, yes.
ALFREDO	**ALFREDO**

(In a blind fury he runs to the door and calls out.)

Or tutti a me.	Everyone - come here!

(All the guests, bewildered, return to the salon.)

TUTTI	**ALL**
Ne appellaste? Che volete?	You called us? What do you want?
ALFREDO	**ALFREDO**

(pointing to Violetta, who is leaning against the table in utter humiliation)

Questa donna conoscete?	You know this woman?
TUTTI	**ALL**
Chi? Violetta?	Who? Violetta?
ALFREDO	**ALFREDO**
Che facesse non sapete?	You don't know what she has done?

VIOLETTA
Ah, taci.

VIOLETTA
Ah, be silent.

TUTTI
No.

ALL
No.

DISC NO. 2/TRACK 10

Alfredo curses Violetta in a brief aria over a cabaletta-style figure in the orchestra. The guests respond wildly (00:58), their incredulity underlined by an unresolved closing chord.

ALFREDO
Ogni suo aver tal femmina
per amor mio sperdea.
Io cieco, vile, misero,
tutto accettar potea.
Ma è tempo ancora! Tergermi
da tanta macchia bramo.
Qui testimon vi chiamo
che qui pagato io l'ho.

ALFREDO
This woman was about to lose
all she owns for love of me;
while I, blinded, vile, wretched,
was capable of accepting everything.
But there is still time! I wish
to cleanse myself of such a stain.
I have called you here as witnesses
that I have paid her all I owe.

(With furious contempt, he throws a purse down at Violetta's feet. Violetta faints in the arms of Flora. As Alfredo is speaking the last few words, his father enters.)

TUTTI
Oh, infamia orribile tu commettesti!
Un cor sensibile così uccidesti!
Di donne ignobile insultatore,
di qui allontanati, ne desti orror!
Va', va', ne desti orror!
Di donne ignobile insultator, *ecc.*

ALL
Oh, what a terrible thing you have done!
You have killed a sensitive heart!
Ignoble man, to insult a woman so,
leave this house at once, you fill us with
horror! Go, go, you fill us with horror!
Ignoble man, to insult a woman, *etc.*

As with all of Germont's music, he responds here in expansive fatherly phrases. Alfredo, realizing what he has done, responds in halting phrases (00:50) as he tries to excuse his actions.

GERMONT

Di sprezzo degno sé stesso rende
chi pur nell'ira la donna offende.
Dov'è mio figlio? Più non lo vedo:
in te più Alfredo trovar non so.

ALFREDO

Ah, sì - che feci! Ne sento orrore.
Gelosa smania, deluso amore
mi strazian l'alma; più non ragiono.
Da lei perdono più non avrò.
Volea fuggirla - non ho potuto!
Dall'ira spinto son qui venuto!
Or che lo sdegno ho disfogato,
me sciagurato! rimorso n'ho.

TUTTI *(a Violetta)*

Oh, quanto peni! Ma pur fa cor.
Qui soffre ognuno del tuo dolor;
fra cari amici qui sei soltanto;
rasciuga il pianto che t'inondò.

GERMONT *(da sé)*

Io sol fra tanti so qual virtude
di quella misera il sen racchiude.
Io so che l'ama, che gli è fedele,
eppur crudele tacer dovrò!

GERMONT

Whoever, even in anger, offends a woman
exposes himself to the contempt of all.
Where is my son? I cannot find him,
for in you I no longer see Alfredo.

ALFREDO

Ah, yes - what have I done? I am horrified.
Maddening jealousy, disillusioned love
torture my heart - I have lost my reason.
She can never forgive me now,
I tried to flee from her - I couldn't!
I came here, spurred on by anger!
Now that I have vented my fury,
I am sick with remorse - oh, wretched man!

ALL *(to Violetta)*

Ah, how you suffer! But take heart,
here, each of us suffers for your sorrow;
you are here among dear friends;
dry the tears which bathe your face.

GERMONT *(to himself)*

I alone among these people know
what virtue there is in this poor woman's
heart. I know she loves him, is faithful to
him, and yet I must keep a pitiless silence!

BARONE *(piano, ad Alfredo)*
A questa donna l'atroce insulto
qui tutti offese, ma non inulto
fia tanto oltraggio - provar vi voglio
che il vostro orgoglio fiaccar saprò.

BARON *(in a low voice, to Alfredo)*
The atrocious insult to this woman
has shocked us all, but such an outrage
shall not go unavenged. I will show you
that I am well able to break your pride.

ALFREDO *(da sé)*
Ohimé, che feci! Ne sento orrore, *ecc.*
Da lei perdono più non avrò.

ALFREDO *(to himself)*
Alas, what have I done, *etc.*
I am horrified she can never forgive me now.

> **DISC NO. 2/TRACK 12**
> This large ensemble, in which everyone expresses their various thoughts at once, brings the act to a stunning conclusion. This convention of nineteenth-century opera does not advance the drama in real time, but allows us to dissect a climactic moment into its various components. Violetta begins in a distant voice, yet is always at the center of the vocal tableau, and builds to an emotional climax while audibly affecting those around her.

VIOLETTA *(riavendosi)*
Alfredo, Alfredo, di questo core
non puoi comprendere tutto l'amore;
tu non conosci che fino a prezzo
del tuo disprezzo provato io l'ho!

VIOLETTA *(regaining consciousness)*
Alfredo, Alfredo you cannot understand
fully the love I have in my heart;
you do not know that even at the risk
of your disdain I have put it to the test!

TUTTI *(a Violetta)*
Quanto peni! fa cor

ALL *(to Violetta)*
How you suffer! But take heart!

ALFREDO
Ohimè! che feci! Ne sento orror!

ALFREDO
Alas, what have I done? I am horrified!

VIOLETTA
Ma verrà tempo in che il saprai -
come t'amassi confesserai.
Dio dai rimorsi ti salvi allora, ah!
Io spenta ancora pur t'amerò.

VIOLETTA
But the day will come when you will know -
You will admit how much I loved you.
May God save you, then, from remorse,
I shall be dead, but I shall love you still.

ALFREDO
Ohimè! che feci! Ne sento orror!

BARONE
Provar vi voglio che tanto
orgoglio fiaccar saprò.

GERMONT
Io so che l'ama, che gli è fedele,
eppur crudele tacer dovrò!

TUTTI
Quanto peni! fa cor! *ecc.*

ALFREDO
Alas, what have I done? I am horrified!

BARON
I will show you that I am well able
to break your pride.

GERMONT
I know she loves him, is faithful to him,
and yet I must keep a pitiless silence!

ALL
How you suffer! Take heart! *etc.*

(Germont leads his son away with him; the Baron follows him. Flora and the Doctor accompany Violetta to her room. The others go out.)

Act 3

Violetta's bedroom. Upstage, a bed with half-drawn curtains; a window with inside shutters; next to the bed a low table with a water-bottle, a glass, various medicines. Downstage, a dressing-table; nearby a sofa; another table with a night-lamp; several chairs and other pieces. The door is to the left; opposite, a fireplace, with a low fire.

(Violetta is in bed, asleep. Annina, sitting in a chair near the fireplace, has dozed off.)

DISC NO. 2/TRACK 13

The Prelude begins with the same sorrowful music we heard in the Prelude to act I. This is followed by an extended lament which seems to express the alternating hope and despair of Violetta's situation.

DISC NO. 2/TRACK 14

The orchestra is muted and Violetta's lines are likewise quiet in this passage. She is barely alive.

VIOLETTA
Annina?

ANNINA
Comandate?

VIOLETTA
Dormivi, poveretta?

VIOLETTA
Annina?

ANNINA
Yes, madam?

VIOLETTA
Were you sleeping, poor child?

ANNINA	**ANNINA**
Sì, perdonate.	Yes. Forgive me.
VIOLETTA	**VIOLETTA**
Dammi d'acqua un sorso.	Give me a sip of water.

(Annina does so.)

Osserva, è pieno il giorno?	Look outside and tell me - is it still day?
ANNINA	**ANNINA**
Son sett'ore.	It's seven o'clock.
VIOLETTA	**VIOLETTA**
Dà accesso a un po' di luce.	Open the blinds a little.

(Annina opens the blinds and looks out into the street.)

ANNINA	**ANNINA**
Il signor di Grenvil!	Doctor Grenvil!
VIOLETTA	**VIOLETTA**
Oh, il vero amico!	Oh, he's a true friend!
Alzar mi vo' - m'aita.	I want to get up. Help me.

(She gets up then falls back on the bed. Finally, supported by Annina, she gets up and walks slowly to the sofa. The doctor enters in time to help her get comfortable. Annina brings cushions and puts them behind her.)

VIOLETTA	**VIOLETTA**
Quanta bontà!	How good you are!
pensaste a me per tempo!	you thought of me in time!
DOTTORE *(Le tocca il polso.)*	**DOCTOR** *(feeling her pulse)*
Sì, come vi sentite?	Yes. How do you feel?

VIOLETTA
Soffre il mio corpo.
Ma tranquilla ho l'alma.
Mi confortò ier sera un pio ministro.
Ah, religione è sollievo ai sofferenti.

DOTTORE
E questa notte?

VIOLETTA
Ebbi tranquillo il sonno.

DOTTORE
Coraggio adunque - la convalescenza
non è lontana.

VIOLETTA
Oh, la bugia pietosa
ai medici è concessa.

DOTTORE *(Le stringe la mano.)*
Addio - a più tardi.

VIOLETTA
Non mi scordate.

ANNINA

(in a low voice, as she shows the doctor out)

Come va, signore?

DOTTORE
La tisi non le accorda che poche ore.

VIOLETTA
My body suffers, but my soul is in peace.
Last evening a priest came to comfort me.
Religion is a great consolation to the
suffering.

DOCTOR
And during the night?

VIOLETTA
I slept quite peacefully.

DOCTOR
Courage, then. Your convalescence is not
far off.

VIOLETTA
Oh, the little white lie
is permissible in a doctor.

DOCTOR *(pressing her hand)*
Goodbye - I'll come back later.

VIOLETTA
Don't forget me.

ANNINA

How is she, sir?

DOCTOR
She has only a few hours to live.

ANNINA Or fate cor.	**ANNINA** Take heart, now.
VIOLETTA Giorno di festa è questo?	**VIOLETTA** Today is a holiday?
ANNINA Tutta Parigi impazza - è carnevale!	**ANNINA** Paris is going mad - it's carnival.
VIOLETTA Ah, nel comun tripudio, sallo Iddio quanti infelici soffron! Quale somma v'ha in quello stipo?	**VIOLETTA** Oh, in all this merrymaking, heaven knows how many poor ones are suffering! How much is there in that drawer?

(pointing)

ANNINA	**ANNINA**

(opening the drawer and counting the money)

Venti luigi.	Twenty louis.
VIOLETTA Dieci ne reca a' poveri tu stessa.	**VIOLETTA** Take ten and give them to the poor.
ANNINA Poco rimanvi allora -	**ANNINA** There won't be much left -
VIOLETTA Oh, mi saran bastanti. Cerca poscia mie lettere.	**VIOLETTA** Oh, for me it will be enough. Then bring in my letters.
ANNINA Ma voi?	**ANNINA** But you, madam?

VIOLETTA	VIOLETTA
Nulla occorrà - sollecita, se puoi.	Nothing will happen - go quickly, please.

(Annina goes out.)

VIOLETTA	VIOLETTA

(She takes a letter from her bosom and reads:)

DISC NO. 2/TRACK 15
Violetta speaks the words of the letter over a solo violin echoing the love theme from act 1. This technique has since been abused by many movies, but remains striking in this context.

"Teneste la promessa - la disfida ebbe
luogo! Il Barone fu ferito però migliora.
Alfredo è in stranio suolo; il vostro
sacrifizio io stesso gli ho svelato; egli
a voi tornerà pel suo perdono; io pur verrò.
Curatevi - mertate un avvenir migliore.
Giorgio Germont."
È tardi!
Attendo, attendo - né a me giungon mai!

"You kept your promise. The duel has
taken place! The Baron was wounded, but
is recovering. Alfredo has gone abroad; I
myself revealed your sacrifice to him; he
will return to ask your pardon; I too shall
come. Take care of yourself. You deserve a
happier future. Giorgio Germont."
It is late!
I wait, I wait - they never come to me!

(She looks at herself in the mirror.)

DISC NO. 2/TRACK 16
Addio del passato. **This famous aria is a masterpiece of construction. Introduced by a melancholy solo oboe, Violetta's farewells are accompanied by halting figures in the orchestra that call to mind her shortness of breath. As she recalls Alfredo's love (00:58) her lines begin to soar, and as she prays for redemption the orchestra presses forward in an ascending harmonic progression (02:05) Having expended all her energies, her line descends, punctuated by isolated chords in the strings, and she ends on an unaccompanied high A (03:26).**

Oh, come son mutata!
Ma il dottore a sperar pure m'esorta!
Ah, con tal morbo ogni speranza è morta.
Addio, del passato bei sogni ridenti,
le rose del volto già sono pallenti;
l'amore d'Alfredo perfino mi manca,
conforto, sostegno dell'anima stanca -
conforto, sostegno -
Ah, della traviata sorridi al desio;
a lei, deh, perdona; tu accoglila, o Dio!
Ah! - Tutto,
tutto finì, or tutto, tutto finì.

Ah, how I have changed!
But the doctor still gives me hope!
Ah, with this disease every hope is dead.
Adieu, sweet, happy dreams of the past,
the roses of my cheeks are already fading.
I miss so much Alfredo's love,
which once solaced my weary soul -
Solaced and comforted -
Ah, smile upon the woman who has
strayed; forgive her, oh God, grant she may
come to thee!
Now all is finished, all is over.

DISC NO. 2/TRACK 17
The revelers outside underline the marked contrast between Violetta's former life and the darkened room in which she now awaits her death.

CORO DI MASCHERE
(dall'esterno)
Largo al quadrupede sir della festa,
di fiori e pampini
cinta la testa.
Largo al piu dociled'ogni cornuto,
di corni e pifferi abbia il saluto.
Parigini, date passo, al trionfo del Bue grasso. L'Asia né l'Africa
vide il più bello, vanto ed orgoglio d'ogni
macello. Allegre maschere, pazzi garzoni,
tutti plauditelo con canti e suoni!
Parigini, date passo,
al trionfo del Bue grasso.
Largo al quadrupede sir della festa,
di fiori e pampini
cinta la testa.

CHORUS OF MASQUERADERS
(from the street)
Make way for the quadruped King of the
festival, Wearing his crown of flowers
and vine leaves. Make way for the tamest of
all who wear horns, greet him with music
of horn and flute. People of Paris,
open the path to the triumphant Fattened
Ox. Neither Asia nor Africa
has ever seen better, this pride and joy of
the butcher's trade. Light-hearted maidens,
and frolicking lads, pay him due honour
of music and song! People of Paris, open
the path to the triumphant Fattened Ox.
Make way for the quadruped King of the
festival wearing his crown of flowers
and vine leaves.

(Annina returns, hastily.)

129

The excitement moves inside as Annina enters. The harmonies remain unstable—their direction uncertain—until we hear the news of Alfredo's imminent return, and all resolves in an optimistic major key.

ANNINA *(esitando)*
Signora!

ANNINA *(hesitating)*
Madam!

VIOLETTA
Che t'accadde?

VIOLETTA
What has happened?

ANNINA
Quest'oggi, è vero, vi sentite meglio?

ANNINA
Today you feel better, don't you?

VIOLETTA
Sì, perché?

VIOLETTA
Yes. Why?

ANNINA
D'esser calma promettete?

ANNINA
Do you promise not to get excited?

VIOLETTA
Sì, che vuoi dirmi?

VIOLETTA
Yes. What do you want to tell me?

ANNINA
Prevenir vi volli -
un gioia improvvisa!

ANNINA
I wanted to prepare you -
A happy surprise!

VIOLETTA
Una gioia! Dicesti?

VIOLETTA
Did you say - a surprise?

ANNINA
Sì, o signora -

ANNINA
Oh yes, madam -

VIOLETTA
Alfredo! Ah, tu il vedesti?
Ei vien! T'affretta.

VIOLETTA
Alfredo! Ah, you saw him?
He is coming! Oh, quickly!

(Annina nods her head, then goes to open the door.)

Alfredo!   Alfredo!

(Alfredo enters, pale with emotion. They are in each other's arms as they exclaim:)

Amato Alfredo! Oh gioia!   Beloved Alfredo! Oh joy!

ALFREDO   **ALFREDO**
Oh mia Violetta. Oh gioia!   My Violetta! Oh, joy!
Colpevol sono - so tutto,   The fault is mine - I know everything now,
o cara.   dear.

VIOLETTA   **VIOLETTA**
Io so che alfine reso mi sei!   I know only that you have come back!

ALFREDO   **ALFREDO**
Da questo palpito s'io t'ami impara,   Let my emotion teach you how I love you.
senza te esistere più non potrei.   I cannot live without you.

VIOLETTA   **VIOLETTA**
Ah, s'anco in vita m'hai ritrovata,   Ah, if you have found me still alive,
credi che uccidere non può il dolor.   it means grief has not the power to kill.

ALFREDO   **ALFREDO**
Scorda l'affanno, donna adorata,   Forget your sorrow, my adored one,
a me perdona e al genitor.   and forgive my father and me.

VIOLETTA   **VIOLETTA**
Ch'io ti perdoni? La rea son io;   What is there to forgive? The guilty one is
ma solo amor tal mi rendé.   me; but it was love alone which made me so.

ALFREDO, VIOLETTA   **ALFREDO, VIOLETTA**
Null'uomo o demon, angel mio,   Now neither man nor demon, my angel,
mai più dividermi potrà da te.   will ever be able to take you away.

Parigi, o cara. **This famous duet, in which the lovers describe an idyllic future together, is often performed in concert. The music is perfectly symmetrical and marvelously intertwined between the two lovers. They are finally together in every sense, but it is too late for them.**

ALFREDO

Parigi, o cara, noi lasceremo,
la vita uniti trascorreremo;
de' corsi affanni compenso avrai,
la tua salute rifiorirà.
Sospiro e luce tu mi sarai,
tutto il futuro ne arriderà.

ALFREDO

From Paris dear, we shall go away,
to live our lives together.
We shall make up for all our heartache,
your health will come back again.
You will be the light of my life,
the future will smile upon us.

VIOLETTA

(echoing him as in a dream)

Parigi, o caro, noi lasceremo,
la vita uniti trascorreremo:

VIOLETTA

From Paris dear, we shall go away,
to live our loves together…

ALFREDO
Sì.
De' corsi affanni compenso avrai.
La tua salute rifiorirà.
Sospiro e luce tu mi sarai, *ecc.*

ALFREDO
Yes.
We shall make up for all our heartache.
Your health will come back again.
You will be the light of my life, *etc.*

We hear Violetta's heart beat faster as she tries to take up her life again, but the low strings repeatedly interject short descending phrases which punctuate her failures.

VIOLETTA
Ah, non più, a un tempio -
Alfredo, andiamo,
del tuo ritorno grazie rendiamo.

VIOLETTA
No more now, Alfredo let us go to church
to offer thanks
for your return.

(She sways, as if to fall.)

ALFREDO	**ALFREDO**
Tu impallidisci -	You are pale -

VIOLETTA	**VIOLETTA**
È nulla, sai!	It is nothing!
Gioia improvvisa non entra mai,	Such sudden joy cannot come
senza turbarlo, in mesto core.	to a sorrowing heart without disturbing it.

(She throws herself down, upon a chair; her head falls back.)

ALFREDO *(spaventato, sorreggendola)*	**ALFREDO** *(holding her up, terrified)*
Gran Dio! Violetta!	Great God! Violetta!

VIOLETTA *(sforzandosi)*	**VIOLETTA** *(with great effort)*
È il mio malore -	It's my illness -
fu debolezza! Ora son forte.	A moment of weakness! Now I am strong.
Vedi? Sorrido.	See? I am smiling.

ALFREDO	**ALFREDO**
Ahi, cruda sorte!	Ah, cruel destiny!

VIOLETTA	**VIOLETTA**
Fu nulla. Annina, dammi a vestire.	It was nothing. Annina, bring me my dress.

ALFREDO	**ALFREDO**
Adesso? Attendi.	Now? Wait.

VIOLETTA	**VIOLETTA**
No - voglio uscire.	No. I want to go out.

(Annina gives her a dress which she tries to put on. Too weak to succeed, she exclaims:)

Gran Dio! Non posso!	Dear God! I cannot!

ALFREDO

(Cielo! Che vedo!)

(to Annina)

Va' pel dottore.

VIOLETTA

Ah! Digli che Alfredo
è ritornato all'amor mio -
Digli che vivere ancor vogl'io.

(Annina goes out. Then, to Alfredo:)

ALFREDO

(Heaven! What is this!)

Go to call the doctor.

VIOLETTA

Tell him that Alfredo
has come back to his love.
Tell him I want to live again.

DISC 2/TRACKS 21 & 22

Violetta realizes the seriousness of her condition, and her music takes on a martial tone, as if she is rebelling aginst fate. Germont's return cheers her slightly but only briefly.

Ma se tornando non m'hai salvato,
a niuno in terra salvarmi è dato.
Ah! gran Dio! Morir sì giovine,
io che penato ho tanto!
Morir sì presso a tergere
il mio sì lungo pianto!
Ah, dunque fu delirio
la credula speranza;
invano di costanza
armato avrò il mio cor!

If in returning you have not saved my life,
then nothing on earth can save me.
Ah! Dear God! To die so young.
when I have sorrowed so long!
To die, when now, at last,
I might have ceased my weeping!
Ah, it was but a dream,
my credulous hope;
to sheathe my heart in constancy
was all in vain.

ALFREDO

Oh mio sospiro e palpito,
diletto del cor mio!
Le mie colle tue lagrime
confondere degg'io -

ALFREDO

My very breath of life, sweet
pulse of my heart!
My tears must flow
together with yours.

Ma più che mai, deh credilo,	But more than ever, ah, believe me,
m'è d'uopo di costanza.	we have need of constancy.
Ah, tutto alla speranza	Ah! Do not close
non chiudere il tuo cor.	your heart to hope.
Ah! Violetta mia, deh calmati,	Ah, my Violetta, be calm,
m'uccide il tuo dolor deh, calmati!	you grief is killing me, be calm!

VIOLETTA

Oh Alfredo! il crudo termine	Oh, Alfredo, what a cruel end
serbato al nostro amor!	for our love!

(Violetta sinks down upon the sofa. Germont enters, followed after a moment by Dr. Grenvil.)

GERMONT

Ah, Violetta!	Ah, Violetta!

VIOLETTA

Voi, signor!	You, sir!

ALFREDO

Mio padre!	Father!

VIOLETTA

Non mi scordaste?	You had not forgotten me?

GERMONT

La promessa adempio.	I am fulfilling my promise.
A stringervi qual figlia vengo al seno,	I have come to embrace you as a daughter.
o generosa!	O generous woman!

VIOLETTA

Ahimè, tardi giungeste!	Alas, you have come too late!

(She embraces him.)

Pure, grate ven sono.	But I am grateful to you.
Grenvil, vedete? Fra le braccia io spiro	Grenvil, see? I am dying in the arms
di quanti cari ho al mondo.	of the only dear ones I have.

GERMONT

Che mai dite!
(Oh cielo - è ver!)

GERMONT

What are you saying!
(Oh, heaven, it is true!)

ALFREDO

La vedi, padre mio?

ALFREDO

Do you see her, father?

GERMONT

Di più non lacerarmi.
Troppo rimorso l'alma mi divora.
Quasi fulmin m'atterra ogni suo detto.
Oh, malcauto vegliardo!
Il mal ch'io feci ora sol vedo!

GERMONT

Don't torture me any longer.
My soul is already devoured by remorse.
Every word she speaks is a thunderbolt.
Oh, rash old man!
Only now do I see the harm I have done.

VIOLETTA

VIOLETTA

(Meanwhile, with great difficulty, she has opened a secret drawer of her dressing table. She takes from it a medallion and gives it to Alfredo.)

DISC NO. 2/TRACK 23

Finally resigned to her fate, Violetta gives her medallion to Alfredo over a funeral march motive in the orchestra which becomes more insistent as Alfredo and his father pour out their despair. As Violetta slips away, the key becomes major (01:07), but it is still punctuated by the funereal figure—we hear both heaven and earth. Over shimmering strings, a solo violin once again announces the love theme (03:22). It grows in intensity as she rallies one last time, and at the peak of her ecstasy, she falls dead and the orchestra hurdles toward its final tragic D-flat minor chord.

Più a me t'appressa -	Come nearer to me -
Ascolta, amato Alfredo.	Listen, beloved Alfredo.

Prendi, quest'è l'immagine de' miei passati
giorni; a rammentarti torni
colei che sì t'amò.

ALFREDO
No, non morrai, non dirmelo -
Dei viver, amor mio.
A strazio sì terribil
qui non mi trasse Iddio.

GERMONT
Cara, sublime, sublime vittima
d'un disperato amore,
perdonami lo strazio recato al tuo bel cor.

VIOLETTA
Se una pudica vergine degli anni suoi sul
fiore, a te donasse il core -
sposa ti sia - lo vo'.
Le porgi quest'effigie;
dille che dono ell'è di chi nel ciel tra gli
angeli prega per lei, per te.

GERMONT
Finché avrà il ciglio lagrime
io piangerò per te.
Vola a' beati spiriti,
Iddio ti chiama a sé.

ALFREDO
Sì presto, ah no, dividerti
morte non può da me.
Ah, vivi, o solo un feretro
m'accoglierà con te.

Take this, it is a portrait painted some years
ago. It will help you to remember
the one who loved you so.

ALFREDO
Ah, you will not die, don't tell me so -
You must live, my darling.
God did not bring me back to you
to face such a tragedy.

GERMONT
Dear noble victim of a hopeless love,
forgive me for having made your heart
suffer.

VIOLETTA
If some young girl in the flower of life
should give her heart to you - marry her -
wish it. Then give her this portrait:
Tell her it is the gift of one who, in heaven
among the angels, prays for her and for you.

GERMONT
As long as my eyes have tears,
so long shall I weep for you.
Fly to the realm of the blessed,
God calls you unto him.

ALFREDO
So soon, oh no, death
cannot take you from me.
Ah, live, or a single coffin
will receive me as well as you.

VIOLETTA (*rianimata*)

È strano!

Cessarono gli spasimi del dolore.

In me rinasce - m'agita insolito vigor!

Ah! ma io ritorno a viver!

Oh gioia!

(She falls down, senseless, upon the sofa.)

FINE

VIOLETTA (*getting up, as if reinvigorated*)

How strange!

The spasms of pain have ceased:

A strange vigour has brought me to life!

Ah! I shall live -

Oh, joy!

END

PHOTO CREDITS

All photographs are copyrighted by the photographers and in some instances by the lending institutions.

Photos Archive Photos / Popperfoto p.39; Bildarchiv Preussischer Kulturbesitz p.10; Christies Images / Super Stock p.68; Courtesy of Glyndebourne Festival Opera: Ira Nowinski/ © Corbis p.27, p.30–31, p.47, p.49, p.79 Hulton-Deutch Collection/Corbis, p.68; Hulton Getty p.12, p.13, p.15, p,21, p.24, p.25, p.33, p.53, p.56; Ira Nowinski/©Corbis, p.34, p.36, p.38, p.44, p.72–73; © 1981 Jack Vartoogian p.18–19, p.22, p.40–41.

LA TRAVIATA

Giuseppe Verdi

COMPACT DISC ONE 67:32:00

1	Prelude	4:31

ATTO PRIMO/ACT ONE

2	Dell'invito tracorsa è gia l'ora	5:02
3	Libiamo ne'lieti calici	3:02
	Alfredo/Violetta	
4	Che è ciò?	2:24
5	Un dì, felice eterea	3:33
	Alfredo/Violetta	
6	Ebben? Che diavol fate?	1:27
7	Si ridesta in ciel l'aurora	1:53
	tutti	
8	È strano	1:28
	Violetta	
9	Ah, fors'è lui	5:59
	Violetta	
10	Follie! Follie!	1:15
	Violetta	
11	Sempre libera	3:49
	Violetta	

ATTO SECONDO/ACT TWO

12	Lunge da lei	1:58
	Alfredo	
13	De'miei bollenti spiriti	1:59
	Alfredo	
14	Annina, donde vieni?	0:44
15	Oh mio rimorso! Oh infamia!	2:53
	Alfredo	
16	Alfredo? Per Parigi or or partiva	4:08
17	Pura siccome un angelo	1:46
	Germont	
18	Non sapete quale affetto	2:11
	Violetta	
19	Un dì, quando le veneri	2:43
	Violetta/Germont	
20	Ah! dite all giovine	4:53
	Violetta/Germont	
21	Imponete. Non amarlo ditegli	1:14
	Violetta/Germont	
22	Morrò La mia memoria	3:48
	Violetta/Germont	
23	Dammi to forza, o cielo!	1:57
24	Che fai?…Ai piedi suoi mi getterò	2:43
	Violetta	

COMPACT DISC TWO 70:26:00

1	Ah, vive sol quel core	2:22
2	Di provenza il mar, il suol	4:35
	Germont	
3	Nè rispondi d'un padre all'affetto	0:32

4	No, non udrai rimproveri	3:52
	Germont	
5	Avrem lieta di maschere la notte	1:02
6	Noi siamo zingarelle	2:43
7	Di Madride noi siam mattadori	2:58
8	Alfredo! Voi!	4:14
9	Invitato a qui seguirmi	2:40
10	Ogni suo aver tal femmina	1:37
	Alfredo/tutti	
11	Di sprezzo degno sè stesso rende	1:48
	Germont/Alfredo/tutti	
12	Alfredo, di questo core	4:18
	Violetta/tutti	

ATTO TERZO/ACT THREE

13	Prelude	4:07
14	Annina? Comandate?	5:13
15	Teneste la promessa	1:57
	Violetta	
16	Addio, del passato	6:06
	Violetta	
17	Largo al quadrupede	0:53
18	Signora! Che t'accadde?	1:53
19	Parigi, o cara, noi lasceremo	4:54
	Alfredo/Violetta	
20	Ah, non più, a un tempio	1:28
21	Ma se tornando...Ah! Gran Dio! Morir sì giovine	3:27
	Alfredo/Violetta	
22	Ah, Violetta! Voi, signor!	1:40
23	Prendi, quest'ä l'immagine...Se una pudica vergine	4:53

CARMEN

CARMEN

Georges Bizet

TEXT BY DAVID FOIL

Additional commentary by William Berger

BLACK DOG
& LEVENTHAL
PUBLISHERS
NEW YORK

Published by
Black Dog & Leventhal Publishers, Inc.
151 West 19th Street
New York, NY 10011

Distributed by
Workman Publishing Company
225 Varick Street
New York, NY 10014

Manufactured in China

Cover and interior design by Elizabeth Driesbach

ISBN-13: 978-1-57912-508-0

h g f e d c b a

Library of Congress Cataloging-in-Publication Data available on file.

*E*verybody knows *Carmen*—the great melodies from Georges Bizet's score are among the most recognized melodies in all of music. But the opera itself is a mesmerizing drama of fatal attraction—still startling in its erotic power and violent intensity, still seductive in its imagination and its potent musical personality. The version of the opera you are about to hear is exactly what the composer intended, restoring the work's original theatrical intensity, both as music and as drama.

You will hear the entire opera on the two compact discs included on the inside front and back covers of this book. As you explore the book, you will discover the story behind the opera and its creation, the background of the composer, biographies of the principal singers and conductor, and the opera's text, or libretto, both in the original French and in an English translation. Special commentary has been included throughout the libretto to aid in your appreciation and to highlight key moments in the action and the score.

Enjoy this book and enjoy the music.

CARMEN

his time I have written a work that is all clarity and vivacity, full of color and melody," the French composer Georges
Bizet told a friend late in 1874, adding, "It will be entertaining. Come along—I think you are going to like it."

At that point, Bizet was genuinely pleased with the new opéra
comique he had just completed, and was looking forward to its
production at the Opéra-Comique in Paris. But this would probably be the last time he felt completely happy about his new

Left: Poster of Emma Calve, a famous early Carmen, circa 1910.
Above: Georges Bizet

Prosper Mérimée

creation, which was called *Carmen*. The rehearsals would be difficult and frustrating; the premiere on March 3, 1875, would be met with apathy. Bizet, who knew he was on to something new in *Carmen*, was bitterly disappointed by this response. Sadly, he did not live to see his work prove a triumphant success only a few years later. He was taken seriously ill shortly after the premiere of *Carmen* and died exactly three months later, early on the morning of June 3, 1875, after the Opéra-Comique gave its thirty-third performance of the opera. Bizet was thirty-six years old.

Carmen has retained more of its allure, magic, and sheer theatrical intensity than almost any other opera in the mainstream repertoire, despite a century of disregard for Bizet's original intentions and a broad popularity that constantly threatens to dump the whole enterprise into the questionable realm of camp. Bizet and his librettists Henri Meilhac and Ludovic Halévy based their work on a dark novella by the French writer Prosper Mérimée. In Mérimée's story, a psychotic soldier, Don José, recounts his obsessive love for an irresistibly carnal creature named Carmen, an obsession that ends with his killing her. In the opera, the bleakness of Mérimée's novella is mitigated somewhat, but the subtle background detail seems to have had a powerful impact on Bizet's music. Making an opera of *Carmen* was apparently his idea and, though he does not have a reputation as a true innovator, he found an uncanny way to reach the bourgeois audience for which he was writing while remaining true to the primal intensity of the material.

Indeed, Georges Bizet's reputation as one of France's greatest composers of the nineteenth century rests almost entirely on *Carmen*. Few composers have shown as much promise as Bizet did as a young man. He was encouraged from an early age by his parents, both of whom were musicians, and entered the Paris Conservatory at the age of nine. As a teenager, he took prizes there in piano and organ performance, and in fugue writing; at the age of nineteen, he was awarded the prestigious Prix de Rome, the seal of approval from the French musical establishment to a young composer. However, Bizet had little interest in writing the kind of music the establishment expected—masses, cantatas, grand symphonic works—and he ran into trouble by trying to write an opera as part of his obligation as the Prix de Rome laureate. (The lighthearted work in question, entitled *Don Procopio*, would not be performed until 1906.) In fact, trouble plagued all of Bizet's many efforts at writing opera. The only other Bizet opera performed today, *Les Pêcheurs de perles* (The Pearl Fishers), completed in 1863, is best known for containing two beautiful arias and a hugely popular duet ("Au fond du temple saint" for tenor and baritone) in an attractive but less than extraordinary score set in an exotic location to a turgid libretto.

An 1878 illustration of *Carmen's* final scene.

The idea of setting *Carmen* as an opera seems to have occurred to Bizet around 1873. His librettists Halévy and Meilhac were a highly esteemed partnership in French opera who wrote, either together or with other collaborators, the librettos for operas by Clement Delibes, Friedrich Flotow, and Jules Massenet and most of Jacques Offenbach's operettas, as well as the plays that inspired the Viennese operettas *Die Fledermaus* and *The Merry Widow*. It seems neither Halévy nor Meilhac—who were consumed with projects they considered more important—thought much of the project or the libretto they fashioned for *Carmen*, and Bizet himself tinkered with the text to bring it to the point where it met his specific demands for the musical score and the drama. The result is a libretto as fine as any in the history of opera, setting the stage for the composition of a score that now seems astonishingly bold.

Bizet's music prior to *Carmen* was unfailingly skillful, attractive, and very much influenced by the work of the respected French composer Charles Gounod, who was his mentor. In his earlier works, Bizet showed a fine gift for melody and an evolving interest in the colors and effects that could be drawn from an orchestra. Yet little of this prepares us for the volatile beauty of the *Carmen* score. The very year he began writing *Carmen*, Bizet had been working on Don Rodrigue, a five-act grand opera about the hero of Spanish history known as El Cid. He abandoned the project because the Opéra burned, temporarily ceasing production and thus eliminating the possibility of a performance; his friend Ernest Guiraud later intimated that the disappearance of the score was a great loss to music. When parts of the *Don Rodrigue* score resurfaced decades later, they revealed another competent but uninspired effort, with little of the genius of *Carmen*, despite a shared Spanish setting.

It is clear that Bizet was both inspired and liberated by the story of *Carmen*,

Composer Charles Gounod
(1818-1893) was Bizet's mentor.

resulting in a score that is surprisingly deft, a quality that heightens the work's ambiguous sensuality and mood. Nothing illustrates this lightness of touch more than the breathtaking signature melody that ignites the opera's prelude. Where did this melody come from? It sounds like nothing else in music. Yes, it suggests Spain and a festive scene, but has something else—a wide-eyed, come-what-may excitement, a shocking virility, and a primal intensity that hints at what Carmen instinctively knows and what Don José is afraid to acknowledge. The detail in Bizet's musical plan is extraordinary. Even though one of the score's most famous passages, the habanera sung by Carmen, relies on the melody of the song "El arreglito" by the Spanish songwriter Sebastián de Yradier, Bizet (who thought it was a folk tune) tweaked the rhythm and shape of the melody in a manner that utterly transformed it. The crowning glory of *Carmen* is the final duet, in which the crazed Don José confronts Carmen in a dazzlingly compact fourth act that lasts barely twenty minutes. After the crowd departs for the bullfight, Bizet draws us into the vortex by echoing the signature theme and dragging it down, down, down chromatically, preparing us for what is about to happen. The duet itself is an exquisitely beautiful showpiece for the two singers, heartbreaking in its inevitability and magical in its streamlined eloquence. No less an orchestral master than Richard Strauss once said, "If you want to know how to orchestrate ... study the score of *Carmen*. What wonderful economy, and how every note and rest is in its proper place."

Rosa Ponselle as Carmen.

Why, then, did audiences and critics scratch their heads and recoil when they first heard *Carmen*? Why did Bizet's score confound and infuriate the orchestra that was to play it for the first time? Some of the singers were puzzled, too. The ladies of the chorus, in particular, resented the fact that they were expected to smoke cigarettes and fight onstage (some of them were taken ill in the process), and there was general uneasiness about the sexual candor of the story. However, Bizet's leading singers supported him and threatened to walk out in protest if any kind of censorship was attempted. There is no evidence to support speculation that Bizet was forced against his will to make extensive last-minute cuts and changes in the score. The morning of the premiere of *Carmen*, in fact, the composer was made a chevalier of the Legion of Honor. At last success seemed to be imminent.

It was not to be. Contrary to legend, *Carmen* was not a failure at its premiere, and it did not directly bring about Bizet's death three months later. It can best be described as being neither a flop nor a hit. At the premiere, Bizet reportedly told the young composer Vincent d'Indy, who came to congratulate him and found him pacing outside near the stage door, "I sense defeat. I foresee a definite and hopeless flop. This time I am really sunk." The audience's unenthusiastic, not to say perplexed, response and the negative reviews only reinforced his fears. His mentor Gounod gracelessly insisted that Bizet had stolen the melody for Micaëla's third-act aria from him, and what hadn't been stolen from him and others was mere "sauce without the fish." Opening-night reviews berated Bizet for the

The cigarette girls in front of a wall covered with graffiti in a set designed in 1981 for the San Francisco Opera by Jean-Pierre Ponnelle.

lack of color in his score and—worst of all, to these critics—for a tendency toward Wagnerian techniques. In the wake of the Franco-Prussian war, any suggestion of Richard Wagner's influence was considered in certain quarters to be an insult to French art. "Fed on the enharmonic succulences of the prophets of the music of the future, Bizet seems to have fed his soul on this diet, thereby killing it," one critic wrote, warming up to continue, "Ingenious details in the orchestra, daring dissonances, and instrumental subtleties cannot portray the uterine agonies of Mademoiselle Carmen and the wishes of her wayward lovers ... the music lacks novelty and distinction. There is no plan, no unity in its style ... it is neither dramatic nor scenic."

The chief prophet of the "music of the future," Wagner in fact abhorred *Carmen*. So intense was his dislike that it widened a long-standing breach between him and the philosopher Friedrich Nietzsche that would never heal. Nietzsche found *Carmen* to be a transcendent work of art because the score manages to be "wicked, subtle, and fatalistic" while remaining accessible. "What is good is easy," Nietzsche wrote as his first aesthetic law, "everything divine runs with light feet." The Russian composer Pyotr Ilich Tchaikovsky was an early fan of *Carmen*, too, and insisted that it would soon enjoy world-wide popularity.

No one would dispute the fact that *Carmen* is a masterpiece, and no one has seriously since its apathetic premiere. Yet the "real" *Carmen* has proved elusive for more than the century that it has been in the repertoire of opera houses all over the world. *Carmen* is not an opera, in the strict grand opera sense of the word, but an opéra-comique. *Opéra-comique* is a French term that has no fixed meaning—not all the works so labeled fit the contemporary understanding of comedy—but it has come to refer to an operatic work with comic elements that also has spoken dialogue. In Paris in the midnineteenth century that dialogue distinguished comic opera from the sober, overstuffed grand operas so popular at the Opéra. The theater known as the Opéra-Comique was an altogether less pretentious place than the Opéra, drawing a more bourgeois crowd, and it provided a more relaxed atmosphere for operatic entertainment.

Dome of the Paris Opéra.

By the early 1870s, Bizet had had no success in writing a grand opera that interested the public, and he decided shortly before he set to work on *Carmen* that he should leave that task to others. He wrote *Carmen* for the Opéra-Comique, certain he had found a level on which to communicate with an audience. He crafted a score with a prelude and twenty-seven musical numbers to be linked by spoken dialogue. He personally corrected the proofs on the published score in this form which was published by the Choudens firm in 1875. Yet, for almost one hundred years, the Choudens score was almost never performed.

Much of *Carmen's* popularity rests on an adaptation of the score by Ernest Guiraud, the gifted New Orleans–born,

Paris–based composer who was one of Bizet's best friends. Guiraud created this new version for the Vienna premiere of *Carmen* in October of 1875, replacing Bizet, who had signed the contract to write the recitatives for the production the day before he died. Guiraud made the score more appealing for the opera

Marilyn Horne in the title role.

Geraldine Farrar as Carmen.

house by composing sung recitatives to replace the spoken
dialogue, as Bizet himself had been contracted to do. There
were some compelling reasons for this change. First of all, the
absence of dialogue and the presence of sung recitative made
Carmen sound more like a grand opera. Second, making it an
opera that was fully sung made the performance easier for
singers who at the time resented the amount of additional
acting they were required to do. Third, opera in the late nineteenth century was not always performed in the language in
which it was written, and the distinctively French opéra-

Jose Carreras as the psychotic Don José.

comique—with its pointillistic interplay of the French language both spoken and sung—lost a great deal in translation. But as Guiraud made *Carmen* a more accessible repertory piece and created the version most audiences know, he blunted the razor-sharp double-edged nature of the true opéra-comique Bizet had envisioned.

Carmen is not a pretty story, despite the image of lusty gypsy women with cascades of hair and roses tucked behind their ears that is traditionally associated with the opera. The title character is a woman who is irresistible to men, with a kind of wild dignity all her own. She does whatever she feels like doing, until she makes the fatal mistake of ruining the life of the deeply disturbed Don José. She chooses to live in a world that tolerates her, a world of deception, thievery, cruelty, and violence. Violence is the flip side of beauty in Bizet's opera—in the text, in the action, and in the music itself—and the cruelty of the actions of everyone involved (except Don José's selfless fiancée Micaëla) is stunning. Slightly later, Italians would claim *Carmen* as the forerunner of verismo opera, a vividly realistic style of opera that flourished in Italy around the turn of the twentieth century. *Cavalleria rusticana* and *I pagliacci* are examples of the verismo style and, ultimately, not unlike *Carmen* in their murderous intensity.

But remember Bizet's description: "... all clarity and vivacity ... It will be entertaining." If the Italians thought *Carmen* prefigured *I pagliacci*, it was probably because they knew Carmen from the Guiraud version, where elements of comedy and Bizet's strikingly ambiguous atmosphere had virtually been eliminated. As in a classic American musical comedy, the dialogue between musical numbers in an opéra-comique tends to underscore the characters' humanity, to reveal subtleties and interesting contradictions in their personalities. Instead of the alluring, vampish prima donna that reigns supreme in Guiraud's version, the Carmen of Bizet's opéra-comique is raunchy, sometimes wickedly funny, petty, tantalizingly remote, and unpredictable. Likewise, Bizet's Don José is not the bellowing overgrown boy he can sometimes seem in the Guiraud version, but a deeply conflicted young man full of repressed rage. He is teetering on the brink of insanity, an obsessive-compulsive who becomes a homicidal stalker. In the case of Don José, the opéra-comique version does not make the character lighter but much, much darker.

For all the criticism of Guiraud's version of *Carmen*, it must be said that the quality of his work was excellent. The recitatives are so effective musically that it is sometimes difficult to know what was written by Bizet and what was written by Guiraud. Its effectiveness made it the accepted version, to such an extent that curiosity about the opéra-comique version was left to scholars. However, in 1964, a musicologist named Fritz Oeser

Gladys Swarthout
as Carmen.

discovered—in a dust-covered, forgotten cupboard at the
Opéra-Comique—a conductor's score and orchestral parts
that allowed him to reconstruct elements of the score Bizet
had not included in the edition published by Choudens in
1875. Oeser's discoveries are fascinating, though Bizet schol-
ar Winton Dean makes a compelling case for viewing the 1875
Choudens score without the Guiraud recitatives as the most
authoritative one. If Oeser's new edition raised a controversy,

it did reintroduce the idea of presenting *Carmen* in its original form, which is now accepted as the ideal in recordings and in the world's major opera houses. Many recordings of *Carmen* since Oeser's discovery have borrowed from Oeser's edition. But this recording, made in 1969–70, led the way in restoring the primacy of Bizet's 1875 Choudens score. At long last, this is the opera—or rather the opéra-comique—that Bizet meant for the world to hear.

THE STORY OF THE OPERA

Act 1

It is a typical, sleepy day in Seville. Soldiers linger in the square outside the armory, next to a cigarette factory, as the townspeople go about their business. So little is happening that, for the soldiers, the highlight of the guards' watch is the appearance of a shy country girl from Navarre named Micaëla. She is looking for Don José. The corporal Moralès tells her that Don José is due shortly with the relief guard and invites her to wait in the guardhouse. Micaëla recoils, taken aback by the laughing soldiers' interest, and tells Moralès she will return later. Don José arrives with the change of guard and learns of Micaëla's visit.

Zuniga, the lieutenant, kids Don José about his country girlfriend and then asks him what he knows about the cigarette factory girls. Don José insists he pays no attention to them. At that moment, a ringing bell signals a smoking break

A scene from Act I in a production at the Houston Grand Opera.

for the factory girls, which attracts a crowd of young men hoping to catch their attention. The girls enjoy the ritual but, in truth, the men are interested in only one girl—the mysterious and alluring Carmen. Carmen is unfazed by their attention, as they beg her to choose one of them as her lover. She answers to the rhythms of the habanera: love is as untamable as a wild bird, as prone to wandering as a gypsy. Her indifference only intensifies the men's interest.

Carmen tosses an acacia flower to the one man in the square who pays no attention to her—Don José, who is repelled by her boldness yet immediately drawn into her spell. He keeps the flower and quickly hides it in his tunic when Micaëla suddenly appears. She brings Don José a letter and some money from his mother, as well as a kiss; they reminisce about their happiness at home. In the letter, Don José's mother begs him to marry Micaëla and, when his tour of duty ends, return to live near her. Embarrassed by the suggestion, Micaëla leaves, saying they will meet again shortly.

At that moment, a fight breaks out in the cigarette factory. Zuniga, surrounded by screaming girls trying to tell him who started it, sends Don José inside to break it up. Don José emerges with a defiant Carmen, who has slashed the face of another girl. She barely offers a defense of her behavior and, when pressed, only sings derisively in Zuniga's face. He leaves to obtain a warrant for her arrest, charging Don José to guard Carmen. She tricks Don José into a conversation and begins to tease him with the prospect of spending an evening (and

more) with her at the tavern of Lillas Pastia, on the outskirts of Seville. He is unnerved by her attention and eventually agrees to untie her hands so she can escape. When Zuniga returns, Carmen is led away and then suddenly pushes Don José to the ground, humiliating him as she runs away laughing,

Placido Domingo as Don José.

her friends thwarting the soldiers' attempts to recapture her. The lieutenant angrily orders a stunned Don José to be arrested and led away to the brig.

Act 2

Carmen is holding court at Lillas Pastia's with her gypsy friends Frasquita and Mercédès. They sing and dance to the great enjoyment of the soldiers who are pursuing them, led by none other than Zuniga. Carmen is cool to Zuniga, who thinks she is angry at him for trying to have her arrested. She is actually piqued that he had Don José thrown into prison, and she is delighted to hear that the unfortunate soldier is being released that night. They are interrupted by the arrival of Escamillo, the great toreador of Granada, who raises the roof of Lillas Pastia's with a toast after Zuniga buys him a drink. Escamillo is immediately drawn to Carmen, who teases and strings him along with her indifference. Zuniga and his men leave with Escamillo, who tells Carmen he will return for her.

Once the crowd has left, a nervous Lillas Pastia tells Frasquita that the smugglers Dancaïro and Remendado have returned. The gypsy women are delighted, however, and learn that the smugglers need their help in bringing in contraband from Gibraltar. All agree that women are indispensable in such an

enterprise, though Carmen surprises them by saying she will not join them. She is, she says, in love. They laugh at her, but she insists that she is only interested in waiting for Don José's release from prison.

When they hear Don José's voice in the distance, Dancaïro suggests Carmen enlist his aid and have him run away with them. She says she will try, as she hustles the smugglers out of the tavern in order to offer a proper greeting to the young soldier. He becomes jealous when Carmen tells him that Zuniga has been pursuing her. She then calms him by dancing for his enjoyment, accompanied by her castanets. As she dances, he hears a bugle call in the distance, summoning the troops back to the barracks. Don José tells her suddenly he must leave. Carmen explodes in rage, ridiculing his passion and his sense of duty, while berating herself for wasting her time on him.

Don José silences her by producing the acacia flower she tossed him in their first encounter. With a feverish intensity, he tells her that the flower has been his emblem of hope during his imprisonment—proof of his passionate love for her.

Carmen sees her opportunity, scoffing at his assurances and insisting that if he really loved her, he would join her and her friends in their new enterprise. Don José is initially seduced by the idea, then recoils at the thought of being a deserter. He prepares to leave, telling her again how much he loves her, when Zuniga enters to confront him. A hysterical Don José draws his sword on Zuniga. Carmen calls for help from Dancaïro and Remendado. They enter with the other gypsies and tell Zuniga that his timing has been unfortunate. When Carmen again asks Don José to join them, he realizes he now has no choice, and she assures him he will come to love the carefree life of the gypsy.

Carmen (Geraldine Farrar) dances for Don José.

Act 3

Months later, the band of smugglers is still hauling contraband over the mountains. They pause to rest, as Dancaïro and Remendado go ahead to find out how to slip unnoticed into the next town. Don José, who is clearly miserable, tells Carmen that his mother lives nearby. The charm of their relationship has worn off for Carmen, and she suggests he return home. He flies into a rage at the idea. As a diversion, Frasquita and Mercédès bring out the tarot cards to read their fortunes. The wisdom of the cards amuses them but Carmen is shocked by what they reveal for herself and Don José—death. Believing

what the cards tell her, Carmen knows now what lies in store. Dancaïro and Remendado return, saying they need the women's help in distracting some customs guards. The increasingly despondent Don José is left to guard the

Frasquita (Gloria Lind, left) and Mercedes (Helen Vanni) read the tarot deck.

Scene from a 1990 production of *Carmen* at the Lyric Opera of Chicago.

loot. A guide appears with Micaëla who is searching for Don José. She tells the guide she will proceed alone without fear. Once she is alone, she gives voice to her fears and prays to God for strength. When Micaëla finally sees Don José, she so startles him that he fires his gun without seeing her.

At that moment, with Micaëla cowering unseen, Escamillo enters and tells Don José that the shot just missed him. After introducing himself, he informs Don José that he is looking for Carmen, with whom he is in love. Don José becomes furious and challenges Escamillo to a knife fight. Escamillo, the superior fighter, humors him but then stumbles and suddenly is at Don José's mercy. Only the arrival of Carmen and the other gypsies saves him. Escamillo laughs at the delicious irony of his salvation and invites Carmen and her friends to be his guests at the bullfight in Seville.

Don José, already beside himself, is stunned when the smugglers find Micaëla hiding in the rocks; she tells him that his mother is calling for him. Carmen tells him to go and, though he resists leaving her to Escamillo's favors, he leaves with Micaëla once he learns that his mother is dying and wants to see him one last time. Don José warns Carmen that their affair is not over. Once he leaves, Carmen's fancy turns to the distant sound of Escamillo's singing.

Act 4

Outside the arena in Seville, excitement is growing in antic-
ipation of the great bullfight that will feature Escamillo. A
huge crowd awaits the ceremonial procession to the bullring,
culminating in the arrival of Escamillo in his toreador regalia,
with a resplendent Carmen on his arm. Frasquita and Mercédès have learned that Don José—who is now pursued by
the army as a deserter—might be in the vicinity. Before entering the arena in the wake of Escamillo's procession, they try
to warn Carmen who dismisses their concern and sends them
on into the arena. Alone in the square, she awaits her destiny. Don José emerges from the shadows to tell her that he
has not come to harm her, and pleads with her to accept the
inevitability of their love. Carmen refuses, and tells him that
they are finished. He does not believe her, begging her to
take him back. Carmen, distracted by the crowd's cheers for
Escamillo, tries to make her way to the bullring but is blocked
by Don José who demands to know if she and Escamillo are
lovers. Carmen answers that she and the toreador are indeed
lovers and that not even the threat of death can make her
deny it. The full weight of Carmen's contempt finally hits Don

Carmen meets her destiny in a 1972 production at the Metropolitan Opera.

José. She further insults him by hurling the ring he had given her in his face. Shattered, his ears ringing with the cheers of Escamillo's admirers, Don José attacks Carmen, stabbing her to death. He collapses over her body, admitting his guilt as he professes his love for her.

THE PERFORMERS

GRACE BUMBRY (Carmen) has had a remarkable career as a mezzo-soprano, with occasional forays into the soprano repertory. Born in 1937 in St. Louis, she began singing in church choirs as a little girl and began attending Northwestern University in 1955 as a student of Lotte Lehmann. Bumbry followed Lehmann to the Music Academy of the West in Santa Barbara, California, to continue the study that would shape her as a singer. Her professional debut came in a concert performance in London in 1959; her operatic debut a year later, where she stunned audiences at the Paris Opéra as a last-minute substitute in the role of Amneris in *Aida*. The fact that she was African-American added to the glamour of the debut, and it created a positive furor when Wieland Wagner subsequently signed her to sing the role of Venus in Wagner's *Tannhäuser* at the 1961 Bayreuth Festival. The triumph Bumbry enjoyed there made her an instant celebrity. Her return to the United States brought her to the Kennedy White House and an important concert tour. Her debut at the Chicago Lyric Opera

Grace Bumbry as Carmen.

in 1963 repeated her Bayreuth success as Venus, and her Metropolitan Opera debut was made two years later as Princess Eboli in Verdi's *Don Carlo*. Bumbry's Carmen created a sensation at the 1966 Salzburg Festival under Herbert von Karajan (a production that was filmed), and it became one of her trademark roles. In the early 1970s, Bumbry took advantage of her remarkable range and began singing soprano roles. The title role in Strauss's *Salome* became a particular favorite, as did the fearsome role of Abigaille in Verdi's *Nabucco*, but she also had great success in the title roles of *Tosca* and *Aida*. (She also continued to sing the mezzo-soprano role of Amneris, just as she began to sing Elisabeth as well as Venus in *Tannhäuser*.) Bumbry also sang Bess in the first Metropolitan Opera production of Gershwin's *Porgy and Bess*. In the 1980s, she returned to the great mezzo-soprano roles upon which her reputation rested. Her voice was always remarkable for its expressive richness, power, and extensive range—qualities largely undiminished when she returned to the Metropolitan Opera for a gala appearance in 1996.

JON VICKERS (Don José) exemplified the art of the dramatic tenor throughout his long and remarkable career. Born in 1926 in Prince Albert, Saskatchewan, he emerged from unlikely beginnings in provincial Canada—where he managed F.W. Woolworth stores and served as a purchasing agent for the Hudson Bay Company—to study voice as a scholarship student at the Royal Conservatory of Music in Toronto. Vickers made his professional operatic debut in 1952 as the Duke in *Rigoletto* at the Toronto Opera Festival, and his tremendous promise began to pay off quickly. Within five years, he was singing in London with the Royal Opera, Covent Garden, where he enjoyed great acclaim in 1958 in the title role in Luchino Visconti's legendary production there of Verdi's *Don Carlo*. The heroic profile and unique intensity of Vickers's singing made him a natural candidate for the heldentenor roles in Wagner's music-dramas. Vickers trod carefully around this potentially dangerous repertoire, sticking primarily (and with great success) with Siegmund in Die Walküre, the title role in *Parsifal* and, for a few years, Tristan in *Tristan und Isolde*. He sang Siegmund at the Bayreuth Festival in 1958 and recorded the role twice but avoided the heavier role of Siegfried. Vickers's repertoire was fascinating in its breadth, and it reflected his highly personal, unusually principled approach to his career. He has had little patience with the superficial glamour

Jon Vickers as Don José and Mirella Freni as Michaëla in a 1968–69 production at the Metropolitan Opera.

and politics of the international operatic scene and has been outspoken in his disdain for those who take for granted the moral dimension of art and of being an artist. If these qualities made him a demanding colleague, they also made him an extraordinary one—Vickers delivered as a performer with astonishing consistency and tremendous dramatic power. Earlier in his career, he sang Jason in Luigi Cherubini's *Medea* opposite Maria Callas in thrilling performances with the Dallas Opera that were captured live on tape. His signature roles included Enée in Hector Berlioz's *Les Troyens* (a long-neglected opera he helped popularize), Canio in Ruggero Leoncavallo's *I pagliacci*, Florestan in Beethoven's *Fidelio* and—perhaps most unforgettably—the anguished title characters in Giuseppe Verdi's *Otello* and Benjamin Britten's *Peter Grimes*.

MIRELLA FRENI (Micaëla) was born in 1935 in Modena, a few months earlier than the city's most famous son, Luciano Pavarotti. As infants, the two singers-to-be—who would later become affectionate colleagues—shared the same wet nurse, and their mothers worked in the same cigarette factory. Freni began studying voice with her uncle, making her first public appearance at the age of eleven with another prodigy, the pianist Leone Magiera, who would become her first husband. She made her opera debut in 1955 in Modena as Micaëla in *Carmen*, inaugurating what would be a stellar international stage and recording career of extraordinary range and longevity. After singing several seasons with provincial Italian houses, Freni made strong impressions in debuts with the Amsterdam Opera (1959), London's Covent Garden (1961), and Milan's La Scala (1962), quickly becoming one of Europe's most sought-after lyric sopranos. The role of Mimì in *La Bohème* became her calling card, especially after her performance in the successful 1963 film of Franco Zeffirelli's La Scala production, conducted by Herbert von Karajan. Freni sang Mimì in her debuts at Moscow's Bolshoi Opera (1964) and New York's Metropolitan Opera (1965). She also excelled in such roles as Susanna in *Le nozze di Figaro*, Violetta in *La traviata*, Zerlina in *Don Giovanni*, Marguerite in *Faust*, and Juliette in *Roméo et Juliette*. In the 1970s, when Freni decided to sing heavier roles—a dangerous choice for a lyric soprano—many critics predicted that it would ruin her voice. Bolstered by a steady technique and the sensitive support of conductors such as von Karajan and Riccardo Muti, she was instead acclaimed for bringing a distinctive lyrical warmth to performances and recordings of the title role in *Aida*, Cio-Cio-San in *Madama Butterfly*, Elisabetta in *Don Carlo*, and Leonora in *La forza del destino*. In 1981, she married the Bulgarian bass Nicolai Ghiaurov, a colleague who virtually became her professional partner, notably after Freni began singing Russian roles such as Tatyana in *Eugene Onegin*. In the 1990s, she has been noted for her performances in the demanding prima donna roles of such verismo warhorses as *Adriana Lecouvreur* and *Fedora*.

KOSTAS PASKALIS (Escamillo) began his career with a seven-year stint in the ensemble of the Athens Opera, where he made his professional debut in 1951 in the title role of *Rigoletto* after studying at the Athens Conservatory. Born in 1929 in Lebadea, Greece, he enjoyed a successful debut at the Vienna Staatsoper in 1958, leading to an international career that would last for the next quarter-century. The dramatic intensity of Paskalis's singing was a fine match for the signature baritone roles in the Italian repertoire. He sang frequently at the Vienna Staatsoper and with Berlin's Deutsche Oper, London's Royal Opera at Covent Garden and, in Russia during the Soviet era, with the Bolshoi and Kirov companies. His Metropolitan Opera debut came in 1965 in the role of Carlo in *La forza del destino*. He also sang with other American companies; in 1979, he was reunited with tenor Jon Vickers in a production of Verdi's *Otello* at the Houston Grand Opera. Because Paskalis came to prominence at a time when the baritones Robert Merrill, Tito Gobbi, Ettore Bastianini, Piero Cappuccilli, and Sherrill Milnes were singing, he did not record as frequently as they did. Yet he was an outstanding singer who had particular success with the challenging role of Escamillo in *Carmen*, which he sang (also with Grace Bumbry and Jon Vickers) in Herbert von Karajan's film of his Salzburg Festival production.

RAFAEL FRÜHBECK DE BURGOS (born Rafael Frühbeck) is the son of a German father and a Spanish mother whose training and repertoire are largely reflective of that heritage. Born in the Spanish town of Burgos in 1933, he began his studies as a violinist at the conservatory in Bilbao in 1950. From 1956 until 1958, he studied conducting with Kurt Eichhorn at Munich's Hochschule für Musik, after which he returned to Bilbao to conduct the city's municipal orchestra. Frühbeck de Burgos quickly emerged as Spain's most promising conductor and, in 1962, was named principal conductor of Madrid's Orquesta Nacional de España, a post he held for fifteen years. He simultaneously served as general-musikdirektor of the Düsseldorf Symphony Orchestra (1966–71) and, for two years, as music director of the Montreal Symphony Orchestra (1975–76). In the United States, Frühbeck de Burgos has had a long association with Washington's National Symphony Orchestra, beginning with a stint as principal guest conductor in 1980. He is a frequent guest with orchestras throughout Europe and the United States. His most recent posts have included music director of Tokyo's Yomiuri Nippon Symphony Orchestra and, beginning in 1990, chief conductor of the Vienna Symphony Orchestra. Though he conducts and records the standard orchestral repertoire, he has been especially admired in Spanish music and that with a Spanish flavor, making him an obvious choice for a recording of *Carmen*.

The Libretto

$\mathscr{A}ct$ 1

Prelude Wild and indefinable, the thrilling melody that begins the opera's prelude becomes a symbol of the title character. It is heard again only once, in the chorus that greets the bullfighters in Act IV, but its vivid, dancing abandon is the very incarnation of Carmen. There is also a contrasting section that quotes the Toreador Song of Act II (01:01), before the principal melody returns. After a deceptive pause, it is followed by a striking motive that will be heard repeatedly an ominous descending melody (02:07), played against a shuddering orchestra, that represents the inexorable force of fate in Carmen's life. It plunges deeper and deeper as it develops, then rises and builds in tension to an almost unbearable point, where it simply and stunningly snaps—and the opera begins.

The factory scene in a production at the Metropolitan Opera.

Sur la place, chacun passe At the conclusion of the opening chorus, which describes a lazy mid-day scene in the square in Seville and introduces Micaëla, Bizet had written a pantomime, to be sung by Moralès, that he cut almost immediately. It is an amusing, charismatic moment (05:54), written to satisfy an underemployed singer and charmingly done, but because it delays the action it is rarely performed. It was heard for the first time when this recording was released on LP and is included here.

SCENE ONE
Introduction

A square in Seville. On the right, the door of a tobacco factory. At the back, facing the audience, a bridge from one side of the stage to the other, reached from the stage by a winding staircase beyond the factory door. The bridge is open underneath. In front, a guard-house; in front of that, three steps leading to a covered passage. As the curtain rises, a file of soldiers (dragoons of Almanza) are grouped before the guard-house, smoking and looking at the passers-by in the square coming and going. The scene is full of animation.

LES SOLDATS
Sur la place
chacun passe,
chacun vient, chacun va;
drôles de gens que ces gens-là!

SOLDIERS
On the square
everyone comes by,
everyone comes and goes;
funny sort of people these!

MORALÈS
A la porte du corps de garde,
pour tuer le temps,
on fume, on jase, l'on regarde
passer les passants.

MORALÈS
At the guard-house door,
to kill time,
we smoke, gossip, and watch
the passers-by.

LES SOLDATS ET MORALÈS
Sur la place, *etc.*

SOLDIERS AND MORALÈS
On the square, *etc.*

Micaëla enters.

MORALÈS

Regardez donc cette petite
qui semble vouloir nous parler.
Voyez, elle tourne, elle hésite.

LES SOLDATS

A son secours il faut aller!

MORALÈS *(à Micaëla)*

Que cherchez-vous, la belle?

MICAËLA

Moi, je cherche un brigadier.

MORALÈS

Je suis là, voilà!

MICAËLA

Mon brigadier à moi s'appelle
Don José ... le connaissez-vous?

MORALÈS

Don José! Nous le connaissons tous.

MICAËLA

Vraiment! Est-il avec vous, je vous prie?

MORALÈS

Il n'est pas brigadier dans notre compagnie.

MICAËLA *(désolée)*

Alors, il n'est pas là?

MORALÈS

Now look at this little lass
who seems to want to speak to us.
Look, she's turning round, she's hesitating.

SOLDIERS

We must go and help her!

MORALÈS *(to Micaëla)*

Whom are you looking for, pretty one?

MICAËLA

I'm looking for a corporal.

MORALÈS

Here I am, look!

MICAËLA

My corporal is called
Don José ... do you know him?

MORALÈS

Don José? We all know him.

MICAËLA

Really! Is he with you, please?

MORALÈS

He isn't a corporal in our company.

MICAËLA *(disappointed)*

Then he isn't here?

MORALÈS

Non, ma charmante, il n'est pas là.
Mais tout à l'heure il y sera,
il y sera quand la garde montante
remplacera la garde descendante.

LES SOLDATS ET MORALÈS

Il y sera, *etc.*

MORALÈS

Mais en attendant qu'il vienne,
voulez-vous, la belle enfant,
voulez-vous prendre la peine
d'entrer chez nous un instant?

MICAËLA

Chez vous?

LES SOLDATS ET MORALÈS

Chez nous.

MICAËLA

Non pas, non pas.
Grand merci, messieurs les soldats.

MORALÈS

Entrez sans crainte, mignonne.
je vous promets qu'on aura, pour votre
chère personne,
tous les égards qu'il faudra.

MICAËLA

Je n'en doute pas; cependant
je reviendrai, c'est plus prudent.
Je reviendrai quand la garde montante
remplacera la garde descendante.

MORALÈS

No, my charmer, he isn't here.
But in a few minutes he will be,
he'll be here when the new guard
comes to relieve the old guard.

SOLDIERS AND MORALÈS

He'll be here, *etc.*

MORALÈS

But while you wait for him to come
will you, my pretty child,
take the trouble
to step inside with us for a moment?

MICAËLA

Inside with you?

SOLDIERS AND MORALÈS

Inside with us.

MICAËLA

No, no.
Many thanks, soldiers.

MORALÈS

Don't be afraid to come in, my dear,
I promise you we shall treat
your dear self
with every due respect.

MICAËLA

I don't doubt it; all the same
I'll come back, that's wiser.
I'll be back when the new guard comes to
relieve the old guard.

LES SOLDATS ET MORALÈS

Il faut rester car la garde montante,
va remplacer la garde descendante.

MORALÈS

Vous resterez!

MICAËLA

Non pas! non pas!

surrounding Micaëla

LES SOLDATS ET MORALÈS

Vous resterez!

MICAËLA

Non pas! Non pas! Non! Non! Non!
Au revoir, messieurs les soldats!

She escapes and runs off.

MORALÈS

L'oiseau s'envole,
on s'en console.
Reprenons notre passe-temps

SOLDATS

Sur la place
chacun passe, *etc.*

MORALÈS

Drôles de gens! Drôles de gens!
Drôles de gens!

SOLDIERS AND MORALÈS

You must stay, because the new guard
is on its way to relieve the old guard.

MORALÈS

You'll stay!

MICAËLA

Indeed I'll not!

SOLDIERS AND MORALÈS

You'll stay!

MICAËLA

Indeed I'll not! No, no, no!
Goodbye, soldiers!

MORALÈS

The bird has flown;
we'll console ourselves.
Let's resume our pastime
and watch the folks go by.

SOLDIERS

On the square
everyone comes by, *etc.*

MORALÈS

Funny sort of people!

The movement of the passers-by which had stopped during the foregoing scene has now resumed with a certain animation. Among the people coming and going is an old gentleman with a young lady on his arm … The old gentleman would like to continue his walk, but the young lady is doing all she can to detain him on the square. She seems anxious, uneasy. She looks to right and left. She is expecting someone, and this someone does not come. This pantomime must fit in very exactly with the following verse.

MORALÈS	**MORALÈS**
Attention! Chut! Attention! Taisons-nous!	Stand by! Sssh! Let's pipe down!
Voici venir un vieil époux,	Look, here comes an old husband
Oeil soupçonneux, mine jalouse,	with a suspicious eye and a jealous look,
Il tient au bras sa jeune épouse;	he's holding on to his young wife by the
L'amant sans doute n'est pas loin;	arm; no doubt the lover's not far off;
Il va sortir de quelque coin.	he'll pop out of some corner.
(avec les soldats)	*(With the soldiers)*
L'amant sans doute n'est pas loin;	No doubt the lover's not far off; he'll pop
Il va sortir de quelque coin.	out of some corner.

At this moment a young man comes quickly on to the square.

Ah! ah! ah! ah!	Ha! ha! ha! ha!
Le voilà.	There he is.

MORALÈS	**MORALÈS**
Ah! le voilà! oui, le voilà! *etc.*	Ah, there he is! Yes, there he is! *etc.*
(avec les soldats)	*(With the soldiers)*
Voyons comment ce tournera.	Let's see how this'll turn out.

The second verse follows and must be faithfully adapted to the scene mimed by the three characters. The young man approaches the old gentleman and the young lady, bows, and exchanges a few words in a low voice, etc.

MORALÈS	**MORALÈS**

imitating the young man's eager greeting

Vous trouver ici, quel bonheur!	What luck, finding you here!

assuming the old husband's sour-tempered look

Je suis bien votre serviteur!

Your servant!

putting on the young man's manner again

Il salue, il parle avec grâce.

He bows, he turns on the charm.

then the old husband's expression

Le vieux mari fait la grimace;

The old husband pulls a face;

imitating the lady's simpering smiles

Mais d'un air très encourageant
La dame accueille le galant.

but the lady is greeting the lover in a very
encouraging manner.

At this moment the young man draws from his pocket a note which he shows to the lady. The husband, the wife, and the young blade all three slowly take a little stroll on the square, the young man endeavoring to slip his love-letter to the lady.

MORALÈS

Ils font ensemble quelques pas;
Notre amoureux, levant le bras,
fait voir au mari quelque chose,

MORALÈS

They walk a few steps together;
our lovebird, raising his arm,
draws the husband's attention to somthing,

The young man, with one hand, points out something in the sky to the old gentleman, and with the other passes his note to the lady.

Et le mari, toujours morose,
Regarde en l'air … Le tour est fait,
car la dame a pris le billet!
Et voilà! Et voilà! Ah! ah!
On voit comment ça tournera!
(avec les soldats)

and the husband, still morose,
looks up in the air … The trick has worked,
for the lady has taken the note.
And that's that! that's that! Ha! Ha!
We see how that'll turn out!
(with the soldiers)

On voit comment ça tournera!	We see how that'll turn out!
Ah! ah! ah! ah!	Ha! ha! ha! ha!
On voit comment ça tournera! *etc.*	We see how that'll turn out! *etc.*

SCENE TWO
March and Chorus of Street Boys

A military march of bugles and fifes is heard in the distance. The relief guard is arriving. The old gentle-man and the young man exchange a cordial handshake, and the young man bows respectfully to the lady. An officer comes out of the guard-house. Soldiers take their muskets and form up in front of the guard-house. The passers-by gather in a group to watch the parade. The military march comes nearer and nearer. At last the relief guard emerges and crosses the bridge. First, two bugles and two fifes. Then a band of street urchins. Behind the children, Lieutenant Zuniga and Corporal Don José, then the troopers.

DISC NO. 1/TRACK 3

This chipper boys's chorus with the unforgettable melody (augmented by tweeting piccolos) forms a severe contrast with the music we will hear associated with Carmen and Don José.

CHOEUR DES GAMINS	**CHORUS OF STREET BOYS**
Avec la garde montante,	Right beside the relief guard,
Nous arrivons, nous voilà.	here we come, here we are!
Sonne, trompette éclatante!	Blow out, loud trumpet!
Taratata, taratata!	Taratata, taratata!
Nous marchons la tête haute	We march with head erect
Comme de petits soldats,	like little soldiers,
Marquant sans faire de faute,	keeping time with no mistakes—
Une, deux, marquant le pas.	one, two—keeping step.
Les épaules en arrière	Shoulders back
Et la poitrine en dehors,	and chest well out,
Les bras de cette maniére	arms this way

Tombant tout le long du corps.

Avec la garde montante, *etc.*

straight down beside the body.

Right beside the relief guard, *etc.*

The relief guard halts facing the guard going off duty. The officers salute with their swords and begin to talk in low voices. The sentries are changed.

MORALÈS *(à Don José)*

Il y a une jolie fille qui est venue to demander. Elle a dit qu'elle reviendrait....

MORALÈS *(to Don José)*

There's a pretty girl been asking for you. She said she'd come back....

JOSÉ

Une jolie fille?

JOSÉ

A pretty girl?

MORALÈS

Oui, et gentiment habillée, une jupe bleue, des nattes tombant sur les épaules....

MORALÈS

Yes, and nicely dressed, a blue skirt, plaits down over her shoulders....

JOSÉ

C'est Micaëla. Ce ne peut être que Micaëla.

JOSÉ

It's Micaëla. It can only be Micaëla.

MORALÈS

Elle n'a pas dit son nom.

MORALÈS

She didn't give her name.

REPRISE DU CHOEUR DES GAMINS

Et la garde descendante
Rentre chez elle et s'en va.
Sonne, trompette éclatante,
Taratata, taratata!
Nous marchons la tête haute
Comme de petits soldats, *etc.*

CHORUS OF STREET BOYS *(reprise)*

And the old guard
goes off home to barracks.
Blow out, loud trumpet!
Taratata, taratata!
We march with head erect
like little soldiers, *etc.*

Soldiers, urchins, and idlers go off at the back; the sound of chorus, fifes, and bugles grows fainter. The commander of the new guard, during this time, inspects his men silently. When the chorus of street boys can no longer be heard, the soldiers are dismissed and enter the guard-house. Don José and Zuniga remain.

ZUNIGA

Dites-moi, brigadier? Qu'est-ce que c'est que ce grand bâtiment?

ZUNIGA

Tell me, corporal, what's that great building?

JOSÉ

C'est la manufacture de tabacs …

JOSÉ

It's the tobacco factory …

ZUNIGA

Ce sont des femmes qui travaillent là? …

ZUNIGA

It's women who work there? …

JOSÉ

Oui, mon lieutenant. Elles n'y sont pas maintenant tout à l'heure, après leur dîner, elles vont revenir. Il y aura du monde pour les voir passer.

JOSÉ

Yes, sir. They're not there now presently, after their dinner, they'll come back. Everyone'll be here to see them go by.

ZUNIGA

Il y en a de jeunes?

ZUNIGA

There are young ones?

JOSÉ

Mais oui, mon lieutenant.

JOSÉ

Why yes, sir.

ZUNIGA

Et de jolies?

ZUNIGA

And pretty ones?

JOSÉ *(en riant)*

Je le suppose … je n'ai les ai jamais beaucoup regardées …

JOSÉ *(laughing)*

I suppose so … I've never taken much notice of them …

ZUNIGA

Allons donc! …

ZUNIGA

Get away with you! …

JOSÉ

… ces Andalouses me font peur, toujours à railler … jamais un mot de raison…

JOSÉ

These Andalusian girls frighten me … always making fun of you … never a word of sense …

ZUNIGA

Et puis nous avons un faible pour les jupes bleues et pour les nattes tombant sur les épaules …

JOSÉ *(riant)*

Ah! mon lieutenant a entendu ce que disait Moralès?

ZUNIGA

Oui …

JOSÉ

Je ne le nierai pas … la jupe bleu, les nattes, c'est le costume de la Navarre … ça me rappelle le pays …

ZUNIGA

Vous êtes Navarrais?

JOSÉ

Et vieux chrétien. Malheureusement, j'aimais trop jouer à la paume … Un jour, un gars me chercha querelle; j'eus encore l'avantage, mais cela m'obligea de quitter le pays. Je me fis soldat! Ma mère me suivit et vint s'établir à dix lieues de Séville … avec la petite Micaëla…

ZUNIGA

And then we've got a weakness for blue skirts and for pigtails down over the shoulders …

JOSÉ *(laughing)*

Ah, sir, so you heard what Moralès said?

ZUNIGA

Yes …

JOSÉ

I won't deny it … blue skirt, pigtails, it's the dress of Navarra … that reminds me of home …

ZUNIGA

You're from Navarra?

JOSÉ

And from an old Christian family. Unfortunately I was too fond of playing paume* … one day a lad picked a quarrel with me; I came off best again, but this forced me to leave the country. I went for a soldier! My mother followed me and came to settle ten leagues from Seville … with the little Micaëla.

DISC NO. 1/TRACK 4

The orchestra plays as José is still talking, expanding into a lazy melody as the young men admire the girls of the cigarette factory. The girls themselves sing a languid melody (02:18), the idleness of their break time and the afternoon heat, as well as the patterns of their smoke, depicted by the woodwinds.

* A kind of fives.

ZUNIGA

Et quel âge a-t-elle, la petite Micaëla?

ZUNIGA

And how old is the little Micaëla?

JOSÉ

Dix-sept ans.

JOSÉ

Seventeen.

ZUNIGA

Il fallait dire cela tout de suite … Je comprends maintenant pourquoi vous ne pouvez pas me dire si les ouvrières sont jolies ou laides.

ZUNIGA

You should have said that at once…. Now I understand why you can't tell me whether the factory-girls are pretty or ugly.

The factory bell is heard.

JOSÉ

Voici la cloche qui sonne, mon lieutenant, vous allez pouvoir juger pour vous-même… Quant à moi, je vais faire une chaîne pour attacher mon épinglette.

JOSÉ

There's the bell ringing, sir, you'll be able to judge for yourself…. As for me, I'm going to make a chain for fixing my priming-pin.

SCENE THREE
Chorus of Cigarette Girls

The square fills up with young men who have come to intercept the cigarette girls. The soldiers come out of the guard-house. Don José sits down on a seat, and remains quite indifferent to all the comings and goings, working on a little chain for his priming-pin.

JEUNES GENS

La cloche a sonné; nous, des ouvrières nous venons ici guetter le retour; et nous vous suivrons, brunes cigarières, en vous murmurant des propos d'amour!

YOUNG MEN

The bell has rung; we've come here to catch the factory-girls on their way back; and we'll follow you, dark-haired cigarette girls, murmuring words of love to you!

At this point the girls appear, smoking cigarettes.

LES SOLDATS
Voyez-les! Regards impudents,
mines coquettes,
fumant toutes du bout des dents la cigarette.

SOLDIERS
Look at them! Impudent glances,
saucy airs,
all of them puffing away at a cigarette.

LES CIGARIÈRES
Dans l'air, nous suivons des yeux
la fumée, la fumée,
qui vers les cieux
monte, monte parfumée.
Cela monte gentiment
à la tête, à la tête,
toute doucement
cela vous met l'âme en fête!
Le doux parler des amants,
c'est fumée!
Leurs transports et leurs serments,
c'est fumée!
Dans l'air, nous suivons des yeux
la fumée, *etc.*

CIGARETTE GIRLS
We gaze after the smoke
as it rises in the air,
sweet-smelling,
towards the skies.
Gracefully it mounts
to your head,
so gently
it exhilarates you!
Lovers' soft talk—
it's smoke!
Their raptures and promises—
smoke!
We gaze after the smoke
as it rises, *etc.*

LES SOLDATS
Mais nous ne voyons pas la Carmencita!

SOLDIERS
But we don't see La Carmencita!

Carmen enters

LES CIGARIÈRES ET LES JEUNES GENS
La voilà!
La voilà!
Voilà la Carmencita!

CIGARETTE GIRLS AND YOUNG MEN
There she is!
There she is!
There's La Carmencita!

She has a bunch of acacia flowers at her bodice, and an acacia flower in the corner of her mouth. The young men come in with Carmen. They follow her, surround her, talk to her. She flirts with them in an offhand fashion. Don José looks up. He glances at Carmen and then quietly resumes his work.

LES JEUNES GENS

Carmen! sur tes pas, nous nous pressons tous!

Carmen! sois gentille, au moins réponds-nous

et dis-nous quel jour tu nous aimeras!

YOUNG MEN

Carmen, we all throng after you!

Carmen, be kind, answer us at least,

and tell us when you're going to love us!

DISC NO. 1/TRACK 5

Quand je vous aimerai? … L'amour est un oiseau rebelle (Habanera) Carmen is introduced to the stage with a rushing melody in the strings suggesting a dangerous character. Actually, the melody is the "Fate" motif heard in the prelude but played three times faster. This leads into the most famous solo of the opera, Carmen's "Habanera" (00:31). A habanera is not a Spanish but a Cuban musical form. It was inspired and inventive for Bizet to borrow the basic melody, a Hispanic-American dance rhythm, from a song popular in France at that time. The gently rocking habanera suggests a mysterious allure that reaches back into ancient and elusive cultures, which sound part gypsy and part Moorish to the modern listener.

CARMEN *(regardent Don José)*

Quand je vous aimerai?

Ma foi, je ne sais pas.

Peut-être jamais, peut-être demain;

mais pas aujourd'hui, c'est certain.

CARMEN *(with a glance at Don José)*

When I'm going to love you?

My word, I don't know.

Perhaps never, perhaps tomorrow;

but not today, that's certain.

Grace Bumbry in a 1968–69 production of *Carmen* at the Metropolitan Opera.

SCENE FOUR
Habanera

CARMEN

L'amour est un oiseau rebelle
que nul ne peut apprivoiser,
et c'est bien en vain qu'on l'appelle,
s'il lui convient de refuser.
Rien n'y fait, menace ou prière,
l'un parle bien, l'autre se tait;
et c'est l'autre que je préfère
il n'a rien dit, mais il me plaît.
L'amour! *etc.*

CHOEUR

L'amour est un oiseau rebelle, *etc.*

CARMEN

L'amour est enfant de bohème,
il n'a jamais connu de loi
Si tu ne m'aimes pas, je t'aime;
si je t'aime, prends garde à toi! *etc.*

CHOEUR

Prends garde à toi! *etc.*
L'amour est enfant de bohème, *etc.*

CARMEN

L'oiseau que to croyais surprendre
battit de l'aile et s'envola—
l'amour est loin, tu peux l'attendre;
tu ne l'attends plus il est là!
Tout autour de toi vite, vite,
il vient, s'en va, puis il revient—
tu crois le tenir, il t'évite,

CARMEN

Love is a rebellious bird
that no one can tame,
and it's quite useless to call him
if it suits him to refuse.
Nothing moves him, neither threat nor
plea, one man speaks freely, the other keeps
mum; and it's the other one I prefer
he's said nothing, but I like him.
Love! *etc.*

CHORUS

Love is a rebellious bird, *etc.*

CARMEN

Love is a gypsy child,
he has never heard of law.
If you don't love me, I love you;
if I love you, look out for yourself! *etc.*

CHORUS

Look out for yourself! *etc.*
Love is a gypsy child, *etc.*

CARMEN

The bird you thought to catch unawares
beat its wings and away it flew—
love's far away, and you can wait for it;
you wait for it no longer—and there it is.
All around you, quickly, quickly,
it comes, it goes, then it returns—
you think you can hold it, it evades you,

tu crois l'éviter, il te tient.	you think to evade it, it holds you fast.
L'amour! *etc.*	Love! *etc.*

CHOEUR

CHORUS

Tout autour de toi, *etc.*

All around you, *etc.*

CARMEN

CARMEN

L'amour est enfant de bohème,
il n'a jamais connu de loi.
Si tu ne m'aimes pas, je t'aime;
si je t'aime, prends garde à toi!
Si tu ne m'aimes pas, je t'aime, *etc.*

Love is a gypsy child,
he has never heard of law.
If you don't love me, I love you;
if I love you, look out for yourself!
If you don't love me, I love you, *etc.*

CHOEUR

CHORUS

Prends garde à toi! *etc.*
L'amour est enfant de bohème, *etc.*

Look out for yourself! *etc.*
Love is a gypsy child, *etc.*

SCENE FIVE

Scene

DISC NO. 1/TRACK 6

Carmen! sur tes pas, nous nous pressons tous! **In the moment following the habanera, Carmen ponders which man might be the recipient of her acacia flower. She looks beyond the men who desire her to one who does not, the otherwise engaged Don José (00:13). As she approaches him, the accompaniment is reduced to a sustained note in the violas (00:41), followed by a dissonant slap of a chord as Carmen tosses the flower at José, laughs, and runs away.**

JEUNES GENS

YOUNG MEN

Carmen! sur tes pas, nous nous pressons
tous! Carmen! sois gentille, au moins
réponds-nous!

Carmen, we all throng after you!
Carmen, be kind, answer us at least!

A pause. The young men surround Carmen, who looks at them one by one. Then she breaks through the circle and goes straight to Don José, who is still busied with his little chain.

CARMEN

Qu'est-ce tu fais là? …

CARMEN

What are you up to there? …

JOSÉ

Je fais une chaîne pour attacher mon épin-glette.

JOSÉ

I'm making a chain to fix my priming-pin.

CARMEN

Ton épinglette, vraiment! Ton épinglette… épinglier de mon âme …

CARMEN

Your priming-pin, really! Your priming pin. … Pin-maker of my heart …

Carmen throws the acacia flower at Don José. He jumps up. The flower has fallen at his feet. Outburst of general laughter.

LES CIGARIERÈS

CIGARETTE GIRLS

surrounding Don José

L'amour est enfant de bohème, *etc.*

Love is a gypsy child, *etc.*

The factory bell rings again. Carmen and the other cigarette girls run into the factory. Exeunt young men, etc. The soldiers go into the guard-house, followed by the lieutenant, who had been chatting to two or three of the girls. Don José is left alone.

JOSÉ

Qu'est-ce cela veut dire, ces façons-là? … Quelle effronterie!

JOSÉ

What's all that mean?—all those carryings-on? … What shamelessness!

He looks at the acacia flower on the ground at his feet. He picks it up.

Avec quelle adresse elle me l'a lancée, cette fleur…

How cleverly she threw it at me, this flower …

Enrico Caruso as Don José.

He smells the flower.

S'il y a des sorcières, cette fille-là en est une.   If there are witches, that girl is one.

Enter Micaëla

DISC NO. 1/TRACK 7

Monsieur mon brigadier? … Ma mère, je la vois The duet of Don José and Micaëla brings some relief after the raw sexual tension that has been building steadily since the curtain rose on Act I. The music is unabashedly sweet, even bucolic in its sound (00:19), reflecting Don José's sentimental feelings for home, for his mother (00:35), and for the virginal Micaëla who has come to find him. It is interesting to note how the orchestration for Don José's music tends to adapt to that of the character he is addressing in a given moment—an apt psychological touch by Bizet. Like the rest of the music in the score associated with Micaëla (a character who does not appear in Merimée's novella), this duet is in a style typical of the French opera then—fluently melodic and tender in its expression (03:46), yet not as overtly passionate as the Italian style.

MICAËLA

Monsieur le brigadier?

MICAËLA

Corporal?

JOSÉ

JOSÉ

hurriedly concealing the acacia flower

Qu'est-ce que c'est? … Micaëla! … Tu
viens de là-bas? …

What's this? … Micaëla! … You've come
from back there? …

MICAËLA

C'est votre mère qui m'envoie…

MICAËLA

It's your mother who sends me …

SCENE SIX
Duet

JOSÉ

Parle-moi de ma mère!

JOSÉ

Tell me about my mother!

MICAËLA

J'apporte de sa part, fidèle messagère,
cette lettre…

MICAËLA

A faithful messenger, I bring from her this
letter …

JOSÉ

Une lettre! *etc.*

JOSÉ

A letter! *etc.*

MICAËLA

Et puis un peu d'argent
pour ajouter à votre traitement.
Et puis …

MICAËLA

And then a little money to add to your pay.
And then …

JOSÉ
Et puis?

MICAËLA
Et puis … vraiment je n'ose,
et puis encore une autre chose
qui vaut mieux que l'argent
qui pour un bon fils
aura sans doute plus de prix.

JOSÉ
Cette autre chose, quelle est-elle?
Parle donc.

MICAËLA
Oui, je parlerai;
ce que l'on m'a donné
je vous le donnerai.
Votre mère avec moi sortait de la chapelle,
et c'est alors qu'en m'embrassant;
"Tu vas", m'a-t-elle dit, "t'en aller à la ville;
la route n'est pas longue, une fois à Séville,
tu chercheras mon fils, mon José, mon
enfant.
Et tu lui diras que sa mère
songe nuit et jour à l'absent,
qu'elle regrette et qu'elle espère,
qu'elle pardonne et qu'elle attend.
Tout cela, n'est-ce pas, mignonne,
de ma part tu le lui diras;
et ce baiser que je te donne
de ma part tu le lui rendras."

JOSÉ *(très ému)*
Un baiser de ma mère!

JOSÉ
And then?

MICAËLA
And then … really, I dare not,
and then yet another thing
worth more than money
and which a good son will surely value
higher.

JOSÉ
This other thing, what is it?
Tell me, then.

MICAËLA
Yes, I'll tell you;
what was given to me
I'll give to you.
Your mother and I were coming out of the
chapel,
And then, as she kissed me,
"You will go to town," she said.
"it's not far; once in Seville
you'll seek out my son, my José, my boy.
And you'll tell him that his mother
thinks night and day of her absent one,
that she grieves and hopes,
that she forgives and waits.
All that, little one,
you'll tell him from me, won't you;
and this kiss that I'm giving you
you'll give him from me."

JOSÉ *(very moved)*
A kiss from my mother!

MICAËLA

Un baiser pour son fils!

José, je vous le rends,

comme je l'ai promis.

MICAËLA

A kiss for her son!

José, I give it to you

as I promised.

Micaëla raises herself on tiptoe and gives Don José a frank, motherly kiss. José, very moved, lets her. He gazes into her eyes. There is a moment of silence.

JOSÉ

Ma mère, je la vois!

Oui, je revois mon village!

O souvenirs d'autrefois,

doux souvenirs du pays!

Doux souvenirs du pays!

O souvenirs chéris!

Vous remplissez mon coeur

de force et de courage!

O souvenirs chéris!

Ma mère, je la vois,

je revois mon village!

JOSÉ

I see my mother!

Yes, I see my village again!

O memories of bygone days,

sweet memories of home!

Sweet memories of home!

O precious memories!

You put back strength

and courage into my heart!

O precious memories!

I see my mother,

I see my village again!

MICAËLA

Sa mère, il la revoit!

Il revoit sa village!

O souvenirs d'autrefois!

Souvenirs du pays!

Vous remplissez son coeur

de force et de courage!

O souvenirs chéris!

Sa mère, il la revoit,

il revoit son village!

MICAËLA

He sees his mother again!

He sees his village again!

O memories of bygone days!

Memories of home!

You put back strength

and courage into his heart!

O precious memories!

He sees his mother again,

he sees his village again!

JOSÉ

his eyes fixed on the factory

Qui sait de quel démon
j'allais être la proie!
Même de loin, ma mère me défend,
et ce baiser qu'elle m'envoie
écarte le péril et suave son enfant!

MICAËLA

Quel démon? quel péril?
Je ne comprends pas bien.
Que veut dire cela?

JOSÉ

Rien! Rien!
Parlons de toi, la messagère.
Tu vas retourner au pays?

MICAËLA

Oui, ce soir même
demain je verrai votre mère.

JOSÉ

Tu la verras!
Et bien, tu lui diras
que son fils l'aime et la vénère
et qu'il se repent aujourd'hui;
il veut que là-bas sa mère
soit contente de lui!
Tout cela, n'est-ce pas, mignonne,
de ma part, tu le lui diras,
et ce baiser que je te donne,
de ma part tu le lui rendras.

He kisses her.

JOSÉ

Who knows into what demon's clutches
I was about to fall!
Even from afar my mother protects me
and this kiss she sent me
wards off the peril and saves her son!

MICAËLA

What demon? What peril?
I don't quite understand.
What do you mean by that?

JOSÉ

Nothing! Nothing!
Let's talk about you, the messenger.
You're going back home?

MICAËLA

Yes, this very evening
tomorrow I shall see your mother.

JOSÉ

You'll be seeing her!
Well then, you'll tell her—
that her son loves and reveres her
and that today he is repentant;
he wants his mother back there
to be pleased with him!
All this, my sweet,
you'll tell her from me, won't you, and this
kiss that I give you
you'll give her from me.

MICAËLA	MICAËLA
Oui, je vous le promets, de la part de son fils	Yes, I promise you; from her son
José je le rendrai comme je l'ai promis.	José I shall give it as I have promised.

JOSÉ	JOSÉ
Ma mère, je la vois! *etc.*	I see my mother! *etc.*

MICAËLA	MICAËLA
Sa mère, il la revoit! *etc.*	He sees his mother again! *etc.*

DISC NO. 1/TRACK 8

Attends un peu maintenant In the original production, the chorus that describes the fight in the cigarette factory (00:25) left the ladies of the Opéra-Comique's original ensemble in a state of frenzy. Already tested by the smoking chorus that introduced them earlier, they were not only required to sing this particularly intricate ensemble, they had to be physically boisterous as well. (Their preferred manner of performing was to stand facing forward and simply sing.) It is a stunning moment, as bloodthirsty and gritty as anything in Italian verismo opera, with Bizet neatly catching the visceral, almost carnal excitement (02:30) the fight has aroused in its witnesses.

JOSÉ	JOSÉ
Attends un peu maintenant… je vais lire	Wait a bit now… I'm going to read her let-
sa lettre …	ter …

MACAËLA	MICAËLA
Je viens de me rappeler que votre mère m'a	I've just remembered that your mother asked
chargée de quelques petits achats …	me to make a few small purchases for her …

JOSÉ	JOSÉ
Attends un peu …	Wait a little while …

MICAËLA	MICAËLA
Non, non … je reviendrai, j'aime mieux	No, no … I'll come back, I'd rather do
cela … je reviendrai, je reviendrai …	that … I'll come back, I'll come back …

She goes out.

JOSÉ

reading

"Il n'y en a pas qui t'aime davantage …
et si tu voulais …" Oui, ma mère, oui,
j'épouserai Micaëla. Quant à cette bohèmi-
enne, avec ses fleurs qui ensorcellent …

JOSÉ

"There's not one of them who loves you
more … and if you wanted to …" Yes,
mother, yes, I'll marry Micaëla. As for that
gypsy with her flowers that bewitch …

Just as he is about to tear the flower from his tunic, an uproar begins in the factory. Zuniga comes on stage, followed by soldiers.

ZUNIGA
Eh bien! eh bien! qu'est-ce qui arrive?

ZUNIGA
Well now, well, what's happening? …

SCENE SEVEN
Chorus

PREMIER GROUPE DE FEMMES
Au secours! Au secours!
N'entendez-vous pas?

FIRST GROUP OF GIRLS
Help! Help!
Can't you hear?

DEUXIÈME GROUPE DE FEMMES
Au secours! Au secours!
Messieurs les soldats!

SECOND GROUP OF GIRLS
Help! Help!
You soldiers!

PREMIER GROUPE DE FEMMES
C'est la Carmencita!

FIRST GROUP OF GIRLS
It's Carmencita!

DEUXIÈME GROUPE DE FEMMES
Non, non, ce n'est pas elle!
Pas du tout!

SECOND GROUP OF GIRLS
No, no, it's not her!
Not a bit of it!

PREMIER GROUPE DE FEMMES

C'est elle! Si fait, si fait, c'est elle!
Elle a porté les premiers coups!

DEUXIÈME GROUPE DE FEMMES

Ne les écoutez pas!

TOUTES LES FEMMES

surrounding Zuniga

Ecoutez-nous, monsieur!
Ecoutez-nous! *etc.*

DEUXIÈME GROUPE DE FEMMES

pulling the officer to their side

La Manuelita disait,
et répétait à voix haute
qu'elle achèterait sans faute
un âne que lui plaisait.

PREMIER GROUPE DE FEMMES

Alors la Carmencita,
railleuse à son ordinaire,
dit "Un âne, pourquoi faire?
Un balai te suffira."

DEUXIÈME GROUPE DE FEMMES

Manuelita riposta
et dit à sa camarade
"Pour certaine promenade,
mon âne te servira!—"

FIRST GROUP OF GIRLS

It's her! It is, it is! It's her!
She started the fighting!

SECOND GROUP OF GIRLS

Don't listen to them!

ALL THE GIRLS

Listen to us, sir!
Listen to us! *etc.*

SECOND GROUP OF GIRLS

Manuelita said, and kept saying
at the top of her voice,
that she'd make sure she bought
a donkey that pleased her.

FIRST GROUP OF GIRLS

Then Carmencita,
in her usual mocking way,
said "A donkey? What for?
A broom will do for you."

SECOND GROUP OF GIRLS

Manuelita retorted,
and said to her friend
"For a certain ride
my donkey will be useful to you!—"

PREMIER GROUPE DE FEMMES	FIRST GROUP OF GIRLS
"—Et ce jour-là tu pourras	"—And on that day you'll be able
à bon droit faire la fière;	to play the lady in your own right;
deux laquais suivront derrière,	two lackeys will follow behind
t'émouchant à tour de bras!"	keeping flies off as best they can!"

TOUTES LES FEMMES	ALL THE GIRLS
Là-dessus, toutes les deux	Thereupon they both started
se sont prises aux cheveux!	to pull each other's hair out!

ZUNIGA	ZUNIGA
Au diable tout ce bavardage!	To the devil with all this chatter!
Prenez, José, deux hommes avec vous	José, take two men in with you
et voyez là-dedans qui cause ce tapage.	and see who's causing all this commotion.

Don José takes two men with him. The soldiers go into the factory. All this while the girls are pushing and arguing among themselves.

PREMIER GROUPE DE FEMMES	FIRST GROUP OF GIRLS
C'est la Carmencita! *etc.*	It's Carmencita! *etc.*

DEUXIÈME GROUPE DE FEMMES	SECOND GROUP OF GIRLS
Non, non, ce n'est pas elle! *etc.*	No, no! It's not her! *etc.*

ZUNIGA	ZUNIGA
Holà!	Stop!
Eloignez-moi toutes ces femmes-là!	Rid me of all these women!

TOUTES LES FEMMES	ALL THE GIRLS
Monsieur! Ne les écoutez pas! *etc.*	Sir, don't listen to them! *etc.*

The soldiers keep the girls back. Carmen appears at the factory door, led by Don José and followed by two dragoons.

The factory-girls go out in a disorderly rush.

ZUNIGA

Voyons, brigadier … Maintenant que nous avons un peu de silence … qu'est-ce que vous avez trouvé là-dedans?

JOSÉ

J'ai trouvé trois cents femmes, hurlant, gesticulant. Il y en avait une qui avait sur la figure un X qu'on venait de lui marquer en deux coups de couteau … en face de la blessée …

On a glance from Carmen he stops.

ZUNIGA

Eh bien?

JOSÉ

J'ai vu mademoiselle …

ZUNIGA

Mademoiselle Carmencita?

JOSÉ

Oui, mon lieutenant.

ZUNIGA

Et qu'est-ce qu'elle disait, mademoiselle Carmencita?

JOSÉ

Elle ne disait rien, elle serrait les dents et roulait des yeux comme un caméleon.

ZUNIGA

Let's see, corporal … now that we've got a moment's silence … what did you find inside there?

JOSÉ

I found three hundred women, yelling and waving their arms about. There was one who had an X on her face that someone had just carved on her with two knife-slashes … Facing the wounded girl …

ZUNIGA

Well?

JOSÉ

I saw the señorita …

ZUNIGA

The señorita Carmencita?

JOSÉ

Yes, sir.

ZUNIGA

And what was she saying, the señorita Carmencita?

JOSÉ

She wasn't saying anything, she was gritting her teeth and rolling her eyes like a chameleon.

The lieutenant looks at Carmen; she, after a glance at Don José and a slight shrug of her shoulders, has become impassive again.

JOSÉ

J'ai prié mademoiselle de me suivre …

JOSÉ

I asked the señorita to come with me …

Carmen turns sharply and looks at José once more.

SCENE EIGHT
Song and Melodrama

DISC NO. 1/TRACK 9

Eh bien! … vous avez entendu? … Tra la la la **Zuniga demands answers from Carmen, whose contemptuous defiance is dazzling. She sings nonsense in his face (00:09), daring him to cut her, burn her, whatever he wishes, but she will tell him nothing. There follows a section called a melodrama, in which Bizet underscored (as in a film score) (01:38) a section leading to spoken dialogue between Carmen and Don José, who is now charged with guarding her. The melodrama is often cut, though it appears in this recording to expand on what is a key moment in the relationship of Carmen and Don José.**

ZUNIGA *(à Carmen)*

Eh bien! … vous avez entendu? … Avez-vous quelque chose à répondre? … parlez, j'attends …

ZUNIGA *(to Carmen)*

Well! … you heard? … Have you anything to answer? … Speak, I'm waiting … Instead of replying, Carmen starts to sing.

Instead of replying, Carmen starts to sing.

CARMEN

Tra la la la, etc.
Coupe-moi, brûle-moi, je ne te dirai rien.
Tra la la la, etc.
Je brave tout, le feu, le fer et le ciel même.

CARMEN

Tra la la la, etc.
Cut me, burn me, I shall tell you nothing.
Tra la la la, etc.
I defy everything—fire, the sword and heaven itself.

ZUNIGA

Ce ne sont pas des chansons que je te demande, c'est une réponse.

ZUNIGA

It's not songs I'm asking you for, it's a reply.

CARMEN

Tra la la la, *etc.*
Mon secret je le garde et je le garde bien!
Tra la la la, *etc.*
J'en aime un autre et meurs en disant que je l'aime.

CARMEN

Tra la la la, *etc.*
I'm keeping my secret and keeping it close!
Tra la la la, *etc.*
I love another and I die in saying that I love him.

ZUNIGA

Ah! ah! nous le prenons sur ce ton-là … *à José* Ce qui est sûr, n'est-ce pas, c'est qu'il y eu des coups de couteau, et que c'est elle qui les a donnés …

ZUNIGA

Aha! So that's the attitude we're taking … to José What's certain, isn't it, is that there had been a knife attack and that it's she who made it …

At this moment five or six women on the right succeed in breaking the line of sentries and rush on to the stage shouting, "Yes, yes, it's her!" One of these women finds herself close by Carmen, who raises her hand and attempts to throw herself upon the woman. Don José stops Carmen. The soldiers haul the women off and this time force them back completely off the stage. A few sentinels remain in sight, guarding the approaches to the square.

ZUNIGA

Eh! vous avez la main leste décidément.
(Aux soldats) Trouvez-moi une corde.

ZUNIGA

Eh! decidedly you have a ready hand.
(to the soldiers) Find me a cord.

There is a moment of silence during which Carmen begins humming again in the most impertinent fashion as she watches the officer.

JOSE

Voilà, mon lieutenant.

JOSE

Here it is, sir.

ZUNIGA

Prenez et attachez-moi ces deux jolies mains.

ZUNIGA

Take this and tie those two pretty hands together for me.

Without offering the least resistance, Carmen smilingly holds out her two hands to Don José.

C'est dommage vraiment, car elle est gentille … si gentille que vous soyez, vous n'en irez pas moins faire un tour à la prison. Vous pourrez y chanter vos chansons de Bohémienne. Le porte-clefs vous dira ce qu'il en pense.	It's a shame, really, for she's pretty … But pretty as you may be, you're nonetheless going to take a stroll to the prison. You can sing your gypsy songs there. The turnkey'll tell you what he thinks of them.

Carmen's hands are bound and she is made to sit down on a stool in front of the guard-house. She remains motionless, her eyes cast down.

Je vais écrire l'ordre. *(à Don José)* C'est vous qui la conduirez …	I'm going to write out the order. (to Don José) It's you who will take her …

He goes out.

CARMEN

Où me conduirez-vous?

CARMEN

Where are you taking me?

DISC NO. 1/TRACK 10

JOSÉ

A la prison, ma pauvre enfant …

JOSÉ

To the jail, my poor child …

CARMEN

Hélas! que deviendrai-je? Seigneur officier, ayez pitié de moi … vous êtes si gentil. Laisse-moi m'échapper, je te donnerai un morceau de la bar lachi, une petite pierre qui te fera aimer de toutes les femmes.

CARMEN

Alas, what will become of me? Noble officer, take pity on me … You are so nice. Let me escape and I'll give you a piece of the bar lachi, a little stone which will make you loved by all women.

JOSÉ

moving away

Nous ne sommes pas ici pour dire des
balivernes … Il faut aller à la prison. C'est
la consigne, et il n'y a pas de remède.

CARMEN

Camarade, mon ami, ne ferez-vous rien
pour une payse?

JOSÉ

Vous êtes Navarraise, vous?

CARMEN

Sans doute.

JOSÉ

Allons donc … il n'y a pas un mot de vrai
… vos yeux seuls, votre bouche, votre teint
… tout vous dit Bohémienne …

CARMEN

Bohémienne, tu crois?

JOSÉ

J'en suis sûr.

CARMEN

Au fait, je suis bien bonne de me donner
la peine de mentir … Oui, je suis
Bohémienne, mais tu n'en feras pas moins
ce que je te demande … tu le feras parce
que tu m'aimes …

JOSÉ

We're not here to talk twaddle … We must
go to the jail. Those are my instructions,
and there's no help for it.

CARMEN

Comrade of my heart, won't you do anything for a fellow-countrywoman?

JOSÉ

You're from Navarra, you?

CARMEN

Certainly.

JOSÉ

Come off it! … There's not a word of
truth in it … your eyes alone, your
mouth, your colouring … everything pro-
claims you a gypsy …

CARMEN

A gypsy, you think?

JOSÉ

I'm sure of it.

CARMEN

In fact, I am very simple to go to the trouble
of lying … Yes, I'm a gypsy, but you'll
do what I want nonetheless … You'll do it
because you love me …

JOSÉ

Moi!

CARMEN

Eh! Oui, tu m'aimes. Cette fleur que tu as gardée—oh! Tu peux la jeter maintenant … cela n'y fera rien. La charme a opéré …

JOSÉ *(avec colère)*

Ne me parle plus, tu entends, je te défends de me parler.

JOSÉ

I!

CARMEN

Ah yes, you love me. That flower you kept—oh, you can throw it away now … that makes no difference. The charm has worked …

JOSÉ *(angrily)*

Don't talk to me any more, d'you hear, I forbid you to talk to me.

DISC NO. 1/TRACK 11

C'est très bien … Près des remparts de Séville (Seguedille) **Carmen has Don José in her sights, and, though her hands are bound, she sings this alluring aria to convince him into letting her escape. The aria begins as a seduction, insinuating and a little mysterious, but when Don José agrees to release her, Carmen repeats the melody with a bold, almost manic intensity (04:09), ending the aria with a shout of joy.**

CARMEN

C'est très bien, seigneur officier, c'est très bien. Vous me défendez de parler, je ne parlerai plus …

CARMEN

That's all right, officer sir, that's all right. You forbid me to talk, I'll not talk any more …

She looks at Don José who backs away.

SCENE NINE
Seguidilla and Duet

CARMEN

Près des remparts de Séville,

chez mon ami Lillas Pastia, j'irai danser la

séguedille,

et boire du manzanilla.

J'irai chez mon ami Lillas Pastia!

Oui, mais toute seule on s'ennuie,

et les vrais plaisirs sont à deux.

Donc, pour me tenir compagnie,

j'emmènerai mon amoureux!

Mon amoureux … il est au diable

je l'ai mis à la porte hier.

Mon pauvre coeur très consolable,

mon coeur est libre comme l'air.

J'ai des galants à la douzaine,

mais ils ne sont pas à mon gré.

Voici la fin de la semaine,

qui veut m'aimer? Je l'aimerai

Qui veut mon âme? Elle est à prendre!

CARMEN

By the ramparts of Seville,

at my friend Lillas Pastia's place,

I'm going to dance the seguidilla

and drink manzanilla.

I'm going to my friend Lillas Pastia's!

Yes, but all alone one gets bored,

and real pleasures are for two.

So, to keep me company,

I shall take my lover!

My lover … he's gone to the devil

I showed him the door yesterday.

My poor heart, so consolable—

my heart is as free as air.

I have suitors by the dozen,

but they are not to my liking.

Here we are at week end;

Who wants to love me! I'll love him.

Who wants my heart? It's for the taking!

Vous arrivez au bon moment!
Je n'ai guère le temps d'attendre,
car avec mon nouvel amant …
Près des remparts de Séville, *etc.*

JOSÉ
Tais-toi! Je t'avais dit de ne pas me parler!

CARMEN
Je ne te parle pas,
je chante pour moi-même;
et je pense … il n'est pas défendu de
penser!
Je pense à certain officier,
qui m'aime, et qu'à mon tour,
oui, à mon tour je pourrais bien aimer!

JOSÉ
Carmen!

CARMEN
Mon officier n'est pas un capitaine,
pas même un lieutenant,
il n'est que brigadier;
mais c'est assez our une bohémienne,
et je daigne m'en contenter!

JOSÉ

untying Carmen's hands

Carmen, je suis comme un homme ivre,
se je cède, si je me livre,
ta promesse, tu la tiendras,
ah! si je t'aime, Carmen, tu m'aimeras?

You've come at the right moment!
I have hardly time to wait,
for with my new lover …
By the ramparts of Seville, *etc.*

JOSÉ
Stop! I told you not to talk to me!

CARMEN
I'm not talking to you,
I'm singing to myself;
and I'm thinking … it's not forbidden to
think!
I'm thinking about a certain officer
who loves me,
and whom in my turn I might really love!

JOSÉ
Carmen!

CARMEN
My officer's not a captain,
not even a lieutenant,
he's only a corporal;
but that's enough for a gypsy girl
and I'll deign to content myself with him!

JOSÉ

Carmen, I'm like a drunken man,
if I yield, if I give in,
you'll keep your promise?
Ah! If I love you, Carmen, you'll love me?

CARMEN	CARMEN
Oui …	Yes …
Nous danserons la séguedille	We'll dance the seguidilla
en buvant du manzanilla.	while we drink manzanilla.

JOSÉ	JOSÉ
Chez Lillas Pastia …	at Lillas Pastia's …
Tu le promets!	You promise!
Carmen …	Carmen …
Tu le promets!	You promise!

CARMEN	CARMEN
Ah! Près des remparts de Séville, *etc.*	Ah! By the ramparts of Seville, *etc.*

Her hands behind her, Carmen goes and re-seats herself on her stool.

Zuniga returns.

SCENE TEN
Finale

DISC NO. 1/TRACK 12

Furtive figures in the cellos play under Zuniga's calm instructions and Carmen's aside, giving us a "secret" peek into the escape plot as it is laid out. Carmen casually repeats snatches of her *Habanera* (00:39) as a flirtation and a warning that she is not to be trifled with.

ZUNIGA *(à José)*	ZUNIGA *(to José)*
Voici l'ordre; partez.	Here's the order; off you go now.
Et faites bonne garde.	And keep a good lookout.

CARMEN *(bas à José)*	CARMEN *(aside to José)*
En chemin je te pousserai,	On the way I shall push you,

je te pousserai aussi fort que je le pourrais ...	I shall push you as hard as I can ...
Laisse-toi renverser ...	Let yourself fall over ...
le reste me regarde.	The rest is up to me.

Carmen places herself between the two dragoons, with José at her side. The girls and others return onstage, kept back by the soldiers. Carmen crosses the stage, moving towards the bridge.

CARMEN

CARMEN

L'amour est enfant de bohéme,	Love is a gypsy child,
il n'a jamais connu de loi.	he has never heard of law.
Si tu ne m'aimes pas, je t'aime;	If you don't love me, I love you;
si je t'aime, prends garde à toi!	if I love you, look out for yourself!

Arriving at the foot of the bridge, Carmen pushes José, who falls. In the confusion Carmen takes to her heels. At the middle of the bridge she stops for a moment, sends her cord flying over the parapet of the bridge, and escapes, while the cigarette girls, with great shouts of laughter, surround Zuniga.

DISC NO. 1/TRACK 13

The orchestra plays a subtle and jaunty military tune which will later be sung by Don José. It is repeated by the basson for the second verse, creating a curiously bouncy, almost comical commentary.

ENTR'ACTE

Act 2

SCENE ELEVEN
Gypsy Song

The tavern of Lillas Pastia. Carmen, Mercédès, Frasquita, Lieutenant Zuniga, Moralès, and another lieutenant are there. A meal has just been finished and the table is in disorder. The officers and gypsy girls are smoking. Two gypsies are strumming guitars in a corner of the room; in the middle, two gypsy girls are singing. Carmen, seated, is watching them dance. An officer is talking to her quietly, but she pays him no attention whatsoever. Suddenly she gets up and begins to sing.

DISC NO. 1/TRACK 14

Les tringles des sistres tintaient (Chanson bohèmien) **The orchestra introduces the Gypsy Song with a hypnotic swirl in the flutes, accentuated on the off-beats by the harps. Carmen and her friends Frasquita and Mercédès sing and dance to the tune with a growing frenzy for the crowd at Lillas Pastia's. Carmen is at last seen and heard in her element, and the effect is mesmerizing—the beat of the last verse of the Gypsy Song (02:50) gets faster and faster until it drops from delirious exhaustion.**

CARMEN

Les tringles des sitres tintaient
avec un éclat métallique,
et sur cette étrange musique
les zingarellas se levaient.
Tambours de basque allaient leur train,
et les guitares forcenées
grinçaient sous des mains obsinées,
même chanson, même refrain.
Tralalalala …

CARMEN

The sistrums's* rods were jingling
with a metallic clatter,
and at this strange music
the zingarellas* leapt to their feet.
Tambourines were keeping time
and the frenzied guitars
ground away under persistent hands,
the same song, the same refrain.
Tralalalala …

* Sistrum: jingling instrument; rattle used by ancient nations.
* Zingarella: Zingara, Zingaro gypsy (It.).

82

During the refrain the gypsy girls dance, and Mercédès and Frasquita join Carmen in singing Tralalalala.

Les anneaux de cuivre et d'argent	Copper and silver rings
reluisaient sur les peaux bistrées;	glittered on dusky skins;
d'orange et de rouge zébrées	orange- and red-striped
les étouffes flottaient au vent.	dresses floated in the wind.
La danse au chant se mariait,	Dance and song became one—
d'abord indécise et timide,	at first timid and hesitant,
plus vive ensuite et plus rapide,	then livelier and faster
cela montait, montait, montait!	it grew and grew and grew!
Tralalalala …	Tralalalala …
Les bohémiens à tour de bras	The gypsy boys stormed away
de leurs instruments faisaient rage,	on their instruments with all their might,
et cet éblouissant tapage,	and this deafening uproar
ensorcelait les zingaras!	bewitched the zingaras!
Sous le rythme de la chanson,	Beneath the rhythm of the song,
ardentes, folles, enfiévrées,	passionate, wild, fired with excitement,
elles se laissaient, enivrées,	they let themselves be carried a way, intoxi-
emporter par le tourbillon!	cated, by the whirlwind!
Tralalalala …	Tralalalala …

At the conclusion of the dance Carmen sinks breathless on to a bench. Lillas Pastia begins to circulate among the officers. She looks worried.

DISC NO. 1/TRACK 15

ZUNIGA	**ZUNIGA**
Vous avez quelque chose à nous dire,	You've something to tell us, Master Lillas
maître Lillas Pastia?	Pastia?
PASTIA	**PASTIA**
Mon Dieu, messieurs …	My God, gentlemen …
MORALÈS	**MORALÈS**
Parle, voyons …	Speak, come now …

PASTIA

Il commence à se faire tard … et je suis, plus que personne, obligé d'observer les règlements.

MORALÈS

Cela veut dire que to nous mets à la porte! …

PASTIA

Oh! Non, messieurs les officiers, oh! non non … je vous fais seulement observer que mon auberge devrait être fermée depuis dix minutes …

ZUNIGA

Dieu sait ce qu'il s'y passe dans ton auberge, une fois qu'elle est fermée …

PASTIA

Oh! Mon lieutenant …

ZUNIGA

Enfin, nous avons encore, avant l'appel, le temps d'aller passer une heure au théâtre … vous y viendrez avec nous, n'est-ce pas, les belles?

Pastia signs to the gypsy girls to refuse.

FRASQUITA

Non, messieurs les officiers, non, nous restons ici, nous.

ZUNIGA

Comment, vous ne viendrez pas …

PASTIA

It's beginning to get late and I, more than anyone, am obliged to observe the regulations.

MORALÈS

That means that you're showing us the door!

PASTIA

Oh no. Officers, oh no! … I only remind you that my inn should have been closed ten minutes ago …

ZUNIGA

God knows what goes on in your inn after closing time …

PASTIA

Oh, sir! …

ZUNIGA

Anyway, we still have time before roll-call to pass an hour at the theatre … You'll come there with us, eh, girls?
Pastia signs to the gypsy girls to refuse.

FRASQUITA

No, officers, no, we're staying here, we are.

ZUNIGA

What, you're not coming?—

MERCÉDÈS	MERCÉDÈS
C'est impossible.	It's impossible.

MORALÈS	MORALÈS
Mercédès!	Mercédès!

MERCÉDÈS	MERCÉDÈS
Je regrette …	Sorry …

MORALÈS	MORALÈS
Frasquita!	Frasquita!

FRASQUITA	FRASQUITA
Je suis désolée …	Ever so sorry …

ZUNIGA	ZUNIGA
Mais toi, Carment, je suis bien sûr que tu ne refuseras pas …	But you, Carmen, I'm quite sure you won't refuse …

CARMEN	CARMEN
C'est ce qui vous trompe, mon lieutenant … je refuse.	That's where you're wrong, Lieutenant, I do refuse.

While the lieutenant is speaking to Carmen, two other lieutenants try to persuade Frasquita and Mercédès.

ZUNIGA	ZUNIGA
Tu m'en veux?	You've got a grudge against me?

CARMEN	CARMEN
Pourquoi vous en voudrais-je?	Why should I have?

ZUNIGA	ZUNIGA
Parce qu'il y a un mois, j'ai eu la cruauté de t'envoyer à la prison …	Because, a month ago, I was cruel enough to send you to prison …

CARMEN

as though she did not remember

A la prison … je ne me souviens pas d'être allée àla prison …

ZUNIGA

Je sais pardieu bien que tu n'y es pas allée … le brigadier qui était chargé de te conduire ayant jugé à propos de te laisser échapper … et de se faire dégrader et imprisonner pour cela …

CARMEN

serious

Dégrader et emprisonner?

ZUNIGA

Il a passé un mois en prison …

CARMEN

Mais il en est sorti?

ZUNIGA

Depuis hier seulement!

CARMEN

Tout est bien, puisqu'il en est sorti, tout est bien.

ZUNIGA

A la bonne heure, tu te consoles vite …

CARMEN

To prison? … I don't recall having gone to prison.

ZUNIGA

I know jolly well that you didn't go there … the corporal who had the job of taking you having opportunely decided to let you escape … and to get himself demoted and imprisoned for that …

CARMEN

Demoted and imprisoned?

ZUNIGA

He's spent a month in prison …

CARMEN

But he's out now?

ZUNIGA

Only since yesterday!

CARMEN

Everything's all right then, since he is out, everything's all right.

ZUNIGA

Well well, you console yourself quickly …

CARMEN

Si vous m'en croyez, vous ferez comme moi, vous voulez nous emmener, nous ne voulons pas vous suivre … vous vous consolerez …

CARMEN

If you take my advice you'll do like me; you want to take us out, we don't want to come with you … you will console yourselves …

MORALÈS

Il faudra bien.

MORALÈS

We'll have to.

The scene is interrupted by a chorus sung in the wings.

SCENE TWELVE
Chorus and Ensemble

DISC NO. 1/TRACK 16

The chorus is heard off-stage as the others inside continue their conversation. Even before we meet Escamillo, the chorus and the heavy brass in the orchestra tell us of his warrior character.

CHOEUR

Vivat! vivat le toréro!
Vivat! vivat Escamillo! *etc.*

CHORUS

Hurrah! Hurrah for the torero!
Hurrah! Hurrah for Escamillo! *etc.*

The dialogue continues during the singing of the above Chorus.

ZUNIGA

Qu'est-ce que c'est que ça?

ZUNIGA

What's all that?

MERCÉDÈS

Une promenade aux flambeaux …

MERCÉDÈS

A torchlight procession …

FRASQUITA

C'est Escamillo … un torero qui s'est fait remarquer aux dernières courses de Grenade.

FRASQUITA

It's Escamillo … a bullfighter who distinguished himself at the last Granada meetings.

MORALÈS

Pardieu, il faut le faire venir … nous boirons en son honneur!

MORALÈS

By jove, we must get him up here … we'll drink in his honour!

ZUNIGA

C'est cela, je vais l'inviter.

ZUNIGA

That's it, I'll invite him.

He goes over to the window.

Monsieur le toréro … voulez-vous faire l'amitié de monter ici? Vous y trouverez des gens qui aiment fort tous ceux qui, comme vous ont de l'adresse et du courage.

Señor torero, will you do us the kindness to step up here? You'll find chaps who are very fond of all those, like yourself, who have skill and courage …

CHOEUR

Vivat! vivat le toréro!
Vivat! vivat Escamillo! *etc.*

CHORUS

Hurrah! Hurrah for the torero!
Hurrah! Hurrah for Escamillo! *etc.*

Enter Escamillo.

ZUNIGA

Nous vous remercions d'avoir accepté notre invitation; nous n'avons pas voulu vous laisser passer sans boire avec vous au grand art de la tauromachie.

ZUNIGA

We thank you for having accepted our invitation; we didn't want to let you go by without drinking with you to the great art of tauromachy.

ESCAMILLO

Messieurs les officiers, je vous remercie.

ESCAMILLO

Gentlemen, I thank you.

SCENE THIRTEEN
Toreador's song

DISC NO. 1/TRACK 17

Votre toast, je peux vous le rendre (Toreador Song) One of the most famous arias in all of opera, Escamillo's Toreador Song is a celebration of the swaggering macho tradition. The arresting verses are in a minor key. In them, the toreador describes his exploits and their dangers. However, the refrain ("Toréador, en garde …") is in the major. This proud, striding melody (01:19) becomes Escamillo's identity as he sings of the love that awaits him when his trials are over.

ESCAMILLO

Votre toast, je peux vous le rendre,
señors, car avec les soldats,
oui, les toréros peuvent s'entendre,
pour plaisirs ils ont les combats!
Le cirque est plein, c'est jour de fête,
le cirque est plein du haut en bas.
Les spectateurs perdant la tête,
les spectateurs s'interpellent à grand fracas!
Apostrophes, cris et tapage
poussés jusques à la fureur!
Car c'est la fête du courage!
C'est la fête des gens de coeur!
Allons! en garde! ah!
Toréador, en garde!
Et songe bien, oui, songe en combattant,
qu'un oeil noir te regarde
et que l'amour t'attend!
Toréador, l'amour t'attend!

TOUT LE MONDE

Toréador, en garde! *etc.*

Carmen refills Escamillo's glass.

ESCAMILLO

I can return your toast,
gentlemen, for soldiers—
yes—and bullfighters understand each
other; fighting is their game!
The ring is packed, it's a holiday,
the ring is full from top to bottom.
The spectators, losing their wits,
yell at each other at the tops of their voices!
Exclamations, cries and uproar
carried to the pitch of fury!
For this is the fiesta of courage,
this is the fiesta of the stouthearted!
Let's go! On guard! Ah!
Toreador, on guard!
And remember, yes, remember as you fight
that two dark eyes are watching you,
that love awaits you!
Toreador, love awaits you!

CHORUS

Toreador, on guard! *etc.*

ESCAMILLO

Tout d'un coup, on fait silence,

on fait silence, ah! que se passe-t-il?

Plus de cris, c'est l'instant!

Le taureau s'élance

en bondissant hors du toril!

Il s'élance! Il entre, il frappe!

Un cheval roule, entraînant un picador!

"Ah! bravo Toro!" hurle la foule;

le taureau va, il vient,

il vient et frappe encore!

En secouant ses banderilles,

plein de fureur, il court!

Le cirque est plein de sang!

On se sauve, on franchit les grilles.

C'est ton tour maintenant!

Allons! en garde! ah!

Toréador, en garde! *etc.*

TOUT LE MONDE

Toréador, en garde! etc.

.... l'amour t'attend!

ESCAMILLO

Suddenly everyone falls silent;

ah—what's happening?

No more shouts, this is the moment!

The bull comes bounding

out of the toril!

He charges, comes in, strikes!

A horse rolls over, dragging down a pica-

dor! "Ah! Bravo bull!" roars the crowd;

the bull turns, comes back.

Comes back and strikes again!

Shaking his banderillas,

maddened with rage, he runs about!

The ring is covered with blood!

Men jump clear, leap the barriers.

It's your turn now!

Let's go! On guard! Ah!

Toreador, on guard! *etc.*

CHORUS

Toreador, on guard! etc.

… love awaits you!

SCENE THIRTEEN B
Toreador's song

FRASQUITA

L'Amour!

ESCAMILLO

L'Amour!

FRASQUITA

Love!

ESCAMILLO

Love!

MERCÉDÈS	**MERCÉDÈS**
L'Amour!	Love!
ESCAMILLO	**ESCAMILLO**
L'Amour!	Love!
CARMEN	**CARMEN**
L'Amour!	Love!
ALL	**ALL**
Toréador! Toréador! L'amour t'attend!	Toreador, Toreador, love awaits you!

They drink and exchange handshakes with the toreador.

DISC NO. 1/TRACK 18

Carmen's initial flirtation is, rather surprisingly, all accomplished in dialogue rather than music. Escamillo's exit from the stage, however, is a swaggering orchestral restatement (00:58) of his Toreador Song.

PASTIA	**PASTIA**
Messieurs les officiers, je vous en prie.	Officers, sirs, I beg you.
ZUNIGA	**ZUNIGA**
C'est bien, c'est bien, nous partons.	All right, all right, we're going.

The officers start to get ready to leave. Escamillo finds himself beside Carmen.

ESCAMILLO	**ESCAMILLO**
Dis-moi ton nom, et la première fois que je frapperai le taureau, ce sera ton nom que je prononcerai.	Tell me your name, and the first time I kill a bull it will be your name that I utter.
CARMEN	**CARMEN**
Je m'appelle la Carmencita.	I'm called Carmencita.

ESCAMILLO

La Carmencita?

CARMEN

Carmen, la Carmencita, comme tu voudras.

ESCAMILLO

Eh bien! Carmen ou la Carmencita, si je m'avisais de t'aimer et d'être aimé de toi, qu'est-ce tu me répondrais?

CARMEN

Je répondrais que tu peux m'aimer tout à ton aise mais que quant à être aimé de moi pour le moment, il n'y faut pas songer!

ESCAMILLO

J'attendrai alors et me contenterai d'espérer …

CARMEN

Il n'est pas défendu d'attendre et il est toujours agréable d'espérer.

ZUNIGA

quietly to Carmen

Ecoute-moi, Carmen, puisque tu ne veux pas venir avec nous, c'est moi qui dans une heure reviendrai ici …

CARMEN

Je ne vous conseille pas de revenir…

ESCAMILLO

Carmencita?

CARMEN

Carmen, Carmencita, as you like.

ESCAMILLO

Well then! Carmen or Carmencita, if I took it into my head to love you and be loved by you, what would you answer?

CARMEN

I should answer that you can love me just as you please, but as for being loved by me just at present, you mustn't think of it!

ESCAMILLO

Then I'll wait, and content myself with hoping …

CARMEN

It's not forbidden to wait, and it's always pleasant to hope.

ZUNIGA

Listen to me, Carmen. Since you won't come with us, it's I who'll come back here in an hour …

CARMEN

I don't advise you to come back …

ZUNIGA

quietly to Carmen

Je reviendrai tout le même.

Nous partons avec vous, torero, et nous
nous joindrons au cortège qui vous
accompagne.

Everybody goes out except Carmen, Frasquita, Mercédès, and Lillas Pastia.

DISC NO. 1/TRACK 19

FRASQUITA *(à Pastia)*
Pourquoi étas-tu si pressé de les fair partir?

PASTIA
Le Dancaïre et Le Remendado viennent
d'arriver …

PASTIA

opening a door and gesturing as he calls out

Les voici …

Enter Dancaïro and Remendado. Pastia closes the doors, puts up the shutters, etc., etc.

FRASQUITA
Eh bien, les nouvelles?

LE DANCAÏRE
Pas trop mauvaises, les nouvelles; nous
arrivons de Gibraltar.

ZUNIGA

I'll come back all the same.

We'll leave with you, torero, and tack
ourselves on to the procession that accompa-
nies you.

FRASQUITA *(to Pastia)*
Why were you so eager to send them away?

PASTIA
Dancaïro and Remendado have just
arrived …

PASTIA

Here they are …

FRASQUITA
Well, the news?

EL DANCAÏRO
Not too bad, the news. We've just come
from Gibraltar.

LE REMENDADO

Jolie ville, Gibraltar! … on y voit des
Anglais, beaucoup d'Anglais, de jolis
hommes les Anglais, un peu froids, mais
distingués.

LE DANCAÏRE

Remendado! …

LE REMENDADO

Patron.

LE DANCAÏRE

Taisez-vous. Nous avons arrangé l'embar-
quement de marchandises anglaises. Nous
irons les attendre près de la côte, nous en
cacherons une partie dans la montagne et
nous ferons passer le reste. Tous nos cama-
rades ont été prévenus … mais c'est de
vous trois surtout ue nous avons besoin
…vous allez partir avec nous.

CARMEN *(riant)*

Pourquoi faire? Pour vous aider à porter
des ballots?

LE REMENDADO

Oh! Non… faire porter des ballots à des
dames … ça ne serait pas distingué.

LE DANCAÏRE *(menaçant)*

Remendado?

LE REMENDADO

Oui, patron.

EL REMENDADO

Nice town, Gibraltar! … you see the
English there, lots of English, nice chaps
the English, a trifle cold, but gentlemanly.

EL DANCAÏRO

Remendado! …

EL REMENDADO

Boss.

EL DANCAÏRO

Shut up. We are arranged to take on board
some English goods. We're going to wait
for it near the coast. We'll hide some of the
stuff up the mountain and run the rest. All
our comrades have been warned … but it's
you three we need principally … you'll
leave with us.

CARMEN *(laughing)*

What for? To help you carry the bales?

EL REMENDADO

Oh no!—make the ladies carry the bales …
that wouldn't be at all the thing.

EL DANCAÏRO *(threateningly)*

Remendado?

EL REMENDADO

Yes, boss.

LE DANCAÏRE

Nous ne vous ferons pas porter de ballots, mais nous avons besoin de vous pour autre chose.

EL DANCAÏRO

We're not going to make you carry any bales, but we do need you for something else.

Mary Garden in the role of Carmen.

SCENE FOURTEEN
Quintet

DISC NO. 1/TRACK 20

Nous avons en tête une affaire (Quintet) **The quintet is a fleet-footed miracle that, like Micaëla's scene with Don José in Act I, comes along like a cooling breeze to relieve all the erotic heat. It introduces outright comedy in the persons of the smugglers Dancaïro and Remendado who, with Frasquita and Mercédès, want Carmen to help them with a shipment of contraband. The men are bent on having the women flirt with the guards so the smugglers can slip past customs at the border. The heightened musical energy (04:02) of the quintet is an imaginative depiction of five sociopaths plotting their next bit of mischief. The subsequent dialogue (05:10) is spoken over the approaching song of Don José, which is a more heroic version of the military tune played for the entr'acte.**

LE DANCAÏRE

Nous avons en tête une affaire.

EL DANCAÏRO

We have a scheme in mind.

MERCÉDÈS ET FRASQUITA

Est-elle bonne, dites-nous?

MERCÉDÈS AND FRASQUITA

Tell us, is it good?

LE DANCAÏRE ET LE REMENDADO

Elle est admirable, ma chère;
mais nous avons besoin de vous.

EL DANCAÏRO AND EL REMENDADO

It's admirable, my dear;
but we require your services.

TOUS LE CINQ

De nous? *etc.*
De vous! *etc.*

QUINTET

Ours? *etc.*
Yours! *etc.*

LES DEUX HOMMES

Car nous l'avouons humblement,
et fort respectueusement;
quand il s'agit de tromperie,
de duperie, de volerie,
il est toujous bon, sur ma foi,

THE TWO MEN

For we humbly
and most respectfully acknowledge
when it's a question of trickery
of deception, of thieving,
it's always good, I swear,

d'avoir les femmes avec soi.
Et sans elles,
mes toutes belles,
on ne fait jamais rien
de bien!

LES TROIS FEMMES
Quoi! sans nous jamais rien
de bien?

LES DEUX HOMMES
N'êtes-vous pas de cet avis?

LES TROIS FEMMES
Si fait, je suis
de cet avis.
Si fait, vraiment je suis.

TOUS LES CINQ
Quand il s'agit de tromperie, *etc.*

LE DANCAÏRE
C'est dit alors; vous partirez?

FRASQUITA ET MERCÉDÈS
Quand vous voudrez.

LE DANCAÏRE
Mais tout de suite.

CARMEN
Ah! permettez!!
S'il vous plait de partir, partez,
mais je ne suis pas du voyage.
Je ne pars pas, je ne pars pas!

to have women around.
And without them,
my lovelies,
no one ever does
any good!

THE THREE GIRLS
What? Without us no one does
any good?

THE TWO MEN
Isn't that your opinion?

GIRLS
Indeed, that's
my opinion.
Yes indeed, really it is.

QUINTET
When it's a question of trickery, *etc.*

EL DANCAÏRO
It's settled then; you'll go?

FRASQUITA AND MERCÉDÈS
Whenever you like.

EL DANCAÏRO
Why, straight away.

CARMEN
Ah! just a moment!
If you want to go, go;
but I'm not in on this trip.
I won't go! I won't go!

LES DEUX HOMMES

Carmen, mon amour, tu viendras—

CARMEN

Je ne pars pas; je ne pars pas!

LES DEUX HOMMES

Et tu n'auras pas le courage
de nous laisser dans l'embarras.

FRASQUITA ET MERCÉDÈS

Ah! ma Carmen, tu viendras.

CARMEN

Je ne pars pas, *etc.*

LE DANCAÏRE

Mais, au moins la raison, Carmen,
tu la diras.

TOUS LES QUATRE

La raison, la raison!

CARMEN

Je la dirai certainement.

TOUS LES QUATRE

Voyons! Voyons!

CARMEN

La raison, c'est qu'en ce moment …

TOUS LES QUATRE

Eh bien? Eh bien?

THE MEN

Carmen, my love, you will come—

CARMEN

I won't go! I won't go!

THE MEN

And you won't have the heart
to leave us in the lurch.

FRASQUITA AND MERCÉDÈS

Ah! My Carmen, you will come.

CARMEN

I won't go! *etc.*

EL DANCAÏRO

But the reason, Carmen,
at least you'll tell us the reason.

QUARTET

The reason, the reason!

CARMEN

Certainly I'll give it.

QUARTET

Let's have it! Let's have it!

CARMEN

The reason is that at this moment …

QUARTET

Well? Well?

CARMEN

Je suis amoureuse!

LES DEUX HOMMES *(stupéfaits)*

Qu'a-t-elle dit?

LES DEUX FEMMES

Elle dit qu'elle est amoureuse!

TOUS LES QUATRE

Amoureuse!

CARMEN

Oui, amoureuse!

LE DANCAÏRE

Voyons, Carmen, sois sérieuse!

CARMEN

Amoureuse à perdre l'esprit!

LES DEUX HOMMES

La chose, certes, nous étonne,
mais ce n'est pas le premier jour
où vous aurez su, ma mignonne,
faire marcher de front le devoir et l'amour.

CARMEN

Mes amis, je serais fort aise
de partir avec vous ce soir;
mais cette fois ne vous déplaise,
il faudra que l'amour passe avant le devoir.

LE DANCAÏRE

Ce n'est pas là ton dernier mot?

CARMEN

I'm in love!

THE MEN *(astonished)*

What did she say?

THE GIRLS

She says she's in love!

QUARTET

In love!

CARMEN

Yes, in love!

EL DANCAÏRO

See here, Carmen, be serious!

CARMEN

Head over heels in love!

THE MEN

This is certainly astonishing,
but it's not the first time,
my pet, that you've been able
to combine love and duty.

CARMEN

My friends, I'd be most happy
to go with you this evening;
but this time—don't be annoyed—
love must come before duty.

EL DANCAÏRO

That's not your final word?

CARMEN

Absolument!

LE REMENDADO

Il faut que tu te laisses attendrir.

TOUS LES QUATRE

Il faut venir, Carmen, il faut venir!

Pour notre affaire,

c'est nécessaire,

car entre nous …

CARMEN

Quant à cela, je l'admets avec vous …

RPRISE GÉNÉRALE

Quand il s'agit de tromperie, etc.

LE DANCAÏRE

En voilà assez; je t'ai dit qu'il faillait venir

et tu viendras … je suis le chef.

CARMEN

Comment dis-tu ça?

LE DANCAÏRE

Je te dis que je suis le chef.

CARMEN

Et tu crois que je t'obéirai?

LE DANCAÏRE (*furieux*)

Carmen! …

CARMEN

Absolutely!

EL REMENDADO

You must relent.

QUARTET

You must come, Carmen, you must come!

It's necessary

for our scheme,

for between ourselves …

CARMEN

As to that, I admit with you that …

QUINTET (*reprise*)

When it's a question of trickery, etc.

EL DANCAÏRO

Enough of that; I told you you must come,

and you will come … I am the leader.

CARMEN

What's that you say?

EL DANCAÏRO

I tell you I'm the leader.

CARMEN

And you think I'll obey you?

EL DANCAÏRO (*furious*)

Carmen! …

LE REMENDADO

throwing himself between Dancaïro and Carmen

Je vous en prie … des personnes si distin-
guées.

LE DANCAÏRE
Amoureuse … ce n'est pas une raison, cela.

CARMEN
Partez sans moi … j'irai vous rejoindre
demain, mais pour ce soir je reste.

FRASQUITA
Je ne t'ai jamais vue comme cela; que
attends-tu donc?

CARMEN
Un pauvre diable du soldat qui m'a rendu
service …

MERCÉDÈS
Ce soldat qui était en prison?

CARMEN
Oui.

LE DANCAÏRE
Je parierais qu'il ne viendra pas.

CARMEN
Ne parie pas, tu perdrais …

José's voice is heard in the distance.

EL REMENDADO

I beg you, such genteel persons.

EL DANCAÏRO
In love … that's not a reason.

CARMEN
Leave without me. I'll come and join you
tomorrow, but for this evening I'm staying.

FRASQUITA
I've never seen you like this. Who are you
expecting?

CARMEN
A poor devil of a soldier who did me a
service …

MERCÉDÈS
That soldier who was in prison?

CARMEN
Yes.

EL DANCAÏRO
I'd bet you he won't come.

CARMEN
Don't bet, you would lose …

SCENE FIFTEEN
Song

JOSÉ

in the far distance

Halte là!
Qui va là?
Dragon d'Alcala!
Où t'en vas-tu par là,
Dragon d'Alcala?—
Moi, je m'en vais faire
mordre la poussière
à mon adversaire.—
S'il en est ainsi,
passez, mon ami.
Affaire d'honneur,
affaire de coeur;
pour nous tout est là
Dragons d'Alcala!

There is no break in the music. Carmen, Dancaïro, Remendado, Mercédès, and Frasquita watch the arrival of José through the half-open shutters.

MERCÉDÈS
C'est un dragon, ma foi.

FRASQUITA
Un beau dragon

LE DANCAÏRE (*à Carmen*)
Eh bien, Carmen, puisque tu ne veux venir
que demain, sais-tu au moins ce que tu
devrais faire?

JOSÉ

Halt!
Who goes there?
Dragoon of Alcala!
Where are you going there,
Dragoon of Alcala?—
Me, I'm going to make
my rival
bite the dust.—
If that's the case,
pass, my friend.
An affair of honour,
an affair of the heart—
that explains everything for us
Dragoons of Alcala!

MERCÉDÈS
Faith, it's a dragoon.

FRASQUITA
A handsome dragoon.

EL DANCAÏRO (*to Carmen*)
Well, Carmen, since you won't come until
tomorrow, d'you know at least what you
ought to do?

CARMEN

Qu'est-ce que je devrais faire?

LE DANCAÏRE

Tu devrais décider ton dragon à venir avec toi et à se joindre à nous.

CARMEN

Ah! … si cela se pouvait! … Mais il n'y faut pas penser … ce sont des bêtises … il est trop niais.

LE DANCAÏRE

Pourquoi l'aimes-tu puisque tu en conviens toi-même?

CARMEN

Parce qu'il est joli garçon donc et qu'il me plaît.

LE REMENDADO *(avec fatuité)*

Le patron ne comprend pas ça, lui … qu'il suffise d'être joli garçon pour plaire aux femmes …

LE DANCAÏRE

Attends un peu, toi, attends un peu …

CARMEN

What is it I ought to do?

EL DANCAÏRO

You ought to persuade your dragoon to come with you and join us.

CARMEN

Ah, if that were possible! … But you mustn't think of it … it's nonsense … he's too simple.

EL DANCAÏRO

Why do you love him, since you yourself admit it?

CARMEN

Because he's a nice boy and he pleases me.

EL REMENDADO *(fatuously)*

The boss, he doesn't understand that … that it's enough to be a nice boy in order to please the women …

EL DANCAÏRO

Wait a moment, you, wait a moment …

Remendado makes his escape and goes out. Dancaïro pursues him and goes out in his turn, dragging along Mercédès and Frasquita who are trying to calm him down.

JOSÉ

Halte là!

Qui va là?

Dragon d'Alcala!

JOSÉ

Halt!

Who goes there?

Dragoon of Alcala!

Où t'en vas-tu par là,
Dragon d'Alcala?—
Exact et fidèle,
je vais où m'appelle
l'amour de ma belle!—
S'il en est ainsi,
passez, mon ami.
Affaire d'honneur,
affaire de coeur,
pour nous tout est là,
Dragons d'Alcala!

Where are you going there,
Dragoon of Alcala?—
Punctual and faithful,
I go where the love
of my fair lady calls me!—
If that's the case,
pass, friend.
An affair of honour,
an affair of the heart,
that explains everything for us
Dragoons of Alcala!

Don José enters.

CARMEN

Enfin … te voilà … C'est bien heureux!

JOSÉ

Il y a deux heures seulement que je suis
sorti de prison.

CARMEN

Qui t'empêchait de sortir plus tôt? Je
t'avais envoyé une lime et une pièce d'or.

JOSÉ

Que veux-tu? J'ai encore mon honneur de
soldat, et déserter me semblerait un grand
crime ... Oh! Je ne t'en suis pas moins
reconnaissant. La lime me servira pour
affiler ma lance et je l'ai gardé comme
souvenir de toi.

holding out the gold coin to her

Quant a l'argent …

CARMEN

At last … so there you are … this is a fine thing!

JOSÉ

It's only two hours since I came out of
prison.

CARMEN

What prevented you from getting out sooner?
I had sent you a file and a gold coin.

JOSÉ

What d'you expect? I still have my soldier's
honour, and to desert would seem to be a
great crime … Oh, I'm none the less grateful to you. The file will be useful to me for
sharpening my lance and I've kept it as a
memento of you.

As for the money …

CARMEN
Tiens, il l'a gardé!

shouting and hammering

Holà! ... Lillas Pastia, holà!

enter Pastia

CARMEN

tossing him the coin

Apporte-nous du Manzanilla ... apporte-nous de tout ce que tu as, de tout ...

PASTIA
Tout de suite, mademoiselle Carmencita.

He goes out.

CARMEN *(à Don José)*
Tu regrettes d't'être fait mettre en prison pour mes beaux yeux?

JOSÉ
Non. On m'a mis en prison, on m'a ôté mon grade, mais ça m'est égal.

CARMEN
Parce que tu m'aimes?

JOSÉ
Oui, parce que je t'aime, parce que je t'adore.

CARMEN
Hullo, he's kept it!

Hi there! ... Lillas Pastia, hi!

CARMEN

Bring us some Manzanilla ... bring us everything you have, everything, the lot ...

PASTIA
At once, señorita Carmencita.

CARMEN *(to Don José)*
You regret having been put in prison for the sake of my lovely eyes?

JOSÉ
No. They put me in prison, they stripped me of my rank, but it's all one to me.

CARMEN
Because you love me?

JOSÉ
Yes, because I love you, because I adore you.

CARMEN

Ton lieutenant était ici tour à l'heure, avec d'autres officiers, ils nous ont fait danser.

JOSÉ

Tu as dansé?

CARMEN

Oui; et ton lieutenant s'est permis de me dire qu'il m'adorait …

JOSÉ

Carmen!

CARMEN

Qu'est-ce que tu as? … Est-ce que tu serais jaloux, par hasard?

CARMEN

Your lieutenant was here just now with some other officers. They made us dance.

JOSÉ

You danced?

CARMEN

Yes; and your lieutenant allowed himself to tell me that he adored me …

JOSÉ

Carmen!

CARMEN

What's the matter with you? … Would you be jealous, by any chance?

Shirley Verrett (b. 1931) made her Metropolitan Opera debut in the title role of Carmen.

JOSÉ	JOSÉ
Mais certainement, je suis jaloux …	Why, certainly I'm jealous …

CARMEN	CARMEN
Eh bien, si tu le veux, je danserai pour toi maintenant, pour toi seul.	Well then, if you want me to, I'll dance for you now, for you alone.

JOSÉ	JOSÉ
Ah! que je t'aime, Carmen, que je t'aime!	Ah, how I love you, Carmen, how I love you!

CARMEN	CARMEN
Je l'espère bien.	So I should hope.

SCENE SIXTEEN
Duet

DISC NO. 2/TRACK 1

Je vais danser en votre honneur Don José arrives, fresh from his stint in prison, and Carmen greets him with some teasing and as a special treat she dances for him alone (00:37) in a way that suggests a tempestuous night of love is ahead for them. But Bizet brilliantly dramatizes the central conflict of the story in a few well-chosen strokes when he has Don José hear the reveille (01:13). Carmen's explosive anger (02:39) when he tells her he must leave has an unsettling effect on Don José, whose psychotic reaction in the end is underlined by the return of the fate motive, heard in the opera's prelude.

CARMEN	CARMEN
Je vais danser en votre honneur,	I am going to dance in your honour,
et vous verrez, seigneur,	and you will see, my lord,
comment je sais moi-même accompagner	how I am able to accompany
ma danse!	my dance!
Mettez-vous là, Don José, je commence!	Sit down there, Don José, I'll begin!

She makes José sit down in a corner, and starts to dance, humming and accompanying herself with her castanets. José is entranced. Bugles are heard in the distance sounding Retreat. José cocks an ear. He comes over to Carmen and compels her to stop.

JOSÉ

Attendez, Carmen, rien qu'un moment,
arrête!

CARMEN

Et pour quoi, s'il te plaît?

JOSÉ

Il me semble, là-bas …
oui, ce sont nos clairons que sonnent la
retraite!
Ne les entends-tu pas?

CARMEN

Bravo! Bravo! J'avais beau faire; il est
mélancholique de danser sans orchestre.
Et vive la musique
qui nous tombe du ciel!

JOSÉ

Wait, Carmen, only for a moment,
stop!

CARMEN

And why, if you please?

JOSÉ

I think, over there …
yes, those are our bugles sounding
Retreat!
Can't you hear them?

CARMEN

Bravo! Bravo! I was trying in vain; it's dismal
dancing without an orchestra.
And long live music
that drops on us out of the skies!

She resumes her song. The bugles sound nearer, pass beneath the windows of the inn, then fade in the distance. José makes a new effort to tear himself from his contemplation of Carmen. He seizes her arm and compels her to stop once more.

JOSÉ

Tu ne m'as pas compris, Carmen, c'est la
retraite;
il faut que moi, je rentre au quartier pour
l'appel

CARMEN

Au quartier! Pour l'appel!

JOSÉ

You didn't understand me, Carmen, it's
Retreat;
I've got to get back to quarters
for roll-call.

CARMEN

To quarters! For roll-call!

Ah! j'étais vraiment trop bête!
Je me mettais en quartre
et je faisais des frais,
oui, je faisais des frais
pour amuser monsieur!
Je chantais! Je dansais!
Je crois, Dieu me pardonne,
qu'un peu plus, je l'aimais!
Taratata!
C'est le clarion qui sonne!
Taratata!
Il part! il est parti!
Va-t'en donc, canari!

Ah! Really I was too stupid!
I went out of my way
and took the trouble,
yes, I took the trouble
to entertain the gentleman!
I sang! I danced!
I believe, God forgive me,
I almost fell in love!
Taratata!
It's the bugle sounding!
Taratata!
He's off! He's gone!
Go on then, canary!*

angrily throwing his cap at him

Tiens; prends ton shako,
ton sabre, ta giberne;
et va-t'en, mon garçon, va-t'en!
Retourne à ta caserne!

Here! Take your shako,
your sword, your bandolier;
and clear off, my son, clear off!
Clear off back to your barracks!

JOSÉ

C'est mal à toi, Carmen, de te moquer de
moi! Je souffre de partir, car jamais, jamais
femme, jamais femme avant toi,
aussi profoundemént n'avait troublé
mon âme!

JOSÉ

It's cruel of you, Carmen, to make fun of me!
It pains me to go, for never, never has a
woman,
never before you has any woman
so deeply stirred my heart!

CARMEN

"Taratata, mon Dieu! C'est la retraite!
Taratata, je vais être en retard!"
Il court, il perd la tête,
et voilà son amour!

CARMEN

"Taratata, my God! It's the Retreat!
Taratata, I'm going to be late!"
He loses his wits, he rushes off,
and that's his love!

* a reference to the yellow tunic of a Spanish dragoon.

JOSÉ	JOSÉ
Ainsi, tu ne crois pas à mon amour?	So you don't believe in my love?

CARMEN	CARMEN
Mais non!	Of course not!

JOSÉ	JOSÉ
Eh bien! tu m'entendras!	Very well! You shall listen to me!

CARMEN	CARMEN
Je ne veux rien entendre!	I won't listen to anything!

JOSÉ	JOSÉ
Tu m'entendras!	You shall hear me!

CARMEN	CARMEN
Tu vas te faire attendre!	You're going to be late!

JOSÉ	JOSÉ
Tu m'entendras! Carmen!	You shall hear me! Carmen!

CARMEN	CARMEN
Non! non! non! non!	No! No! No! No!

JOSÉ	JOSÉ
Oui, tu m'entendras!	Yes, you shall hear me!
Je le veux! Carmen,	I insist! Carmen,
tu m'entendras!	you shall hear me!

He reaches inside his tunic and takes out the acacia flower Carmen threw him in Act One.

DISC NO. 2/TRACK 2

La fleur que tu m'avais jetée (Flower Song) **The Flower Song is the tenor's big solo moment in Carmen, a beautiful aria that challenges the singer to deliver it with passion and, at the same time, a kind of neurotic tenderness. It is one of those arias with such beautiful surfaces that one does** not have to look beneath them to appreciate it. Yet it is a disturbing moment in the context of the opera—a quality captured in Jon Vickers's performance on this recording—that ends with passionate declaration that rises (03:19) to an eerily soft high B-flat.

La fleur que tu m'avais jetée,	The flower that you threw to me
dans ma prison m'était restée.	stayed with me in my prison.
Flétrie et sèche, cette fleur	Withered and dried up, that flower
gardait toujours sa douce odeur;	always kept its sweet perfume;
et pendant des heures entières,	and for hours at a time,
sur mes yeux, fermant mes paupières,	with my eyes closed,
de cette odeur je m'enivrais	I became drunk with its smell
et dans la nuit je te voyais!	and in the night I used to see you!
Je me prenais à te maudire,	I took to cursing you,
à te détester, à me dire	detesting you, asking myself
Pourquoi faut-it que le destin,	why did destiny
l'ait mise là sur mon chemin?	have to throw her across my path?
Puis je m'accusais de blasphème,	Then I accused myself of blasphemy,
et je ne sentais en moi-même,	and felt within myself,
je ne sentais qu'un seul désir,	I felt but one desire,
un seul désir, un seul espoir	one desire, one hope
te revoir, ô Carmen, oui, te revoir!	to see you again, Carmen, to see you again!
Car tu n'avais eu qu'à paraître,	For you had only to appear,
qu'à jeter un regard sur moi,	only to throw a glance my way,
pour t'emparer de tour mon être,	to take possession of my whole being,
ô ma Carmen!	O my Carmen,
et j'étais une chose à toi!	and I was your chattel!
Carmen, je t'aime!	Carmen, I love you!

DISC NO. 2/TRACK 3

Non! tu ne maimes pas! Carmen sees the potential for exploiting Don José's vulnerability and, in a rhythmically seductive phrase beginning with the words "Là-bas, là-bas ..." (00:19), she insists (much as she insisted in the Seguedille) that he join her and her smuggler friends.

CARMEN	**CARMEN**
Non, tu ne m'aimes pas!	No, you don't love me!

JOSÉ
Que dis-tu?

CARMEN
Non, tu ne m'aimes pas,
non! Car si tu m'aimais,
là-bas, là-bas,
tu me suivrais.

JOSÉ
Carmen!

CARMEN
Oui!—
Là-bas, là-bas, dans la montagne,

JOSÉ
Carmen!

CARMEN
là-bas, là-bas, tu me suivrais.
Sur ton cheval tu me prendrais,
et comme un brave à travers la campagne,
en croupe, tu m'emporterais!
Là-bas, là-bas dans la montagne!

JOSÉ
Carmen!

CARMEN
Là-bas, là-bas, tu me suivrais,
Si tu m'aimais!
Tu n'y dépendrais de personne;
point d'officier à qui tu doives obéir
et point de retraite que sonne

JOSÉ
What are you saying?

CARMEN
No, you don't love me,
no! For if you did,
you'd follow me over there.

JOSÉ
Carmen!

CARMEN
Yes!—
Away over there into the mountains,

JOSÉ
Carmen!

CARMEN
away over there you'd follow me.
You'd take me up behind you on your
horse and like a daredevil you'd carry me
off across the country!
Way over there into the mountains!

JOSÉ
Carmen!

CARMEN
Away over there you'd follow me,
if you loved me!
There you'd not be dependent on anyone;
there'd be no officer you had to obey,
and no Retreat sounding

pour dire à l'amoureux

qu'il est temps de partir!

Le ciel ouvert, la vie errante,

pour pays l'univers;

et pour loi ta volonté,

et surtout la chose enivrante

la liberté! la liberté!

JOSÉ

Mon Dieu!

CARMEN

Là-bas, là-bas dans la montagne,

JOSÉ

Carmen!

CARMEN

là-bas, là-bas, si tu m'aimais,

JOSÉ

Tais-toi!

CARMEN

là-bas, là-bas tu me suivrais!

Sur ton cheval te me prendrais …

JOSÉ

Ah! Carmen! hélas! tais-toi!

tais-toi! mon Dieu!

CARMEN

et comme un brave, à travers la campagne,

our, tu m'emporterais, si tu m'aimais.

to tell a lover

that it is time to go!

The open sky, the wandering life,

the whole wide world your domain;

for law your own free will,

and above all, that intoxicating thing

Freedom! Freedom!

JOSÉ

Oh God!

CARMEN

Away over there into the mountains,

JOSÉ

Carmen!

CARMEN

away over there, if you loved me,

JOSÉ

Stop it!

CARMEN

away over there you'd follow me!

You'd take me up on your horse …

JOSÉ

Ah, Carmen! Alas! Stop!

stop! Oh God!

CARMEN

and like a daredevil

you'd carry me off

across the country, if you loved me.

JOSÉ

Hélas! Hélas!

CARMEN

Our, n'est-ce pas,

là-bas, là-bas tu me suivras,

tu m'aimes et tu me suivras!

Là-bas, là-bas emporte-moi!

JOSÉ

Pitié! Carmen! Pitié!

O mon Dieu, hélas!

Ah! Tais-toi! Tais-toi!

Non! Je ne veux plus t'eécouter!

Quitter mon drapeau … déserter …

c'est la honte, c'est l'infamie!

Je n'en veux pas!

CARMEN

Eh bien, pars!

JOSÉ

Carmen, je t'en prie!

CARMEN

Non, je ne t'aime plus!

JOSÉ

Ecoute!

CARMEN

Va! Je te hais!

Adieu! Mais adieu pour jamais!

JOSÉ

Alas! Alas!

CARMEN

Yes, isn't it so,

you will follow me there,

you love me and you'll follow me!

Take me away over there!

JOSÉ

Pity, Carmen! Have pity!

Oh God, alas!

Ah, stop, stop!

No! I won't listen to you!

To abandon my colours … to desert …

that's shameful, that's dastardly!

I'll have none of it!

CARMEN

All right then, go!

JOSÉ

Carmen, I implore you!

CARMEN

No, I don't love you any more!

JOSÉ

Listen!

CARMEN

Go! I hate you!

Good-bye! And good-bye forever!

JOSÉ	JOSÉ
Eh bien, soit … adieu, adieu pour jamais!	All right, so be it … good-bye forever!

CARMEN	CARMEN
Va-t'en!	Get out!

JOSÉ	JOSÉ
Carmen! Adieu! Adieu pour jamais!	Carmen! Goodbye, good-bye forever!

CARMEN	CARMEN
Adieu!	Good-bye!

Don José hurries towards the door; just as he reaches it, somebody knocks.

SCENE SEVENTEEN
Finale

DISC NO. 2/TRACK 4

Holà Carmen! Holà! Holà! **In the second-act finale, just as the smugglers arrive to collect Carmen, Zuniga blunders in, looking for Carmen. He is held captive, leaving Don José no recourse but to join the smugglers. The "Là-bas" melody (03:51) returns with militancy, for an entire band of smugglers is now gathering, transforming Carmen's insinuating siren song into a galloping hymn to the rogue's life and bringing the act to an end.**

ZUNIGA *(au dehors)*	ZUNIGA *(outside)*
Holà! Carmen! Holà! Holà!	Hallo there, Carmen! Hallo! Hallo!

JOSÉ	JOSÉ
Qui frappe? qui vient là?	Who's that knocking? Who's there?

CARMEN	CARMEN
Tais-toi! Tais-toi!	Keep quiet!

ZUNIGA

forcing the door

J'ouvre moi-même et j'entre.

sees Don José—to Carmen

Ah! fi, ah! fi, la belle!
Le choix n'est pas heureux; c'est se mésallier
de prendre le soldat quand on a l'officier.

to Don José

Allons! Décampe!

JOSÉ
Non!

ZUNIGA
Si fait, tu partiras!

JOSÉ
Je ne partirai pas!

ZUNIGA

striking him

Drôle!

JOSÉ

drawing his sword

Tonnerre! Il va pleuvoir des coups!

ZUNIGA

I'm opening up myself, and coming in.

Ah! Fi, fi! My lovely lady!
This isn't a happy choice; it's demeaning
to take the soldier when you've got the officer.

Off with you, get moving!

JOSÉ
No!

ZUNIGA
You certainly will go!

JOSÉ
I shall not go!

ZUNIGA

Scoundrel!

JOSÉ

By thunder! It's going to rain blows!

116

CARMEN

throwing herself between them

Au diable le jaloux! *(appelant)*
A moi! A moi!

Gypsies appear from all sides. Carmen points to Zuniga. Dancaïro and Remendado hurl themselves upon him and disarm him.

CARMEN

Bel officier! Bel officier, l'amour
vous joue en ce moment un assez vilain
tour.
Vous arrivez fort mal, hélas! Et nous
sommes forcés,
ne voulant être dénoncés,
de vous garder au moins … pendant une
heure.

LE DANCAÏRE ET LE REMENDADO

Mon chere monsieur,
nous allons, s'il vous plaît,
quitter cette demeure;
vous viendrez avec nous?

CARMEN

C'est une promenade.

LE DANCAÏRE ET LE REMENDADO

Consentez-vous?

TOUS LES BOHÉMIENS

Répondez, camarade.

CARMEN

Devil take the jealous! *(calling)*
Help! Help!

CARMEN

My fine officer! My fine officer, love
at the moment is playing you a rather dirty
trick.
Your arrival is most untimely; and alas,
we are compelled,
not wishing to be betrayed, to detain you
… for at least an hour.

EL DANCAÏRO AND EL REMENDADO

My dear sir,
if you please, we are going to leave this
establishment;
you'll come with us?

CARMEN

Just for a stroll.

EL DANCAÏRO AND EL REMENDADO

Do you consent?

ALL THE GYPSIES

Answer, comrade.

ZUNIGA

Certainement,

d'autant plus que votre argument

est un de ceux auxquels on ne résiste guère,

mais gare à vous! Gare à vous plus tard!

LE DANCAÏRE

La guerre, c'est la guerre!

En attendant, mon officier,

passez devant sans vous faire prier!

LE REMENDADO ET LES BOHÉMIENS

Passez devant sans vous faire prier!

ZUNIGA

Certainly,

the more so since your argument

is one of those that can hardly be resisted;

but take care! Look out for yourselves later!

EL DANCAÏRO

War is war!

Meantime, my good sir,

carry on without further argument!

EL REMENDADO AND THE GYPSIES

Carry on without further argument!

The officer is led out by four gypsies armed with pistols.

CARMEN *(à Don José)*

Es-tu des nôtres maintenant?

JOSÉ

Il le faut bien.

CARMEN

Ah! Le mot n'est pas galant,

mais qu'importe, va, tu ty feras

quand tu verras

comme c'est beau, la vie errante;

pour pays, l'univers,

et pour loi ta volonté,

et surtout, la chose, enivrante

la liberté! La liberté!

TOUS *(à Don José)*

Suis-nous à travers la campagne,

viens avec nous dans la montagnen,

CARMEN *(to Don José)*

Are you one of us now?

JOSÉ

I have no alternative.

CARMEN

Ah! that's not gallantly put,

but no matter, go, you'll take to it there

when you see

how fine is the wandering life;

the whole world your domain,

your own free will for law,

and above all that intoxicating thing

Freedom! Freedom!

ALL *(to Don José)*

Take to the country with us,

come with us into the mountains,

suis-nous et tu t'y feras
quand tu verras, là-bas,
comme c'est beau, la vie errante;
pour pays, l'univers,
et pour loi, ta volonté!
Et surtout, la chose enivrante
la liberté! La liberté!
Le ciel ouvert, la vie errante,
pour pays tout l'univers;
pour loi ta volonté,
et surtout la chose enivrante:
la liberté, La liberté!

come with us and you'll take to it there
when you see, away over there;
how fine is the wandering life:
the whole world your domain,
your own free will for law!
And above all that intoxicating thing
Freedom! Freedom!
The open sky, the wandering life,
the whole wide world your domain;
your own free will for law,
and above all that intoxicating thing
Freedom! Freedom!

SCENE EIGHTEEN
Introduction

The curtain rises on a wild and rocky scene; the night is dark and the solitude complete. During the musical prelude a smuggler appears at the top of the rocks, then another, then two more, and finally twenty here and there, climbing and scrambling over the rocks. Some of them are carrying heavy bales on their shoulders.

DISC NO. 2/TRACK 5

Entr'acte One of Bizet's most beautiful melodies appears in the entr'acte, apropos of nothing really—a soaring flute solo heard over arpeggios in the harp. The melody is never heard again but it effectively removes the audience from the bustle of Seville, placing the action in the country and perhaps reflecting Don José's sad reminiscence of happier times.

DISC NO. 2/TRACK 6

The smugglers appear singing a hushed chorus with a tinge of melancholy exhaustion.

CHOEUR	**CHORUS**
Ecoute, écoute, compagnon, écoute,	Listen, friend, listen,
la fortune est là-bas, là-bas,	fortune lies over there,
mais prends garde pendant la route,	but take care along the way,
prends garde de faire un faux pas!	and watch your step!
LE DANCAÏRE, LE REMENDADO, JOSÉ, CARMEN, MERCÉDÈS ET FRASQUITA	**EL DANCAÏRO, EL REMENDADO, JOSÉ, CARMEN, MERCÉDÈS AND FRASQUITA**
Notre métier est bon,	Our calling is a good one,
mais pour le faire il faut	but to follow it you must
avoir une âme forte!	have a stout heart!

Et le péril est en haut, il est en bas,	There's danger up above, and down below,
il est partout, qu'importe!	it's everywhere—what of it!
Nous allons devant nous	We go forward
sans souci du torrent,	without worrying about the torrent,
san souci de l'orage,	without worrying abut the storm,
san souci du soldat	without worrying about the soldier
qui là-bas nous attend,	who's waiting for us over there,
et nous guette au passage—	and keeping a sharp lookout for us—
sans souci nous allons en avant!	we go forward without worrying!

TOUS

Ecoute, compagnon, écoute, *etc.*

ALL

Listen, friend, listen, *etc.*

LE DANCAÏRE

Halte! Nous allons nous arrêter ici ... ceux qui ont sommeil pourront dormir pendant une demi-heure.

EL DANCAÏRO

Halt! We're going to stop here ... those who feel sleepy can doss down for half an hour.

LE REMENDADO

EL REMENDADO

stretching himself out voluptuously

Ah!

Ah!

DISC NO. 2/TRACK 7

LE DANCAÏRE

Je vais, moi, voir s'il y a moyen de faire entrer les marchandises dans la ville ... une brèche s'est faite dans le mur d'enceinte et nous pourrions passer par là.

EL DANCAÏRO

Me, I'm going to see if there's some way of getting the stuff into the town ... a gap has been made in the outer wall and we could get through that way.

calling out

Remendado!

Remendado!

LE REMENDADO	**EL REMENDADO**
waking up	
Hé?	Hé?
LE DANCAÏRE	**EL DANCAÏRO**
Debout, tu vas venir avec moi.	Get up, you're coming with me.
LE REMENDADO	**EL REMENDADO**
Mais, patron …	But, boss …
LE DANCAÏRE	**EL DANCAÏRO**
Qu'est-ce que c'est?	What's that?
LE REMENDADO	**EL REMENDADO**
getting up	
Voilà, patron, voilà!	Here we are, boss, here!
LE DANCAÏRE	**EL DANCAÏRO**
Allons, passe devant.	Right, go on ahead.
LE REMENDADO	**EL REMENDADO**
Et moi qui rêvais que j'allais pouvoir dormir … C'était un rêve, hélas! c'était un rêve!	And I who thought I was going to be able to sleep … It was a dream, alas, it was a dream!

He goes out, followed by Dancaïro. During this scene between Carmen and Don José, a few gypsy men light a fire, by which Mercédès and Frasquita come and sit down; the others roll themselves up in their cloaks, lie down and go to sleep.

JOSÉ	**JOSÉ**
Voyons, Carmen … si je t'ai parlé trop durement, je t'en demande pardon faisons la paix.	Look, Carmen … if I spoke to you too harshly, I ask your forgiveness. Let's make up.

CARMEN

Non.

JOSÉ

Tu es le diable, Carmen?

CARMEN

Oui, qu'est-ce que tu regardes là, à quoi penses-tu?

JOSÉ

Je me dis que là-bas il y a une bonne vieille femme qui croit que je suis encore un honnête homme …

CARMEN

Une bonne vieille femme?

JOSÉ

Oui; ma mère.

CARMEN

Ta mère. Eh bien, tu ne ferais pas mal d'aller la retrouver.

JOSÉ

Carmen, si tu me parles encore de nous séparer …

CARMEN

Tu me tuerais, peut-être?

José does not answer

CARMEN

No.

JOSÉ

You're worried, Carmen?

CARMEN

Yes, what's that you're looking at there, what are you thinking of?

JOSÉ

I'm telling myself that down there is a good old woman who believes me still to be an honest man …

CARMEN

A good old woman?

JOSÉ

Yes, my mother.

CARMEN

Your mother. Well then, you'd do no harm by going to find her.

JOSÉ

Carmen, if you talk to me any more about us separating …

CARMEN

You would kill me, perhaps?

A la bonne heure … Mêlons! Coupons! (Card Trio) **This is the moment that, for Carmen, is the crux of the action in the opera. Frasquita and Mercédès are playing with tarot cards. When Carmen tries her hand, the cards reveal her dire fate (03:27) She is hurtling toward death, and there is nothing she can do about it. She is devastated and almost instantly resigned to what seems inevitable. The section of the scene beginning with "En vain pour éviter les réponses amères" (04:05) reveals her fatalistic attitude in a mournful melody that develops with the same staggering intensity as the fate motive. It is perhaps the most substantial and beautiful solo moment Carmen has in the entire opera.**

CARMEN

A la bonne heure … J'ai vu dans les cartes
que nous devions finir ensemble.

CARMEN

Well and good … I've seen in the cards
that we are to finish together.

JOSÉ

Tu es le diable, Carmen?

JOSÉ

You're worried, Carmen?

CARMEN

Mais oui, je te l'ai déjà dit …

CARMEN

Why yes, I've already told you so …

SCENE NINETEEN
Trio

She turns her back on José and goes and sits down by Mercédès and Frasquita. After a moment of indecision, Don José moves off in his turn and goes and stretches himself out upon the rocks. During the final exchanges in the foregoing scene, Mercédès and Frasquita have been spreading out playing cards in front of them.

FRASQUITA ET MERCÉDÈS

Mêlons! Coupons!
Bien, c'est cela!
Trois cartes ici …

FRASQUITA AND MERCÉDÈS

Shuffle! Cut!
Good, that's that!
Three cards here …

Quatre là!
Et maintenant, parlez, mes belles,
de l'avenir, donnez-nous des nouvelles;
dites-nous qui nous trahira,
dites-nous qui nous aimera!
Parlez, parlez!

FRASQUITA
Moi, je vois un jeune amoureux,
qui m'aime on ne peut davantage.

MERCÉDÈS
Les mien est très riche et très vieux,
mais il parle de mariage.

FRASQUITA
Je me campe sur son cheval,
et dans la montagne il m'entraîne.

MERCÉDÈS
Dans un château presque royal,
le mien m'installe en souveraine!

FRASQUITA
De l'amour à n'en plus finir,
tous les jours, nouvelles folies!

MERCÉDÈS
De l'or tant, que j'en puis tenir,
des diamants, des pierreries!

FRASQUITA
Le mien devient un chef fameux,
cent hommes marchent à sa suite!

four there!
And now speak, my lovelies,
give us news of the future;
tell us who's going to betray us,
tell us who's going to love us!
Speak! Speak!

FRASQUITA
Me, I see a young suitor,
no one could love me more.

MERCÉDÈS
Mine is very rich and very old,
but he talks of marriage.

FRASQUITA
I settle myself firmly on his horse
and he carries me off into the mountains.

MERCÉDÈS
In an almost royal castle
mine installs me in queenly state!

FRASQUITA
Never-ending love,
every day new raptures!

MERCÉDÈS
As much gold as I can take,
diamonds, precious stones!

FRASQUITA
Mine becomes a famous leader,
a hundred men march in his train!

MERCÉDÈS

Le mien en croirai-je mes yeux?
Oui … il meurt!
Ah! je suis veuve et j'hérite!

MERCÉDÈS

Mine … can I believe my eyes?
Yes … he dies
Ah! I'm a widow and I inherit!

REPRISE DE L'ENSEMBLE

Parlez encor, parlez, mes belles, etc.

TOGETHER REPRISE

Speak again, speak, my lovelies, etc.

They begin to consult the cards again.

MERCÉDÈS

Fortune!

MERCÉDÈS

Fortune!

FRASQUITA

Amour!

FRASQUITA

Love!

CARMEN

Voyons, que j'essaie à mon tour.

CARMEN

Let's see—let me have a try.

She starts to turn up the cards.

Carreau, pique … la mort!
J'ai bien lu … moi d'abord.
Ensuite lui … pour tous les deux la mort!

Diamond, spade … Death!
I read it clearly … me first.
Then him … for both of us, Death!

in a low voice, while continuing to shuffle the cards

En vain pour éviter les réponses amères,
en vain tu mêleras;
cela ne sert à rien, les cartes
sont sincères et ne mentiront pas!
Dans le livre d'en haut
si ta page est heureuse,
mêle et coupe sans peur,
la carte sous tes doigts se tournera joyeuse,

In vain to avoid bitter replies,
in vain will you shuffle;
that achieves nothing, the cards
are truthful and will not lie!
If your page in the book
up above is a happy one,
shuffle and cut without fear,
the card under your fingers will turn up

t'annonçant le bonheur.	nicely, foretelling good luck.
Mais si tu dois mourir,	But if you are to die,
si le mot redoutable	if the terrible word
est écrit par le sort,	has been written by Destiny,
recommence vingt fois, la carte impitoyable	begin twenty times—the pitiless card
répétera la mort!	will repeat Death!

turning up the cards

Encor! Encor! Toujours la mort!	Again! Always Death!

FRASQUITA ET MERCÉDÈS
Parlez encor, parlez mes belles, etc.

FRASQUITA AND MERCÉDÈS
Speak again, my lovelies, speak! etc.

CARMEN
Encore! le désepoir!
Toujours la mort!

CARMEN
Again! Despair!
Always Death!

Dancaïro and Remendado return

CARMEN
Eh bien? …

CARMEN
Well? …

LE DANCAÏRE
Eh bien, j'avais raison de ne pas me fier de Lillas Pastia. Nous avons aperçu trois douaniers qui gardaient la brèche.

EL DANCAÏRO
Well, I was right not to trust Lillas Pastia. We spotted three customs men guarding the gap.

CARMEN (*en riant*)
N'ayez pas peur, Dancaïre, nous vous en répondrons de vos trois douaniers …

CARMEN (*laughing*)
Have no fear, Dancaïro, we'll take care of your three customs men for you …

JOSÉ (*furieux*)
Carmen!

JOSÉ (*furious*)
Carmen!

LE DANCAÏRE	**EL DANCAÏRO**
Ah! tu vas nous laisser tranquilles avec ta jalousie. Tu vas te placer là, sur cette hauteur. Dans le cas où tu apercevrais quelqu'un, passes ta colère sur l'indiscret. En route alors …	Ah, you will give us a rest from your jealousy. You will post yourself there on that height. If you should happen to spot anyone, take your anger out on such an ill-advised person. On our way, then …

to the women

Mais vous me répondrez vraiment de ces trois douaniers?	But you really will answer to me for these three customs men?
CARMEN	**CARMEN**
N'ayez pas peur, Dancaïre.	Have no fear, Dancaïro.

DISC NO. 2/TRACK 9

As the three women go to distract the customs official with their charms, they sing a jaunty counterpoint that inspires the chorus to join in a risqué parody of an operatic call-to-arms.

SCENE TWENTY
Ensemble with Chorus

CARMEN, MERCÉDÈS ET FRASQUITA	**CARMEN**, **MERCÉDÈS** AND **FRASQUITA**
Quant au douanier, c'est notre affaire, tout comme un autre il aime à plaire, il aime à faire le galant; ah! laissez-nous passer en avant!	As for the customs man, he's our affair; just like the next man he loves to please, he loves to play the gallant; ah! leave us to go on ahead!
TOUTES LES FEMMES	**ALL THE GIRLS**
Quant au douanier, c'est notre affaire, *etc.*	As for the customs man, he's our affair, *etc.*

TOUS

Il aime à plaire!

MERCÉDÈS

Le douanier sera clément!

TOUS

Il est galant!

CARMEN

Le douanier sera charmant!

TOUS

Il aime à plaire!

MERCÉDÈS

Le douanier sera galant!

FRASQUITA

Oui, le douanier sera même entreprenant!

TOUS

Oui, le douanier c'est notre/leur affaire,
tout comme un autre il aime à plaire,
il aime à faire le galant,
laissez-nous/les passer en avant!

CARMEN, MERCÉDÈS ET FRASQUITA

Il ne s'agit plus de bataille,
non, il s'agit tout simplement
de se laisser prendre la taille
et d'écouter un compliment.
S'il faut aller jusqu'au sourire,
que voulez-vous, on sourira!

EVERYONE

He loves to please!

MERCÉDÈS

The customs man will be easy on us!

EVERYONE

He is gallant!

CARMEN

The customs man will be charming!

ALL

He loves to please!

MERCÉDÈS

The customs man will be gallant!

FRASQUITA

Yes, the customs man will even be forward!

ALL

Yes, the customs man is our/their affair;
just like the next man he loves to please,
he loves to play the gallant;
let us/them go on ahead!

CARMEN, MERCÉDÈS AND FRASQUITA

It's no longer a question of battle;
no, it's simply a question
of letting ourselves be taken by the waist
and listening to a compliment.
If it's necessary to go as far as a smile,
what of it?—we'll smile!

TOUTES LES FEMMES	ALL THE WOMEN
Et d'avance, je puis le dire,	And here and now I can say
la contrebande passera!	the stuff will get through!
En avant! Marchons! Allons!	Forward! On our way! Let's go!

TOUT LE MONDE	ALL
Oui, le douanier c'est notre/leur affaire, *etc.*	Yes, the customs man is our/their affair, *etc.*

Everyone leaves, Don José brings up the rear, examining the priming of his carbine; just before he disappears, a man is seen moving behind a rock. It is Micaëla's guide. The guide advances cautiously, then signals to Micaëla that the coast is clear.

DISC NO. 2/TRACK 10

LE GUIDE	THE GUIDE
Nous y sommes.	We're there.

MICAËLA MICAËLA	MICAËLA

entering

C'est ici.	This is the place.

LE GUIDE	THE GUIDE
Oui, vilain endroit, n'est-ce pas, et pas rassurant du tout?	Yes, nasty spot, isn't it, and not at all reassuring?

MICAËLA	MICAËLA
Je ne vois personne.	I don't see anybody.

LE GUIDE	THE GUIDE
Ils reviendront bientôt. Ils n'ont pas emporté toutes leurs marchandises … prenez garde … l'un de leurs doit être en sentinelle et si l'on nous apercevrait …	They'll come back soon, for they haven't taken away all their goods … take care … one of their men must be on sentry–go, and if we were seen …

MICAËLA

Je l'espère bien qu'on m'apercevra …
puisque je suis venue ici justement pour
parler à un de ces contrebandiers …

MICAËLA

I sincerely hope someone will see me …
since that's just what I've come here for, to
speak to one of these smugglers …

LE GUIDE

Eh bien, vous pouvez vous vanter d'avoir
du courage … venir ainsi affronter ces
Bohémiens …

THE GUIDE

Well now, you can boast of having courage
… to come here like this to face these gypsies …

MICAËLA

Je n'aurais pas peur, je vous assure.

MICAËLA

I shouldn't be afraid, I assure you.

LE GUIDE

Bien vrai?

THE GUIDE

Truly?

MICAËLA

Bien vrai.

MICAËLA

Truly.

LE GUIDE *(naïvement)*

Alots je vous demanderai la permission de
m'en aller. Si ça ne vous fait rien, j'irai vous
attendre à l'auberge au bas de la montagne.
Vous restez décidément?

THE GUIDE *(naïvely)*

Then I'll ask your permission to take
myself off. If it's all the same to you I'll go
and wait for you in the inn at the foot of
the mountain.
You're determined to stay?

DISC NO. 2/TRACK 11

Oui, je reste! … Je dis que rien ne m'épouvante (Micaëla's Air) At this depressing point in the opera,
the air Bizet wrote for Micaëla is always welcome. It is an elegant, glowing testament to her
faith in her love for Don José (00:27). Like the first-act duet, it would not be out of place in an
opera of Gounod or Massenet. The orchestration is particularly effective, with a prominent
role given to the evocative and reflective French horn. The melody is borne on the swirling
arpeggios in the cellos, as if to suggest the uncertainty that surrounds her unshakable fidelity
to her beloved.

Hilde Gueden, an Austrian lyric
soprano as Micaëla.

MICAËLA
Oui, je reste!

MICAËLA
Yes. I'm staying!

LE GUIDE
Que tous les saints du paradis vous soient
en aide alors, mais c'est une drôle idée que
vous avez là …

THE GUIDE
May all the saints in paradise come to your
aid then, but it's a funny idea you've got
there …

MICAËLA

looking around her

Mon guide avait raison … l'edroit n'est
pas bien rassurant.

MICAËLA

My guide was right … it's not a very reas-
suring spot.

SCENE TWENTY-ONE
Aria

MICAËLA
Je dis, que rien ne m'épouvante,
je dis, hélas! que je réponds de moi;

MICAËLA
I say that nothing frightens me, I say, alas,
that I have only myself to depend on;

mais j'ai beau faire la vaillante,	but I have tried in vain to be brave,
au fond du coeur, je meurs d'effroi!	at heart I'm dying of fright!
Seule en ce lieu sauvage,	Alone in this wild place,
toute seule j'ai peur,	all alone, I'm afraid,
mais j'ai tort d'avoir peur;	but I do wrong to be afraid;
vous me donnerez du courage,	you will give me courage
vous me protégerez, Seigneur.	you will protect me, Lord.
Je vais voir de près cette femme	I shall get a close look at this woman
dont les artifices maudits	whose evil wiles
ont fini par faire un infâme	have finished by making a criminal
de celui que j'amais jadis	of the man I once loved
elle est dangereuse, elle est belle,	she is dangerous, she is beautiful,
mais je ne veux pas avoir peur,	but I won't be afraid,
je parlerai haut devant elle.	I shall speak out in front of her,
Ah! Seigneur,	Ah! Lord,
vous me protégerez!	you will protect me!
Ah! je dis, que rien ne m'épouvante, *etc.*	Ah! I say that nothing will frighten me, *etc.*
… protégez-moi, O Seigneur,	… protect me, O Lord,
Protégez-moi, Seigneur!	protect me, Lord!
Mais … je ne me trompe pas … sur ce	But … I'm not mistaken … on that
rocher, c'est Don José.	rock—it's Don José.

calling out

José! José! José! José!	José! José! José! José!

Terrified

DISC NO. 2/TRACK 12

Mais … je ne me trompe pas Micaëla hides when she sees Don José fire his gun at a figure who turns out to be Escamillo. The air is thick with testosterone in the vigorous duet that follows (00:34), in which Don José boldly challenges the man he sees as his rival while Escamillo—obviously a far more skilled fighter—is amused by his passion. Though the second half of the duet is often cut, it is heard in its entirety here (02:23), revealing that Escamillo spares Don José's life when he has the better of him, even though Don José was ready to kill him.

Mais que fait-il? … Il arme sa carabine, il ajuste … il fait feu.	But what is he doing? … He's cocking his carbine … he's aiming … he fires.

A shot is heard.

Ah! mon Dieu, j'ai trop présumé de mon courage …	Ah, my God, I overestimated my courage …

She disappears behind the rocks. At the same moment Escamillo comes in, holding his hat in his hand.

ESCAMILLO

ESCAMILLO

Quelques lignes plus bas, et ce n'est pas moi qui aurais le plaisir de combattre les taureaux que je suis en train de conduire …	A little lower … and it isn't I who would have the pleasure of fighting the bulls I'm about to drive …

Enter José

JOSÉ

JOSÉ

carrying his cloak

Qui êtes-vous? Répondez.	Who are you? Answer.

ESCAMILLO

ESCAMILLO

very calm

Eh là … doucement!	Eh eh … gently!

ESCAMILLO

Je suis Escamillo, Torero de Grenade!

JOSÉ

Escamillo!

ESCAMILLO

C'est moi!

JOSÉ

returning his knife to its sheath

Je connais votre nom,

soyez le bienvenu; mais vraiment, camarade,

vous pouviez y rester.

ESCAMILLO

Je ne vous dis pas non,

mais je suis amoureux, mon cher, à la folie,

et celui-là serait un pauvre compagnon,

qui, pour voir ses amours, ne risquerait sa vie!

JOSÉ

Celle que vous aimez est ici?

ESCAMILLO

Justement.

C'est une zingara, mon cher.

JOSÉ

Elle s'appelle?

ESCAMILLO

I'm Escamillo, the Granada matador!

JOSÉ

Escamillo!

ESCAMILLO

That's me!

JOSÉ

I know your name,

you're welcome; but truly, comrade,

that could have been the end of you.

ESCAMILLO

I'm not denying it, but, my friend, I am
madly in love,

and he would be a wretched fellow

who wouldn't risk his live to see his ladylove!

JOSÉ

The girl you love is here?

ESCAMILLO

Exactly.

She's a gypsy girl, my friend.

JOSÉ

Her name?

ESCAMILLO
Carmen.

JOSÉ
Carmen!

ESCAMILLO
Carmen! oui, mon cher.
Elle avait pour amant
un soldat qui a déserté pour elle.
Ils s'adoraient, mais c'est fini, je crois.
Les amours de Carmen ne durent pas
six mois.

JOSÉ
Vous l'aimez cependant!

ESCAMILLO
Je l'aime!
Oui, mon cher, je l'aime à la folie!

JOSÉ
Mais pour nous enlever nos filles de
bohème, savez-vous bien qu'il faut payer?

ESCAMILLO
Soit! On paiera.

JOSÉ
Et que le prix se paie à coups de navaja!

ESCAMILLO
A coups de navaja!

JOSÉ
Comprenez-vous?

ESCAMILLO
Carmen.

JOSÉ
Carmen!

ESCAMILLO
Carmen! Yes, my friend.
She had as a lover
a soldier who once deserted on her account.
They adored each other, but it's over, I think.
Carmen's affairs don't last six months.

JOSÉ
Yet you love her!

ESCAMILLO
I love her!
Yes, my friend, I love her to distraction!

JOSÉ
But to take our gypsy girls away from us
you know that you have to pay?

ESCAMILLO
All right! I'll pay.

JOSÉ
And that the price is paid with the knife!

ESCAMILLO
With the knife!

JOSÉ
You understand?

ESCAMILLO

Le discours est très net.

Ce déserteur, ce beau soldat qu'elle aime,

ou du moins qu'elle aimait—

c'est donc vous?

ESCAMILLO

You put it very clearly.

This deserter, this fine soldier she loves,

or rather, used to love—

is you, then?

JOSÉ

Oui, c'est moi-même!

JOSÉ

Yes, myself!

ESCAMILLO

J'en suis ravi, mon cher,

et le tour est complet!

ESCAMILLO

I'm delighted, my friend,

and the wheel's come full circle!

Both draw their knives and wrap their left arm in their cloaks.

JOSÉ

Enfin ma colère

trouve à qui parler!

Le sang, je l'espère,

va bientôt couler, *etc.*

JOSÉ

At last my rage has found an outlet!

Blood, I hope,

will soon flow, *etc.*

ESCAMILLO

Quelle maladresse,

j'en rirais vraiment!

Chercher la maîtresse

et trouver l'amant! *etc.*

ESCAMILLO

What a predicament,

I could laugh at it, really!

To look for the mistress

and find the lover! *etc.*

ENSEMBLE

Mettez-vous en garde,

et veillez sur vous!

Tant pis pour qui tarde

à parer les coups!

En garde! Allons! Veillez sur vous!

TOGETHER

Put up your guard,

and look out for yourself!

So much the worse for the one

who's slow at parrying!

On guard! Come on! Look out for yourself!

They take up positions on guard at some distance from each other.

ESCAMILLO

Je la connais, ta garde navarraise.

Et je te previens en ami,

Qu'elle ne vaut rien …

ESCAMILLO

I know it, your Navarrais-style guard,

and I warn you, in a friendly way,

that it's no good …

Without answering, Don José advances upon the matador.

A ton aise.

Je t'aurai du moins averti.

As you like.

At least I'll have warned you.

Fight. Incidental music. The matador, very calm, attempts only to defend himself.

JOSÉ

Tu m'épargnes, maudit.

JOSÉ

You're not trying, you devil.

ESCAMILLO

A ce jeu de couteau

je suis trop fort pour toi.

ESCAMILLO

At this knife-play

I'm too good for you.

JOSÉ

Voyons cela.

JOSÉ

Let's see.

A swift and very lively hand-to-hand engagement. Don José finds himself at the mercy of the matador, who does not strike.

ESCAMILLO

Tout beau,

Ta vie est à moi, mais en somme

j'ai pour métier de frapper le taureau,

Non de trouer le coeur de l'homme.

ESCAMILLO

Steady,

your life belongs to me, but in short

my job is to kill bulls,

not to bore holes in men's hearts.

JOSÉ

Frappe ou bien meurs … Ceci n'est pas
un jeu.

JOSÉ

Strike, or die … this isn't a game.

ESCAMILLO	ESCAMILLO

disengaging himself

Soit, mais au moins respire un peu.	All right, but at least get your breath.

Reprise of ensemble

JOSÉ	**JOSÉ**
Enfin ma colère	At last my rage
trouve à qui parler *etc.*	has found an outlet, *etc.*

ESCAMILLO	**ESCAMILLO**
Quelle maladresse,	What a predicament,
j'en rirais vraiment! *etc.*	I could laugh at it, really! *etc.*

DISC NO. 2/TRACK 13

All of the opera's dramatic themes, and many of its musical themes, are juxtaposed in the confrontations of this finale. Escamillo's music grows calm after his fight with Don José, and he exits (02:07) to a breezy reprise of the Toreador Song played in the lower strings. Micaëla reappears and attempts to pull José back home with a recap of the most lyerical of the music she sang to him in Act I. Carmen's response elicits an almost psychotic explostion of rage from José (05:00), foreshadowing his music in the final confrontation duet in Act IV. After he leaves, (07:30) there is a final quote of Toreador Song in the distance. All the interpersonal issues of the characters and the forces driving them are thus laid out for the final confrontation in Act IV.

SCENE TWENTY-THREE
Finale

They fight. The matador slips and falls. Enter Carmen and Dancaïro; she rushes forward and stays José's hand. The matador gets to his feet; Remendado, Mercédès, Frasquita, and the smugglers have meanwhile come upon the scene.

CARMEN

Holà, holà! José!

ESCAMILLO

Vrai, j'ai l'âme ravie
que ce soit vous, Carmen, que me sauviez
la vie!
(à Don José)
Quant à toi, beau soldat,
je prendrai ma revanche,
et nous jouerons la belle,
le jour où tu voudras reprendre le combat!

LE DANCAÏRE

C'est bon, c'est bon, plus querelle!
Nous, nous allons partir.

to Escamillo

Et toi, l'ami, bonsoir!

ESCAMILLO

Souffrez au moins qu'avant de vous dire au
revoir, je vous invite tous aux courses de
Séville. Je compte pour ma part y briller de
mon mieux
et qui m'aime y viendra!

to José, who makes a threatening gesture

L'ami, tiens-toi tranquille,
j'ai tout dit et je n'ai plus ici
qu'à faire mes adieux!

CARMEN

Stop, stop, José!

ESCAMILLO

Really, I'm overjoyed
that it should be you, Carmen, who saved
my life!
(to Don José)
As for you, my fine soldier,
I'll take my revenge,
and we'll play for two out of three
whenever you wish to renew the fight!

EL DANCAÏRO

Enough, enough, no more quarreling!
We must get going.

And you, my friend, good night!

ESCAMILLO

Allow me at least, before I say goodbye,
to invite you all to the bullfights at Seville.
I expect to be at my most brilliant there,
and who loves me will come!
to José, who makes a threatening gesture

Friend, keep calm,
I've had my say, and I've nothing more
to do here but make my farewells!

Leisurely exit of Escamillo. Don José tries to attack him but is held back by Dancaïro and Remendado.

JOSÉ *(à Carmen)*
Prends garde à toi, Carmen, je suis las de souffrir!

JOSÉ *(to Carmen)*
Take care, Carmen, I'm weary of suffering!

Carmen answers him with a slight shrug of her shoulders and walks off.

LE DANCAÏRE
En route, en route, il faut partir!

EL DANCAÏRO
Let's get going! We must be off!

TOUS
En route, en route, il faut partir!

ALL
Let's get going! We must be off!

LE REMENDADO
Halte! quelqu'un est là qui cherche à se cacher.

EL REMENDADO
Stop! There's someone there trying to hide!
He brings in Micaëla.

He brings in Micaëla.

CARMEN
Une femme!

CARMEN
A woman!

LE DANCAÏRE
Pardieu, la surprise est heureuse!

EL DANCAÏRO
Lord, a pleasant surprise!

JOSÉ
Micaëla!

JOSÉ
Micaëla!

MICAËLA
Don José!

MICAËLA
Don José!

JOSÉ
Malheureuse!
Que viens-tu faire ici?

JOSÉ
Poor girl!
What are you doing here?

MICAËLA

Moi, je viens te chercher.

Là-bas est la chaumière,

où sans cesse priant

une mère, ta mère,

pleure, hélas sur son enfant.

Elle pleure et t'appelle,

elle pleure et te tend les bras;

tu prendras pitié d'elle,

José, ah! José, tu me suivras!

CARMEN

Va-t'en! Va-t'en! Tu feras bien,

notre métier ne te vaut rien!

JOSÉ

Tu me dis de la suivre?

CARMEN

Oui, tu devrais partir!

JOSÉ

Tu me dis de la suivre

pour que toi, tu puisses courir

après ton nouvel amant!

Non! non vraiment!

Dût-il m'en coûter la vie,

non, Carmen, je ne partirai pas,

et la chaîne qui nous lie

nous liera jusqu'au trépas!

Dût-il m'en coûter la vie, *etc.*

MICAËLA

Ecoute-moi, je t'en prie,

MICAËLA

I've come looking for you.

Down there is the cottage

where, praying unceasingly,

a mother, your mother,

weeps, alas, for her son.

She weeps and calls you,

she weeps and holds out her arms to you;

you will take pity on her,

José, ah José, you will come with me!

CARMEN

Go on! Go on! You'll do well to go;

our business means nothing to you!

JOSÉ

You're telling me to go with her?

CARMEN

Yes, you ought to go!

JOSÉ

You're telling me to go with her

so that you can run after

your new lover!

No! Not likely!

Though it should cost me my life,

no, Carmen, I shall not go away,

and the bond which unites us

shall unite us till death!

Though it should cost me my life, *etc.*

MICAËLA

Listen to me, I implore you,

ta mère te tend les bras,
cette chaîne que te lie,
José, tu la briseras!

**FRASQUITA, MERCÉDÈS,
REMENDADO, DANCAÏRE, CHOEUR**
Il t'en coûtera la vie,
José, si tu ne pars pas,
et la chaîne qui vous lie
se rompra par ton trépas.

JOSÉ *(à Micaëla)*
Laisse-moi!

MICAËLA
Hélas, José!

JOSÉ
Car je suis condamné!

**FRASQUITA, MERCÉDÈS,
REMENDADO, DANCAÏRE, CHOEUR**
José! Prends garde!

JOSÉ *(à Carmen)*
Ah! je te tiens, fille damnée,
je te tiens, et je te forcerai bien
à subir la destinée
qui rive ton sort au mien!
Dût-il m'en coûter la vie,
non, non, non, je ne partirai pas!

CHOEUR
Ah! prends garde, prends garde, Don José!

your mother holds out her arms to you,
that bond which unites you,
José, you will break it!

**FRASQUITA, MERCÉDÈS,
REMENDADO, DANCAÏRO, CHORUS**
It will cost you your life,
José, if you don't go,
and the bond which unites you
will be broken by your death.

JOSÉ *(to Micaëla)*
Leave me!

MICAËLA
Alas, José.

JOSÉ
For I am doomed!

**FRASQUITA, MERCÉDÈS,
REMENDADO, DANCAÏRO, CHORUS**
José! Take care!

JOSÉ *(to Carmen)*
Ah! I've got you, accursed girl,
I've got you, and I shall compel you
to bow to the destiny
that links your fate with mine!
Though it should cost me my life,
no, no, no, I shall not go!

CHORUS
Ah! Take care, take care, Don José!

MICAËLA

Une parole encor, ce sera la dernière.
Hélas! José, ta mère se meurt, et ta mère
ne voudrait pas mourir sans t'avoir pardon-
né.

JOSÉ

Ma mère! Elle se meurt?

MICAËLA

Oui, Don José.

JOSÉ

Partons, ah, partons!
(à Carmen) Sois contente, je pars, mais
nous nous reverrons!

He hurries off with Micaëla.

ESCAMILLO *(au loin)*

Toréador, en guarde! etc.

MICAËLA

One word more, this will be the last.
Alas! José, your mother is dying, and she
doesn't want to die without having forgiven
you.

JOSÉ

My mother! She's dying?

MICAËLA

Yes, Don José.

JOSÉ

Let's go, ah, let's go! *(to Carmen)*
Be satisfied! I'm going, but we shall meet
again!

ESCAMILLO *(in the distance)*

Toreador, on guard! etc.

Don José stops at the back, on the rocks. He hesitates, but, after a moment, goes on his way with Micaëla.
Carmen rushes in the direction of the voice. The gypsies take up their bales and prepare to leave.

ENTR'ACTE

Act 4

SCENE TWENTY-FOUR
Chorus

A square in Seville, with the walls of the old arena in the background. The entrance to the ring is closed by a long curtain. A builfight is about to take place, and there is great excitement. Hawkers move about offering water, oranges, fans, etc.

DISC NO. 2/TRACK 14

Entr'acte **The dramatic and flavorful introduction to the last act places the action squarely back in the city, amid the excitement before a bullfight. The darting, dancing rhythms and the unpredictable flair of the orchestration suggest vivid images that will appear when the curtain rises.**

CHOEUR	CHORUS
A deux cuartos! A deux cuartos!	Two cuartos! Two cuartos!
Des éventails pour s'éventer!	Fans to cool yourselves!
Des oranges pour grignotter!	Oranges to nibble!
Le programme avec les détails!	Programme with details!
Du vin! De l'eau! Des cigarettes!	Wine! Water! Cigarettes!
A deux cuartos! A deux cuartos! etc.	Two cuartos! Two cuartos! etc.
Yoyez! A deux cuartos!	Look! For two cuartos!
Señoras et caballeros!	Señoras and caballeros!

ZUNIGA	ZUNIGA
Des oranges, vite!	Some oranges, look sharp!

145

PLUSIEURS MARCHANDS	SEVERAL FRUITSELLERS

running up

| En voici, | Here you are, |
| prenez, prenez, mesdemoiselles. | take these, ladies. |

UN MARCHAND — **ONE OF THEM**

to Zuniga, who pays

| Merci, mon officier, merci. | Thank you, officer, thank you. |

LES AUTRES MARCHANDS — **THE OTHERS**

| Celles-ci, Señor, sont plus belles. | These ones here, sir, are better. |
| Des éventails pour s'éventer, *etc.* | Fans to cool yourselves, *etc.* |

ZUNIGA — **ZUNIGA**

| Holà! des éventails! | Here you! Some fans! |

UN BOHÉMIEN — **A GYPSY**

running forward

| Voulez-vous aussi des lorgnettes? | Want some opera glasses too? |

A scene from the final act in a production staged by the San Diego Opera.

A deux cuartos! The opening chorus of Act IV is one of the most exciting moments in opera, as the crowd gathers for the toreador's procession before the bullfight. Finally, after a brief introduction, we hear the principal theme that is introduced in the opera's prelude (02:46), as the chorus sings in counterpoint, hailing the spectacle that comes to a grand conclusion at the arrival of Escamillo with Carmen on his arm. Carmen and Escamillo make a subdued yet very public declaration of their love, after which (07:26) Frasquita and Mercédès share their concerns with Carmen. Their dialogue is underscored by a curiously melancholy repeated figure in the flutes.

REPRISE DU CHOEUR
A deux cuartos! A deux cuartos!
Voyez! voyez! A deux cuartos! etc.

CHORUS *(reprise)*
Two cuartos! Two cuartos!
Look! Look! Two cuartos! *etc.*

ZUNIGA
Qu'avez-vous donc fait de la Carmencita?

ZUNIGA
But what have you done with Carmencita?

FRASQUITA
Escamillo est ici, la Carmencita ne doit pas
être loin.

FRASQUITA
Escamillo is here, Carmencita can't be far
off.

ZUNIGA
Ah! c'est Escamillo, maintenant?

ZUNIGA
Ah! It's Escamillo now?

FRASQUITA
Et son ancien amoureux José, qu'est-il
devenu?

FRASQUITA
And her former lover Don José, what's
become of him?

MERCÉDÈS
Il est libre.

MERCÉDÈS
He's at large.

ZUNIGA
Pour le moment.

ZUNIGA
For the moment.

FRASQUITA

Je ne serais pas tranquille à la place de
Carmen, je ne serais pas tranquille du tout.

FRASQUITA

I shouldn't feel easy in Carmen's place,
I shouldn't feel easy at all.

From outside loud shuts are heard, trumpet calls, etc. The Cuadrilla is arriving.

SCENE TWENTY-FIVE
Chorus and Scene

CHOEUR

Les voici! Voici la quadreille!
La quadrille des toréros!
Sur les lances le soleil brille!
En l'air toques et sombreros!
Les voici! voici la quadrille,
la quadrille des toréros!
Voici, débouchant sur la place,
voici d'abord, marchant au pas,
l'alguazil à vilaine face!
A bas! à bas! à bas! à bas!
Et puis saluons au passage,
saluons les hardis chulos!
Bravo! viva! gloire au courage!
Voici les hardis chulos!
Voyez les banderilleros!
Voyez quel air de crânerie!
Voyez! voyez! voyez! voyez!
Quel regards, et de quel éclat
étincelle la broderie
de leur costume de combat!
Voici les banderilleros!

CHORUS

Here they come! Here's the cuadrilla!
The toreadors's cuadrilla!
The sun flashes on their lances!
Up in the air with your caps and hats!
Here they are! Here's the cuadrilla,
the toreadors's cuadrilla!
Here, coming into the square
first of all, marching on foot,
is the constable with his ugly mug!
Down with him! Down with him!
And now as they go by
let's cheer the bold chulos!
Bravo! Hurrah! Glory to courage!
Here come the bold chulos!
Look at the banderilleros!
See what a swaggering air!
See them! See them!
What looks, and how brilliantly
the ornaments glitter
on their fighting dress!
Here are the banderilleros!

Un autre quadrille s'avance!	Another cuadrilla's coming!
Voyez les picadors!	Look at the picadors!
Comm ils sont beaux!	How handsome they are!
Comme ils vont du fer de leur lance,	How they'll torment the bull's flanks
harceler le flanc des taureaux!	with the tips of their lances!

At last Escamillo appears, accompanied by a radiant and magnificently dressed Carmen.

L'Espada! Escamillo!	The Matador! Escamillo!
C'est l'Espada, la fine lame,	It's the Matador, the skilled swordsman,
celui qui vient terminer tout,	he who comes to finish things off,
qui paraît à la fin du drame	who appears at the drama's end
et qui frappe le dernier coup!	and strikes the last blow!
Vive Escamillo! ah bravo!	Long live Escamillo! Ah bravo!
Les voici! Voici la quadrille! etc.	Here they are! Here's the cuadrilla! etc.

ESCAMILLO *(à Carmen)* **ESCAMILLO** *(to Carmen)*

Si tu m'aimes, Carmen, tu pourras, tout à l'heure,	If you love me, Carmen, soon you can be proud of me.
être fière de moi.	

CARMEN **CARMEN**

Ah! je t'aime, Escamillo, je t'aime,	Ah! I love you, Escamillo, I love you,
et que je meure si j'ai jamais aimé	and may I die if I have ever loved
quelqu'un autant que toi!	anyone as much as you!

TOUS LES DEUX **TOGETHER**

Ah! je t'aime!	Ah! I love you!
Oui, je t'aime!	Yes, I love you!

LES ALGUAZILS **ALGUAZILS**

Place, place! place au seigneur Alcade!	Make way! Make way for his worship the Mayor!

During a little orchestral march the Mayor enters and crosses the stage, preceded and followed by an escort of constables. Meanwhile Frasquita and Mercédès draw near to Carmen.

FRASQUITA

Carmen, un bon conseil, ne reste pas ici!

CARMEN

Et pourquoi, s'il te plaît?

MERCÉDÈS

Il est là!

CARMEN

Qui donc?

MERCÉDÈS

Lui, Don José!

Dans la foule il se cache; regarde.

CARMEN

Oui, je le vois.

FRASQUITA

Prends garde!

CARMEN

Je ne suis pas femme à trembler devant lui.

Je l'attends, et je vais lui parler.

MERCÉDÈS

Carmen, crois-moi, prends garde!

CARMEN

Je ne crains rien!

FRASQUITA

Prends garde!

FRASQUITA

Carmen, a word of advice, don't stay here!

CARMEN

And why, if you please?

MERCÉDÈS

He's there!

CARMEN

Who?

MERCÉDÈS

Him, Don José!

He's hiding among the crowd; look.

CARMEN

Yes, I see him.

FRASQUITA

Take care!

CARMEN

I'm not a woman to tremble in front of him.

I'm expecting him, and I'll speak to him.

MERCÉDÈS

Carmen, believe me, take care!

CARMEN

I'm not afraid of anything!

FRASQUITA

Take care!

The mayor's cortège has entered the arena. Behind him, the procession of the cuadrilla resumes its march and goes into the ring. The crowd follows … and in withdrawing has revealed Don José, leaving him and Carmen alone downstage.

SCENE TWENTY-SIX
Duet and Final Chorus

DISC NO. 2/TRACK 16

C'est toi! C'est moi! **The spectacular opening and its delicate denouement bring the listener to the greatest pages in the entire score, the final confrontation between Don José and Carmen. The fugitive Don José emerges from the shadows as the magnificently dressed Carmen, barely surprised, awaits her destiny. He is pitiful, crying to her in sobbing phrases (00:55) that he wants another chance to love her. She dismisses him coldly, which only makes him beg more fervently. The melody that he sings to the words "Carmen, il est temps encore" (01:50) reveals the depth of his agony, but Carmen sings the same melody back to him as she denies him, even in the face of death. When Don José realizes that she means what she is saying (03:47), he makes one last desperate attempt to convince her.**

CARMEN

C'est toi!

JOSÉ

C'est moi!

CARMEN

L'on m'avait avertie
que tu n'etais pas loin, que tu devais venir;
l'on m'avait même dit de craindre pour
ma vie
mais je suis brave et n'ai pas voulu fuir.

CARMEN

It's you!

JOSÉ

Yes, me!

CARMEN

I'd been warned
that you were about, that you might come here;
I was even told to fear for my life,
but I'm no coward and had no intention of running away.

JOSÉ

Je ne menace pas, j'implore, je supplie;
notre passé, Carmen, je l'oublie.
Oui, nous allons tous deux
commencer une autre vie,
loin d'ici, sous d'autres cieux!

CARMEN

Tu demandes l'impossible,
Carmen jamais n'a menti;
son âme reste inflexible.
Entre elle et toi, tout est fini.
Jamais je n'ai menti;
entre nous, tout est fini.

JOSÉ

Carmen, il est temps encore,
oui, il est temps encore.
O ma Carmen, laisse-moi
te sauver, toi que j'adore,
et me sauver avec toi!

CARMEN

Non, je sais bien que c'est l'heure
je sais bien que tu me tueras;
mais que je vive ou que je meure,
non, non, je ne tu céderai pas!

JOSÉ

Carmen, il est temps encor.
Ô ma Carmen, laisse-moi
te sauver, toi que j'adore;
ah! laisse-moi te sauver
et me sauver avec toi!
O ma Carmen, il est temps encore, *etc.*

JOSÉ

I'm not threatening, I'm imploring,
beseeching; our past, Carmen,—I forget it!
Yes, together we are going to begin
another life,
far from here, under new skies!

CARMEN

You ask the impossible,
Carmen has never lied;
her mind is made up.
Between her and you everything's finished.
I have never lied;
all's over between us.

JOSÉ

Carmen, there is still time,
yes, there is still time.
O my Carmen, let me
save you, you I adore,
and save myself with you!

CARMEN

No, I'm well aware that the hour has come,
I know that you are going to kill me;
but whether I live or die,
no, no, I shall not give in to you!

JOSÉ

Carmen, there is still time,
O my Carmen, let me
save you, you whom I adore;
ah! let me save you
and save myself with you!
O my Carmen, there is still time, *etc.*

CARMEN

Pourquoi t'occuper encore
d'un coeur qui n'est plus à toi?
Non, ce coeur n'est plus à toi!
En vain tu dis "Je t'adore",
tu n'obtiendras rien, non, rien de moi.
Ah! c'est en vain,
tu n'obtiendras rien, rien de moi!

JOSÉ

Tu ne m'aimes donc plus?

Carmen is silent.

Tu ne m'aimes donc plus?

CARMEN

Non, je ne t'aime plus.

JOSÉ

Mais moi, Carmen, je t'aime encore;
Carmen, hélas! moi, je t'adore!

CARMEN

A quoi bon tout cela? que mots superflus!

JOSÉ

Carmen, je t'aime, je t'adore!
Eh bien, s'il le faut, pour te plaire,
je resterai bandit, tout ce que tu voudras—
tout, tu m'entends? Tout!
Mais ne me quitte pas,
ô ma Carmen,
ah! Souviens-toi, souviens-toi du passé!
Nous nous aimions naguère!

CARMEN

Why still concern yourself
with a heart that's no longer yours?
No, this heart no longer belongs to you!
In vain you say "I adore you,"
you'll get nothing, no nothing, from me.
Ah! It's useless,
you'll get nothing, nothing, from me!

JOSÉ

Then you don't love me any more?

Then you don't love me any more?

CARMEN

No, I don't love you any more.

JOSÉ

But I, Carmen, I love you still;
Carmen, alas! I adore you!

CARMEN

What's the good of this? What waste of words!

JOSÉ

Carmen, I love you, I adore you!
All right, if I must, to please you
I'll stay a bandit, anything you like—
anything, do you hear? Anything!
But do not leave me,
O my Carmen,
ah! Remember the past!
We loved each other once!

Ah! Ne me quitte pas, Carmen,
ah, ne me quitte pas!

CARMEN
Jamais Carmen ne cédera!
Libre elle est née et libre elle mourra!

CHOEUR ET FANFARES *(dans le cirque)*
Viva! viva! la course est belle!
Viva! sur le sable sanglant
le taureau, le taureau s'élance!
Voyez! voyez! voyez!
Le taureau qu'on harcèle
en bondissant s'élance, voyez!
Frappé juste, en plein coeur,
voyez! voyez! voyez!
Victoire!

Ah! Do not leave me, Carmen,
ah, do not leave me!

CARMEN
Carmen will never yield!
Free she was born and free she will die!

CHORUS AND FANFARES *(in the arena)*
Hurrah! Hurrah! A grand fight!
Hurrah! Across the bloodstained sand
the bull charges!
Look! Look! Look!
The tormented bull
comes bounding to the attack, look!
Struck true, right to the heart,
Look! Look! Look!
Victory!

During the chorus, Carmen and José remain silent, both listening. Hearing shouts of "Victory!" a cry of delight escapes Carmen. Don José's eyes are fixed upon her. The chorus over, she takes a step towards the main entrance of the ring.

The final confrontation between Carmen and Don José in a production at the Metropolitan Opera.

Où vas-tu? Don José quickly unravels, and the music dizzily and sickeningly reflects the quick, violent action that follows when Carmen tries to escape and go to Escamillo, whose triumph echoes
from the arena. The confrontation turns ugly and vicious—Carmen insults Don José with a deri-
sive shout of "Tiens!" (There!) (01:50) when she throws the ring he gave her in his face. Unafraid,
she strides confidently toward the arena (01:58) and an enraged Don José steps forward and stabs
her to death. As she falls lifeless to the ground—the fate motive triumphant at last in the orchestra (02:22)—he weeps over her, singing of his love as the opera ends on a grim final chord.

JOSÉ	JOSÉ
blocking her way	
Où vas-tu?	Where are you going?
CARMEN	**CARMEN**
Laisse-moi!	Leave me alone!
JOSÉ	**JOSÉ**
Cet homme qu'on acclame,	This man they're cheering,
c'est ton nouvel amant!	he's your new lover!
CARMEN	**CARMEN**
Laisse-moi! Laisse-moi!	Leave me alone! Leave me alone!
JOSÉ	**JOSÉ**
Sur mon âme,	By my soul,
tu ne passeras pas,	you won't get past,
Carmen, c'est moi que tu suivras!	Carmen, you will come with me!
CARMEN	**CARMEN**
Laisse-moi, Don José, je ne te suivrai pas.	Let me go, Don José, I'm not going with you.
JOSÉ	**JOSÉ**
Tu vas le retrouver. Dis … tu l'aimes donc?	You're going to him. Tell me … you love him then?

CARMEN

Je l'aime!

Je l'aime, et devant la mort même,

je répéterais que je l'aime!

shouts and fanfares again from the arena

CHOEUR

Viva! La course est belle! *etc.*

JOSÉ

Ainsi, le salut de mon âme,

je l'aurai perdu pour que toi,

pour que tu t'en ailles, infâme,

entre ses bras, rire de moi!

Non, par le sang, tu n'irais pas!

Carmen, c'est moi que tu suivras!

CARMEN

Non! non! jamais!

JOSÉ

Je suis las de te menacer!

CARMEN

Eh bien! Frappe-moi donc, ou laisse-moi passer!

CHOEUR

Victoire!

JOSÉ

Pour la dernière fois, démon,

veux-tu me suivre?

CARMEN

I love him!

I love him, and in the face of death itself

I would go on saying I love him!

CHORUS

Hurrah! A grand fight! *etc.*

JOSÉ

So I am to lose

my heart's salvation so that you

can run to him, infamous creature,

to laugh at me in his arms!

No, by my blood, you shall not go!

Carmen, you're coming with me!

CARMEN

No! No! Never!

JOSÉ

I'm tired of threatening you!

CARMEN

All right, stab me then, or let me pass!

CHORUS

Victory!

JOSÉ

For the last time, you devil,

will you come with me?

CARMEN

Non! non!
Cette bague autrefois,
tu me l'avais donnée,
tiens!

She throws it away.

JOSÉ

advancing on Carmen, knife in hand
Eh bien, damnée!

Carmen draws back, José following, as fanfares sound again in the ring.

CHOEUR

Toréador, en guarde!
Et songe bien, oui, songe en combattant,
qu'un oeil noir te regarde,
et que l'amour t'attend!

Don José stabs Carmen; she falls dead. The curtains are thrown open and the crowd comes out of the arena.

JOSÉ

Vous pouvez m'arrêter.
C'est moi qui l'ai tuée.

Escamillo appears on the arena steps. Don José throws himself upon Carmen's body.

Ah! Carmen! ma Carmen adorée!

THE END

CARMEN

No! No!
This ring that you
once gave me—
here, take it!

JOSÉ

advancing on Carmen, knife in hand
All right, accursed woman!

CHORUS

Toreador, on guard!
And remember, yes, remember as you fight
that two dark eyes are watching you,
and that love awaits you!

JOSÉ

You can arrest me.
I was the one who killed her!

Ah! Carmen! My adored Carmen!

THE END

PHOTO CREDITS

CARMEN

Giuseppe Verdi

LIBRETTO BY MEILHAC & HALEVY

COMPACT DISC ONE

| 1 | Prélude | 3:27 |

PREMIER ACTE/ACT ONE

2	Sur la place, chacun passe	9:01
	Choeur/Moralès/Micaëla	
3	Avec la garde montante	4:25
	Choeur/Moralès/José/Zuniga	
4	C'est bien là, n'est-ce pas … La cloche a sonné	4:33
	Zuniga/José/Choeur	
5	Quand je vous aimeria? … L'amour est un oiseau rebelle *(Habanera)*	4:48
	Carmen/Choeur	

6	Carmen! sur tes pas	1:38
	Choeur/Carmen/José	
7	Monsieur le brigadier? … Ma mere, je la vois	9:11
	Micaëla/José	
8	Attends un peu maintenant … Au secours!	3:37
	José/Micaëla/Zuniga/Choeur	
9	Eh bien! … vous avez entendu? … Tra la la la …	2:10
	Zuniga/Carmen/José	
10	A la prison	1:02
11	C'est tres bien … Près des remparts de Séville *(Seguedille)*	4:33
	José/Carmen	
12	Voici l'ordre *(Finale)*	2:01
13	Entr'acte	1:41
	Orchestre	

DEUXIEME ACTE/ACT TWO

14	Les tringles des sistres tintaient	4:00
	Carmen	
15	Vous avez quelque chose à nous dire	1:34
	Zuniga/Pastia/Moralès/Frasquita/Mercédès/Carmen	
16	Vivat! vivat le Toréro!	1:14
	Moralès/Choeur/Zuniga/Mercédès/Frasquita/Escamillo	
17	Votre toast, je peux vous le rendre *(Chant du Toreador)*	4:53
	Escamillo/Choeur/Frasquita/Mercédès/Carmen	
18	Messieurs les officiers	1:24
	Pastia/Zuniga/Escamillo/Carmen	
19	Eh bien! vite, quelles nouvelles?	0:51
	Frasquita/Pastia/Dancaïre/Remendado/Carmen	
20	Nous avons en tête une affaire *(Quintet)*	7:23
	Dancaïre/Mercédès/Frasquita/Remendado/Carmen	

COMPACT DISC TWO

1	Je vais danser en votre honneur	4:48
	Carmen/José	
2	La fleur que tu m'avais jetée *(Flower Song)*	4:16
	José	

3	Non! tu ne m'aimes pas!	3:57
	Carmen/José	
4	Holà Carmen! (Finale)	4:47
5	Entr'acte	2:38

TROISIÈME ACTE/ACT THREE

6	Écoute, écoute	4:00
	Choeur/Dancaire/Remendado/José/Carmen/Mercedes/Frasquita	
7	Reposons-nous une heure ici, mes camarades	1:00
	Dancaire/Remendado/José/Carmen	
8	A la bonne heure … Mêlons! Coupons! (Card Trio)	7:04
	Carmen/José/Frasquita/Mercédès	
9	Eh bien?	3:34
	Carmen/Dancaïre/José/Mercédès/Frasquita/Choeur	
10	Quante au douanier, c'est notre affaire	0:43
11	Oui, je reste! … Je dis que rien ne m'épouvante	5:44
	Le Guide/Micaëla	
12	Mais … je ne me trompe pas	5:57
	Micaëla/Escamillo/José	
13	Holâ, Holâ! José!	8:41
	Carmen/Escamillo/Dancaire/José/Micaëla/Frasquita/ Mercedes/ Remendado/Choeur	
14	Entre'acte *(Orchestre)*	2:13

QUATRIEME ACTE/ACT FOUR

15	A deux cuartes!	9:02
	Choeur/Zuniga/Plusieurs Marchands/In Bohèmien	
16	C'est toi! C'est moi!	6:02
17	Où vas-tu?	3:31